GREECE THROUGH IRISH EYES

By the Same Author

All for Hecuba: The Dublin Gate Theatre 1928-1978 (1978)

Oscar Wilde (1983/97)

The Dublin Gate Theatre 1928-1978 (1984)

The Dandy and the Herald: Manners, Mind and Morals from Brummell to Durrell (1998)

Brian Friel and Ireland's Drama (1990)

Dark Fathers into Light: Brendan Kennelly (1994, editor)

Lawrence Durrell: the Mindscape (1994/2005)

The Thief of Reason: Oscar Wilde and Modern Ireland (1995)

Music in Ireland 1848-1998 (1998, editor)

To Talent Alone: the Royal Irish Academy of Music 1848-1998 (1998, with Charles Acton)

The Diviner: the Art of Brian Friel (1999)

2RN and the Origins of Irish Radio (2002)

Music and Broadcasting in Ireland (2005)

Creativity, Madness and Civilisation (2007, editor)

The Literatures of War (2008, editor, with Eve Patten)

Nostos: Proceedings of the Durrell School of Corfu 2002-2005 (2008, editor)

Charles: the Life and World of Charles Acton 1914-1999 (2010)

Theodore Stephanides, Corfu Memoirs and Poems (2011, editor)

Judith – an unpublished novel by Lawrence Durrell (2012, editor)

The Disappointed Bridge: Ireland and the Post-Colonial World (2014)

GREECE THROUGH IRISH EYES

Richard Pine

The Liffey Press

Published by
The Liffey Press Ltd
Raheny Shopping Centre, Second Floor
Raheny, Dublin 5, Ireland
www.theliffeypress.com

© 2015 Richard Pine

A catalogue record of this book is
available from the British Library.

ISBN 978-1-908308-73-3

All rights reserved. No part of this publication may be
reproduced or transmitted in any form or by any means,
including photocopying and recording, without written
permission of the publisher. Such written permission must also
be obtained before any part of this publication is stored in a
retrieval system of any nature. Requests for permission should
be directed to The Liffey Press, Raheny Shopping Centre, Second
Floor, Raheny, Dublin 5, Ireland.

Printed in Spain by GraphyCems

Contents

List of Illustrations

Foreword

Denis Staunton

The sovereign debt crisis that hit Greece and Ireland in 2010, leaving Athens and Dublin at the mercy of the European Commission, the European Central Bank and the International Monetary Fund, might have been expected to bring these two countries at opposite edges of Europe closer together. For their creditors and the international financial press, Greece and Ireland did indeed belong together, along with similarly indebted Portugal and Spain, dubbed the PIGS, or more politely the "peripheral" EU states. But for the politicians in Dublin and Athens, any comparison between the two countries was odious in the extreme. "Ireland is not Greece," proclaimed the Irish, as they sought to secure their position as the star pupil among eurozone debtors. "Greece is not Ireland," insisted the Greeks, as they sought to explain why it was more difficult for them to escape from beneath their debt burden.

A few months before the crisis broke, Richard Pine had started contributing regular Letters from Greece to *The Irish Times*, his personal, often idiosyncratic and always erudite observations on life in his adopted country. Most reporting on the Greek crisis had come from the capitals – Athens, Brussels, Berlin or Washington – but these Letters came from a village twenty-five miles outside Corfu town, from the very periphery of the periphery. Their preoccupations were often the same as those of the news reports from Greece – political turbulence, the financial crisis – but they were informed by a thoroughly different sensibility. They used literary, cultural and historical references to reveal connections between the Greek and Irish experiences and to help Irish readers to understand what was happening in Greece. The tone was light and often self-deprecating, as in one of the first Letters, about the prevalence of political violence in Greece:

> Death threats are in fact fairly common. I myself have received one, but it was half-hearted and, dare I say it, well-intentioned – more of a warning than an ultimatum – ironically, for apparently "condoning" terrorism in an *Irish Times* article.

The Letters from Greece made for unwelcome reading in the Greek embassy in Dublin, not least because of the unsparing picture they drew of a dysfunctional Greek state and the bribery, cronyism and tax evasion endemic throughout the country. One Greek diplomat paying a courtesy call to *The Irish Times* began by declaring "I am NOT going to speak about Mr Richard Pine," before launching into a tirade about his latest disobliging dispatch from Corfu. But if he was rigorous and unrelenting in his criticism of the Greek political class, he was equally constant in his affection and respect for the Greek people as he observed the impact of the crisis on the lives of his neighbours.

Richard was among the first international commentators to understand that the Greek debt crisis was not so much about economics as about national identity, and that the measures imposed from outside threatened to undermine something more profound even than national sovereignty, something he calls Greekness. This book is at its heart an exploration of this concept of Greekness, the essential spirit that distinguishes the Greeks and that helps to explain many of the characteristics of Greek society, both good and bad. He shows how history, geography and culture have shaped today's Greece and draws on his experience as one of Ireland's most distinguished literary and musical critics to provide an insightful survey of contemporary Greek music, literature, film and drama.

As an outsider in both Greece and Ireland, with an intimate knowledge of both, he is quick to spot what the two countries have in common as formerly rural societies that experienced wars of independence and civil wars, but equally alert to what sets them apart. His disappointment at the ungenerous response of Ireland's political leaders to Greece's enduring difficulties is expressed more in sorrow than in anger – in contrast to his outrage at the behaviour of the eurozone's creditor countries, led by Germany. It is not necessary to share his conclusion about Europe's political future to admire the love of Greece, Ireland and Europe that inspires it. And regardless of how you view the Greek crisis, this book will help you towards a much deeper understanding of it.

Denis Staunton
Deputy Editor
The Irish Times
Dublin, July 2015

Update

Three Tense Weeks in July: Lessons Learned and Unlearned

In the immediate aftermath of the Greek referendum of July 2015, and in the depths of the Greek political and economic crisis, it is difficult to avoid final remarks which concentrate only on the current context. A few words are certainly needed, to supplement the brief references to the referendum in the main text (pages 272, 276, 284, 290, 319), especially since, living in Greece among Greeks, my antennae have been particularly attuned to the voices in the *agorá*, in the olive grove and in the *kafeneío*.

By the time you read this, an election may have been won and lost, with a reconstructed centre-left government and a left-left opposition. In the interim, a Government of National Unity (aka National Chaos) is the most likely means of survival for Alexis Tsipras, a hostage to fortune.

The key clichés in the journalism of this crisis (and there are many) include:

- euroscepticism at the point where the European concept may be dead

- the blatancy of German aggression towards Greece and movement towards European hegemony

- a democratic deficit: the supersession of the unelected over the elected and abrogation of national sovereignty

- increase in mutual blindness between Europe south and north

- Greece "on a collision course with reality"

- "compromise" has morphed into "hypocrisy" and "make-believe"

- money is both real and virtual.

But these labels ignore the perennial facts of Greek life:

- the unmoving geopolitical context in the Balkans and the Levant, which western Europe seems unable to appreciate

- the utterly local nature of the Greek domestic polity

- debate and resistance as innate qualities of the Greek DNA

- an aversion to realities which, for millennia, have proved insupportable.

The perennials outweigh the clichés because, ultimately, the EU is a blip on the radar of Mediterranean history.

The labels do, however, indicate icebergs of disquiet: each suggests a design fault in the way the EU conducts its business. Journalists such as Fintan O'Toole (in *The Irish Times*) and economists like Thomas Piketty and Nobel laureate Paul Krugman have argued that the *fracas* over Greece has left a stain on Europe and its sense of democracy.

There are issues of accountability: finance minister Yanis Varoufakis realised that EU proposals, presented to eurozone ministers, suppressed the supporting documents on which their decisions were based. On a "need-to-know" basis, ministers were asked to approve recommendations but didn't need to know why. As Varoufakis commented, the "Eurogroup" was, in law, "a non-existent group [with] the greatest power to determine the lives of Europeans [but] not answerable to anyone".

There are issues of governance: previously coy references to Germany's expansionary and hegemonic intentions have grown into explicit statements (by, for example, a former IMF director, Ashoka Mody) about a phenomenon which a teenager in the village described to me as "winning the war by other means". My account of lectures given in Berlin in 1942, setting out Germany's plans for a post-war "European Economic Community" (see pp. 301-2) suggest that those plans are coming to fruition today. Four newspaper editors declined my account on grounds of political correctness, while Derek Scally of *The Irish Times* and James Kirkup of *The Telegraph* say that raising such a question is disgraceful and offensive: they disregard the fact of German dominance of Europe and its hard-line attitude to the smaller states.

July 2015 confirmed especially that German Chancellor Angela Merkel and her finance minister Wolfgang Schäuble intended to crush Tsipras and Syriza and, if that also meant sending Greece to perdition, so be it. Greece had offended the prevailing conservative consensus and must be punished.

There are issues of pragmatism: the bailout conditions may have begun in 2010 as well-intentioned, but the events of July have shown them to be not only unnecessarily vindictive, but based on stupidity. As Krugman has repeatedly argued, if you know a debtor cannot repay his debt, there is no point whatever in forcing him to repay it. July 2015 was like a schoolyard scrap: it simply proved that aggression does not require intelligence. As I write, the acknowledgement of the long-denied need for Greek debt relief is emerging, even from Berlin.

There are issues of humanity: I live in a Greek village, with real Greeks. Peasants. Entrepreneurs who want to do business. Young people who would prefer not to emigrate. People who want to get on with being Greek, and are finding it incompatible with being European. I have been at pains in my *Irish Times* column to emphasise that none of this crisis can be laid at the door of the ordinary folk I meet every day: my neighbours Hercules, Antigone, Perikles and Aristotle suffer unjustifiably from the rottenness of the Greek system. Their already precarious lives are further diminished by decisions over which, even in a referendum, they have little control. I am more than ever conscious of the unnecessary severity of the bailout. Ordinary folk display hopelessness and dismay, but nevertheless a sad resilience. The crisis has deepened their sadness and aggravated their frustration. As journalist Alexis Papachelas wrote last week, "the people are desperate for a new narrative".

Of course there are many faults in the Greek system, but not, I believe, in the Greek character. This is the crucial factor absent from all the crisis negotiations. Decades of abuse through cronyism, nepotism, bureaucratic inefficiency and obfuscation, bribery, corruption and tax evasion have created the present crisis, but the average man in the street (or man in the olive grove) has little or nothing to do with it.

This is, essentially, a country of creative, industrious, honest people; a good country that could be better if it did not subscribe to Europe's oligarchy and self-deception. Point to the corruption in Greece, and then look at the land rezoning, the phone licences and clientelism in Ireland. Point to the famous "Lagarde List" of Greeks who sifted away money in HSBC accounts in Geneva, and then look at the Irish names on that list.

In discussions with the EU, Tsipras and Varoufakis called for a political, rather than an economic, solution, indicating their insistence that without a political recognition of Greece's situation a bailout was inappropriate. But behind that insistence was an unspoken call for a *moral* and *philosophical* recognition, not merely of national sovereignty and self-determination (since so much had already been surrendered in the Nice, Maastricht and Lisbon treaties), but of the *spirit of Greece.*

Angela Merkel's or Enda Kenny's or Jean-Claude Juncker's blindness to that need speaks volumes about their intellectual incapacity and their moral poverty. Merely to have acknowledged that the crisis in Greece was humanitarian would have improved their media ratings immeasurably. But Tsipras, in appealing to them, failed to recognise their emotional deficit.

Since January 2015 (when the Syriza government was elected), some letter-writers to *The Irish Times* have expressed outrage that the Greeks have the effrontery to ask for further help. Others express outrage that politicians and financial institutions refuse to acknowledge the humanitarian crisis. Both are right, but both suffer from prejudice and ignorance. Anyone in Ireland who asks, "Why should we bail out the Greeks?" should also ask, "Why do we send aid to Africa?" Few of the Africans we help can be blamed for drought or famine. The less fortunate deserve care, whatever their background, whatever their plight.

Throughout this book, I stress the need for balance: between strengths and weaknesses, hopes and fears, beauties and ugliness.

But these must be measured against the hinterland of the Greek character, rooted in landscape, family and the home – aspects of the psyche which are non-negotiable. While the Greek *economy* (in macro terms) is in jeopardy, Greek people's sense of their own *oikonomía* – the laws relating to the conduct of the household – remains intact. We now have to find a new balance: between certainty and uncertainty.

This book seeks to interpret Ireland and Greece to one another. The hypocritical self-serving of Enda Kenny and Michael Noonan has at times made that near-impossible, but since they are mere politicians they will have no place in the history of ideas.

The crisis has confirmed my portrait of Greece as a country troubled by the efficiencies demanded by modernity but untroubled in its people. And my belief that, like Ireland, Greece has no organic or systemic place in "Europe" (Chapter 10) has been intensified and corroborated.

The crisis has highlighted Greece's attempt, throughout its history, to define itself and to establish self-esteem, even when that process involves deep divisions. It has underlined the fact that Greeks are by nature polemical (see p. 36), and prone to civil conflict. Alexis Tsipras has carried that polemic into the heart of Europe: without immediate effect, but indelibly and irrevocably.

The election of the first ever left-wing government in January 2015 brought to a political system that was intellectually and morally bankrupt a prospect of change based on honesty and self-assurance. It failed. Horace Walpole said, "No country was ever saved by good men", and Tsipras has proved that there is not a good – or bad – man in Greece capable of saving his country.

The chief agents of the subjection of Greece were Angela Merkel and Wolfgang Schäuble, abetted by the satellite states which, to its shame, include Ireland. By shamefully attempting to intimidate Greece and destroy the Syriza government, they were denying the Greek people their democratic right to be wrong. And this bullying will continue.

The damage caused to the fabric of Greek society by the ill-conceived austerity programme has angered Greeks, especially in exacerbating the brain-drain of its brightest young graduates. But it has not damaged their Greekness – *ellenikótita*.

The successive bailouts – three at this stage – have been like a Greek family continually mortgaging its house – a step no Greek would contemplate. No one can predict whether Greece will survive in its present form, or even whether the third bailout (if it happens) will succeed where the others failed. If one loves Greece, one could not wish to attempt such a forecast. Uncertainty has assumed a life of its own and imposed itself as the future conditional.

July 2015 will mark Europe's failure to honour its commitment not to the Greek economy but to the Greek people. The arguments against Greece may be economic in origin, but they are profoundly homophobic: fear of anything different. As gay people have always known, otherness has a high price. Those who cling to the concept of a united Europe have not examined the cost of unity.

As I write, I am certain only of the integrity and courage of Greeks in their persistence that they are Greeks first, and, if necessary, Europeans afterwards. The Greeks I know are frantically grasping for an enabling idea that will stand the test of time, not a mirage that fades after a few weeks or months. Never before have so many perennial truths of the Greek character been clustered on the head of a single crisis.

Richard Pine
Corfu, Greece
20 July 2015
πανηγύρι του Αγιου Νλιας –
feast of the prophet Elijah

ACKNOWLEDGEMENTS

My first thanks are due to Roy Foster: it was his suggestion that I should write this book, and he once wrote to me, "Greece is a country that I both love and mourn", which has been a *caveat* to me while writing.

Having written for *The Irish Times* since 1974, in a variety of epiphanies, I have many debts to the respective editors who commissioned my work: the Foreign Editors (chronologically): Patrick Smyth, Denis Staunton, Peter Murtagh and Chris Dooley; the editors responsible for the Opinion pages: Patrick Smyth (again), Fintan O'Toole, Enda O'Doherty, Fionnuala Mulcahy. To the Features and Arts Editors: Fergus Linehan, Brian Fallon, Paddy Woodworth, Gerry Smyth. And the Editors: Conor Brady, Geraldine Kennedy and Kevin O'Sullivan. Thanks to them all.

Another journalist and friend, Damian Mac Con Uladh, originally from County Mayo and now working in Athens, on *ENet* (the online edition of the daily newspaper *Eleutherotypia* and formerly the lamented *Athens News*, has contributed substantially to my appreciation of modern Greek society. I owe him a massive debt.

In Corfu Town, I have been aided by: Dr Spiros Giourgas, President and founder of the Albert Coen Foundation; Costas Ilvanidis, custodian of Vidos island; Spiros Kasimis, *restaurateur extraordinaire*; Spiros Kolouris and his wife Elizabeth Parker, whose interest in, and encouragement for, this book, aided it on its way; Mary Lemis (née Delahunt, from Wicklow) who, with her late husband, Spiro (Irish honorary consul), was – and is – the centre of the small Irish community in Corfu; Theresa Nicholas, whose graphic memories of Corfu "then and now" provide such a valuable record; Vangelis, computer wizard; Jim Potts (author of the authoritative *The Ionian Islands*) and his wife Maria Strani-Potts (author of the stories *The Cat of Portovecchio*) for their insights into Corfiot and Epirot character; Ljubomir Saramandič, curator of the Serbian Museum; the late Penny Simpson; Lucy Steele (former British vice-consul); Sylvia Demetriades Steen (saviour of the Skyros horses); Dr Anthony Stevens (Jungian psychiatrist who taught me much about myself without actually sending me an invoice); Kostas and Stavros for the banquets at "Bellissimo"; Babis, Yianni and the two Spiros at "Chrysomallis" (the name means "Golden Fleece"); all at the Konstantinoupolis hotel; and, at Lawrence Durrell's home at Kalami, Daria and Tassos Athenaios.

At the Ionian University in Corfu: Kostas Kardamis, Haris Xanthoudakis, William Mallinson and Paschali Nikolaiou and, until his departure for greener fields, Theodoros Buchelos. At the National and Kapodistrian University of Athens, Dr Chara Ramma of the Library of Public Law.

In Athens, many journalists including Nick Malkoutzis, Yannis Palaiologos (author of *The 13th Labour of Hercules*) and Kostas Karkagiannis (all at *Kathimerini*). I also take a wry satisfaction from the fact that several online journals, including *GreekReporter. com* and *prothemanews.com* have "borrowed" my *Irish Times* columns for reproduction and comment.

In mainland Greece: Tony Buckby, director of the British Council; Tom Cameron (owner of the "James Joyce" pub in Athens); David Connolly, translator working at the University of Thessaloniki; Eleni Calligas, historian of the Ionian *enosis* and great-great-granddaughter of Panos Kalligas, author of *Thanos Vlekas*; Apostolos Doxiadis, novelist and film-maker; Alexia Stephanides-Mercouri (who graciously gave me permission to edit the memoirs of her father, Theodore Stephanides) and her husband Spiros Mercouris; Charles Sheehan, former Irish Ambassador to Greece, his successor Noel Kilkenny, and all the staff at the Embassy in Athens; Ersi Sotiropoulos, avant-garde writer; Yiorgos Yatromanolakis, professor and outstanding novelist; Katerina Levidou, musicologist at the University of Athens was a valuable guide in the matter of musical nationalism.

Neni Panourgiá, at Columbia University, whose book *Dangerous Citizens* is required reading for anyone interested in the condition of the Left in Greece, was generous in commenting on parts of this book.

Denise Harvey (dedicated publisher of Alexandros Papadiamandis) spontaneously made available the essay "The Other Mind of Europe" by her late husband, Philip Sherrard, in characteristic generosity of spirit which pervades all her work as a publisher; Sherrard's ability to live in, and celebrate, the strengths of Greece, while acknowledging its weaknesses, has been a compelling model.

In Ireland, to Rev. Patrick Comerford; Gerald Dawe and Dorothea Melvin; Ninian Falkiner; Patricia Kavanagh, a companion for some of the journey; Olivia O'Leary; Eve Patten; Ruairi Quinn.

I am grateful to the following for their advice, support and interest: Roderick Beaton (who has forgotten more about Greece than most Greeks will ever remember); Brewster Chamberlin and his wife Lynn-Marie Smith, of the Conch Republic, for numerous serious and not-so-serious discussions; Lee Durrell (and Colin Stevenson) for constant interest in her late husband, Gerald Durrell; the late Penelope Durrell; Nicholas Gage (né Gatzoyannis, whose moving tribute to his mother, *Eleni*, brought us to his home village of Liá in Epirus); Anna Lillios, editor of *Lawrence Durrell and the Greek World*; Sir Michael Llewellyn Smith (whose study of the Anatolian Catastrophe, *Ionian Vision*, is essential reading); Peter Mackridge (the pre-eminent expert on the evolution of the Greek language); Patrick Salmon (former Irish diplomat in Athens and president of the Irish-Hellenic Society); and Paul Watkins (who gave me space in the *Anglo-Hellenic Review* for many of my ideas). The fact that all of them participated in seminars of the Durrell School of Corfu is an extra gratification.

Two of these, Roderick Beaton and Peter Mackridge, are eligible for some kind of sainthood, for the fact that two of the most eminent figures in the world of Hellenic studies were prepared to answer my – at times – pedestrian questions with tact, patience, good humour, erudition and clarity, and in fact answered more questions than I had asked. Deepest thanks on both a professional and a personal level.

Simon and Linda Baddeley, residents of Ano Korakiana, were instrumental in guiding me towards the work of Corfiot sculptor Aristeidis Metallinos, and in obtaining permission from the sculptor's grand-daughter, Angeliki, to reproduce his work. Yiorgos Chouliaras, a remarkable diplomat and poet (who introduced me to the work of Irish novelist Patrick McGinley) has been a friend and advisor for many years, even though we disagree on a few matters.

Maria Vlachou was a most helpful and conscientious research assistant, who greatly eased the burden of finding rare publications and items in newspaper archives.

My fellow villagers have contributed to this book more than they know and, indeed, just by being there: Darryl and Paula Bill, for the protein; James and Wendy Chatto, pioneers of writing about Corfu; Spiro and Lola Dimitras and their truly wonderful children Sotiris, Marietta and Angelos; John and Jackie Knowles; Thelma Miller and Steve Grocott; Lefteris Parginos; Philip Parginos; Polymeros, Mary and Spiro Kassaris, on the terrace of whose *kafeneío* many sections of this book were conceived; Harry Salvanos and family for so many taverna evenings; Mrs Salvanos for all the bread and for all the mutually incomprehensible conversations we have had over the years; Tomas and Vasso Siriotis at Ano Perithia, whose inspired cuisine was a source of sustenance beyond description; Paul and Ursula for the lifts; and Ilias, phone wizard.

The names of Lawrence Durrell and Peter Levi will appear frequently as character witnesses, whose writings on Greece are far finer than anything I could conceive, and have been in my consciousness throughout my own writing.

To David Givens, at The Liffey Press, thanks for his ready acceptance of the book, and his helpful and persuasive editorial eye.

To Pavla Smetanová whose happy and loving friendship was – and is – essential to this book's existence, my heartfelt thanks. In fact, it probably would not have been written without her and her husband, Andreas Damaskinós.

And to my wonderful daughters, Emilie and Vanessa, who have learned to live with an absent father and (I think) still love him.

My greatest debt is to the man to whom this book is dedicated, and who, after almost fifty years of friendship, made it possible, by a generous legacy, for me to undertake some necessary journeys within Greece.

Richard Pine
Villa Ipothesi
Perithia
Corfu

"Ochi" Day, 28 October 2014 –
Independence Day, 25 March 2015

In loving memory

Neil (Bruce) Holman

1949-2013

best and dearest friend

PREFACE

I've written this book for three principal reasons: firstly, to give Irish readers an indication of the Greek character and how Greek society has developed from the time of the war of independence (1821-30) to the present day; secondly, to suggest some of the parallels between the Greek and Irish experiences and achievements in history, culture, politics and economics.

My third reason is more complex: to explain why I love Greece and yet, as my friend Kostas Karkagiannis (a journalist with *Kathimerini* newspaper) puts it, "to do that, you have to be *hard*". He means that, in order to love Greece, one has to accept that the country – but only *some* of the people – has been damaged by unplanned tourism, and crippled by political and economic mismanagement and graft. Due to these unpalatable factors, Greece and the Greeks have been misrepresented and misunderstood. I therefore hope to explain why this should be so. My talks with neighbours, academics, historians and journalists produce expressions ranging from "doom and gloom" to "we can win through". Some unhappy people even say "bring in the tanks – at least under the Colonels (the military regime 1967-74) we had stability and increased prosperity". I, like many people from Ireland throughout modern history, am a *Philhellene* – a person who loves Greece and Greek things. But I have to be responsible about it. And that's why this book will, at times, be an argument, not a travel brochure.

There now, with its current crisis, arises a fourth reason: the need to express the very severe – and possibly fatal – condition of Greece, its economy, its administrative system, its geopolitical

1

position, its people, in terms which go beyond the daily grind of austerity and its causes, and provide a portrait of "Greece entire": its adherence to beliefs and behaviours so deeply engrained in the Greek psyche, so radically affected by its ecology, so celebrated and yet so misunderstood. To keep faith with this "Greece entire", to understand first and celebrate after, is an imperative that was intensified for me, as a resident of Greece, since the advent of the Syriza government in January 2015. The imperative supersedes that of merely loving and criticising, because it looks for that which is perennial and perduring, which cannot be changed or destroyed. Political crises have sought to affect Greekness, but the Greece I have found and which I describe in these pages cannot be affected by mere politics or the vagaries of the marketplace.

Therefore, this is *not* a guidebook, nor a survey of local customs, folklore or festivals, so I won't be telling you about where to find good bouzouki music or sponge-diving or authentic weaving, nor will I be extolling the beauties – or otherwise – of Greece's cities, towns and islands. There are plenty of these guides available, some of them very instructive and helpful, others misleading, factually incorrect or simply lacking in what the visitor really wants to know. Where this book *does* offer some guiding principles, it points you towards what I regard as the essential "Greekness" (a word we'll encounter often in this book); above all, it asks you to respect its customs – they are what makes Greece Greek and therefore your principal reason for being there – and to be aware of both the strengths and weaknesses of Greek society.

Nor is this an exhaustive history of Greece, nor a comprehensive account of its modern experiences. Of course it's a subjective view – "from where I sit" – which I have presented to the Irish public in the form of my "Letters from Greece" in *The Irish Times*. Many readers have commented, most of them criticising me for bias, blindness, stupidity or wilful dismissal of the facts. I hope that the result is at least honest and, if it's also convincing, or alerts you to the wider picture, it will have fulfilled a valuable and necessary function.

I couldn't have called this book "In Praise of Greece" because there is more in Greece than its praiseworthiness, especially today.

To write a hagiography would be unforgivable. One of the motifs running through this book is that Greece is a country to both love and mourn. As Cromwell said to his portraitist Sir Peter Lely, "I desire you would not flatter me at all, but remark on all these roughnesses, pimples, warts and everything as you see me". Some of Greece's "roughnesses" are, to my eyes, among its virtues, but there are so many points at which its beauty is impaired by factors more serious than merely facial accidents. If I extol aspects of Greece – for example its vibrant culture – it is not to "flatter" them but to set them beside the imperfections amid which we live our lives.

Because there is so little human traffic between Ireland and Greece (other than tourists), one of the reasons for "Letters from Greece" has been to explain Greece and Greek affairs to Irish readers, and this has led to the present book. One can meet ignorance about Greece in high places. In 2012, for example, Ireland's finance minister, Michael Noonan, made disparaging remarks about Greece that demonstrated not only his appalling lack of diplomacy but also his extreme ignorance, when he suggested that, apart from holidays, Irish people know little of Greece except *feta* cheese.

If there is any truth in his snide remark, it's that not enough has, so far, been written about Greece for Irish readers. Hence this book. In much of my writing in the past fifteen years, I've tried to concentrate on Greek-related topics, as much to explain myself to Greece as to explain Greece to myself. And as a result, I've been blessed with a certain level of recognition and inclusion, as much as any *xénos* (from the Greek, ξένος meaning "guest" or "stranger") can expect.

This is therefore a book about Greece, from an Irish perspective, for those who would like to develop a serious interest in the country, its people, their history and their culture. Naturally, the attractions of tourism – the treasures of archaeology, the climate, beaches and idyllic islands – are discussed in the appropriate parts of the book, but my general intention is to make you aware of the beauties you might not otherwise suspect, and not only beauties: the Eleusinian mysteries and the Delphic oracle were central to Greek society and its beliefs; today, we have mysteries rather darker and more disturbing to the modern mind: the internal wrangling of politicians, bribery and corruption, problematic bureaucracy and financial mismanagement. We should not overlook Heraclitus' description of the oracle: "It neither speaks plainly, nor conceals, but gives signs ['ουτε λεγει 'ουτε κρυπτει, αλλα σημανει]." In other words, It doesn't tell the truth, it doesn't tell lies, but it *hints* [*simaíno – I signify*]. Much of modern Greece (which thus provides us with the term "semantics") is found in between the hints, the lines of sign-language, and we need a semantics of "Greekness" to elucidate it.

"Greek", "Greekness", and "Hellenic" will be interchangeable. The term "Hellenic" refers to the people known as Hellenes – the Greeks. The Greeks would call it ελλενικότιτα, *ellenikótita* or Greekness.[1] I have employed it as a general description of the *spirit* of Greece. Today, "Greece" is a term used outside the state, whose official name is "The Hellenic Republic" (or "Democracy": Ελληνική Δηοκρατία).[2] "Greek" and "Greece" are, in fact, foreign terms applied to the lands of the Hellenes. Perhaps the use of "Hellenic" in preference to "Greek" is best illustrated by the term "Hellenisation", meaning the extension of Greek culture throughout the empire of Alexander the Great (356-323 BC); "Grecification" doesn't sound the same. Similarly, I've allowed the terms "Turkish" and "Ottoman" an interchangeability in describing the military and political forces which dominated the Balkans for so many centuries.

Part of this book will examine the different strategies by which Ireland and Greece achieved their independence (Ireland from Britain, Greece from the Turks and, in the Ionian islands, the Venetians). It will also offer an assessment of the different experiences of independence – its freedoms, its constraints, its abuses and the challenges to both countries in the greater European context (Chapter 10). The post-colonial imagination is common to both cultures, and is deeply imbued.

To the general reader, Greece represents two ideas that have become clichés: historically, it's a land of great antiquity in terms of art, drama and epic poetry, the birthplace of philosophy and democracy; today, it's a holiday destination of sun, sea, sand and sex. But the Irish reader knows more than this. The financial crash in both countries in 2010 has brought them together into the same frame of reference in the larger geo-political and geo-economic picture, and this in turn has made citizens in Greece and Ireland more aware of each other – areas in which they have much in common. So this book will attempt to elucidate those common areas of experience and achievement.

The overview (Chapter 1), like the "Letters from Greece", reflects my concern for the country in which I live, and my connection with its people. Culture, tradition, character on one side; economics, social transformation, international relations on the other. In between, scandals, clientelism, the weight of history versus the imperatives of the future. These are the outward manifestations of the inner debate. My journey from Ireland to Greece has brought me from one edge of Europe to the other, from one of the "bad boys" of the eurozone to the other (not forgetting the Spanish, Portuguese and Italians who have also had to submit to the acronym "PIGS"). I am attempting to bring the characters of the two into communion, and bring together the two extremes of my own experience (geographically and intellectually) in such a way that they might coalesce.

This is, of necessity, a personal account: subjective, selective and not entirely dispassionate. At its back is my own "odyssey" from London to Ireland to Greece, which makes me ask: Why do we travel to a foreign country? And decide to live there? For some, it's a retirement dream – a place in the sun (very few want to retire to Finland or Ireland). For others, the need to be elsewhere haunts them because, perhaps, they lack something vital in their life so far, something that might be available at the end of a journey.

One magnificent Greek word which, for me, encapsulates so much of what is attempted by Greece's *voyeurs*, is *skiagraphy*: technically, it's a term for the process of x-raying (and also the construction of sundials) but literally it means "writing with shadows", *skiá* being a shadow. This is what we do, those of us who try to describe Greece, whether we are insiders or visitors: we engage with the shadows that are all Greece is prepared to offer us, and we try to make pictures from the shadows. Maybe we achieve nothing more than a silhouette; maybe our "x-ray" reveals perspectives that might otherwise remain hidden. Who knows?

It may surprise you that, with such a long experience of cultural policy and, especially, literature and drama, I have placed two chapters on culture towards the end of the book, suggesting that its relevance is subservient to history and politics. You will see, however, that "culture", in every aspect of Greek creativity, not only mirrors this history and politics, but, in a sense, sums it up.

Chapter 1, in which I describe my reasons for coming to Greece, is inevitably autobiographical, and I trust it will be accepted in the spirit in which it is written: in order to establish how one Irish critic has come to observe the society in which he now lives. Being who I am, and who I have been, were essential factors in my decision to relocate, and the very large step out of the known into the unknown which that involved. So, too, the "Afterword" is a personal reflection on why that life has been possible.

Also, it has been inevitable that my personal prejudices about the condition of Europe – and especially the status of Greece and Ireland – should be obvious in Chapter 10, in which I argue that neither Ireland nor Greece truly belongs to Europe.

"Through Irish eyes"... hmm. Forty years ago I might have written a book on "Ireland through English eyes". But those forty years, while they haven't entirely eradicated my Englishness, have imbued me with a strong sense of what Ireland is and what it means to be Irish, so much so that I feel justified in saying that the eyes with which I see Greece today are Irish.

I have to acknowledge Peter Levi's admonition: "there is something phoney about 'going native' – to try to lose one's identity is a mistake which I have avoided."[3] Me too. One can never *become*, or even *pretend* to be, Greek; but one's identity does undergo a sea-change. Nicholas Gage wrote: "So pervasive and all-powerful are the land and climate of Greece that to live in the country for any significant period is to become Greek."[4] Gage *is* Greek so he would say that, wouldn't he? I can't quite agree; you can take the man out of the north but you can't take the north out of the man. I've tried to reconcile two statements, each of which has a relative truth: T.S. Eliot said, "The man who returns will have to meet the boy who left",[5] while Hannah Arendt said, "Conscience is the anticipation of the fellow who awaits you if and when you come home."[6] Odysseus may have "come home", not only physically to Ithaca but to a new truth; if one could only imagine the same at the end of one's own odyssey – if, that is, it has an ending ... Where I do agree with Nicholas Gage is in that question of *home*: someone said "home is where you want to be buried" and, knowing where that is for me (see Afterword) establishes my sense of home.

Living anywhere is give-and-take; whether we live alone or with our family, there's an inevitable need for expression, to articulate in some way aloneness or togetherness. Whether it's a poem or a drama or just a letter to the folks back home – which in my case is the "Letters from Greece" – it's a way of making sense of the distance between where we've come from and where we are now.

All of which is my long answer to my short question: why do we decide on a far place and then try to reach it, to land on its shore, to make friends with the "natives", and to achieve some kind of acceptance? A new place. And, as I point out in this book, *place* has a spirit which affects us profoundly. It makes the Greeks Greek, and it makes the outsider less of an outsider. That's all we can hope for.

We must also acknowledge the phenomenon that any researcher disturbs the "field" in which he or she works. If I live in, and write about, Greece, I thus inevitably become part of the "field", and report it with *my* eyes, not Derrida's or Malinowski's or Lévi-Strauss's. A man will see Greek society quite differently to the society seen by a woman, however objective they believe themselves to be. A Marxist will see the evolution of modern Greece as a lost cause; a venture capitalist as a gross opportunity; a politician as a means to an end. This book is the view of a literary critic (male) living in a small village on a small, rather untypical, Greek island, with "an Irish eye".

A westerner, trained in linear thinking, will find lack of connections between apparently different and discordant aspects of Greece. Philip Sherrard wrote of this problem most sympathetically in his essay "The Other Mind of Europe", in which he introduced this western logic to its Greek counterpart: he called the former a "very arrogant and self-complacent mentality" which could not

admit a mindset "still untrammelled in a network of beliefs and un-
derstandings which [...] we could only call superstitious, meaning
they didn't correspond to any reality". He therefore found himself
"led [...] into much unknown and unexpected territory" which had
"been written off the map of European history [and] the map of the
modern western consciousness".[7] That journey into "unknown and
unexpected" territory has been mine, too. Like Sherrard, I have
found the "other mind of Europe" and in this book I have tried
to describe it and introduce it to its western "other". In doing so,
maybe the timbre of Greece will resonate, if only slightly, within
the reader, as it resoundingly does for me.

Ultimately, as Lawrence Durrell wrote at the opening of his
memoir of Corfu: "Other countries may offer you discoveries in
manners or lore or landscape; Greece offers you something harder – the discovery of yourself."[8] Whether as a tourist, a would-be
resident or a commentator, what we express in those postcards,
snapshots or "letters" is a discovery of Greece *and* oneself.

1

GREECE AND IRELAND:
A PERSONAL PERSPECTIVE

First Steps in Greece

I knew Greece before I knew Ireland. I came here fifty years ago as a fifteen-year-old schoolboy, in a group organised by the classics teachers in my school. Our three weeks in Greece encompassed Athens, Delphi, a comprehensive tour of the Peloponnese, and Rhodes. As a junior scholar I could read, write and speak classical Greek. The high point of the holiday was, for me, to stand on the stage of Epidaurus, one of the most famous amphitheatres in the Hellenic world (home today to a world-famous festival), and recite lines from Euripides' *Hecuba*; we took it in turns to speak and then to appreciate the incredible acoustics which made even a "stage whisper" audible in every seat. We did this not only to please our teachers, but to find an emotional and cultural experience – and a humbling one.

Although I did not realise it at the time, that immersion in the classics pre-conditioned me to love Greece; it was a floodgate. But what did I – and do I – mean by "Greece"? My subsequent life in Ireland accustomed me to thinking of "the other", a *difference* which was welcoming, accessible and rewarding. It's what Philip Sherrard calls "the other mind of Europe" (and as an Anglo-Irishman he would have known that intimately). And it's possible that Greek tragedy-drama enabled me to see the modern Greek world as a place of fate, a place where people accept, with fortitude, what is offered. But if there is any truth in this, it is also true that I knew

9

the joys and satire of Aristophanes, and could see in today's Greek a spirit of excitement and humour. I was neither blinkered nor partisan.

I subsequently revisited Athens four years later, as an undergraduate at TCD, during the military junta. Looking back, it was probably a journey I should not have taken, had I been aware of the severity of the Colonels' regime and the offence to democracy which it represented. But in Ireland we were more aware of, and concerned by, the beginnings of the northern civil rights crisis and the pandemic of student revolutions in Berkeley (1965 and 1967) and Paris (1968); the student revolt of 1973 in Athens, which was crucial to the downfall of the junta, was still four years in the future.

Two years later (1971), when I gave my inaugural address as President of TCD's Philosophical Society, one of my platform speakers was the redoubtable Helen Vlachos (Eleni Vlachou, to give her her formal Greek name), at that time living in London in self-imposed exile, having suspended publication of her newspaper, *Kathimerini*, for the duration of the junta, 1967-74.[1] Meeting her was a revelation to me of how the death of one of our most basic rights and abilities – freedom of expression – can disfigure the concept of humanity.

During my days in a hostel in Athens in 1969, the concierge suggested we go to a café to meet some of his friends. They were interested in life in Britain and Ireland. The conversation went as follows:

"In London, how much freedom of speech do you have?"

"Complete freedom."

"We don't believe you."

"Provided we don't say anything blasphemous or treasonable, we can say whatever we like."

"What kind of things?"

"If I stand outside the Houses of Parliament and shout 'Down with the government' no-one will arrest me. Or if I stand outside Buckingham Palace and shout 'The Queen is an idiot' I might be taken to a psychiatric unit as a harmless lunatic, but otherwise we have complete freedom of speech."

"We don't believe you."

Suddenly, one of my new friends gave a signal and we left the café in haste. Outside I asked, "What is happening?" to which the answer was, "A man in that café is a police informer and he has gone to the telephone. If we hadn't moved, we would have been arrested." If there had been mobile phones at that time, our exit might have been less successful. The stories of what happened to dissidents and critics of the Colonels' regime in those years have been told by Peter Murtagh in *The Rape of Greece*. At the time, it was I who was shocked by my companions' disbelief that freedom of expression could be so basic a part of society. Reading Natalie Bakopoulos's *The Green Shore* (2012), portraying the domestic exile of dissidents under the junta, brings home the immediacy of the fear, apprehension and pain experienced at that time.

Today, when Greece is once more threatened – but, one must hope, ineffectually – by a resurgence of fascism, the era of the Colonels, and their defeat in 1974 by factors including the rebellion of university students of my own age, is recalled as vividly as the brutality of the civil war (1945-49), when so many were summarily executed by government forces in order to defeat partisan opinion.

Apart from the spiritual experience of the recitation at Epidaurus, I have three abiding memories of that time in the Peloponnese in 1965. The first is being in Olympia, partly because we were able to stand in the stadium where the original Games took place, and partly because, in the (at that time) tumbledown structure that constituted Olympia's museum, I saw the "Hermes" of the great sculptor Praxiteles, as close as I am now to my own hand. The second is standing before the Lion Gate at Mycenae (the modern Mikenes), and wondering at the power which it still exudes – something I did not again experience until I entered the prehistoric gate of Dun Aengus on Inishmore: the legacy of millennia and the proofs of history. It forces one onto one's knees – at least metaphorically.

The third Greek epiphany was a simple shock for a northerner: for the first time in my life, seeing an orange tree and *being able to pick the fruit*; this was in the main street of Sparta, while we were waiting for a bus, and I'm not ashamed to say that it meant as much as Sparta itself. Today, with a dozen orange trees in my own garden, I still have a sense of adventure and surprise as the fruit ripens to my northern eyes. A new mindset was being offered to me.

First Steps in Ireland

Going to Ireland as an undergraduate in 1967 was far more of a culture shock than my first encounter with Greece. Despite the inescapable genetic implant of the Celtic (my maternal great-grandfather was Irish and my paternal grandmother was Cornish, thus making me almost 40 per cent Celtic, with Pyrenean, Provençal and rustic English making up the rest), I knew almost nothing of Ireland – its language, culture, history – so much so that, thinking that I was entering a Protestant anglophile enclave of TCD in a city of Catholic republicans, I thought it would be essential to order English newspapers, since I assumed Irish newspapers were written in the Irish language.

All that changed, almost overnight. Ireland became my home, my domicile. I worked for twenty-five years in Raidió Teilifís Éireann (RTÉ, the national broadcaster), first in the Music Division, with principal responsibility for the orchestras, and thereafter in Public Affairs. Parallel with these backstage assignments I pursued my own career as a broadcaster, literary and music critic.

I wrote about Brian Friel, and other Irish dramatists and poets such as Brendan Kennelly and Oscar Wilde; I wrote the official history of the Dublin Gate Theatre; I became a governor of the Royal Irish Academy of Music; I wrote music criticism for *The Irish Times*; I was a founder, and Secretary, of the Irish Writers' Union. I was therefore closely associated with some of the key elements in Irish (especially Dublin) cultural life, and for many years this sustained me emotionally and intellectually.

I had married young and, after ten years of marriage, which had produced our two wonderful daughters, it came to its natural conclusion. I had come to dislike Dublin, since it had changed so greatly from the city with which I had fallen in love. My second relationship lasted a little longer than my marriage, but it, too, came to an end. I had started to commute between Dublin and Connemara, where we had given the children their holidays, and I envisaged a life divided between Connemara and Corfu. But a life divided is not a true life, and, for the sake of integrity and fulfilment, I took the decision to up roots completely, however reluctant I was to move away from my family and friends.

The catalyst to my removal to Greece came in 2000, when I attended a conference in Corfu organised by the International Lawrence Durrell Society. I was the author of a critical study, *Lawrence Durrell: The Mindscape* and I had long considered and cherished the possibility of establishing a forum in which Durrell's work – and that of his younger brother Gerald – could be discussed. They had lived in Corfu from 1935 to 1939 and written about it: Gerald in what is now known as the *Corfu Trilogy* (the first part of which is the well-known *My Family and Other Animals*) and Lawrence in *Prospero's Cell*. As a student I had met Gerald, and Lawrence became a friend about whom I wrote two books. My visit to Corfu convinced me that it was the most appropriate venue for such a forum, an ongoing seminar in Durrellian studies, so I settled here and the Durrell School of Corfu, a multi-disciplinary, cosmopolitan seminar of scholars, came true after I took early retirement from RTÉ and it thrived until 2013.

What I am saying in these pages is that I love Ireland, where my children live, where my intellectual life was based for four decades, where my long-term friends still live, and that I also love Greece, where I conducted that dream seminar for twelve years, and where I am increasingly inspired by the new intellectual world with which I am becoming acquainted, in particular with the work of Greek writers and writers on Greek affairs.

But I was now a stranger in three countries: England, from which I had all but permanently emigrated; Ireland where, despite my long residence there (forty years), I still feel a slight unease; and Greece, where my northern way of thinking and my ineptness with the modern language stamp me indelibly as a *xénos*.

The Greek Spirit

When you enter Greece, whether by land, sea or air, and present your passport you are – to put it prosaically – crossing a political border. But *entering* Greece means much more: becoming a part, if only for a short time, of an "other" world. So it isn't the land mass defined as "national territory" but something that lies behind the idea of a nation, which inheres in the landscape – in the sea, the mountains, the clusters of small towns and villages, the language – and which has made the Greeks the type of people they are, just as the Irish landscape has shaped the minds and destinies of its peoples without recourse to boundaries.

Is there an "essential" Greece? Many have written that in Greece a "spirit" is being encountered which *inheres* in a place; they are not hallucinating. However insensitive to antiquity one may be, one becomes inevitably and inescapably aware of this spirit in and through the stones, as in later life I found myself encountering the spirit of the Connemara mountains – the two horseshoes of the Bens and the enclosing presence of the Inagh valley. My friend Tim Robinson has, I think, convinced many readers of his books on Connemara and Inishmore of that presence, that sense of being "here" and at the same time in an "other" place. One need not know how to pray, and if you do so, you probably pray to a lesser god; as T.S. Eliot wrote in *Four Quartets*, "You are here to kneel, where prayer has been valid"[2] – thus acknowledging the continuing presence of a power larger than a religion or a personality. To this I would add Edmund Burke's "venerate where we are not presently able to understand".[3] It has nothing to do with scale or immensity; it is not merely physical but metaphysical in its effect. And humbling, because that immensity makes it frighteningly clear that we are so much less than what has been here before. We will never be able to comprehend the whole, but we can nevertheless put ourselves in a position to admire what is beyond us.

Among Greeks such as the poets George Seferis and Odysseas Elytis, and among philhellenes like Peter Levi and Philip Sherrard, the voyage towards a belief in the possibility of transcendence sometimes becomes a theism by which, as a profoundly irreligious and atheistic person, I am out of sympathy. Transcendence in itself is welcome, even reassuring, until one reaches the point where it requires submission to a higher authority; in my rejection of such authority I am an unreconstructed Protestant and so, I believe, are the Greeks. Not, of course, in the denominational sense, but in the political meaning of holding *protest* as a higher good than submission.

In the natural world, we relish the examples of the *deus loci*, the exclamation *numen inest!* which, astonishingly perhaps, has no Greek equivalent beyond πνεύμα του τόπου – *pneúma tou tópou*, the "spirit of place" or *genius loci*. The title of Elytis' poem "Axion Esti" ("It is Worthy") is probably Greece's nearest expression of this belief in spirit of place. It expresses *immanence*, a presence within landscape which is also a presence within Greekness. Seferis called it "Hellenic Hellenism" rather than the Hellenism detected by outsiders.

In so far as I can – and want to – recognise that immanence, and to discover it in Greekness which is primal, originary, and in constant danger of dilution, diminution, even extinction by the modern, I find the place where I can love Greece.

So there is an indefinable *spirit* in Greece. It's indefinable because it cannot be reduced to any specific source or cause. Wherever you are in this multi-faceted country, a factor which is not – necessarily – the sky or the sea or the language attracts you as an "other", a place apart, ultimately unexplorable but worth the journey of discovery.

Philip Sherrard, using Elytis as an example, spelled out the fact that in the *interbellum* of 1918-39 Greeks were conducting, on common ground with poets and novelists, an excavation of values which seemed to have lost their meaning. He emphasised that the Greeks'

> search for identity tends [...] to take the form of an immense preoccupation with the question of what it means to be Greek. They cannot take their quality of Greekness for granted; and the result is that the discovery and exploration of Greece as the embodiment or personification of the values of Hellenism is or tends to be a necessary and quite conclusive stage in the discovery and exploration of their personal identity.[4]

Greece is not simply the land of Greece today (which only reached fulfilment with the accession of the Dodecanese islands in 1947): it is an accretion of geographical and philosophical ideas, or – to combine those two concepts – the influence of *place* on the *mind*. It is the peoples in the various places who, over the period 1821-1947, became Greece; it's the eleven million individual Greeks who will maintain their individuality and that of their families in preference to loyalty to the state, but who will unhesitatingly and proudly proclaim "I am a Greek!"

It's the peoples who came to the Greek state as refugees or repatriates – the Anatolian survivors in 1922, the Pontine Greeks even today; it's the Greek people living in the USA, Canada, Britain, Australia…

It's the Greek people who still, by various accidents of history, live outside the state: in southern Albania (aka northern Epirus), Macedonia, Istanbul… It's the Phanariot Greek tradition from Constantinople (Istanbul); it's the fierce regionalism of the mainland: Attica, Thessaly, Epirus, the Peloponnese, and of the islands: the Ionians, the Dodecanese, Cyclades, Sporades, and Crete, which they express in their cultural differences – dialect, cuisine, understanding of history.

It's the Jewish Greeks, those (approximately ten per cent of the total) who survived the mass exportation to the extermination camps. It's the Greeks of Cyprus, who attempted, in the 1950s, to become a part of Greece (through *enosis*, meaning "union"), but who now live in an unhappy relationship with the Turks who, since 1974, illegally occupy the northern part of their country.

It's the Greek works of art in the museums of the world, but especially the sculptures taken from the Acropolis and known as the "Elgin Marbles". It's the husband of Queen Elizabeth II (a prince of Greece, born in Corfu) and her cousin, the Duke of Kent (whose mother, Marina, was a princess of Greece).

It's the rich (the Onassis, Niarchos, Leventis, Chandris dynasties) and it's the poor who constitute almost 30 per cent of the overall population.[5] It's the big fat Greek mamma and it's the slim, fashion- and health-conscious teenage girls. It's the Orthodox *pappas* (priest) in his stovepipe hat, and the businessman in his Armani suit.

It's the world-famous concert artists like opera diva Maria Callas or the composer Mikis Theodorakis or, today, violinist

Leonidas Kavakos, and the everyday unknown artist in the local café who, like his Irish counterpart, will make, and transmit, music and tradition in his close community.

It's the fascists[6] trying to take over the state and it's the terrorists trying to abolish it. It's the politicians and the civil servants who take bribes and the entrepreneurs and ordinary citizens who bribe them. It's an administrative system that has failed the state, bringing it to its knees, economically, socially and spiritually.

So, what is "Greekness" in its everyday – and I mean everyday – epiphany? It's:

- a strong sense of family

- a strong sense of honour and self-esteem

- a generosity of spirit

- a love of dispute

- a suspicion of foreigners, despite an inherent natural hospitality

- a respect for land and the sea and man's place in it

- a love of art as a sign of man's creativity.

None of this threatens the Greek way of life or the modernisation/ Europeanisation of Greece. What threatens Greece?

- harmonisation/equalisation when Greeks know that we are *not* equal

- imposition of external power and influence

- diminution of self-esteem, pride, self-control

- any collectivity which impairs the family and extended family.

It's necessary here to emphasise that "austerity" is nothing new to Greece. The word – αυστηρότητα (*austirótita*) – means "roughness" or "sternness", terms which we can easily see in the response to the harshness of the physical environment on land and at sea. We must also link this with the word *agón*, which can mean "struggle" or "battle" or "contest" depending on the severity of the context. If we go further, and add that the "pride" or "self-esteem" comes from the Greek word φιλοτιμία – *filotimía* – meaning "love

of honour", which has a further meaning of "obstinacy" and "perti-
nacity", we start, I hope, to appreciate that the Greek character is a
mindscape of honour, unfazed by the need for struggle in the face
of austerity. Very few, if any, Greeks would accept the motto "anything for a quiet life". As a young supporter of Syriza said recently,
"Without protests there can be no achievements".

Where does this fierce attachment to liberty emanate? The
landscape. If the land and the sea are so unforgiving, so relentless,
then they breed ferocity of spirit, the basic strategies of survival
become almost entirely the business of life. So many Greeks –
even city-folk – have family memories of poverty in an inhospitable land. The Irish can understand this: the ruggedness of Aran,
between land and sea, the fact of the emigrant's exile, famine, endurance. One learns either to live in endurance or to submit. If the
best option is the emigrant ship, the accompanying baggage is an
innate knowledge of who you are and where you have come from:
the stones that gave you birth, the sacrifice that may, or may not,
(with apologies to W. B. Yeats) make a stone of the heart.[7]

So we still love Greece. Why?

To say that the sum is greater than the parts is to move into the
dangerous territory of "unity in diversity" or, to employ the fascist
slogan, "strength through unity". In fact, many would argue that
the parts are greater than the sum: the individual strands in the
fabric of Greek life are holding the tapestry together and widening
its horizons, rather than *vice versa*.

Although, as you will see from my euroscepticism in Chapter 10, the phrase "unity in diversity" can become offensive, it can
be helpful, in an attempt to explain/explore what it means to be
"Greek", what "Greekness" is. In 1984 Declan Kiberd asked:

> Do the families of suburban Dublin wake up sweating under
> the burden of Irish tradition? Do their children feel ravaged
> by crises of national identity as they reach for the multi-
> national snap-crackle-and-pop? The answer is clearly no.[8]

In Greece today, the answer would be Yes, and possibly Kiberd's
own answer would be different, thirty years on. As Yiorgas Chouli-

aras says, "To be a practicing Greek [...] can be both exceptionally rewarding and taxing".[9]

Greece may seem, to the average non-Greek observer, to be chaotic and undeveloped, and it seems like that to many Greeks, too. In terms of economic and social development, it is probably today at a point where Ireland found itself forty years ago. Similarly, words such as "disorganised" and "backward" were frequently levelled at Irish people and the Irish administration before and during the accession to membership of what is now the European Union (EU). Not only was Greece a fundamentally rural, minimal society but, like Ireland, it had no industry and only a sub-standard infrastructure.

Greece was slower than Ireland to discover the merits of the "begging bowl" which Irish governments held out to Brussels with the "poor mouth". Ruairi Quinn, Minister for Finance in the Irish coalition government of 1994-97 (who had studied as an architect in Athens in the 1960s), told me that Ireland had succeeded in attracting "cohesion funds" from the EU which had been intended for Greece, because Greece had yet to discover how to knock on the right doors in Brussels – a deficit they have subsequently rectified.

Today, the tension between the inherent strengths of Greece – the Hellenic spirit – and its current weaknesses is not a conflict between ancient and modern, nor a matter of watching the inexorable march of "progress" before which the past must tremble. It's much more profound than that. Many in Greece today are confident that "Greekness" complements modernity and will enable them to prevail in the adverse conditions the country is experiencing.

There has certainly been a clash between the traditional, conservative agents of history and the progressive modernisers, as in any society, especially noticeable, I suppose, in Ireland. But this clash does not necessarily mean the extinction of one in favour of the other. To put it at its simplest, the enduring Hellenic spirit is capable of distinguishing between the good and the not-so-good of modernism; it can accommodate what it needs in order to survive, and reject the rest. This is the crux of the current debate in Greece about sovereignty, autonomy, identity, self-respect and their place in a global society.

This is not to say that there aren't huge problems affecting that spirit, which appear to be the fuel of tradition, but are in fact eating it from within. But there are aspects of Greekness which a Eurocrat can't eradicate, and some of these characteristics – procrastination, evasion, denial – may be deplorable in circumstances where modernisers are anxious to plough through the slothful economy and administration. They are well matched by the entrepreneurial achievements of Greeks in, for example, international shipping, and their creative genius in literature, film and music; all these characteristics are simultaneously and indivisibly aspects of "Greekness". And in all of these we can recognise the capacity to embrace modernism, to face its challenges and take advantage of its positive energies.

Not all is black. In 2004 Greece won the European football championships and in 2005 the Eurovision Song Contest (matters of huge national pride). It had opened a new international airport with a rail link to the city (something Dublin cannot boast) and had successfully staged the Olympic Games, also in 2004. It had a Hellenic Tiger tugging at the economy, making it, after Ireland, the most successful in Europe.

But this is completely at variance with the horizons and experience of the majority of Greek people, especially the large proportion living below the poverty line, and it disturbs a deep resonance within the collective memory. History is a cruel mistress. A Greek is someone who, as novelist Vangelis Hatziyannidis puts it, "spends more time planning the past than he does planning the future".[10] Or, as journalist Antonis Karakousis says, "Our country and its people, for the most part, like to live with myths, while ignoring reality".[11]

Those of us who live in Greece cannot ignore the present crisis, nor should any tourist, however innocent, be unaware of the social and political upheaval. Athens was the birthplace of democracy, and it is again today the debating chamber of national change and the high point of street protest. Greeks are naturally disputatious; I see this every day in the village. The raised voice, the clenched fist, the in-your-face refutation, are merely ways of saying, vehemently, "Sorry, I don't agree with you" or "What kind of eejit are you?"

I am constantly irritated – but no longer surprised – when foreigners criticise the Greeks, usually for their laziness, procrastination and, in the public service, inefficiency. It's as if they don't encounter those defects in their own countries. This is particularly the case with the German and British condescension and patronising behaviour towards, and dismissiveness of, Greekness. I have asked why anyone would wish to live in a country in which they seem to dislike the people, the system and, indeed, the weather (too cold and rainy in winter, too hot in summer) and have seldom received any convincing explanation, other than that whingeing seems to be as much a British national pastime as backgammon is for the Greeks.

The man to whom this book is dedicated often chided me for, as he called it, my "post-colonial guff", insisting that after 180 years of freedom any country should have established itself as a viable independent state and have divested itself of any *angst* about foreign domination. Nothing I could say to him would persuade him that that *angst* had imprinted itself on a people's DNA, nor could I persuade him that Ireland, too, exhibited similar symptoms of an enduring "slave mentality". My friend's viewpoint was encapsulated in an editorial in the *Sunday Tribune* of 1986 which argued that "identity is not the issue [...] This obsession [...] is a foolish and indulgent diversion from what we should be about".[12] But identity *is* the issue: if you cannot be Greek, you cannot be anything in the international arena, and many Greeks, from all parts of the political spectrum, whether rightly or wrongly, argue that Greece has not yet become an independent, autonomous state, in command of its own assets and knowing its own destiny.

Life in the Village

I lived in Corfu Town – a magnificent cosmopolitan city of history, culture and commerce – for several years before I bought and renovated a house in a small village twenty-five miles from Town. The Town is alive almost twenty-four hours with café-bars, tavernas, smart and not-so-smart hotels, markets, arcaded streetscapes, medieval and modern fortresses, four museums of national importance, and the richly decorated and much-venerated shrine of the island's patron, Saint Spiridon.

Sitting at the Mikro Café in Corfu Town I can see, within a radius of ten yards, a silversmith, a goldsmith, the elegant Apostrophos bookshop, two clothes boutiques, two wine bars, a *kafeneío* (local bar), a pizzeria, a former English-language bookshop and newsagent which is now a fish-spa, a sign advertising a long-defunct municipal children's library, a boutique for household decorations, and, of course, a church. Here, one can carry on that essential task of watching the world go by. I've never been much of a museum man. I prefer to look at living things and people, at movement and emotion. It is somehow – I'm not sure exactly why – reassuring that an elderly man can spontaneously jump up from his chair and sing a traditional ballad for the delectation of his companions and the obvious respect of his younger auditors.

Corfu successfully marries the *chic* with the pagan, town with country. By contrast to the town, the village is lively but unsophisticated: all human life is there. It's a working village. There's a winery, a joinery, a blacksmith, an oilery where you take your olives for the pressing, a post office, two tavernas, two multi-purpose shops, one *kafeneío*, an ice-cream parlour, a car hire office and a petrol station doubling as a DIY store.

The villagers know more about you than you know about yourself. In this, it has many parallels with the villages in the west of Ireland where I have lived: Roundstone and Ballyconneely. Writing here about "Greekness" is like sitting in Roundstone and writing about "Irishness".

My personal experience of Greece has shown me most dramatically that the popular perception of a sun-soaked paradise, where picturesque peasants ride around the countryside on equally picturesque donkeys, and taverna waiters launch into "Zorba's Dance" at the drop of a drachma for the delight of touristic onlookers, is, even though partially true, far from the full picture. Ireland, too, suffers from its picturesqueness, which is of such importance to the tourist industry: "offbeat bacchanalian encounters with a sincere, earthy folk [...] friendly because they have been seen as pre-modern".[13]

The similarities between Greece and Ireland are inescapable in the village, especially in microcosm: my friend Brian Friel has written that the whole world can be seen in the daily life of Glenties, his mother's village, and this has earned him the reputation of "the Irish Chekhov" – Chekhov who said that in his stories he described simply what he saw by looking out of the window. In Greece, Odysseas Elytis said the same: "you will come to learn a great deal if you study the insignificant in depth".[14]

I puzzled the villagers by calling my house *Villa Ipothesi* – starting up a debate as to its meaning. A "hypothesis" is an idea: schoolchildren are trained to deduce what is the author's "hypothesis" in the set text. So they look at the sign on my gate and puzzle: "what's he getting at?" I try to explain that it's all "hypothetical", the world-as-if. If a writer is "at home" in exile, there can be no "home place" except in conjecture and abstraction. So *ipothesi* indicates "home-as-if".

On my terrace, the breeze lifts the olive leaves from green to silver; at night, the garden lit up with teeming fireflies, I hear the mating call of the skops owl. It's difficult to think that upcoming elections are causing heated debates just 200 metres up the lane at the *kafeneío*. There would be as many as six backgammon games at one time, besides a card game of such Byzantine complexity that its players frequently argue as to the interpretation of the rules – if there are rules as such. In the absence of a village hall/community centre, the *kafeneío* serves as a venue for meetings of the village council and associated purposes. Because it is also the local post office, it is a rendezvous for everyone paying their telephone and electricity bills; such is the complexity of the latter that long attempts at analyses of the bills take up a considerable part of the week when they arrive.

In 2013, Frank McNally questioned whether the term "tight-knit" as a description of Irish communities was as valid today as it had been, suggesting that perhaps Aran would be one of the few remaining communities to merit that adjective.[15] In Greece, there are strong indications that a sizable number – as many perhaps as 1.5 million – are considering a move from city to countryside, while other sources indicate the feelings of younger people whose disillusion with both the city and its politics point them towards the land, with organic farming as an attractive alternative lifestyle.

But "tight-knit" can mean closing ranks to both "foreigners" and themselves. During the civil war, one man in the village gave the names of his young partisan contemporaries who became some of the many "disappeared"; he was allowed to buy goods in the village shop, but was otherwise ostracised until he died, fifty years later.

A young man from the village visited last year with his American wife and young son. He was brash, anxious to display his acquired wealth and thus to indicate how smart he had been to leave not only the village but Greece itself for the challenge and rewards of the USA. Every gesture in speech and body language was condescending towards those among whose families he had been a child. It transpired that he owned an amusement arcade in Coney Island, NY. Big shot. In Ireland he would be called a "returned Yank"; in the village, he was called the *amerikános* – an epithet which can be far from complimentary.

The village communities remain "tight-knit" in their allegiance to family and the land (what the French call *terroir*), and in Corfu, that largely means the olive trees (all 3.5 million of them) which are the chief source of both wealth and sustenance.

The village got its first *graffito* last year: *Strength Trough Unit.* That's the slogan of the Golden Dawn (fascist) party, which has a surprisingly large following in Corfu, higher than its already high national average. I think the graffitist was either a little lacking in English, or the party bosses told him to go easy on the paint. But no-one has erased it. It's there outside the *kafeneío* for all to admire.

Loving or Mourning?

Many of my *Irish Times* readers have been puzzled by my apparent tolerance for political chicanery, bribery and corruption and clientelism, which have without doubt weakened public perception of Greece. But in Chapters 5 and 6 I will attempt to put these undeniable problems into context, and to point out that many of these problems also blight the Irish social and political landscape (planning permissions, banking arrogance, clientelism, for example).

While not condoning or excusing such activity, these chapters will try to explain why they are inherent in both Ireland and Greece. For example, I'll particularly address the issue of *clientelism* which bedevils both Ireland and Greece and on which their social structure has been built in recent decades.

What is there to love about Greece?[16] Quite apart from its spectacular scenery, its climate, its extant antiquities, and the fact that it was – perhaps still is – "the cradle of civilisation", there is something much more fundamental: the intimate relationship between landscape and character, which makes Greece and its people so attractive and so challenging.

This relationship has created a grittiness which inheres in all Greeks, whether townies or villagers. It enabled the Greek army to repulse the Italians on the Albanian border in 1940-41 – the first victory by the Allied countries in World War II. During that war, it enabled the Greeks to form an effective resistance movement against occupying German forces, despite appalling famine in Athens and other cities. It fuelled the debate about the future identity of the country during the ensuing civil war. And it provided the animus which preserved it from the military junta of 1967-74, especially the students (many of whom were killed) who eventually defeated that regime.

What is there to mourn about Greece? First, the perennial irredentism which makes Greeks long for restitution of its antique glory, including the idea of recapturing Constantinople (Istanbul), which led to the Anatolian Catastrophe of 1922 and which was a major factor in the political and economic upheavals from the 1920s onwards. Next, the era following the exit of the colonels in 1974, when successive governments, first under New Democracy and then PASOK, created a "welfare state" based on clientelism and cronyism, encouraging a dependence on a "We'll fix it" mentality which, along with other factors, has contributed to the present crisis.

Other aspects of Greek society which must be bewailed are the inferior educational system at all levels, which sees billions of euros being spent privately by parents to ensure a better future for their children. The lack of industrial development, which Ireland has overcome by attracting multinational manufacturing and financial services, has been a major absence in the Greek economy: there was an ambition, a part of the irredentism in the heart of every Greek, that Athens could become the financial hub of the burgeoning Balkan economic world, but that was never realised.

The lack of planning in the development of tourism, which is not only Greece's major export industry but also coterminous with its attraction as a social and cultural magnet, leaves Greece competing badly with neighbouring countries in the provision of, for example, golf courses (there are only twelve courses in the entire country) and marinas, of which very few are of any significant size or have adequate management.

Perhaps most serious of all is the transition from a rural to an urban society which leaves many villages depopulated, without creating any technological or wealth-creating nodes on which to build.

Loving or mourning. Which?

The love and the plusses outweigh the bewailing and the minuses. But, for the most ardent philhellene, the gap is closing.

One could never despair of a country and a people which exhibits, in the face of adversity, such *joie de vivre* that pushes their bewilderment and misery into a corner. In the village, local expressions of opinion at the *kafeneío* are heated one minute and the next subside, as the evening continues, into equally heated games of cards and backgammon.

Greece may not be a modern, forward-looking society, keeping pace with the northern march towards unification and "progress". Not least because of the idea of *terroir* – the rootedness of people in their locale, that intimate relationship between land and people which makes them more concerned about their vines and their olives than about a factory in a nearby town. Only the sea – *thálassa* – has been a challenge to the land, and even then, despite Greece's continuing domination of the shipping industries, it benefits only a few millionaires and the crews of its merchant navy.

Greece's potential is in so many areas untapped, even though the areas highlighted by economists and technocrats may not be those I am thinking of: the areas to be exploited are those that create the reasons for loving Greece; the areas where Greece is mourned are possibly those where mourning is inappropriate.

Greece and Ireland[17]

I am sometimes asked why Irish readers should be concerned about the fate of the Greeks. Quite apart from the similarities in the depression of the two countries, the extent of the collapse of Greek society, on both macro and micro levels, has repercussions for Ireland.

The reasons for needing to know about Greece are threefold: first, the fact that we are all within the EU – at least for the present – means that we do not ask for whom the bell tolls: it tolls for us. Second, we need to appreciate that a country considered principally as a two-dimensional holiday destination is actually populated by real people with real lives to lead outside the holiday season: we have severe winters here!

Third, Greece gave us concepts such as "democracy", "economy", "philosophy", "aesthetics", "semantics", and, admittedly, "plutocracy" and "kleptocracy" – in fact, about one-third of our vocabulary (see Appendix). Unless you've had a classical education (which is rare these days in Irish schools) you may not realise how much the English language owes to Greece. Where would we be without "psychiatry" and the "telephone"? Even the alphabet (and that's a Greek word, too) is different – so different that you know that the words represent something different to the way western alphabets speak our thoughts.

That Greece should today lose its sovereignty, its status, even its attraction as a holiday magnet, is a matter for all of us to regret, and to recognise that we can do nothing about it. And – here is the real tragedy – neither can the Greeks.

Whether or not we applaud or deplore membership of the EU and the pressures it exerts in the interests of standardisation (what I have called "Merkelisation"), and whether or not we acknowledge the need for the austerity measures that were imposed by the EU and the International Monetary Fund (IMF), on both Ireland and Greece after their respective economic collapses, we must also acknowledge that the raising of standards in both countries, as a criterion for continued EU membership, has benefited more than it has disadvantaged.

Yet I would not be alone in suggesting that Greece's slowness to conform is due to inherent characteristics which make its EU membership questionable. Some would call these characteristics inherent *flaws* or *defects*, but they are so typical of Greekness that to denounce them is tantamount to calling Greece itself, and all Greek people, flawed and defective. That is most emphatically not the case, but I have to admit that, in certain company, I am in a minority. I want to paint a picture of a country, and a people, and a culture, which I love and respect as much as, if not more than, I love and respect Ireland and its people and its culture.

Another "whether or not": whether or not one supports Ireland's EU membership, and all the vulnerability to external pressures in fiscal and geopolitical matters, the fact that Ireland and Greece have so much in common in terms of ancient and modern history, in literature, in nationalism and the independence movement, and in economic affairs, makes it difficult not to reflect on the characteristics which make soulmates of these two countries: one on Europe's western edge, the other where Europe meets the east – the Levant, the cradle of modern civilisation and dissent. As I shall demonstrate (Chapter 3), Greece's Balkan and Levantine position places it irrevocably in the context which begins in Thessaloniki and continues southward through Turkey, Syria, Israel, Palestine, Lebanon, Jordan and Egypt. Yet what Ireland and Greece have in common is greater than what separates them, namely, the western European landmass.

1453 and 1690

In an extremely cryptic, but typical, remark, W.B. Yeats once said that "Until the Battle of the Boyne, Ireland belonged to Asia".[18] He meant that at that date (1690) Ireland became a part of the west-European way of thinking that relied on logic, reason and order more than on the imagination and its multiple possibilities. And that *before* then, Ireland had exhibited, in its poetic and independent character, aspects of a more oriental, rather than occidental, culture: a culture which thrived on speculation, multiplicity and, in particular, a relationship with the uncanny which the march of western logic and narrative history would diminish and all but extinguish.

Yeats may have been too insistent, but he wanted to make the claim that Protestant William's defeat of Catholic James at the Boyne represented the last stand of that imaginative way of life which was nourished on the principles of dissent, inclusion rather than exclusion (the idea that we could consider "both/and" rather than making a choice of "either/or") and daily, unmediated commerce between this world and "the other".

In modern Greek literature that commerce continues to be manifested as a quality of life. If Ireland was, until the eighteenth century, such a place of the imagination, Greece remains in the mindset which accommodates both east and west. Physically, it borders the Middle East and the Balkans; culturally, it absorbed so much of Turkish culture and organisation during the Ottoman domination (1453-1830) that typical items such as coffee, tobacco, much of its music and its most treasured shadow-puppet *Karagiózis* are of Turkish origin, while, in the Ionian islands, under Venetian rule (1386-1797), an Italianate culture prevailed. These are not merely the surface signs of behaviour: they permeate the Greek character, which, despite assumptions to the contrary, is profoundly multi-ethnic and multi-cultural. Greece is indeed the meeting place of west and east.

It's been written that "East is East and West is West and never the twain shall meet", but Kipling's poem continues (and this is seldom quoted):

> But there is neither East nor West, Border, nor Breed,
>   nor Birth
> When two strong men stand face to face, tho' they come
>   from the ends of the earth![19]

Ireland and Greece may not always be "strong men", but in Greece and, in Yeats's mind, once-upon-a-time in Ireland, west and east *do* meet – perhaps that is what makes it so challenging and so exciting.

The year 1453, when Constantinople, the centre of the Hellenic world, was conquered by the Ottomans, may seem a very long time ago, but it has lingered in the Greek conscience, not least because, as historians have pointed out, Hellenism became a homeless idea. There would be no Greek state for nearly 400 years. The passing of 400 years is no great distance for the Irish memory either. So 1453 for Greece and 1690 for Ireland remain fixed points in the memory, signals of farewell to a secure identity and of entry into an uncertain future.

And there are many other parallels: 1821, when Greeks first declared the war of independence, and 1916 in Ireland; 1830, when the Greek state was established, 1921 for the Irish; and in 1921-22 Ireland immediately had its civil war, while Greece had to wait until after the Nazi retreat in 1944 to inaugurate five years of internecine fighting. But that is only in political history; there are many others, across the social and cultural spectrum.

In Greece it was always a reaching out to "the glory that was Greece",[20] an appeal to ancient wisdom, art and military prowess. That memory has supplied the motive power for an irredentism which still persists: Greeks regard southern Albania as, properly speaking, northern Epirus, its inclusion in the modern Albanian state as an unfortunate accident of history; in this, they have some justification: Saranda, Albania's southernmost city, was a Greek settlement, its name relating to the "Forty Saints" by which the town was then known (*Agioí Saránta*). There are many Greeks still living in southern Albania, and Greece would like to reclaim them; at present, Greek Orthodox citizens in southern Albania are at risk from nationalist attacks.

But perhaps the most tragic and foolhardy show of Greek irredentism was the attempt, in 1920-22, to recapture Constantinople/Istanbul. Greece has yet to recover from the disgrace and humiliation of that catastrophe which it brought on itself and catalysed many of the political problems of the twentieth century. The Greeks say *fós tís Anatolís* (φώς τής Ανατολής), "the light of Anatolia" or "light from the east" – *anatolia* meaning "the rising of the sun". To lose it is to lose a vital part of your identity. So Greece and its borders remain as question marks over that identity, as surely as the Irish border continues to trouble the Irish conscience.

Similarities and Dissimilarities

There are both considerable differences between Ireland and Greece and considerable likenesses. The geographical and climatic conditions are so obvious that they need no comment from me. These different conditions are part of what makes southern Europe so attractive to northerners. But because of Ireland's geographical location, on the northwestern edge of Europe, it also has much in common with Greece, on Europe's southeastern edge. In the same way that Greece is a meeting point of east and west, so Ireland, too, is on the cusp of Europe, a meeting point of old and new, the land mass and the ocean: it holds them together, and at the same time is vulnerable to both.

Like the Greeks, the Irish have been travellers to far places since the beginning of history. The Irish diaspora (in Greek, διασπορά meaning "dissemination" or "spreading") is as significant as the Greek; it's just that they didn't invent the word, or build an empire. Very few Irish people have reached Greece, however, either in history or as modern tourists; the population of Irish in Greece is, officially, less than 500,[21] while the number of Greeks, including Cypriots, in Ireland stands at approximately 1,000.[22]

Greece may, like Ireland, be under-industrialised, and it certainly has failed to attract any of the pharmaceutical and communications giants which contribute so much to the Irish economy and exchequer. But Greece is nevertheless an economic force and, more significantly and perhaps sinisterly, Greece is the plaything of international powers such as the USA, Russia and China; it has been such a plaything since it was set up in the 1830s with a foreign monarch, and in fact its independence has been safeguarded by those powers (originally, Britain, Prussia, Turkey and Russia) only because it has always been a vital pawn in the geopolitical game being played, then and now, in the eastern Mediterranean (Chapter 3). Is Ireland so different?

Athens and Dublin have little in common: in 1831, when the Greek state came into existence, Athens was merely a small town huddling around the great monument to its former glory, the Acropolis (meaning "top of the town") with the Parthenon as its major symbol of the Hellenic spirit – so much so that, until 1834, it was unfit to be Greece's capital city, a role assigned to Nafplion, in the south of the Peloponnese. So Athens lacks the Georgian grandeur of Dublin. It's mainly a nineteenth century city, with many neo-classical buildings such as the royal palace (now the parliament), banks and universities; twentieth century additions included several art deco constructions such as theatres. Athens' central square is Syntagma (meaning "Constitution"). The "posh" equivalent of Dublin's Merrion or Fitzwilliam Square is in nearby Kolonaki, just beneath the Acropolis and Mount Lykabettos, but as well as a highly desirable residential area, it also houses the up-market boutiques such as Gucci, Louis Vuitton and Cartier.

The Plaka is the oldest part of pre-independence Athens, a village huddling on the slopes of the Acropolis; it became a market area with cafés, antiquarian shops and museums; the market itself (*agorá* in Greek) could be compared to Dublin's Moore Street, which Lawrence Durrell described as "a background of scabrous backchat worthy of Aristophanes".[23] Both have changed hugely in recent years, and Peter Levi, writing in 1980, mourned that, after the restrictions imposed on social activity by the Colonels, "the Plaka became the hideous parody it now is".[24] Levi's favourite café, Flocca, has gone, replaced by a "Flocafe franchise".

Athens has a very extensive and efficient underground railway; Dublin has none. Excavations for new lines or stations are frequently halted to allow archaeologists to document the finds, which are often incorporated into the new structures, thus literally carrying the past into the present.

The Athens port of Piraeus, which services the ferries for most of the Aegean islands, is comparable to Ireland's Dún Laoghaire – but it's a modern city of such unsightliness (and, I think, pointlessness) that it makes Dún Laoghire seem graceful.

The very considerable difference between Greece and Ireland, geographically speaking, is the enormous number of Greek islands (approximately 1,200, apart from uninhabitable islets), which constitute one-fifth of Greece's land mass; many of them are lucrative tourist destinations, relying on safe and efficient air and sea connections. Where Irish islands like Inishbofin and Tory are still denied operative landing strips for small aircraft,[25] the larger Greek islands such as Rhodes, and many of the much smaller ones such as Skíathos, have airports that can accommodate tourist-sized planes.

In the Aegean islands, however, the neglect is in the lack of sewage treatment, fresh water and adequate infrastructure (especially roads) which not only disadvantages the tour operators but also makes life outside the season bleak and dangerous for residents. In the winter of 2014-15, islands in the Cyclades such as Tinos and Andros were cut off, with neither water nor electricity.

On a cultural level, the similarities are more subliminal and subcutaneous than overt. Greece has no dramatist (in modern times) to place beside Brian Friel, or any of the Irish dramatists of cultural nationalism (Wilde, Yeats, Synge, Shaw, O'Casey). But Greece, like Ireland, has two Nobel poets – George Seferis (1900-71) and Odysseas Elytis (1911-96) from Greece, W.B. Yeats and Seamus Heaney from Ireland. In cinema, Theo Angelopoulos (1935-2012) is a more than a match for Irish directors such as Neil Jordan and Jim Sheridan, while some of the more *avant garde* or "deviant" of Greek films would raise eyebrows even in today's Ireland. Perhaps the most compelling comparison I know, in modern Greek and Irish cinema, is *The Wind that Shakes the Barley* (admittedly by an English director, Ken Loach) and *Deep Soul* (*Psyhi Bathia*) by Pantelis Voulgaris, both depicting their countries' fratricidal civil wars. In music, too, I think Greece outweighs Ireland, where few major composers have emerged in recent decades and almost none – Gerald Barry excepted – have found international recognition.

Ireland has the huge advantage that most literature is in English and therefore accessible to a worldwide readership. Greek is a minority language and to reach a similar readership a writer needs to find a reliable translator and a viable publisher. I'm not sufficiently grecophone to be able to read in the original, so that is as remote from me as a book in Irish would be from the average Greek reader. There is, however, a vast treasury of literature, mostly post-independence, some of which is available in translation.

The antiquity of both Ireland and Greece is obvious to the enquiring traveller, even though Ireland's prehistory is less well known than Greece's, and figures far less prominently in the tourist brochures. Although not considered of the same historical significance today, the Boyne valley has megalithic tombs comparable with any sites in Greece.

In brief:

- both countries conducted a war of independence

- both countries experienced a civil war

- both countries missed out on the industrial revolution

- Ireland and Greece were predominantly rural societies which are now rapidly becoming predominantly urban

- both had a single dominant political party for many decades

- both suffer from the practice of clientelism

- both have a strong literary and storytelling tradition

- both have an infrastructure which is improving but remains inadequate

- both have entered an economic crisis and experienced its consequences

- both are developing the already strong business in tourism

- both Ireland and Greece launched Europe's top two low-price airlines, Ryanair and EasyJet[26]

- where the British complained that whenever they found the answer to "the Irish Question", the Irish changed the question, Greece has, particularly recently, succeeded in the same obfuscation and ambiguity

- both peoples exhibit "a type of intelligence and of thought, a way of knowing [which] implies a complex but very coherent body of mental attitudes and intellectual behaviour which combine flair, wisdom, forethought, subtlety of mind, deception, resourcefulness, vigilance, opportunism".[27]

But:

- Greece has borders with many more countries than Ireland

- Greece is not Anglophone, nor does it speak the language of its former colonisers

- there are far more Greek words in the English language than English (or Irish) words in Greek

- Ireland is one big island with several small offshore islands, totalling 68,890 square kilometres, whereas Greece has over 1,200 islands, with a consequent total coastline of 13,600 kilometres and a land mass of 132,000 square kilometres

- Ireland has no maritime/shipping industry and no merchant navy

- in Greece military service is compulsory for men over 19; there is no such requirement in Ireland

- in Ireland, the smoking ban was 99 per cent successful from the outset, while in Greece it is impossible to implement (Chapter 4)

- Ireland's laws on same-sex unions are in advance of Greece's

- Greece was directly involved in both world wars; Ireland, as a state, was not, despite the large numbers of Irishmen who fought with the British forces

- Ireland was not invaded in the second world war, and, despite aerial attacks, did not succumb to the privations, indignity and misery of a ruthless and brutal army of occupation, as did the Greeks

- the Jewish population of Ireland was not deported to death camps; the Greek Jews were

- in Ireland, prostitution is neither legal nor regulated; in Greece, prostitution is legalised, prostitutes are medically checked, and are represented by their own trade union (with 5,000 members). There is even an internet map showing the authorised Athens brothels; I have yet to see the Dublin equivalent.

2

BRIEF HISTORY LESSONS

A Circular Narrative

History repeats itself: a maxim which Greece continually proves and, it seems, approves. Greece fought a war of independence from the Turks in the 1820s. Today, its independence is once more at stake, and the subject of intense polemics (*pólemos* being the word for war). Its civil war was officially fought from 1945 to 1949; in effect it, too, began in 1821 and continues in the divisions of society today. The strengths and weaknesses of the Greek character – industry and prevarication, openness and intrigue, xenophilia and xenophobia, love and bitterness – continually reassert themselves to both the honour and the detriment of this nation-state which, before 1821, was neither a nation nor a state, and, one could argue, is neither now.

Greeks' submission to foreign powers began with the Otto-man capture of Constantinople in 1453; it continued with their liberation by Britain, France and Russia in the 1820s; today, external forces direct its future, both political and economic; financial surveillance dates not from 2009-10 but from the mid-nineteenth century.

Thus the Greek mind is inured to these cycles of experience. Historians will argue not about *what* happened, but *how often* it recurred. One might call it "continually re-inventing the wheel"; the discontinuities of the Greek experience, its cyclic nature, constantly surprise us in the discomfort with which they imbue life today. To write anything about Greece pre-2010 seems to be painting a scenario of a disaster-waiting-to-happen, and in a sense the systemic collapse of Greece in our own time can be seen in the upheavals which punctuate this history since 1821.

The history of Greece – from ancient to modern – is the history of an idea: a spirit, a response to the landscape, a way of thinking, a culture, a crucible of dispute.

First, it was the idea that shaped the concept of a social polity. Second, it was the aesthetic concept which shaped the sculptures and public buildings and wrote its dramas – all intimately related to the interplay between men and gods. Third, it was the idea of "Greekness" which permeated the empire of Alexander ("the Great").

Then, fourth, during the long silent centuries after the disintegration of the empire and its conquest by Rome, it was the spirit that kept Hellenism alive in men's minds and hearts. Fifth, it became the idea of a modern Greek state, based on romantic principles, which Greek poets and intellectuals in exile encountered in the capitals of Europe and which fuelled the independence movement.

Sixth, it was the ill-fated idea that Greece should recover, by whatever means, its former glory (the *Megáli Idéa*).[1] Seventh, it was the idea of resistance to anything threatening the autonomy of the individual, the family and the immediate community.

This reduction serves history ill, yet it provides us, in a prism, with the many ideas that constitute the lifeblood of Greece today.

Although I have implied that these ideas appear in the Greek character chronologically, they are in fact present throughout history: the ideas of civil order, aesthetics, loyalties, self-expression and land ownership are all aspects of Greekness. Thanassos Cambanis believes that "there is no such thing as national character – just culture and history", to which he attributes the Greek problems.[2] He is missing the point: culture-plus-history *is* national character.

Greece is a myth that grew out of many myths, which are narratives: the basis of storytelling by which wisdom is transmitted down the generations and binds a community together in belief and behaviour. Today's Greeks are hardly different from their ancestors, in that they subscribe to myths, some of which are enabling, others disabling. So the "myth" has a much broader and deeper meaning than the mere word suggests to the western mind, where it usually connotes something unbelievable. The complexity of Greece is summed up in the final five words from Odysseas Elytis' 1959 poem "Axion Esti" ("It is Worthy"): "This small, this great world!" (Αιέν ο κόσμος ο μικρός, ο Μέγας! *Aién o kósmos o mikrós, o Mégas*).

"To deal with a matter so complex as Greek pre-history or even early history," wrote Lawrence Durrell, "one must be something like a water-diviner or a soothsayer."[3] I am neither. Therefore I am pressing the fast-forward button to bring the kaleidoscope of five key episodes in Greek history into immediate focus and thus to present them in their modern context.

Alexander the Great can be blamed for a lot. His native Macedonia was the *fons et origo* of his Greek empire, which embraced parts of Italy in the west, northern Asia (today's Afghanistan and Pakistan) to the east, and Egypt to the south (especially Alexandria, the Greek city founded by Alexander in 331 BC – a megalopolis or cosmopolis, in fact). It was financed by gold mines in Macedonia which are even today the source of local debate.[4] Greek colonists founded the port of Marseilles, with its strategic importance near the mouth of the Rhône. Palestine, Persia, Armenia, most of the Balkans, the Black Sea, Anatolia and north Africa all came within the ambit of the Hellenic influence: in many respects, they became "Greek", and the concept of the *pólis* (the conduct of the affairs of the state) permeated their cultures.[5]

It was this expansion that created not only a territorial empire, but also an empire of thought. This spirit of Hellenism pervaded that huge space and influenced the minds, first, of the peoples with whom it came into contact and, later, as an abiding ubiquitous influence in matters of thought, governance and comportment in the western imagination.

Irredentism began with the fall of Constantinople in 1453, which led almost immediately to ballads and other imprecations for the restoration of the city to the Hellenic world. Constantinople was a thesaurus of Greek works of art and manuscripts and the centre of Christian Orthodoxy. The Greek name for "Istanbul" remains "Constantinou-polis" – literally, the city of Constantine, which remained the focus, and last hope, of Hellenism. Its loss left an empty space at the centre of Greekness. The "Song of Agia Sophia" (the city's central church) promised that, one day, it would become "ours once more". The Irish equivalent aspiration, "a nation once again", will be obvious. The irredentist ambitions of republicans who see the unity of Ireland north and south as the only acceptable (to them) long-term strategy for Irish destiny echo similar ambitions in Greece.

In a sense – brutal though it may seem – there was no Greek history between 1453 and the first stirrings of nationalist thought in the 1780s. There is a massive period of empty time until the war of independence. It was one of the projects of Greek nationalism, in the later eighteenth and nineteenth centuries, to re-connect itself with the ancient past, with its dignity and the tropes of civilisation which its ancestors had given to the world.

Nikos Kazantzakis referred to "the double-born soul of the modern Greek", persisting in the idea of an ancient people and attempting to synthesise that with the modern world. The dilemma is at the base of the issues: what constitutes a "nation", what constitutes a "state", and how do they make a "nation-state"? Kazantzakis opened a highly divisive issue when he referred to the Greek's "Oriental bowels": "the East, all darkness and mystery, rises up from deep within him".[6] The tension of the east-west debate remains central to the question of Greek identity.

It may be due to this bipolar condition that Greeks have acquired a reputation for mendacity. Perhaps the most appropriate way of discussing this problem is in terms of the great "Liar's Paradox" of the Greek mind, which has exercised philosophers, logicians and even mathematicians since at least 600 BC: a Cretan tells you "All Cretans are liars". This means that the speaker is a liar; so how do you believe him? If he is to be believed – which on his own admission he isn't – then Cretans are truthful, thus disproving his statement. If the statement is true, then it is false; if it is false, then it is true. The paradox illustrates perfectly the difficulty in discovering the truth or otherwise of any given situation. As Lawrence Durrell put it, "to accept two contradictory ideas as simultaneously true".[7] The beauty of the paradox – and all paradoxes are beautiful – lies in its circularity. Much of modern Greece can be better understood or translated if one keeps this paradox in mind, and thus accepts both of the contradictory ideas.

At the risk of gross over-simplication and sins of omission, I shall briefly describe five key episodes in modern Greek history:

- the War of Independence, 1821-30

- the *enosis* (union) of the Ionian Islands with the Greek state in 1864

- the Balkan wars of 1912-13, the First World War and the Anatolian campaign and catastrophe, 1920-22

- the Second World War, 1940-44 and the Civil War, 1943-49

- the military junta 1967-74.

You'll note that these almost all concern strife and dissension, while the intervening years are marked by civic disputes, rapid changes of government, the arrivals and departures of monarchy, the struggle to establish a constitution, the challenge of modernisation, and the economic malaise that has always beset a country without appreciable industry or adequate infrastructure. They punctuate the flow of a society's narrative as it struggles towards its own identity, making that narrative discontinuous.

The War of Independence, 1821-30

The Greek flag was raised in defiance (*epanástasi*) in the Peloponnese, on 25 March 1821, by Bishop Germanos of Patras. Or was it? There is a strong likelihood that the date, the location and the flag-raiser were constructed from separate episodes in order to create a sense of unity and urgency.

Like most ambitions for independence, the momentum in Greece, as in Ireland, was intellectual before it was military, and preceded the opening signals of armed revolt (Greece 1821, Ireland 1916) by several decades.

Due to its history of discontinuities, Greece staggered towards statehood and unity; the foundation of the state, and its recognition and guarantee by the Great Powers of Britain, France and

40

Russia (which had in effect brought it into existence) were the beginning of a process of amalgamation and accommodation, during which the state moved from a small geographical area to the
country we know today.

The process of Greek territorial unification (in four major
tranches) was, however, far from simple, since it was accompanied
by a perennial debate about the nature and purpose of the state
– in fact, the role and ontology of Hellenism – which continues
to the present. Attempts at unity have been both embraced and
thwarted by all patriotic Greeks who find co-operation, concord

The extension of the Greek national territory from 1864 (union with
Ionian islands) to 1947 (accession of the Dodecanese islands). The
temporary acquisition of land lost to Turkey in 1922 is shown on
the west coast of Turkey.

41

and conciliation to be central difficulties in organising a modern political entity.

The nucleus of nationalism was the *Filikí Etaireía* (Society of Friends),[8] founded in Odessa in 1814 by merchants rather than intellectuals, but incorporating ideas current among Greek exiles for at least thirty years before that. It was an *ad hoc* amalgam of desperation, combining merchants, landowners, priests, bandits (*klephts*) and warlords. *Klephts* occupy an ambiguous position in Greek history: they were "outlaws" in the sense that they denied conventional authority under the Ottomans, retreating to the mountains to escape reprisals. While they were thus hostile to the Turks, they also conducted a "highwayman" existence; "brave, brutal, anarchic and cunning, but men of honour in the traditional Greek sense".[9] Their energy and resourcefulness was successfully harnessed to the cause of independence, after which their tradition passed subliminally to those who conducted similar guerrilla resistance during the Second World War.

As a gross exaggeration, to say nothing of misrepresentation, I think we can see a genealogy of the Left, a connection between the historical *klephts* and their successors, the "Left" of twentieth-century politics, as discussed by Neni Panourgiá in *Dangerous Citizens*: the Left have, in effect, been the outlaws of political life; after the Civil War communism was illegal; under the junta the Left was excoriated, from their cultural leaders such as Mikis Theodorakis to the humblest foot-soldier. One can readily appreciate the expression of a committed socialist in conservative Greece, disputing the location of the true *pólis*.

Those most in favour of the revolution (apart from the philhellenes and intellectuals) were the rising merchant and professional classes, who smelled the chance of placement, power and profit – as does the bourgeoisie in any such situation; but in some minds, mainly those of the peasantry, the exchange of one type of master for another would be of little consequence; the same held true of the semi-autonomous feudal landlords (*kotzambasidhes*), provided that it was they who remained the masters. Most lords and peasants lived on the *latifundia* (in Greek, the Turkish term *tsiflíki* is current) which were not abolished (with redistribution of land) until 1923; for them, the family and the village were of paramount – perhaps the only – importance, and local issues such as access to water or the imposition of taxation were more demanding than the idea of founding a "state" or constituting a "nation".[10] In these local loyalties we can see the resistance to any form of centralised government that removed power from the locality, and even the reluctance to put faith in the idea of elected representatives of the people.

Campbell and Sherrard see some dissension among the revolutionaries in 1823-24 as a "virtual" war; Koliopoulos and Veremis also refer to this period as "civil war". Campbell and Sherrard specifically refer to the situation after the assassination of Iannis Kapodistrias, the first president of Greece, in 1831 as "civil war", as does Misha Glenny, while Doumanis sees that event as "the country descend[ing] again into chaos".[11] It's essential to recognise this fact, since it bears directly on later dissensions.

The next attempt to unify the country was the imposition of a foreign monarchy. Thus, the dispute as to whether Greece should be a republic or a monarchy, which ended in 1974, was already in place in 1831. The monarchy was always at risk: as Prince Leopold of Saxe-Coburg (a potential occupant of the Greek throne) is said to have quipped, "whoever becomes King of Greece had better keep his bags packed".[12]

The inner momentum of nationalism would not have been sufficient to overthrow Turkish domination and establish a nation state without the supervening will of the "Great Powers", at that time still engaged in the "struggle for mastery in Europe". Greece was a side-show in the fall-out from the Congress of Vienna of 1815, which mastered the dismemberment of the Napoleonic empire and the consequent reorganisation of their client states in central Europe.

Greece was to depend thereafter on the political will of these powers for its security, financial fortunes (and misfortunes) and definition of its national boundaries.

Greece was an unpopular and insecure monarchy until 1974. The Great Powers canvassed the courts of Europe for a suitable candidate, many of whom declined the honour before appointing, in 1832, Otto (Otho), the seventeen-year-old son of Ludwig I of Bavaria. He was accompanied by a regent and a court of Bavarian advisers who established a Greek-free administration and a standing army, again almost entirely Bavarian. But the only "King Otto" acclaimed by the Greek people was Otto Rehhagel, who coached the Greek football team to victory in the European Cup in 2004.[13]

It is ironic that the state was the result of "the first major successful war of independence by a subject population against an imperial power since the American Revolution",[14] which led to "the first polity created in Europe where nationality and modernism were formally recognized as the organizing principles of the state",[15] yet it was also the first problematic state created by the Great Powers with which they had to contend and manage.

One of the most significant lessons to be learnt from the economic struggles of the new state was its financial indebtedness to external powers: in the War of Independence, a debt of four million pounds was incurred to Britain alone in respect of capital provision, armaments and interest repayments. Greece has, in fact, been in debt to the Great Powers ever since its creation; it had been bankrupt in 1843, and subject to international supervision since 1856, which was formalised in 1897 with an International Financial Commission to control Greek finances (not unlike the role of the International Monetary Fund today), thus indicating a loss of national sovereignty which was to become a major crisis in the economic collapse of 2010.

Otto promised constitutional reform, a promise he did not keep, which led in 1862 to his ousting and replacement by another foreigner, a prince of Denmark (like his predecessor, he too was seventeen years old) who took the throne as George I in 1863, the year preceding the Ionian *enosis*. He was titled "King of the Hellenes", as distinct from Otto who had been "King of Greece" – the semantic difference indicating, in George's case, the wish to see the state embracing Greeks living outside the frontiers of the state.[16] The connection with European royalty was strengthened by George's being the brother-in-law of Britain's future king Edward VII and Tsar Alexander III, the uncle of Britain's future George V and cousin to the monarchs of Norway, Denmark, Spain, Belgium, Romania and Yugoslavia.

With the advent of George I it seemed that Greece might look forward to a "crowned democracy" – not a million miles away from the idea, promoted at exactly the same time (1864) by Sir William Wilde as a measure of Home Rule for Ireland, of a "regal republic".

Ionian *Enosis*, 1864

The *enosis* (union) of the Ionian islands with the thirty-year-old state of Greece in 1864 was its first territorial accretion (the last of which would be the Dodecanese[17] islands in 1947), but it was also an accretion of intellectual and cultural acumen. Greece needed both a greater territory and an invigoration of *nous*.

In 1844, John Kolettis, a major parliamentary figure in the first decades of Greek independence,[18] had stated that "The Greek Kingdom is not the whole of Greece, but only a part, the smallest and poorest part".[19] It was a signpost to expansion and one of the first instances of the *Megáli Idéa* – a term which originated with Kolettis: a national sense of mission which appealed to the "inextinguishable nostalgia of the Greek race".[20]

If Greece as a whole is a meeting-point of east and west, Corfu and the other Ionians are the meeting-place of Greece and Italy. They are both east and west, displaying characteristics and behaviour patterns, even today, which you will not encounter on the mainland or in the Aegean. They are the cusp of European Greece, as the Dodecanese are its eastern meniscus.

As a result of the international treaty of Constantinople in 1800 (the first of many affecting both the Ionians and Greece), a Heptanese (or Septinsular) Republic[21] was established; it has been described as "the first Greek state to be established [since] 1453",[22] and, as such, "a beacon to the mainland Greeks."[23] With the defeat of Napoleon in 1814/15 another treaty, in Paris, assigned the islands to a reluctant Britain, which created a "protectorate", known technically as "the United States of the Ionian Islands" but, in effect, under British rule, with an indigenous parliament subject to the authority of the High Commissioner. The principal language of public affairs remained Italian, with Greek spoken almost exclusively by the peasantry: thus the drama of the islands was enacted in Italian, dubbed into English with Greek subtitles.

Ionian *enosis* was not a simple matter of whether or not the islands would vote for union with Greece, or whether Greece would welcome the islands (although the vote was hotly disputed, and the result was greeted with some misgivings in Athens). The islands were in fact dangled before Greece as a carrot to induce acceptance of the new king, so that Greece would both acquire the constitution it had sought unsuccessfully under Otto, and much-needed territory.

••

Irish Philhellenes

Two Irishmen were among the administrators of the Ionian islands: George Nugent Grenville (1788-1850) from County Westmeath, became Lord Nugent in 1813; he was an early member of the London Hellenic Committee; High Commissioner 1832-35, he demonstrated his philhellenism by publishing a literary periodical, the Ionian Anthology.[24] Sir John Young (1807-1826), from County Cavan, a former MP for Cavan and Chief Secretary for Ireland 1852-55, was High Commissioner 1855-58.[25]

A Dubliner of Huguenot descent, Edward Blaquière (d.1832), was, in 1823, one of the founders of the London Hellenic League which included Thomas Moore, Byron and Jeremy Bentham among its supporters; it was instrumental in raising funds for the war of independence and subsequently to stabilise the fledgling provisional government.

Charles Napier (1782-1853) who identified with the Greeks as much as the Irish, was the cousin of Lord Edward Fitzgerald, and as such may have shared Fitzgerald's sense of republicanism. Napier exhibited his philhellenism as a British administrator by falling out with the Governor of Corfu and as a result being posted to Kephalonia; there he hosted Byron, loved a Greek woman with whom he had two daughters, and wrote an important survey of the island's infrastructure. His subsequent career took him to the Indian north-west frontier, where, as a conquering general, he sent the one-word telegram to London, "peccavi" – "I have Sind". C.M. Woodhouse, whom we shall encounter later, considered that such as Napier "found in foreign causes a sublimation for their own nationalism",[26] and Napier himself said: "The Greeks are more like the Irish than any other people, so like, even to the oppression they suffer, that as I could not do good to Ireland the next pleasure was to serve men groaning under similar tyranny".[27]

Sir Richard Church (1784-1873), of Quaker origins in Cork, was probably the most experienced and distinguished of the philhellenes to be actively engaged in the war itself. He had participated in the capture of the Ionian islands. After service with the King of Naples, he returned to Greece in 1827 as commander-in-chief of the Greek army; when he led a victorious entry to the Peloponnese that year, he was greeted as "our father!". However, he resigned after disagreements with Kapodistrias, but subsequently served in the post-independence Greek military, becoming governor of Roumeli and was part of the coup which almost deposed King Otto in 1843, resulting in a form of constitutional government. Having become a Greek citizen, he made his home in Athens for the last twenty years of his life, and on his death in 1873 his gravestone recorded that he had "given himself and all that he had to rescue a Christian race from oppression and to make Greece a nation". A street in Athens is named after him.

Sir Thomas Wyse (1791-1862), a former MP for Tipperary and Waterford, author of a treatise on education and the husband of Napoleon's niece, was British ambassador to Greece in 1849 and remained sympathetic to the Greek cause. His son, William Bonaparte-Wyse, was briefly considered as a candidate for the throne of Greece after the abdication of King Otto in 1863.

Another Quaker, James Bourchier (1850-1920), from County Limerick, worked as the Times correspondent in the Balkans from 1888 and was decorated by the Greek government for his reports. He covered the first Olympic games in 1896 before moving to Crete to cover the anti-Turkish rebellion of 1896-97. He actually became an adviser to the Greek government on Cretan affairs and, as a friend of Prince George, was instrumental in the latter becoming Greece's representative in Crete; he played a vital role as a go-between in the fracas between the prince and the up-and-coming Cretan politician Eleftherios Venizelos who later became Greek prime minister.

And, much later in the century, Ireland pioneered much work in Hellenic studies, with J.P. Mahaffy (Provost of TCD), author of many works on Greece including Rambles and Studies in Greece, Greek Life and Thought, What Have the Greeks Done for Modern Civilisation and Social Life in Greece, in which he provided the first frank discussion in English of Greek homosexuality, and in which he acknowledged *the assistance of "my old pupil Mr Oscar Wilde". Wilde himself accompanied Mahaffy on a visit to Greece in 1879, after which he claimed "I was the first undergraduate to visit Olympia".[28] He also told W.B. Yeats, "We Irish are [...] a nation of brilliant failures, but we are the greatest talkers since the Greeks".[29]*

The Irish Institute of Hellenic Studies in Athens was established in 1995: see J.V. Luce et al. (eds.), The Lure of Greece: Irish Involvement in Greek Culture, Literature, History and Politics.

. . . .

The Balkan Wars, the First World War and the "Anatolian Catastrophe", 1912-22

The 1880s saw a huge extension in the railways and a programme of road-building which transformed Greece's infrastructure. The 1880s and 1890s also saw two elements in rural depopulation: emigration, mainly to the USA,[30] and movement towards the cities and the creation of an urban, professional middle class. Success in political life was dictated by the need of MPs (as in Ireland's TDs) to maintain their local support by means of clientelism, which inhibited the development of political parties with identifiable ideologies and policies.

It was not enough to emulate the appearance of a western democracy: the values of such a society must be inculcated into an administration built on graft, nepotism and lack of discipline.

As part of the treaty of Berlin in 1881, Greece's second major territorial gain came in Thessaly (to the north of the existing Greek mainland, between Athens and Macedonia). This, for the first time, gave Greece a significant continental identity, but it continued to look enviously at its northern border with Bulgaria and, as always, at Anatolia.

As a result of the Balkan Wars, Greece gained the key cities of Thessaloniki (together with much more of Macedonia, on the northern border with Bulgaria) and Ioannina (in Epirus, on the western mainland). These wars thus opened the possibility of a major advance by Greece in the realisation of the *Megáli Idéa*. The British Prime Minister, Lloyd George, an admirer of his Greek counterpart, Eleftherios Venizelos, considered the Greeks to be "the people of the future in the eastern Mediterranean",[31] but he also made clear the juniority of Greece in any negotiations when he stated in 1912 "the future of Greece will be decided in London, not Athens". The immediate and direct origins of an apparent British support for Greece's Asia Minor ambitions came in 1915 with the offer of a trade-off: the acquisition by Greece of the coastal lands (Anatolia) in exchange for Greek support in the war. As Michael Llewellyn Smith wryly remarks: "It was easier to offer what belonged to others."[32] One is reminded of the (no doubt) apocryphal story that, entering the peace conference at Versailles (when the victorious Powers, in 1918-19, once more carved up the European landmass into their respective spheres of influence), Lloyd George asked one of his aides, "Is it Upper or Lower Silesia that we are giving away?"

In the period 1909-13 Greece had increased its territory by almost 70 per cent, and its population from 2.7 million to 4.4 million. But the shopping list was far from satisfied, if all the lands inhabited by Greek peoples (including Anatolia and the Pontus (the southern shore of the Black Sea)) were to be brought within its embrace. Nevertheless, Greeks could be forgiven for thinking that, for once, history was being kind to them.

The Anatolian Catastrophe saw the culmination and extinction of the *Megáli Idéa* which had been one of the main determinants in the establishment of the aspirational Greek state, and one of the most divisive. Those who saw it as the duty of Greeks to pursue the irredentist claim, and to put it into effect by achieving the ultimate goal of Constantinople, were driven irrationally towards the catastrophe from which Greece continues to suffer.

Anatolia remained the prize for Greece which seemed possible only if Greece were backed internationally against Turkey. It had been one of the first areas colonised by the Greeks. The centre was Smyrna, with other famed cities such as Ephesus (today, Turkish Efes) and Trebizond (Trabzon). The hinterland was a fertile plain of farming land, in which a life of simple husbandry was conducted.

Venizelos tried to persuade the king that it was possible, by alliance with the British, "to save Hellenism in Turkey and to secure the creation of a truly great Greece, including almost all the territories in which Hellenism has been active during its long history".[33] With encouragement, but no military support, from Britain, France and the USA, Greece was foolishly optimistic.[34] In May 1919, the Greek army occupied Smyrna – prosperous, vibrant, and nationalist, "the heart of Hellenism in Asia Minor",[35] frequently called "the Paris of the Levant" and "the Joy of Asia". The King had visited the city and proclaimed to his troops: "You are fighting for the Hellenic idea which produced in this very place that incomparable civiization which will never cease to merit the admiration of the whole world".[36] This neatly encapsulated the spatial, intellectual and moral superiority of the Greek claim to Asia Minor.

The peoples whom the Idea wished to assimilate were the "unredeemed Greeks" – the very term implying a self-criticism that Greece had so far failed to incorporate their Greekness into the reality of the state. Until that was achieved, these unredeemed Greeks constituted a state (of mind) outside the "real" state whose borders would be read on the map as a reproach.

The Greek army was outmanoeuvred by the Turks and fled ignominiously. The Turks destroyed the city, eradicating all signs of Greekness. But the aftermath was the real catastrophe, with the uprooting and exchange of the two populations – the Anatolian Greeks to a country they had never known, and the Turks in eastern Greece to their own homeland – over one million Anatolians were exported to Greece, after which refugees accounted for 25 per cent of Greece's population, and a definite Turkish element was directly imported into Greek society and culture (see Chapter 7 for the phenomenon of *Rebétiko*). The Anatolian refugees had to be accommodated and settled, the cost of the extra burden on the exchequer being ameliorated only slightly by Red Cross aid and US cash. They were Greeks but not yet Greek. And they carried their Anatolia with them, building new settlements such as the Athens suburbs of "Nea Smyrna", "Nea Ionia" and "Nea Chalkidona".

As Lawrence Durrell wrote, only thirty-five years after the catastrophe:

> The tragedy of his expulsion from Anatolia still weighs
> heavily upon the heart of the modern Greek, whether he

is a metropolitan or an exile from the bountiful plains and wooded mountains of Asia Minor. He cannot forget it. If he is an exile he returns again and again to Anatolia in his dreams: he broods upon it [...] But it is more than the injustice, the cruelty, the madness of the whole episode which sticks in the mind of the modern Greek. It is also a sense of a lost richness, a lost peace of mind [...] It has become a memory which he touches from time to time, like a man fingering a cicatrice.[37]

Once the war outside the state was removed as the unifying force of the *Megáli Idéa*, the different ambitions vested in it became a "war" within the state. The Civil War was born once more in 1922.

The Anatolian Catastrophe therefore brought to the surface a further, and perhaps deeper, set of distinctions which was aggravated by the collapse of this unifying principle, the *Megáli Idéa*: between those who believed that Greece, as a state, had never been properly conceived, established or promulgated, and those whose pragmatism induced them to accept the art of the possible and to find compromise and the middle way as the exemplars and warrantors of stability and the route to continued prosperity. What was Greece? A territorial reality or a state of mind? A republic or a monarchy? A traditional, domestic society based on conservative, time-honoured values, or a modern polity playing a role in the international community? A society in which plutocracy overrode merit, in which the rich became richer and the poor poorer, or one in which workers, both urban and rural, could share any new prosperity?

In 1935, after a succession of attempted coups threatening civil war, the king, George II, established a right-wing government led by General Ioannis Metaxas, who rapidly declared a state of emergency and suspended parliament.[38]

The 1940-45 War and the Civil War

On 28 October 1940, the Italian dictator, Mussolini (whom Metaxas admired), demanded access to Greek territory by his troops through the border with Albania. Albania had been an Italian

ΔΗΜΟΤΙΚΟ ΠΕΡΙΦΕΡΕΙΑΚΟ ΘΕΑΤΡΟ ΚΕΡΚΥΡΑΣ

OH! WHAT A SURPRISE FOR THE DU-CE!

(HE CAN'T PUT IT OVER THE GREEKS)

ΠΩ ΠΩ ΤΙ ΕΠΑΘΕ Ο ΜΟΥΣΟΛΙΝΙ!

ΔΕΥΤΕΡΑ 28 ΟΚΤΩΒΡΙΟΥ 2013

Poster advertising a celebration of "Ochi Day", 28 October, in Corfu in 2013, showing a Greek soldier in traditional fustanella dress pitchforking a diminutive Mussolini.

puppet during the 1930s, and its king had fled when the Italian army entered in June 1939, ahead of the opening of the world war. When he received Mussolini's demand, the response of Metaxas was "*Ochi!*" – "No!" Thereafter, not only has 28 October become "Ochi Day", one of the major national holidays, but a symbol of all Greeks' defiance of intrusion on their privacy. Cynics might say that "Ochi" did not signal an achievement, since it inevitably preceded invasion, but that would be to ignore the fact that it was a direct act of resistance which would be such a marked feature of Greece's war. "Ochi" resonates for all Greeks as a statement of defiance and the right to dissent.

The Greek army, which the Italians presumably assumed would offer little opposition, was mobilised and a severe war ensued on the Greek-Albanian border (in the northwest), resulting, after five months, in the defeat of the Italians – the first such defeat of an Axis power by the Allies in the history of the war. But it immediately sealed Greece's fate, as the response was a swift and thorough German invasion through Greece's northeast. Control of Greece was shared between Germany and Italy until Italian capitulation in 1943, whereupon the German control of Greece was, in theory, complete, but in practice was restricted to cities and towns, while the resistance occupied the mountains.[39]

The left-wing EAM (*Ethnikón Apelftherotikón Métopon* – National Liberation Movement) had its military wing in ELAS (*Ethnikós Laikós Apelevtherotikós Stratós* – National Popular Liberation Army, appropriating the name of the state, Hellas). EAM/ELAS was the kernel of the resistance. Tens of thousands of Greek citizens were murdered by the Germans in reprisals against partisan raids, sometimes involving wholesale slaughter and villagers being burned alive, with which the name of Kurt Waldheim (at that time a German officer in northern Greece and later secretary-general of the United Nations and president of Austria) has been linked.[40]

It is no doubt callous to suggest that the Civil War was of greater significance than the German occupation. How can one overlook the fact that almost the entire Jewish population of Greece was deported to the death camps?[41] How can one ignore the fact that 250,000 people died of starvation (in 1941, in Athens alone, 35,000-40,000) as a result of German appropriation of available food?[42] Or that an estimated 500,000 people (seven per cent of the population) died in the war? Or that inflation pushed the price of bread from ten drachmas in 1940 to 34 million drachmas in 1944? But the *transitus* of resistance into civil war in fact caused more damage to the fabric of Greek society than that of the war against the Germans.

In a tragic sense World War II segued seamlessly into the Civil War. It was a long time coming: it had been conceived in 1821. The issues had been present since before the foundation of the state. In C.M. Woodhouse's words, it was a "moral and psychological struggle for the hearts and minds of the Greek people".[43] Greeks were presented with rival political orientations, rival squadrons of paramilitaries and rival foreign powers bidding for their adhesion.

The question(s) of what Greece actually was, and would be, in the nineteenth and twentieth centuries had divided all classes and sectors of society: tradition-versus-modernism, rural-versus-urban, and, above all, the capacity of Greece to make its own decisions on economic policy. The economic turmoil of the 1920s and 1930s had been the seedbed of the discontent which the Metaxas dictatorship of 1936 was intended to suppress.

Historians disagree as to when the Civil War started and when it ended. Some date its starting point to 1943, others to 1945 and 1946; and its end to 1948, 1949 or 1950.[44] From 1941 the split was obvious but silent; from 1943, overt civil war was only a dice throw away. If the Metaxas dictatorship had not been overtaken by that of the Nazis, the Civil War would most likely have become overt much earlier. Greece had been on the brink of civil war from 1936, as it had in 1824-25, 1862 and 1916.

Those of the Left who had conducted the guerrilla campaign against the Germans, alongside their right-wing counterparts, now found themselves at odds with their fellow countrymen, because it now became obvious that the German occupation had been a temporary interruption in the process of conflict between left and right. In more than a physical sense, the *antártes* (guerrillas, partisans, rebels) of the self-styled "Democratic Army", like the brigands and *klephts* before them, remained in the mountains which were their natural terrain, both physically and metaphysically. It can be reasonably suggested, too, that the spirit of the *antártes* is to be found in the resistance and opposition to the state in today's terrorists and anarchists. The mountain warriors have become urban guerrillas.

It was clear that German retreat left the way open for a debate on how Greece would then be governed, and at first it seemed that this might be conducted peacefully; but, in the absence of a common enemy, the disparate groups turned on each other and on the residual British troops in Athens who were directed by Britain's monarchist orientation.[45] The language question was also part of the division: the provisional government of the Left declared that demotic was the language of education, legislation, judicial decisions and official documents.[46] This debate would also surface under the junta, and for the same reasons.

The post-war relief offered by Britain and the USA was, we now know, conditional on Greece eliminating communism. Thus the British, whose aid to the partisans in the anti-Nazi guerrilla campaign had been so crucial, were now backing their political opponents in the pursuit of Balkan and Levantine stability. Some bewilderment has been caused by the fact that the British should turn against their former allies, after Liberation, and suppress them in order to ensure the return of the monarchy. A sage interpretation of this apparent contradiction is Nicos Svoronos's view that, all along, Britain saw "the need to use [...] EAM-ELAS for military operations with however the ultimate aim of preventing by any means its eventual acquisition of power".[47]

The common interest (shared by Britain and the USA) was the defeat of communism, or at least its containment within the

Stalinist sphere of influence and definitely not beyond the northern borders of Greece with Bulgaria, Yugoslavia and Albania –
feeders for the resistance which had once been the common ally
and was now the enemy. The defeat of communism and (due to
the particular insistence of Churchill) the restoration of a democratic monarchy as the "legitimate" body of the state, was the
bottom line, aided enormously by the cessation of supplies from
Greece's three northern communist neighbours and the closure
of the borders.

It was important for them that Greece should remain aloof
from the communist bloc in the rest of the Balkans, for ideological reasons, but more importantly for its strategic position. The
exclusion of Greece from that bloc had been part of a deal between
Churchill and Stalin in 1944 (and assented to by Roosevelt) which
has all the flavour of Lloyd George's "which are we giving away?"
gambit.[48]

The involvement of Britain and the
USA in post-war Greek affairs was a
matter of geopolitics. On one side, the
returning government and its army
was backed – and militarily supplied –
by Britain and the USA. On the other,
EAM/ELAS, predominantly but not
exclusively communist, was backed
initially by Yugoslavia, Albania and
Bulgaria. This gives us a stark indication of the polarisation of the conflict,
which was in effect the first, and most
serious, demonstration of the Iron
Curtain and the Cold War. The extermination of communism, and the
fighting force which had been so crucial to Britain's Mediterranean strategy
in the world war, was Churchill's and
Truman's chief objective. It was a case
of excluded middle. *Either* a communist (or at least left-wing) republic *or*

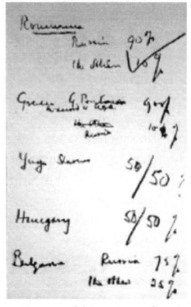

*A page of the memorandum
handwritten by Winston
Churchill, allocating control
of Greece to Britain and of
Romania to the Soviet Union;
the positive tick is Stalin's.*

a conservative monarchy. A scenario where the former EAM or KKE, *Kommounistikón Kómma Elládas*, the Communist Party, as representative of the left, might be admitted to power-sharing was inconceivable.

US bias against communism (with the lowering of Churchill's "Iron Curtain") was, if anything, more paranoid than Churchill's,[49] and led the US not only to give vital – and brutal – support to the right in the Civil War, but also to support it in Greek politics almost up to the present day.

While it was Churchill who had negotiated the western hegemony over Greece, the USA in 1947 became the dominant partner in this geopolitical deal, with the "Truman Doctrine" which specifically committed economic support for Greece in order to exclude Soviet interests. Elizabeth Barker suggests that the British were obliged to leave Greece "by their own grave financial and economic difficulties" but that "they did not leave until they were confident the Americans would take their place".[50] Greece became "the biggest beneficiary per capita of American largesse in the world – receiving more than $3 billion in military and economic assistance by 1963".[51] The revival of the Greek economy was due largely to this investment, but we also see a rehearsal for the EU's frustrations with Greek administrative problems in that the Americans found the Greek civil service "a depressing farce", and the modernisation of the system was too "politicized, rigid and insensitive to the needs of ordinary citizens".[52]

The essence of the Civil War's legacy is that anyone known to have been actively associated with EAM or to be politically inclined towards the left was blacklisted and remained a non-citizen during the post-war and junta periods; even with the restoration of democracy under New Democracy in 1974, a conservative distrust of the left continued to jeopardise the possibility of dissent.

In 1946, on 25 March (Independence Day), Kazantzakis's play *Kapodistrias* was performed at the National Theatre. Kazantzakis chose Kapodistrias as a historical figure who might be taken as a symbol of the continuing Greek quest for freedom, this time from the Nazis. Kazantzakis was a witness to – and a participant in – this quest. The idea of Greece re-inventing its freedom arose, in his mind, with the onset of Civil War. In late 1949, with the defeat of the left, he wrote "slavery has oppressed us once again [...] in order to free ourselves, we have need of a new 1821"; and eight months later, "It is our duty to stare at the abyss with dignity and faith".[53] The idea that one is indentured to despair permeates his novels, such as *Christ Recrucified* (written 1949 but not published until 1954), *Freedom or Death* (1953) and *The Fratricides* (1963). Wary and distrustful of giving his novels contemporary contexts, Kazantzakis (like the South African André Brink)[54] employed allegory as a strategy to both escape censorship and make connections with past events that resonate in the folk memory and conscience. *Christ Recrucified* provides "implicit and sustained allusions to the [...] civil war".[55] *Freedom or Death* is a book of despair: "man who wants to be free, today is done for" said its author,[56] and the novel's subtitle is, "He says he wants to be free. Kill him". Kazantzakis' title is deliberately ironic, since "freedom or death" was the war cry in the War of Independence (and the symbol of the *Filikí Etaireía*).

Military Junta (the Colonels), 1967-74

From the end of the Civil War, an unofficial cadre of middle-ranking army officers (probably descended from the "IDEA" group[57] formed among the army-in-exile in 1944, and also the "X" group of pro-royalist paramilitaries, which had taken the monarchist side in the Civil War)[58] fostered a pervasive sense of the need to reimpose a strict government, preferably with a civilian frontispiece, to repair and rebuild what they saw as a state still troubled by left-wing ideas. (This was the reason for the junta being dubbed "the Colonels", since it was not the generals but these middle-rankers who planned the coup, of which even the chief-of-staff was unaware.)

Since 1949 an unstable society was proof that, despite a definitive ceasefire, the Civil War had not ended. After six years of conflict, society needed peace and harmony. This, however, was – and remains – elusive. With the eclipse of the left (KKE was banned) successive governments nevertheless failed to establish an acceptable form of democracy. Constantine Tsoucalas puts this in context:

The search for a national identity, which had been the major preoccupation of the Greek ruling class through-out the nineteenth century, had finally and sadly failed. It was the realization of this failure that had been the main stimulant for the search for new directions during the thirties.[59]

The conflict was now between liberals and conservatives, with US influence brought heavily to bear on the promotion of the latter. Elections in 1950, 1951 and 1952 were inconclusive, with Sophokles Venizelos (son of Eleftherios) failing to punch even below his father's weight.[60] Attempts at new political parties and various coalitions reflected the fluidity which the Colonels would eventually describe as a "chaos" which only they could quell. During this period, the US carrot was the withholding of finance for post-war reconstruction (reminiscent of the EU's threats to more recent Greek governments), and, it was made clear to the British ambassador, "the US government have now committed themselves to a definite and overt interference in the internal affairs" of Greece;[61] it was orchestrated by ambassador John Peurifoy (who two years later, as ambassador to Guatemala, engineered a right-wing coup there). It's been said that his name became synonymous with "the vile and brutal way the Americans treated their subjects".[62] When the US Congress questioned America's role in supporting the jun-ta, Deputy Defense Secretary David Packard testified that "I am not supporting the attitude of the government, but I am simply saying that our military considerations are overriding".[63]

The military figurehead was Colonel Yiorgos Papadopoulos (a former member of "IDEA", which had already attempted a coup in 1951), who became President of Greece in the absence of the king. In Peter Levi's opinion, he was "a fanatic with no brains" while his right-hand man, Brigadier Stylianos Pattakos, was "a sadistic buf-foon". The government collectively was "like the Marx brothers without the talent".[64] Fanaticism and sadism were indeed evident in the junta's proceedings, but there were brains, too, but perhaps little or no talent.

In its first days, the junta announced, "We have long been witnessing a crime committed against our people and our nation" perpetrated by the media and political parties, involving a "methodical attack on and undermining of all institutions [...] paralysis of state machinery [...], moral decline" leading to "an atmosphere of anarchy, chaos, hatred and discord" and "the brink of national catastrophe".[65] The Colonels would counter this by a move "towards radical change [...] prosperity and progress [...] social justice [...] moral and material improvement of society as a whole and especially of the peasants and workers of the poorer classes".[66] No one on the left would have argued with the first part of that statement, and it gives us a pre-echo of the self-justification of terrorist/anarchist groups in present-day Greece. The note of alarm appealed to a middle class sense of stability, the need for order out of chaos and the elimination of the causes of "anarchy".

Papadopoulos and his spokesmen went on to claim, in 1971, that "democracy has already been achieved in Greece" and "Greece is the most democratic country in southeast Europe and the Middle East"[67] – the second part of which might, in a tight corner, be arguably true, the first part of which was so flagrant an untruth that to call it "inane" is mild.

The rhetoric, such as it was, of the junta was, as in the early years of independent Greece, a linguistic sleight of mouth. The word for revolution, *epanástasis*, meaning "uprising" would have resonated with Greeks as it had done 140 years earlier, suggesting Christ's resurrection (*anástasis*) and thus reassuring citizens that Greece was Christian and therefore an integrated nation.

The Greeks were confronted with a minority government with draconian powers, ranging from arrest without warrant, imprisonment without trial, interrogation, torture, murder and – the ultimate penalty of the dispossessed – to become one of the "disappeared". This was not merely an insult to democracy, because "democracy" itself had become a much-abused term, but what seemed, in George Seferis's words, a "*coup de grâce*" to all that is meant by Greekness.[68]

S. Victor Papacosma suggests: "The combined effects of brutal force, skill, considerable luck, and a divided opposition provided the junta with several years to prove that authoritarian rule rather than the traditionally turbulent parliamentary system could offer more effective, honest government".[69] Furthermore, the economy improved: the average annual per capita income increased from $700 in 1967 to $1,200 in 1973. And as we shall see in relation to popular support for Golden Dawn vigilantism (below, p. 135), the regime was greeted in some quarters for those improvements: Peter Levi was told "no more strikes. [The buses] come on time now [...] The working man likes this government" and as for democracy, "people need a little but not too much".[70]

A context of fear inhibited people's ability to protest openly: one of Levi's friends "disappeared" for ten days; "he came back with the marks of someone who had been badly beaten up, but he refused to talk about how, or by whom".[71] Peter Murtagh (at that time an editor at the *Guardian* and today with *The Irish Times*) has given us (in his *The Rape of Greece*, 1994) painfully graphic descriptions of torture inflicted on suspected dissidents.

The lesson to be learned was: the price of progress is cohesion; the price of life is uniformity.

Only with a seminal and provocative statement by Seferis and the publication in 1970 of *Eighteen Texts* (a collection of essays, stories and poems by young and old writers) were acts of defiance articulated.

In his statement (broadcast by the BBC, heard and also disseminated in print in Athens) Seferis called the dictatorship a "compulsory paralysis in which whatever spiritual values we have succeeded in keeping alive, with toil and suffering, are on their way [...] to be drowned in stagnant and marshy water". The junta was "absolutely and utterly opposed to the ideals for which our world, and so gloriously our people, fought in the last world war."[72]

During the junta, Theo Angelopoulos made his film *Days of '36*, an allegorical narrative of political assassination by a right-wing government (that of Metaxas). He referred to his strategy as "a film about dictatorship during a time of dictatorship, so it was impossible for me to use direct references. I sought a secret language. The allusions of History."[73]

Peter Mackridge, who lived in Athens during the junta, called it "a particularly inane dictatorship".[74] He expanded on this comment by remarking on the content and "excruciating language" of the junta's public pronouncements, their imposition of dress codes for men and women, and their manipulation of the media.[75] Mackridge also pointed out that the language issue was raised yet again by the junta's insistence that "*katharévousa* [...] was the only variety of Greek worthy of being called the 'national language' whereas demotic was no more than a debased, corrupt, and barbaric idiom".[76] With this strategy, the Colonels probably did more to foster resentment of their policies than the severe restrictions on other freedoms, since it implied that to be acceptable as a "proper" Greek one must conform to certain codes, or be judged "barbaric" – outsiders, expelled from civility and the *pólis*.

The statements by the junta, to which Mackridge refers, and the counter-statements by such as Seferis, employ the same mental images and almost the same vocabulary, for the same reason: they attempted to appeal to the patriotism of Greeks, to enlist their support for a concept of Greekness; one, on the "right", insisted on a "purity" of Greekness in language, thought and deed; the other, on the "left", argued for a wider, more inclusive, more liberal persuasion rooted not in political terms such as "democracy" but in the emotional, affective nature of freedom.

Seferis had, with unconscious precision, anticipated the junta when he wrote, in early 1967, an appreciation of the late George Theotokas, in the form of an imaginary conversation in which Theotokas says: "Now that I have passed an entire lifetime [1906-66] ravaged by military revolutions, dictatorships, political upheavals, risings, calamities and despair [...] I must end in the conclusion that we have not made one inch of progress in these matters".[77]

Forty years later, Mark Mazower believed that "the fear of civil strife, which haunted Greeks for most of the twentieth century and exploded into life during both World Wars, has finally been laid to rest".[78] That is a forecast incapable of either proof or disproof, but seems to me to rest on foundations that are less than firm.

3

GEOPOLITICS: GREECE, THE
BALKANS AND THE LEVANT

Otherness and Difference

One of the most important facts of life for the traveller – whether short-term tourist or intending resident – is that in entering Greece one is leaving Europe behind and entering that geographical area which, in the last 200 years, has become known as "the Balkans" – an area stretching historically from Hungary and Romania in the north to Cyprus in the south, from Corfu in the west to Constantinople/Istanbul in the east; and which merges, at certain points imperceptibly, with the "Levant", which carries the mind from Thessaloniki to Cairo.

Leave behind everything except a toothbrush and perhaps a change of clothes. Leave behind *Baedeker*, the *Guide Bleu* and the *Rough Guide*. Even a passport in these parts is a dubious document. Leave behind, in particular, preconceptions, and any baggage that will impede mental progress. Any setting out from home or base is both an *ex*cursion and an *in*cursion from the known into the unknown, however well mapped it may appear.

We live in a world on edge: we are on the edge of other people's worlds and they on ours. Like tectonic plates, these edges grind against each other. Greece's location as the cusp of east and west makes it seem at times as if there is no sensation other than tectonic torsion.

In entering the Balkans, today's traveller is not leaving behind irrevocably the cultures – religions, languages, political and social structures – of Europe, but encountering a society, or series of so-cieties inter-related like the most complex of families, where those cultures undergo severe metamorphosis and are deeply affected by those corresponding characteristics of the host countries.

Greece is perhaps the most westernised of the Balkan states, all of which came into existence officially in the past 200 years, many contemporaneous with Ireland and some much more recently: Montenegro in 2006 and Kosovo in 2008. But it is nevertheless composed more substantially of the customs and mindsets of the east than of the west. It is *different*.

The Balkans have historically been an amorphous, indecisive, promiscuous, indeterminate, indefinable series of shifting bound-aries, populations, religions, seldom without strife and seldom with prosperity or, indeed, hope.

The essential difficulty for westerners – but not perhaps for the Irish reader – is the matter of *difference* or *otherness*. An Anglo-Greek writer[1] who is unreservedly philhellene, recently suggested to me that despite such love of Greece, a western-trained intel-ligence will find it frustrating and occasionally enfuriating to en-counter an intelligence which is trained in a different style – one might almost say a different medium. "They don't connect" ex-presses this western, logical, sequential way of thinking when con-fronted with a non-western system which has its own logic. For the philhellene, it's the case once again of "loving *and* mourning". The spectacle of political leaders and bureaucrats as "uncouth" (to use my correspondent's term) also expresses a qualitative differ-ence, not merely the non-democratic style of government through which Greece and the whole of the Balkans and Levant have passed, and are still passing, but also the strangeness of their pre-occupations and methodology.

One can extrapolate that frustration of philhellenism to apply it to what we might call "balkanophilia" or "levantophilia": an easy tendency to misunderstand, to misjudge, to misperceive the situa-tion in which one finds oneself.

So the disconcerted visitor or foreign resident – the *xénos* – should, if life is to become possible, appreciate the otherness and difference which make the people and systems qualitatively alien to his or her own intellectual hinterland. Even the term "Balkans" infers a dangerous place and a hostile people, while "Levant" has a more exotic, more alluring, even forbidden flavour.

And in a sense that is a reasonable starting point. On the binary presumption of "us" and "not us", what is *not* western is "other". As I suggested in relation to Ireland and Asia (in Yeats's phrase, above, p. 28), this exclusion of a middle, intermediate, inclusive possibility makes it difficult for us to see any distinction other than "us" and "them". This obstacle to inclusion and mutual understanding characterises the problems of communication and co-operation between the West and the Balkans, between west and east, between north and south of the Mediterranean basin, between, in particular, Greece and Turkey.

These are the challenges to the traveller. The challenges to Greeks today, at home in their uncertainty, are tugging in the opposite direction. Mark Mazower, for example, says that, from a historical perspective, the Balkans were "in Europe but not of it".[2] When, on the eve of EU membership, Constantinos Karamanlis proclaimed "Ανήκωμεν εις τήν Δύσιν" (*Aníkomen eis tín Dúsin* – "We belong to the West",) he was placing a major question mark over Greece's future because it went to the heart of Greekness: at the crossroads of three continents, where does Greece belong? East and west are so deeply embedded in both history and culture, in intellect, poetry and landscape, that it is impossible to make such a declaration without also demanding a personality change, a relocation of all those elements which constitute the complex nature of Greekness.

Geopolitics, to put it bluntly, is interference by greater powers in the affairs of smaller powers, manipulating transnational interests which are not necessarily the interests of the smaller countries ("which are we giving away...?"). The greatest example of this in the present context is Churchill's "acquisition", from Stalin, of postwar Greece as a sphere of influence.

The essence of today's geopolitics in southeast Europe, as far as Greece is concerned, is that an EU member state, which ever since independence has quested for a consensual identity, is now expected to reimagine that elusive identity in the light of changes to the EU, changes in the balance of political and economic power in the eastern Mediterranean, and the pressure of social changes within Greece itself.

The Balkans

"Freedom of choice is always limited for small countries."[3] Elisabeth Barker's chilling words perfectly illustrate Greece's position as a state whose historical and cultural significance far outweighs its size and wealth, but whose very location, as a strategic character in geopolitics, outweighs history and culture.

But the fact that the Balkans and Levant have been perennially diminished, directed and impoverished by greater forces is only one side of the scenario: the Greeks' search for a Greek identity, for some defining text, icon or historical moment which would encapsulate Greekness, is motivated by, and rooted in, the very fact that its "Balkanisation" fragments it into competing claims for identity in language, religion, geography, in fact all aspects of culture. The permeable borders on the physical map are also porous membranes of the mind; the identities are vulnerable, even frangible, if they are surrendered without the *agón* between past and present, east and west, north and south, man and woman, fidel and infidel, which is at the heart of "Greece".

If Greece is a meeting-point of east and west, the Balkans as a whole have been the macrocosm of which Greece is the microcosm. The area of the Balkans was, politically speaking, amorphous until the rise of nationalism in the nineteenth century encouraged the definition of ethnicity, rather than religious affiliation, as the principal criterion of nationhood.

Even the word "Balkans" is etymologically vague, and the description of the Balkans as a "peninsula" is in my opinion misleading (it in no way resembles a land mass which is "almost an island"). But the term has been applied since the nineteenth century by outsiders wishing to describe this unknown region.

"Discovery" and "invention" are inter-related concepts, both etymologically and practically. The Balkans were "discovered" in the course of Europe's eighteenth century curiosity, and at the same time, in the western imagination, they were "invented" as surely as "Ruritania", a formulaic identity to satisfy Europe's inherent difficulty with comprehending "the other".

Greece is a stepchild of history; within the boundaries it has been given, its ability to cultivate its potential is severely inhibited. Greece has never accepted this, struggling against history to reestablish itself more fully, yet always knowing the hopelessness of its ideals.

The Balkans is a "rough neighbourhood [...] where nation-states have a relatively short history, national frontiers are not generally considered as sacrosanct, and ethnic minorities are frequently manipulated in order to destabilize neighbours and thus lay claim on a possible future redrawing of political maps".[4]

In this entire region, history gives us plentiful evidence of the ways that identity and culture have been the victims of fear and hatred, lust, and the terrible balance between hope and sperectomy, the ideal (which is freedom) and the real (which is subservience). Predominantly, until the evolution of the nation-state, religion was an even stronger signal of identity than ethnicity. It was in fact Greek orthodoxy, supporting, and supported by, Greek language and learning, that underpinned resistance to the Ottomans, since the Greek faith found its connection with that of the Russian churches (due largely to the endeavours of a Corfiot, Evgenio Voulgaris).[5]

"There are few areas in the world where geography has influenced history as profoundly as in the Balkan Peninsula".[6] Mark Mazower observes that "the process of nation-building in the Balkans occupied the entire nineteenth century. It was protracted and experimental and left many of the region's 'little people' still subjects of imperial power".[7] For example, the creation of Yugoslavia and Czechoslovakia demonstrated that smaller nationalist groupings (Serbs, Bosnians, Croatians and others in the former, Czechs and Slovaks in the latter) were obliged, temporarily at least, to submerge their aspirations for self-determination in what was perceived, and argued, not least by the supervening powers, as a greater good (and of course a greater convenience). Temporarily, until the break-up of Yugoslavia, this was a partial success in suppressing what Mazower calls "the principle of nationality" as "a recipe for violence".[8]

The Bosnian war of 1992-95 gave horrific evidence of its resurgence, of which we have the interpretation of filmmakers in Milcho Manchevski's *Before the Rain* (2009), set in Macedonia, and Danis Tanovic's *No Man's Land* (2001), showing aspects of the Bosnian war. Sometimes with poor or deliberately naïf cinematography, these films crudely but with compassion tell us what a routine newspaper report can only hint at: the personal pain out of which grows a people's grief, resentment and fury.

Elizabeth Pond, in *Endgame in the Balkans* (2006), optimistically believed that the Europeanisation of the Balkans would overcome the "blood and soil nationalisms" of the region.[9] The very idea that, in order to come within the European embrace, candidate states must conform to the bourgeois, mercantilist criteria of the west amounts to a declaration that unless these criteria are not met, the candidate is a non-state: the twenty-first-century equivalent of "the infidel". Such states could be part of a United Nations, but not of a United Europe.

The nation-state may be in decline, but is nationalism dead? If people regard themselves as a community with strong cultural, linguistic, religious or ethnic bonds, are they not entitled to seek to articulate this distinctive identity by means of self-determination? If a Greek cannot become a German, or an Irishman become a Finn, then the argument that "We are all Europeans" is meaningless. If nationalism is the residual value of the ailing nation-state, then its expression in terms of a flag, a currency, a parliament, a national library – all symbols of this communal identity – is undeniable.

The new countries gave eastern Europe an entirely new profile with the collapse, in 1918, of the Austro-Hungarian empire: Hungary, Transylvania, Wallachia, Croatia, Bosnia, Herzegovina, Montenegro, Kosovo and Macedonia came into focus, demonstrating idiosyncratic cultural and political characteristics. The creation of the Yugoslav Federation, as a kingdom in 1918 and a republic in 1945, was an attempt to weld many of these disparate characters into a manageable unity, the failure of which after the death of "Tito" (Josip Broz, who ruled 1945-80) led to the resurgence of seven republics and the continuing ethnic and religious disputes in Kosovo and Macedonia.[10]

In 1986 I had first-hand experience of the "de-Tito-isation" of Yugoslavia: lecturing on "cultural democracy" at the Serbian Centre for Cultural Research, I was invited also to attend the congress being held in Belgrade of a cultural association concerned with European identities. Two memories emanate from my experiences in Belgrade: the first was the fact that, unknown to me, one of my lectures on cultural democracy had been surreptitiously recorded and broadcast on the principal channel of Serbian Radio (imagine RTÉ's Radio 1 devoting a morning hour to such a topic...) and the second was that, at a session of the congress, I tried to approach a huddle of organisers and was sternly warned off: my guide indicated that certain secret topics were being discussed which would change the shape of the Balkans. It was only on my return to Ireland that I discovered the significance of the secret discussions on "de-Tito-isation", as reported in the international press.

The process, which has become known as "balkanisation", means, in its first sense, decentralisation, peoples seeking separation on the basis of cultural or religious or racial distinctiveness in order to assert their identity. This was the term used to describe the scenario after 1918, but it had negative connotations: as Gerasimos Augustinos argues, the region was regarded post-1918 as "a uniformly negative construction indicating a place prone to political fragmentation and violence".[11]

Mazower suggests that "the First World War was the culmination of this entangling of Balkan liberation struggles with the European state system".[12] While it may be called *a* culmination (in the wake of the Balkan wars which preceded it) it was by no means *the* culmination, since the entire geopolitical system expanded immeasurably with the entry into the game of the USA and the formation of the League of Nations. Thereafter, while the "European state system" went into decline with the Second World War and the emergence of the EU, the "entanglement" continued, with the "great powers" of Europe joined, and diminished, by greater powers with equal, if not more urgent, interests in the Balkans, the Levant and the Middle East.

At the conclusion to his *Struggle for Mastery in Europe,* A.J.P. Taylor pronounced "in January 1918 Europe ceased to be the centre of the world. European rivalries merged into a world war [...] All the old ambitions [...] became trivial and second-rate, compared to the new struggle for control of the world."[13]

In 1918, the promulgation of the "Fourteen Points" document by US president Woodrow Wilson indicated that America, at least, recognised that the small countries could never, by dint of militarism, establish their independence, which must, therefore, be achieved by other means. This did not, however, pass the baton to those countries themselves, but called for a new form of supervision by the "great powers" – transparency and honesty. If any small country had harboured a dream – a *Megáli Idéa* – from then onwards it had to be renegotiated in the light, firstly, of a new Europe and, secondly, of a Europe in which America would be a major player.

"Transparency" morphed into "diplomacy" and "honesty" into "statecraft". But if nothing else, it opened the way for those smaller countries, once they had achieved statehood, to become equal members of the League of (later United) Nations.

Throughout the nineteenth century, when Greece was finding its feet on the European model of a nation-state, the dominant powers – Britain, France, Austro-Hungary, Russia and, after unification, the Italian and German mini-states (in, respectively, 1860-70 and 1871) – maintained a mutually suspicious watch on each others' territorial and strategic ambitions. In Greece's case, this meant the successful attempts by Britain and France to restrict Russian naval access to the Mediterranean from the Black Sea via the Dardanelles and the Bosporus, in which the Ottoman empire was a vital player.

Today, fear of Russia is not primarily military but economic, as Russian investment in the Mediterranean economies increases, in competition with that of China. That latter fact alone indicates that the globalisation of capital has irrevocably changed the face of geopolitics, which is now concerned with metaphysical as well as physical space: supranational rather than international.

Greece's former dependence on the military strength of its neighbours and masters has become an economic dependence from which, like almost any other small country – Switzerland excepted – it cannot escape. As Alexis Papachelas wrote in 2014: "We feel humiliated because our economic dependence has eroded the country's sovereignty [...] We need to find our own way. We need a good dose of self-confidence and a good plan. But we also need to keep mind of the facts."[14] In this, Ireland and Greece have so much in common (as discussed in Chapter 10).

Much of the previous chapter was concerned with the influence – both decisive and indecisive – of the "great powers" on the fortunes of modern Greece. A note of caution is necessary: it is too easy to ascribe all of Greece's misfortunes (and, indeed, good fortunes) to these supervening powers. Firstly, because Greece has attempted, as best its leaders were able, to assert its independence, within the constraints of such independence. Secondly, because these "powers" are no longer the major players in the globalised economy. Thirdly, because it has not been merely the effect of the "great powers" that has caused Greece much discomfort: "the fault, dear Brutus, lies in ourselves that we are underlings".

However, to take this argument to the wider geophysical area of the Balkans, this discomfort and inhibition is common to all the lands which were formerly under Ottoman rule. From the point in the late eighteenth century where the western phenomenon of the "Enlightenment" brought new concepts of idealism, romanticism, nationalism and selfhood to these lands (with specific examples in the American and French revolutions of 1776 and 1789), the exertion of power by those who, for military and financial reasons, were to dictate the future shape of Europe became the decisive factor in the emergence of the new nation-states.

The character of the Balkan experience during this emergence has been called the "politics of oscillation", in the sense that the tennis match between west and east, between Christianity and Islam, between democracy and absolutism, made an already unsettled and uncertain region dependent on power-politics to an increasingly violent extent. Indeed, Mazower refers to "the bloody intersection of regional Balkan quarrels and Great Power competitiveness"[15] as a condition of life.

Levant

Greece is the foster parent of the Levant, that equally complex stretch of multi-racial, multi-cultural lands southwards from Turkey through Cyprus, Syria, Lebanon, Israel, Palestine and Jordan to Egypt, where Alexandria is, today, the ghost of the great Greek city it once was.[16] And those lands look over their shoulder with increasing anxiety at the Middle East: Iraq, Saudi Arabia, Iran, the Emirates and Afghanistan. Throughout the Levant – with its classical, biblical and historical associations so tangibly evident today as living presences – Greek culture remains a significant element in the soup-mix. With powder kegs such as Syria and Kurdistan, and the relatively new phenomenon of the supraphysical "Islamic State", to say nothing of Turkey and Cyprus, Greece's geostrategic position recycles its history well into the future.

We can easily describe the physical area of the lands that constitute "the Levant", but it is impossible to delineate the mix of mindsets, the intricate way that the Levant is wedded to north, south and east, its "betweenness" negotiated over millennia by a usually peaceful co-existence of Muslims, Christians and Jews – as, indeed, was the case with the Balkan lands.

To Greeks, "Levant" rhymes with "Anatolia" since it means the same thing: light from the rising sun. The principal port cities of the Levant are Thessaloniki, Smyrna, Beirut and Alexandria, all, except Beirut, *Greek* cities. Thessaloniki, Athens, Smyrna, the Dodecanese. And then we add Cyprus to the equation: the Greek island at the centre of Greek-Turkish disputes, and of international attempts – abjectly failing so far – to achieve a reconciliation of the two parts of this partitioned island which has been fought over for hundreds of years.

Greece, in fact, by virtue of its centrality between the Balkans and the Levant, is more important than any survey of its diplomatic or military strengths could indicate.

Thessaloniki – or Salonica to give its more popular name – was once (as a significantly Jewish city), "the Jerusalem of the Balkans"; to look back no further than 1900, it has been a city in flux, unsure of its location or its destiny. It has been almost completely erased on four occasions: the Balkan war (1912-13), the First World War, the Anatolian Catastrophe and the Second World War. Thessaloniki was a meeting-point not only of east and west, but of almost every race, language and culture of the Balkans and the Levant: Bulgarians, Macedonians, Greeks, Albanians and Jews; a medieval town thrown through several crises into the twentieth century: "a microcosm of a cosmopolitan, Levantine way of life that was simply inconsistent with the industrialised world and its attachment to nation states".[17] And today it remains a disputed entity between Macedonia and Greece, its significance as the second city emphasised annually by Greece in the International Trade Fair, customarily addressed by the Prime Minister, and the attendance by the president at the "Ochi Day" celebrations on 25 October.

Greece and Turkey

Irish readers will easily understand what it means to have been dominated by a neighbouring country for 400 years. The underlying hostility between governors and governed, and between different segments of the governed, emanated in eastern Europe from what Mazower calls "the deep rift of incomprehension that lies between the worlds of Christianity and Islam, which for more than a millennium [...] were locked in a complex struggle for territory and minds in Europe".[18] Nowhere is that more explicit than in the experience of Greek peoples both within the Greek heartland and its diaspora, under the hegemony of the Muslim Ottomans. The eternal vision of Constantinople as the lighthouse of orthodox Christianity kept alive Greek resentment of Turkish rule, and determination to restore Christian Hellenism in its place, ensuring continuation of "the *danse macabre* between Greeks and Turks".[19]

Due to the centuries-long dominance of the Ottomans, the Balkans have been called "European Turkey" or "Turkey in Europe". But there is a point at which the fusion and interpenetration of east and west stop abruptly: Turkey itself. The Turks were never European, and their cultural, social and religious differences from European norms and *mores* remain an obstacle to their admission to the EU.

Leaving aside religion as a boundary and violence as its manifestation, the cultural mindset of Turkey has more affinity with its Middle East hinterland and the recent idea (one might call it, in Greek, a *Megáli Idéa*) of an "Islamic State" – a metaphysical rather than a specifically physical state. No one would wish to deny the validity of Ottoman history or question its motive forces *per se*; to do so would be to lack all respect for a culture and a civilisation which has made a significant impact, in aesthetic terms, on world civilisation. But the expression of Islam in statecraft, the blatant demands of Turkey regarding oil exploration, and the forty-year-old illegal occupation of northern Cyprus make Turkey an incongruous candidate for EU membership alongside its old vassals Greece, Bulgaria, Romania and of course Cyprus itself.

As I've hinted, the islands of the eastern Aegean – those closest to the Turkish coast – are the subject of border disputes. The islands, which although predominantly Greek in population, were under Turkish rule, were awarded (as in pass-the-parcel) to Italy in 1912-13 and to Greece in 1947, by a series of international treaties which Turkey today repudiates.

In 1987 and 1999 Turkey and Greece were on the threshold of war, as if their common threshold of disputed frontiers were the inevitable *tópos* of conflict. Discussion of any joint exploration of mineral deposits is impossible for Greece while Turkey maintains a permanent threat of war; on Greece's side, the narrowly avoided war in 1987 and 1996 was provoked by Turkey's commencement of oil exploration based on its alleged ownership of some of the Aegean islands.

The defence budgets of both countries exemplify the situation: mutual fear leads to mutual escalation in armaments. Greece spends more *per capita* on purchase of new weaponry, including its airforce, than any other European state.

Turkey strives to establish the exact designation of its continental shelf to enable it to explore for oil. A minuscule but extremely potent example of this designation is the Greek islet of Kastelorizo, only two kilometres from the Turkish coast with a population of less than 500 and an area of five square miles. It is neighboured by several other islets, mostly uninhabited, which lie on the Greek-

Turkish sea border. Ownership of all is disputed by Turkey, which has no strategic interest other than that of oil and gas exploration. Greek threats of retaliation against Turkish military "invasion" of its airspace have been an accident-waiting-to-happen for decades. In 2014, the danger of violence reappeared when Turkey designated an area of Greek airspace as a space for its own air exercises. These are not merely petty squabbles over a few uninhabited rocks, nor are they entirely about the mineral wealth beneath them: the atavism of racial memory also plays a crucial role. Thus a resource which might have brought Greece and Turkey closer to a real *rapprochement* of co-operation has become a potential battlefield. It seems to be a problem for which there is no solution.

Albania

Albania was perhaps the most complex society in the Balkans in that, as it did not exist as a state until 1912-13, it had little lien on international sympathy. As a mountainous land, with deep tribal animosities between north and south, Albania historically "enjoyed" (in the eyes of the few outsiders who penetrated its countryside: see Further Reading) a reputation for fierceness, individuality and blood feuds. Much of their character seems to be dictated by the mountainous conditions in which almost all Albanians lived until the start of urbanisation. The brigands or bandits who were a feature of Albania noted by English travellers in the early twentieth century continued to live a (by western standards) outlandish existence until very recently, and maybe still do so. As it was explained to Edith Durham in the early 1900s:

> You think you in England are civilised and can teach us. There is no one here who would commit crimes as are found in London. Our brigands are poor. They rob to live, and do so at the risk of their lives. Your brigands have often been to a university and rob to obtain luxuries by lies and false promises. But you call us savages because we shoot people.[20]

The same might well be said of the Greek *klephts*, such a pervasive force in modern Greek history and any other of the Balkan peoples whose circumstances made such a living a necessity rather than a choice.

Why is Albania important to an account of modern Greece? In the village where I live, it seems that the Albanian mountains are at the end of the street. Corfu is, in fact, closer to Albania than to most of mainland Greece. This proximity brings into sharp focus the melting pot of the Balkans: the transience of borders, the porous nature of customs, beliefs and languages, the transhumant lives of shepherds and their flocks (as inconsiderate of frontiers as the Sámi people of Scandinavia).

Each region breeds its own people. Albania is almost entirely mountainous and I am not the first to apply the word "forbidding": these mountains have formed tribal people, fierce in their desperation. Where southern Albania ends and northern Greece begins, no one is quite sure. The perplexity of the tranhumant peoples is expressed dramatically and passionately in Sotiris Dimitriou's stories *May Your Name Be Blessed*. The uncertainty has caused at least three major international disputes.

Seldom has the word "cusp" been more appropriate: "border" or "frontier" seem quite inadequate. There *are* no borders in the Balkans, a fact which has been both its strength and downfall.

That flags and other symbols can also be a cause of violence is evident from the appearance of a flag representing "Greater Albania" during a football match between Serbia and Albania in Belgrade. Albanian supporters had been banned from the game, but the flag was flown by an aircraft above the stadium, provoking expressions of extreme violence on the part of the Serbian crowd. The flag showed the predominantly Albanian region of Kosovo, and parts of Montenegro, Macedonia and Greece, as "Greater Albania". Irredentism works both ways. As an Ulsterman might say, "Give us back our twenty-six counties".

Under the dictatorship of Enver Hoxha (1945-85), Albania was oriented not towards the other communist states in eastern Europe, but to Maoist China (for a sarcastic account of the relationship, see Ismail Kadaré's novel *The Concert*). Until, that is, China disavowed its interest; as Misha Glenny puts it, "the Chinese just disappeared in the late 1970s, leaving only bizarre traces of their once eternal friendship".[21] One trace of communist aesthetics was – and is – the concrete blocks of apartments and offices which constitute its townscapes; another was the demolition of all churches and mosques. Dissidence was unheard, both within and outside the state.

Hoxha's sole achievement, in nationalist terms, was to make Albania totally independent. Ideologically it was watertight and peopletight. Often, looking across the "Corfu Straits" – the two kilometres-wide waterway separating Corfu from Albania – I think of those Albanians who, desperate to escape the Hoxha regime, swam across that channel, in many cases to be smashed by the frequent ferries passing through, or captured by coastguards and sent back for execution. Albania was a fortress which is only now emerging from the "siege mentality" which Irish people can see only too clearly in the north of their island. Today it struggles to establish itself as a modern, responsible society, ready for the EU membership which would allow it to turn its back on a past that is long on folklore and tradition, short on urban or cosmopolitan living.

Albania is in fact two countries which seem to live in a symbiosis of mutual ignorance and denial: the "modern" Albanians live in the new cities and pursue contemporary norms; the traditional people still occupy the hinterland and live according to tradition – chiefly the *kanun*.

In 2009 Albania lodged its formal application for EU membership, and suddenly the two ends of Europe fall into place: when Albania is enfolded into the EU, it will bring with it the concept of the *kanun*, the code which governs the conduct of a blood-feud, which seems to be an ineradicable element in Albanian social culture. The leading Albanian novelist, Ismail Kadaré, has described its origins and current practices in his novel *Broken April*. It's a chilling as well as a gripping read about how the *kanun* affects every aspect of life from the cradle to the grave. In addition to prescribing the protocol for honour killings, the *kanun* also governs most social activity, including marriages and property, all under the rubric of loyalty, hospitality and "right conduct" (*Sjellja*). Integrity and morality are paramount, and infringement of the rigid rules governing conduct is punishable with extreme penalties.

With existing deaths for "family dishonour" among Muslims throughout Europe, whose perpetrators regard themselves as obeying a law higher than that of the host country,[22] the EU is especially anxious that Albania stamps out the blood-feud before it can be seriously assessed as an EU applicant. Albania has established a "Committee of Nationwide Reconciliation" to address the phenomenon, but its pervasiveness, especially in remote rural areas in the north of the country, where tribal customs still predominate over national laws, makes it almost impossible to suppress entirely. As a team of Serbian sociologists reported in 2004, "it is difficult to comprehend the character, mentality and pattern of behaviour of Albanians without taking into account the *Kanun*. Not only is it far from being eradicated, but, down to the present day, its norms continue to regulate many of the Albanians' daily life matters."[23]

Although the *kanun* (or "code") does not appear in any part of the Albanian constitution, it is an integral part of Albanian life (and death), and MPs are at the forefront of finding ways to minimise the impact of the custom. Outlawed under Hoxha's communist regime, it has found new acceptance not only in Albania itself but in Albanian enclaves in Kosovo, Macedonia and Montenegro. In five years in Kosovo forty killings related to blood-feuds were reported; the *kanun* is particularly prevalent in the mountains of Kosovo, where it is reported that over a period of eighty years, two families had inflicted thirty-two killings: the responsibility for revenge is passed down through the generations.

Recent legislation imposes stiff penalties not only for feud-related killings but for the very existence of a feud, in a desperate attempt to end the practice, but local traditions weigh much more heavily than laws passed in Tirana. Reconciliation seems to have a much greater potential, since it is locally based, with the *besa*, or temporary suspension of the feud, becoming the preferred solution, since it is itself embedded in the Code. As one MP put it, "people don't trust justice and that's why they return to the *kanun*. They lack confidence in their problems being solved by legal means." In 2003, the newspaper *Koha Jone* went so far as to state that people reverted to the *kanun* because "the government is so corrupt that law as a mechanism of society's functioning has been discredited".

The *kanun* principally governs the revenge that must be exacted by one family when one of its members has been killed by another. Traditionally, a blood-feud would be initiated over dishonour by one family to another, or in a dispute over land ownership. Not unlike an Italian *vendetta*, it requires that if I kill you, your family must kill me. Then one of my family must avenge me, and so on *ad infinitum*. More seriously, the *kanun* has taken on a new lease of life with the advent of drugs gangs operating under cover of the *kanun*.

In the period 1998-2003, official figures put the number of feud-related deaths at 330; today's it's approximately 10 per cent or less of all murders in the country. In one southern town, twenty-eight deaths have been directly identified with a single blood-feud over a seven-year period. The only place where a potential feud victim is safe is in his own home. Some of those living in fear have not left the immediate environs of their homes for over fifty years. It is officially reckoned that at present over 1,000 families, throughout Albania (of whom 177 live in the capital, Tirana), live in isolation for fear of feud reprisals, a drop of over 50 per cent in a four-year period, due to the reconciliation process.[24] The children of these families are home-educated, their numbers estimated variously at between 200 and 800 across the country.

Many years ago, the late Paul Adamidi-Frascheri, Cambridge-educated chamberlain to King Zog and son of Zog's minister for education, explained to me the rigorous rules which even extend to hospitality: if someone you are supposed to kill comes to your house, you must give him bed and board for as long as he wants to stay, and you may not touch a hair of his head, because, in the words of the *kanun*, "the Albanian's house belongs to God and the guest". But, as Paul explained with what I can only describe as a mixture of relish and *sang froid*, "my dear chap, as soon as he left my property, I simply blew his head off". So much for a Cambridge education.[25, 26]

The 2010 film *The Forgiveness of Blood*, directed by Joshua Marston, is frightening because it shows the *kanun* not in any his-

torical setting but in the present day. Although it carries the dis-
claimer "any similarity to actual persons or actual entities is purely
coincidental", the entity *is* the *kanun*, and its presence in a community where text-messaging and phone-cameras are the norm for
young people underlines its immediacy and the perduring nature
of its social control.

The EU criteria not only demand a radical change in human
rights but also the same attention to statistical and fiscal matters as
any other candidate state. A senior Irish economist who has been
consulted by the Albanian government in recent years tells me that,
after initial study, he was obliged to decline any further involvement because it was impossible to analyse statistics which did not
exist: the numbers of young people, the proportion of them who
had third-level education, the numbers abroad who might re-enter
the home workforce – in fact, a complete inventory of the national
labour force on which a policy for job creation and youth employment might be based. The lack of such statistics suggests that Albania is in an even more delicate position than was Greece before the
latter took the route of falsification and invention of statistics which
eventually won it admission to the EU (see Chapter 6).

Macedonia

If ancient Macedonia was one of the starting points for the Greek
Megáli Idéa of Alexander's empire, it is one of the stumbling-
blocks of Greece's progress as a Balkan leader, and for much the
same reasons. Where Alexander had his roots in the lands north
of present-day Greece, Macedonia today, as a former constituent
of the Yugoslav Federation, seeks its new identity, of which its
name and flag are the outward symbols. Macedonians objected to
Oliver Stone's film *Alexander the Great*, not on sexual grounds (as
in Greece) but because it purported to show Alexander as Greek
rather than Macedonian. Greece stands in the way of a Macedonian state, because of that "greatness" which Alexander brought to
the sense of being Greek.

Irredentism is an issue here, too, since Macedonian nationalists
lay claim to land and people beyond its current border, that there is
a Macedonian ethnic minority in northern Greece which should be

included in the new state, including part of Bulgaria and the city of Thessaloniki, which, they assert, would be the new capital.

Misha Glenny suggests that the stability of not only Greece but also Bulgaria and Serbia is jeopardised by the problem of reconciling "Macedonia" with "Macedonians" – an ethnic *idea* without a physical reality: "nationalism and national identity in the region are built on fragile foundations".[27] "Macedonia" at present exemplifies the amorphous nature of the entire Balkan area in the west's inability to produce acceptable definitions of what it means to be Macedonian/Albanian/Greek.

In 1900, Macedonia was nothing more than an aspiration articulated by political means. In the frustration of today's impasse with Greece, it might well seem to be little else.

Greece's ambition, to realise, at least in part, a semblance of the *Megáli Idéa* by taking the lead in the economic affairs of the Balkans, by means of statecraft, has been wrecked by its intransigence over the renaming of "FYROM". Macedonia points out that, as the "Republic of Macedonia" within the Yugoslav Federation for fifty years, Greece never objected to its name.

Greece's refusal today to agree to Macedonia becoming "Macedonia" has impressed no one, but the diplomatic impasse it has caused has led to the involvement of United Nations negotiators over the past quarter century, whose success in suggesting compromises such as "New Macedonia", "Northern Macedonia" or "Republic of Upper Macedonia" has been consistently stonewalled by Greece. At the time of writing, the dispute is not only unresolved but shows no possibility whatever of reaching any kind of compromise.

Greekness has many heartlands, due to its regional character. Macedonia is one of them. In Kazantzakis's novel *The Fratricides* an army captain exhorts his men about Macedonia and Albanian Epirus: "This soil [...] is kneaded with Greek blood and Greek sweat and tears, and has been for thousands of years. It's ours and we aren't going to let anyone else set foot in it".[28] Mark Dragoumis relates that, in the 1880s, the Greek ambassador to Germany was asked at a dinner party, "*voulez vous un peu de macedoine?*" to which he replied, "I don't just want some, I want all of Macedonia".[29]

As the Macedonian politician Ivica Bocevski has said: "The very name Macedonia is the backbone of the Macedonian identity and ethnicity. We cannot define our culture, traditions, religion as other than Macedonian."[30] This is precisely what Greece refutes: "Macedonia" is also the *fons et origo* of *Greek* identity.

For a time, Greece even imposed an embargo on Macedonian imports and exports via Greece. And it has also gone to the extent of bulldozing Macedonian cemeteries and erasing parish registers in that area in order to deny this ethnic claim.

And there is aggression on both sides. Not only the name, but also the flag, has been a matter of contention. The adoption by Macedonia of the "Vergina Sun" or "Star" as its flag was a – perhaps unintended – provocation, since the "Vergina Sun" is an ancient Greek symbol, and Vergina, a town south of Thessaloniki, is believed to be the burial site of Philip of Macedon, father of Alexander. In re-cent years, the most gratuitous provocation by Macedonia towards Greece was the erection, in the centre of Skopje, of a massive (22-me-tres high) bronze equestrian statue of Alexan-der. Athens fulminated. As I review this chap-ter (May 2015) Macedonia is violently split by nationalist factions, creating yet another in-ternational politial crisis which threatens the stability of the Balkans.

Cyprus

One of the most severe examples of geopolitics is Cyprus. Cyprus won its freedom from Britain in 1960, yet today remains an ex-ample of history's infinite capacity for repeating itself, with Greece, Turkey, Russia and the UN using it as a cat's paw of competing pow-ers.[31] Disraeli is said to have regarded it as "the key to Western Asia".

Turkey's dispute over the ownership of the Greek islands ex-tends to Cyprus, a situation much more severe and with much greater geopolitical repercussions.

Cyprus became a British protectorate in 1878 (Gladstone called it "an insane covenant") and a colony in 1925; in the 1950s nationalists (with the acronym EOKA: *Ethnikí Orgánosis Kipria-koú Agónos* or "National Organisation of Cypriot Struggle") made a vigorous but unsuccessful attempt to win its freedom from Britain in order to effect an *enosis* with Greece. After the accession of the Dodecanese in 1947 it would have been the final jewel in Greece's crown. The movement provoked anti-Greek riots in Istanbul proclaiming "Cyprus is Turkish" – a pre-echo of Turkish aggression in 1974.

Eventually, Britain conceded and left in 1960, with the establishment of Cyprus as an independent republic, with Archbishop Makarios as its president: 77 per cent of the island's population was Greek, 18 per cent Turkish. Britain, however, retained 100 square miles as a sovereign territory, which would be of use to both British and US surveillance in this crucial part of the eastern Mediterranean.

William Mallinson reproduces two examples of geopolitics in recent history. In the first, Henry Kissinger, US Secretary of State, wrote to his opposite number, James Callaghan, the British Foreign Secretary, in the mid-1970s, when Britain was contemplating withdrawal from its military bases in Cyprus, which it considered of minimal strategic importance. Kissinger emphasised the view of the US that withdrawal "could have a destabilizing effect on the region as a whole, encouraging the Soviet Union and others to believe that the strategic position of the West has been weakened in that area". There is no question, judging by Callaghan's weak-kneed reply, but that this was an act of international bullying on Kissinger's part over an independent state where neither the US nor Britain had any moral rights.

The second episode occurred during a phone conversation between Kissinger and Callaghan later in 1976, after the latter had become British Prime Minister, on the eve of a UN resolution on the division of the island between Greek and Turkish Cypriots. It suggests that Callaghan was not merely Kissinger's gofer, but, as Prime Minister and former Foreign Secretary, hadn't a clue what was going on: "I'm on holiday really. I am in touch all right. But I haven't been following this one in particular except in the newspapers." Kissinger was anxious that Britain would have other EU countries on its side – as the lackey of the US, of course. The French, Kissinger said, "are pushing a very pro-Greek line". Callaghan: "What's the line-up at the moment then? Anybody with the French?" "You and the Italians". "We're with the French, are we, at the moment?"[32]

Today, the British sovereign base in Cyprus houses one of the world's most sophisticated surveillance stations, capable of intercepting web and fibreoptic messages throughout the Middle East, one purpose of which is to monitor Russian satellite signals.[33] British-US co-operation did not stop with Kissinger. As Richard Clogg points out, Cyprus' membership of the EU "has the thoroughly anomalous consequence that one EU country, Britain, exercises sovereignty over sizeable chunks of the territory of another EU member in the shape of the two sovereign base areas of Akrotiri and Dhekella".[34]

In its last days, in 1974, the Greek military junta ("the Colonels") staged a short-lived coup against Makarios and installed a pro-*enosis* puppet, possibly to bolster its (non-existent) popularity at home with an irredentist gesture. While this involved no militant action against Turkish Cypriots, Turkey was apprehensive for their safety and invaded the island, concentrating on the north coast where most Turkish Cypriots lived. The Turkish action was the second blow to the Colonels (the first being the student uprising of the previous year) and the junta collapsed. As Peter Levi commented in Athens at the time, "out of the disaster of Cyprus came the freedom of Greece".[35]

Anthony Eden, Britain's Foreign Secretary at the time of the *enosis* crisis, acknowledged that "in geography and in tactical considerations, the Turks have the stronger claim on Cyprus; in race and language the Greeks; in strategy the British".[36]

In a sense, therefore, the Turkish action was advantageous to the Greek people, but its illegality, condemned by the UN, its continued expansion of territory across the north of Cyprus (it now controls 40 per cent of the island), and its unilateral declaration in 1983 of the "Republic of Northern Cyprus", have remained the most fundamental obstacles to any *entente* between Greece and Turkey. The fact that a candidate for EU membership actually illegally occupies 40 per cent of another member state must be one of the greatest ironies and anomalies of recent European history, comparable, in the eyes of hardline Irish republicans, to British "occupation" of Northern Ireland.

If it had not been for the Turkish invasion of northern Cyprus in 1974, the country, as a sovereign state, might have been able to conduct its own affairs (within the rules of the geopolitical game, of course), in communication with Greece but not officially aligned to it.

The island remains partitioned; the "Green Line", marking a no-go zone, separates Greeks and Turks and even passes through Nicosia, the island's capital. In 2009 Greek Prime Minister George Papandreou, echoing many other politicians and activists, called for the removal of the wall as the last such symbol of divisiveness in Europe: he was, however, overlooking the "peace lines" that still separate Catholics and Protestants in Belfast.

The Cypriot dilemma has been exacerbated in recent years for the same reason as that of the Turkish continental shelf: oil. Cyprus has begun exploration around its shores, on the basis of an "exclusive economic zone" (EEZ); Turkey retaliated by sending its own seismic survey vessel into Cypriot waters, entering blocks that have already been awarded by Cyprus to US oil companies and an Italian-Korean partnership which are already part of the Cyprus exploration. An estimate running into trillions of cubic metres is at stake.

The Turkish action in this new form of invasion has had the result of putting into abeyance all bilateral negotiations on the island's future. The Cypriot situation has led to warships from both sides patrolling the exploration fields. Escalation of naval aggression is unlikely, but such posturing does nothing to advance the co-operation which both sides ostensibly support. The presence of warships off the Cyprus coast from the Russian Black Sea fleet increases apprehension about an escalating situation. Both Turkish and Greek naval commanders state they are working to undisclosed "rules of engagement" to protect their countries' interests. It has been said that in confronting Turkey, which, as in 1922, is militarily much the stronger, Greece "is bringing a sword to a gunfight".[37]

One might expect the US to intervene, but the balance of power in the entire Balkan-Levant region is once again at stake, as the US needs Turkish co-operation in relation to a solution in Syria, the "Islamic State" and the downturn in Turkish-Israeli relations, making Greece a small potato in the overall seed-bed. It's a wait-and-see situation in which the stronger powers – Washington, Berlin, Brussels and even Moscow – will not commit to any process which might even further destabilise the region. Thus the "sick man of Europe" has regained some of his former health, if not strength, to the disadvantage of Greece and Cyprus.

With Greece and Cyprus courting both Israel and Egypt in matters of oil, diplomacy enters a phase unknown to Greece since the Second World War.

Viewed in parallel with the issue of immigration into Europe and North America, and the dangers represented by "Islamic State", the nexus of politics and economics complicates even the simplest of situations, and Greece, Turkey and Cyprus are *not* a simple situation. When oil greed meets irredentism and any form of *Megáli Idéa*, the complexity and profundity increase exponentially. The geopolitical game in play is in fact more serious than anything since the division of spoils in 1918-19.

Global Finance

Lost among the geopolitical maelstrom is the fact that Cyprus, too, underwent an economic collapse in 2013 and submitted to a bailout. Like the Irish situation, but unlike the Greek, the economic crisis in Cyprus was caused by banking errors. But in all three cases, concern was more evident for any domino effect outside the country than for its internal misery. Protection of foreign interests, it seems, overrode the interests and feelings of ordinary people in the states where these mistakes were made. The word "contagion" in itself suggests that somehow Greece, Ireland and Cyprus are some kind of financial lepers.

In Cyprus, large Russian investment was at stake, which raised much greater issues than in Greece or Ireland. Russian interests in Cyprus (as in Greece) are primarily financial, of course, but to recipients of its investments it brings much extra baggage.

In Cyprus's case, Russian support at the UN is a vital element in maintaining the island's sovereignty. On the other hand, the West seems apprehensive that Russian support for Cyprus might lead to a takeover, excluding western interests.

It is said that in 2009-2010, Prime Minister George Papandreou was offered financial aid by either or both Russia and China, but that he was warned off by Brussels: taking non-EU aid would be tantamount to leaving the EU. Whether or not that is true, the mutual wooing of Greece and China, and the continued interest of both Russia and China in Greek affairs, is a sign that Greece may be a pivotal spot in an *entente* between east and west as an economic trading place.

With the severe differences between Greece and the EU over renegotiation of the bailout following the election of the Syriza-led government in January 2015, the idea that Greece might look elsewhere gains momentum. Papandreou was weak; Prime Minister Alexis Tsipras is determined. His coalition partners, who are more anti-EU than Tsipras, have said, "If Germany remains rigid and wants to blow apart Europe" then the Greek "Plan B" would be "to get funding from another source. It could be the United States at best, it could be Russia, it could be China".[38] Not only did Tsipras make a special visit to Moscow in April 2015, but his deputy was simultaneously in detailed discussions with China's vice-premier in Beijing.

Yet another layer of geopolitics has been added in the past six years, with Chinese investment in Greece. Not only has the Chinese company Cosco bought the freight terminal of Piraeus port – the heart of the Greek maritime industry – but another Chinese company, Fosun, has also signed deals with Greece worth many billions of euros. The site of the old Athens airport, a controlling interest in the management of the new airport, the remainder of Piraeus port, the Greek rail transportation system (as a hub for exports to China and central Europe), are all elements in an extensive investment in the ailing economy, as is an anticipated exponential growth in Chinese tourism to Greece.

The geopolitics of global finance are clear from Prime Minister Antonis Samaras' statement in mid-2014 that "Greece can become the main European entry point for China thanks to our strategic location".[39] But the economy is not the only geopolitical signpost: Samaras also indicated that joint naval exercises between the Greek and Chinese navies were part of the bilateral agreement to include a naval base for China in Crete. "Greece is the friendliest and most reliable country in Europe for China," he said.[40] What the joint operations might involve is unclear; Greece's friendliness is, of course, encouraged by the already massive Chinese financial presence in the Greek marketplace and Greece's continued global vulnerability. And it deepens the region's complexity on economic, military and diplomatic fronts. Tourism is merely a symptom of involvement on all these fronts.

Conclusion

In 2000, Mark Mazower wrote that, despite ongoing threats to peace in southeast Europe – of which the Cypriot problem was the most serious – it "will take more than an earthquake to improve". Nevertheless, Greek-Albanian tensions over "Northern Epirus/ Southern Albania", or "Bulgarian dreams of Macedonia" are "faint and meaningless echoes" of earlier issues.[41] This may have been a reasonable view in 2000, but in 2014-15 those issues, among many others, are as urgent as ever: Mazower could not, perhaps, have foreseen the divisiveness of the oil and gas possibilities, nor might the extent of globalisation have been apparent as a factor in geopolitics, but these are without doubt factors which make the region as fragile today as it ever was. Only the names have changed.

Having described as succinctly as possible what is involved in the geopolitics of today's Greece, as the central player in the Balkan/Levant region, I am left contemplating the helplessness of Greeks who continue to ask, "Who am I?" "Who are we?" When so much sovereignty has been surrendered, for economic or political or strategic reasons, and Brussels, Washington, Beijing, Moscow have fists rather than fingers in the pie, the questions of identity and self-determination sometimes seem diminished beyond remedy: these questions were being asked in the 1820s; they are as valid today, with mastery residing not in parliament or the national bank, but outside the state.

4

PEOPLE

Society and Politics

In separating a discussion of "society", in this chapter, from one of "politics" in the next, I am guilty of segregating two elements which, together, constitute the Greek reality: society, in the sense of people and the way they organise their lives, is inseparable from politics, the organisation of the *pólis*, the place to which people gather in order to establish a consensual *polity*.[1] A Greek person without a view of politics – even the most humble widow in the remotest village – is inconceivable. Involvement in political life, however peripheral, is inescapable. The state is the image of the people and the people *are* the state. But in Greece (where voting is compulsory, although not enforced), opinion on all matters relating to the *pólis* is ever present; action is ubiquitous; and participation, at whatever level of state, is a prerogative exercised daily, even if it consists merely of hot-tempered debates in the *kafeneío*. The man in the street – or the man in the olive grove – may not readily express himself in concepts, but hypotheses and ways of seeing the world are embedded within the Greek mind.

There is, however, an ever-present danger of a *lacuna* between the *idea* of political life and its *reality*, between what citizens assume and expect, and what their representatives actually undertake. This has its roots in the difference, in everyday life, between appearance and reality; this will become a central feature of this chapter and the two following.

There are two ways of describing the strata of Greek society and its organisation. One is the top-down approach, starting with the Constitution and the mechanisms of law, justice and administration. The other is the view from the grassroots: how Greek ideas and arrangements about law, justice and administration are perceived by the man in the street/olive grove and how they affect him or her. The difficulty, as probably in most societies, is the meeting-point of these two approaches, somewhere in the middle of the government-society axis, where individual and local and communal interests interact with the overriding provisions for the egalitarian organisation of life.

I have confined the practical concrete aspects of the Constitution, administrative and education systems, Church-State relationships and party politics to the next two chapters in order to concentrate here on the nature of the Greek mind and character from which political life emanates. It is, primarily, private, and thence derive its public aspects. Even within the house, with its age-old concept of *economics* (*oikonomía*), we see political life in embryo, because in order to understand the structures, one must first understand the people, their customs and traditions, *mores* and values, their behaviour in and out of the home: in short, their culture.

Difference and Mindscape

H.D.F. Kitto, in his invaluable survey *The Greeks* (1951 and still in print), opens with an enticing gambit:

> In a part of the world that had for centuries been civilized, and quite highly civilized, there gradually emerged a people, not very numerous, not very powerful, nor very well organized, who had a totally new conception of what human life was for, and showed for the first time what the human mind was for.[2]

I don't think you will regard it as special pleading when I suggest that the *different* way the ancient Greeks conceived of the meaning of life and the purpose of the human mind remains valid and, yes, still *different*. Lawrence Durrell, in his persuasive essay on "Landscape and Character", referred to the

> constant factor that we discern behind the word 'Greek-ness' [...] the enduring faculty of self-expression inhering in landscape [...] the restless metaphysical curiosity, the tenderness for good living and the passionate individual-ism [...] Human beings are expressions of their landscape.[3]

In Durrell's terms, "landscape values" become human values. This is no less evident in the transhumant Sarakatsani people of northern Epirus, studied so effectively by J.K. Campbell in *Honour, Family, Patronage*, than it is in the way that the Anatolian refugees tried to replicate their previous lives on arrival in Greece in 1922-23, or the response of today's urban dwellers to their streetscapes and *agorá*. Greece is a landscape which has bred a national char-acter preoccupied with curiosity, individualism, good living and sensuality, which are as evident in all aspects of today's society as they were in classical Athens.

Kitto also refers to "a sense of the wholeness of things" as "per-haps the most typical feature of the Greek mind".[4] Here again, the passion for integration (and, with it, integrity), for the principles which hold society together, is the contested ground of modern politics: the insistence, on one hand, on cohesion, consensus as a super-glue, and the denial of the validity and efficacy of that glue by those who dispute the way in which the elements of the State have been stuck together in the manner of an Airfix kit.

It was Aeschylus (in the tragedy *Agamemnon* of 458 BC) who put into the mouth of his tragic hero, "Call no man happy until he is dead". The maxim remains true of Greece today: as Kitto ob-serves, "Life, and consequently thought, were built very close to the bed-rock of Necessity, and a certain hardness, and therefore resilience, was the result".[5] It requires little intelligence to per-ceive the same stoicism in the austerity (*austirótita*, harshness) of Greece post-2010.

In the run-up to the 2015 elections, an Athenian journalist re-ferred to the "weird aloofness [of Greeks] to the risks of the day".[6] It can be argued that that aloofness, a disavowal of risk, a concentration, instead, on more durable values and certainties, has always been a characteristic of the Greek mind, from the Stoics in the third century BC to the *klephts* and *antártes* of the nineteenth and twentieth centuries, and today's rigid espousal of anarchist and antinomian tenets. The same journalist suggested that "this country has neither ethical nor institutional foundations", by which he meant that an "aloof" people has the capacity to distrust any system which is lacking an ethical basis, and which he believed was represented in the – as he saw it – ungovernability of the country.

The fraught relationship of citizens and the state is best seen in the early days of independence, when the question of *language* became divisive. If Greeks had found their unifying factors in religion and language, the identity which these conveyed to them became problematic when the question arose of how that identity was to be, literally, articulated. At the time of independence, the number of intellectuals was very small, the number of educated leaders of the revolution even smaller,[7] cities almost non-existent and the vast majority of the population were rural, illiterate peasants. Two languages were spoken: the "posh" or "mandarin" of the leadership and the "vulgar" or "demotic" of the majority. The refined version was known as *katharévousa*, and the debate between this and demotic would run until 1976. But the country as a *nation* could not continue without an agreed common tongue.

It was in the educational system that the most intense debate took place, because the acculturation of the young mind was the principal means of creating citizens loyal to the state and supportive of its national consciousness.

It was a vital process of nation-building through consciousness and articulation – vital in the sense of being a life-or-death issue. The emergence of the Greek used today is a narrative of the triumph of pragmatism over idealism; as Peter Mackridge calls it, "a language in the image of the nation", as true a representation of Greekness as compromise and experience will allow, and again exemplifying Greece's between-ness in the Balkans and Levant: the process, as Mackridge calls it, of transforming "a language which clearly displayed the influence of Italian and Turkish as well as its relationship with Ancient Greek and which embodied and expressed a common Balkan culture" into a working instrument which is also "capable of embodying and expressing a common modern European culture".[8]

It thus represents the journey of a twilight people into a fully-lit sense of identity and purpose, however much that identity may still be debated in the political arena. In this process the majority of citizens have been passengers for most of the time.

Home, the Family and Economics

The idea of "home" as a sacred place for the family is central to the Greek mind, whether urban or rural: the focus of birth, well-being, prosperity and co-operation; the place to which the wanderer returns, whether he is the eighth-century Odysseus to Ithaca, or the "returned Yank" to any one of the thousands of villages from which his parents or grandparents departed.[9] It's the place where individuality is honed and the solidarity, honour and values of kinship are pledged; it's the origin of the term *economics* – οικονομία (iko-nomía) from *οίκος* = house and *νόμος* (*nómos*) = law – the laws of the house, or "household management". Writ large, it becomes the national budget, but in each house it's not merely the financial side of life but the way the family organises its existence, responds to, and tries to transcend, the harshness of life in the village or, today, the austerity of life in the global marketplace.

One has only to read the novels of the nineteenth century to realise how transient were the villages of the peasants, how easily moved or destroyed. Only the stone-built houses of merchants and the public buildings, churches and manor houses had any chance of endurance. Mud, thatch, wattle, were evanescent, as short-lived as their occupants. But, as Thomas Gallant observes,[10] the terminology for both *house* and its *occupants* – *oíkos* in classical times, and *spíti* today – encompasses house *and* household. *Oikogénia* (meaning engendering within a house) as the word for "family" underlines this identification of place and people. Thus its transience was a threat to its continued existence, as much as its rootedness guaranteed it.

Maybe Mr Micawber was Greek: the idea of being in debt to another – whether monetarily or in any other way – is to be beholden, creating a bond and limiting one's freedom. With the advent of a money economy, the need to avoid falling into debt was paramount: the Greek word for "obligation", *ipochréosi*, literally means "in debt", suggesting the inferiority of the debtor to the creditor, and is closely related to the concept of *honour*, of which the family is the custodian.[11]

"Home" is where the hearth is, the *estía*, the source of warmth, storytelling, reassurance and, in de Valera's terms, the wisdom of old age. Throughout the era of Turkish domination it was the family and the home, rather than any idea of nation or fatherland, which was at the forefront of resistance. It is also the focus of *filotimía*, the sense of dignity, self-esteem and, above all, *honour* which guides the family in all its transactions. In this, Greeks are not a million miles from the Islamic sense of honour which has such frightening manifestations for non-Muslims in its recourse to violence in order to maintain family values. Indeed, the evidence of similar violence within the Greek family can be found readily in novels and films.

Gallant points out that a Greek man will use "deception, prevarication, intimidation and even violence" to protect and enhance his household. I would omit the word "even". These are the strategies applied to desperate situations; for most rural Greeks throughout history, and for *all* Greeks today, the situation is sufficiently desperate that deception and prevarication will come to the fore as weapons for individuals as well as governments. It is the fierceness of the average Greek's determination to exercise personal freedom that bewilders non-Greeks.

The Table

Why is this important? Because the kitchen is the centre of the house and household, it is part of the *oikogénia*. Its function is cultural and political: the dinner table is the place of discussion and the transmission of values.

The first fact to be noted about Greek cuisine is its regionality and even its parochiality. The second is that, as in *Rebétiko* music and *Karagiózis* drama, it embodies significant elements of Turkish ingredients and dishes.

Even terms such as *mezes* (small dishes of appetisers) have a Turkish origin: meatballs (*keftedes* and *soutsoukakia*), pastries and sweets (*baklava* and *halva*) and the *kebab* and *souvlaki* (from *soúvla*, the roasting spit). *Ouzo*, the "national" anis-flavoured spirit, is a version of the Turkish *mastika* (and a cousin of absinthe and pastis).[12] This mixture of the two cultures (or two aspects of the same culture) gives an added dimension to the millennial disputes between Greece and Turkey.

A Touch of Spice is the English-language title of Πολιτικη Κουξινη (*Politiki Kouzini*, 2003, directed by Tassos Boulmetis) which means "The Kitchen of Constantinople". It encompasses the aftermath of the Anatolian Catastrophe, the purge of Greeks from Constantinople/Istanbul in 1955-56 and again in 1964. The experience of the exiles, resettled in Athens, is expressed as "The Turks expelled us as Greeks. The Greeks regarded us as Turks. Greece was more beautiful in our minds than what we found when we came." Throughout the film, which is a tender exploration of childhood love and adult disillusion, the focus on the Kitchen is inseparable from that experience: "Our cuisine is tinged with politics. It's made by people who left their dinner unfinished somewhere else." The central character "carries his grandfather's cuisine as his way of clinging to memory".

As Vefa Alexiadou insists, "the culture and history of Greece are deeply embedded in the recipes".[13] For example, Lenten fasting imposes restrictions on food intake which are in fact liberating, as they encourage new approaches to what is permissible. Different fish, meat and herbs offer different tastes, depending on the season. Alexiadou quotes from the Anglo-Greek character of Basil, in his journey of self-discovery in *Zorba the Greek*: "I at last realized that eating was a spiritual function and that meat, bread and wine were the raw materials from which the mind is made".[14] Zissimos Lorenzatos shares the spirituality of this impression as he enjoys a traditional meal of bread, cheese, eggs, goat's meat and wine which represents "our culture in its most enduring aspects".[15]

Leaving aside the staples of the Greek diet – bread, *feta* cheese, yogurt, *moussaka*, bean soup, *keftedes*, a large range of pasta dishes, and the various purées of chickpea (*hummous*), codsroe (*tarama*) and aubergine (*melitsanosalata*) – there is a dizzying variety of regional foods, depending on the environment and the family pocket. Fish in proximity to the sea, breads and pies in the mountain villages. Roast meat is still a rarity for many, a spit-roasted lamb at Easter sometimes affording the family their only substantial meat dinner of the year.

Greek pride inheres in local produce: the quality of *feta* cheese – salty, crumbly, hard, milky, or even "angry cheese" as some mountain cheese-makers sell it during fermentation – depends in every case on the pasture and, of course, whether it is made from sheep's or goat's milk, or a mixture of the two. In the village where I live, the *feta* is of a distinctly creamy texture due to the very high altitude of the pasture; at the same altitude we get honey almost as black as treacle and perfumed with the wild flowers of the valley, predominantly lavender. Village rivalries over such produce are very prevalent, as they are even today over the quality of the water from the local wells. There is in fact no reason why the microclimates of Greece should not yield distinctive foods and cuisine as they do in other matters of culture.

If Greece is ungovernable, as so many commentators suggest, it's worth recalling Charles de Gaulle's comment on France: how do you govern a country with 246 types of cheese? Or, to quote a recent study, "how many Greeks does it take to buy a watermelon?" The answer to both questions underlines their impossibility.

Many Greek chefs are anxious to move away from the usual suspects of the taverna menu and experiment with a very Greek form of *nouvelle cuisine*: using fresh organic vegetables, fish and meat, they create variations on familiar themes and also introduce new dishes. The staples of beans (in many varieties), cereals, greens, herbs and spices, wine, cheese and, above all, olive oil, are capable of unlocking a myriad of tastes (*gévseis*). In Corfu Town, I recently met a roasted kid (the four-legged kind) in an egg, lemon and spinach sauce that would grace any *table nouvelle*. But this experimental phase is not confined to the towns and cities: Kyria

Salvanos spends the winter imagining new tastes and, as the only customer on many a night, I am the guineapig for her pork fillets in a wild mushroom and white wine sauce, or her welcome innovations on pasta, while at the right time of the year local eels, marinaded in home-made olive oil with wild vegetables (*horta*), is something to look for and, once located, to treasure.

Nevertheless, the move to the city has encouraged the consumption of convenience foods, rather than those which are only seasonally available. This leads to the importation of fruit, vegetables, meat and fish in which (with the exception of fish due to depletion of Mediterranean stocks), Greece is quite capable of self-sufficiency. Greece imported €11.7 million (15,500 tons) of tomatoes in 2011.

Standardisation is another factor: packaging and presentation are more important to city-dwellers than to those who have tomatoes growing in the garden, but *taste* is becoming less important than availability of imported produce which is in danger of winning air-miles bonuses. And the lack of any co-ordinated export policy means that, outside Greece, the likes of Michael Noonan could be forgiven for thinking that *feta* is the only export: Greek olive oil and wines could compete successfully with the Spanish and Italian products to be found on supermarket shelves if the conditions for marketing them were put in place.

The Role and Status of Women

As in most marriages, the Greek home is a negotiated space between husband and wife and, at times, a contested space. Traditional roles in rural society, where the man works outdoors to garner a subsistence while the woman keeps the house and rears the children, may have diminished in significance with the growth in urban living and the equality of women and men. But even recent studies indicate that the points of demarcation and coalition of roles within the home remain characteristic of Greek families in general.

Most of Chapter 3 was concerned with a westerner's comprehension of Greece in the Balkans as "other", of "us" and "them" as it has formed our understanding of difference in cultural terms.

Another, equally profound, borderland exists between one kind of "us" and one kind of "them": woman as "other". No man writing on gender in modern Greece, however persuaded by feminism or women's studies, can escape the danger of thinking in "man" terms. The emphasis in Ireland for "gender balance" on, for example, state management boards, is not to be found in Greece, where "tradition" views woman as a domestic person, especially as *mother*.

A very strong case can be made for the fact that, until revisionism began to create new memories, not only was history written by the winners (rather than the losers) but also that it was the history of men rather than women. With the sole exception of Laskarina Bouboulina (1771-1825), whose role in the war of independence became legendary,[16] no woman features prominently in any account of modern Greek politics, until the film star Melina Mercouri (daughter of an MP and herself an activist against the junta) became Minister of Culture in the PASOK administrations of 1981-89 and 1993-94, when, among other achievements, she inaugurated the campaign for the return to Greece of the Parthenon (or "Elgin") Marbles.

The life of the home, and of the family, however, has been exhaustively studied by anthropologists, ethnologists, sociologists and sexologists and it is predominantly women who provide the central feature, and subject, of the home. One anthropologist has suggested that "we might see *all* Greeks in this history as 'women', for they are the ruled and the written about".[17]

However, I find the fieldwork of Jill Dubisch, Michael Herzfeld and others lacking in the wider apprehension of their focus: while they can extrapolate a general truth from a focussed study, they seem not to see that the field in which they work is constantly changing – exponentially in the case of women – so that their work is suspended in a time-warp that is in danger of becoming persuasive long after its time has passed.

Moreover, anthropology and sociology seem to consist too often of counting heads and dividing by the number of perceived customs. They are sciences, not wisdom. Undeniable gems such as Campbell's work among the Sarakatsani (which *does* offer us wisdom) are as important as the day they were written, but they must be continually revisited (as, too, the studies of Arensberg and Kimball in Ireland) in order to check on their continuing relevance.

I find a significant difference between what is said about people's behaviour and what they actually *do*, simply because to report it is to translate it into a different set of meanings from the life in which it was lived. In the case of marriage, which has been the predominant subject of ethnography, it can no longer be considered exclusively, without reference to the increasing factor, in cities, of single women, single mothers and unmarried couples. Indeed, the city itself is a different world from that traditionally studied by the ethnographers and sociologists, and a much more complex and challenging one.

Nevertheless, the women of Greece are, largely, unspoken. That does not, of course, mean that they are, as a gender, unsung heroes. It merely makes it difficult to depict the "typical" Greek woman.

Nicholas Gage states quite clearly that "as in most western countries, the winds of women's liberation and the sexual revolution have had a dramatic impact on the roles and rights of women".[18] He points to the legalisation of abortion, the permissibility of divorce, the outlawing of the dowry, and the opening of professional positions to women. At the same time, Gage also emphasises the essential factor in the Greek mind, which regards a working wife as "a blot on the household's masculinity and ability to provide". Coming from a village background and then immersed in Greek-America,[19] he may be extolling an idea long past when he says "women at every level of Greek society were brought up to coddle their men", but I have personal experience of the fact that a Greek boy-child can do no wrong, and may not be corrected by his mother for any wrong-doing.[20]

It might be best to think of Greek women throughout modern history as occupying a similar position, and having a similar nature, to the rights and obligations enshrined and delineated in the Constitution: in the sense that there is a meeting-point, within the house, of the woman, with specific, if undefined, rights and obligations and the man, with his own rights and obligations. Perhaps all marriages and domestic arrangements are like this: in effect, a compromise where the rules of the house – the *oikonomía* – are regulated between the parties to the marriage, which is also the household.

There is one biological fact which we cannot ignore: when the Irish philhellene John Pentland Mahaffy was challenged to state the difference between a man and a woman he neatly answered "I cannot conceive". The role of Greek woman as mother is more important than that of wife, even though one is usually the consequence of the other. A feminist critic could write in 1986 that women were still "locked in their reproductive roles".[21]

In his novella *The Murderess* (*I Fonissa*, 1903), Alexandros Papadiamandis depicts a woman who sees it as her god-given mission to save young girls from a life-long fate – especially where there might be no possibility of the essential dowry – by ending their brief lives.

> She had never done anything except work for others. As a child, she had worked for her parents. When she married, she became her husband's slave – yet because of her own character and his weakness she had also been his guardian; when she had children, she became their servant; when her children had children, she became her grandchildren's servant as well.[22]

Reflecting on her own condition makes her empathise with that of others yet unborn.

While the reality of life at that time in a small island (Papadiamandis's birthplace of Skíathos) bears little resemblance to the lives of Greek women today, the psychology remains an underlying symptom of women's secondary social position: for "dowry" read "glass ceiling".

The days of women's subservience, even in the remotest islands, are finished, yet certain conventions still apply: on the day that my neighbour, Hercules, died, his wife (now his widow), who up to then had habitually worn colourful clothes, immediately donned widow's black, conforming to a tradition that is unlikely to disappear in the near future. She is identified in her status now by her clothing, and thus *performs*, in communion with the other widows in the village, a role distinct from that of wife, demonstrating the relationship between the living and the dead. (In some villages you will still find "mourners" who "perform" at wakes just as the *caointeoir* "keens" the Irish dead.)

Although the public "performance" by women of their household chores, such as shopping, is no longer subject to the former social restrictions which controlled their movements as in a formal dance, it's still the case that in seven years I have never seen a woman at any social or political gathering in the village (other than celebration of weddings, baptisms and funerals): the *kafeneío* is strictly, if silently, the purlieu of the men. The idea that a woman would sit in the evening at a game of cards or backgammon, or simply take a drink and watch television, is inconceivable (excuse my pun). And I know of one in a neighbouring village to which women are not admitted – similar to the case in some Dublin pubs until very recently.

But that's in the village. In town, women are cosmopolitan, liberated, enfranchised, sitting alone or with other women at cafés, while the women students are increasingly open about a life of sexual freedom that was until recently subdued and covert.

A further aspect of the dilution of traditional values is *exogamy*: marriage outside the immediate "tribe", as opposed to *endogamy*, marriage within. Marriage of Greek women with non-Greek men, or vice versa, is not exactly rampant, but it is an increasing phenomenon, for example in the number of Irish women in Greece married to Greek men.

In studying "women" as performers in society – whether as wives, mothers, writers, or politicians (especially the latter) – I do *not* subscribe to the view of woman as a "sub-culture", as do many anthropologists. In fact, women writers in particular have constantly presented themselves as equal to men, and, in issues requiring an understanding of love, compassion and commitment, more effective.

I experienced one instance, however, of the traditional male concept of the woman as inferior when the secretary of the Durrell School of Corfu visited the bank for some transaction; she had a power of attorney sworn by myself, but could make no headway with the bank. Eventually I was called in to provide my signature; when I protested to the manager that our secretary had all the necessary legal authority, he merely said: "But you are the *man!*" This attitude no doubt persisted from the time, prior to 1982, when a woman could not establish a business without her husband's consent.

The Prefect of the Athens region, Rena Dourou, recounts that, during her election campaign the former deputy Prime Minister, Theodoros Pangalos, said that he could not stand the sight of her "filthy face" on election posters, and that he would like to see her campaigning in a bikini. She also recalled that Evangelos Venizelos, leader of PASOK and deputy Prime Minister, had told a female MP that "she should be pregnant".[23]

The Union of Greek Women was founded in 1879, and in 1890 the first female student was admitted to the University of Athens – fourteen years ahead of her Irish sister at Trinity College, Dublin. Many other women's organisations came into existence, of which the League for Women's Rights, founded in 1920, was suppressed by the Metaxas dictatorship in 1936, as were women's "political" organisations, such as the Panhellenic Union of Women (established in 1945) by the 1967 junta. The conservatism of the junta extended not only to "restoring" traditional Greekness in religion and the suppression of communism, but also in insisting on the integrity of the family as the basic social unit, which any "liberation" of women would undermine. The junta even imposed dress codes for women (as in Franco's Spain) and forbade mixed social gatherings of students.

The idea of e-man-cipation for women only returned to the Greek agenda in 1981 with the first PASOK administration and the leadership of the Prime Minister's American wife, Margaret Papandreou. Under PASOK, the equality of men and women, both in the workplace and in the home, was enforced, abolishing a husband's legal right to prevent his wife from working, decriminalising adultery, and facilitating abortion (another area in which Greece predates Irish law).

Despite these changes in the status of women, there remains, in the view of Eleni Stamiris, "the old patriarchal assumptions still firmly rooted"[24] in the cadres of society traditionally dominated by males such as trades unions, political parties, parliament and the legal profession, which have failed to integrate women fully into their executive strata. To date, only one political party has had a woman leader (Aleka Papariga, leader of KKE, 1991-2013) and one chair of an incipient party (Maria Mamanaki, of Synaspismos, 1991-93, which evolved into Syriza, "Coalition of the Radical Left" (Συνασπισμός Ριζοσπαστικής Αριστεράς, Synaspismós Rizospastikís Aristerás)). In 1956, the 300-seat parliament held only two women; by 1985 that had grown to thirteen; today, the percentage is almost 20 per cent (56/300).

It remains undeniable, however, that "the family is the significant unit of social and economic structure in the Greek village community".[25] Women do continue with household chores, although many traditional occupations, such as spinning (the most prevalent of female domestic functions), have almost completely disappeared. In the village I see widows collecting *horta* (wild greens) for their supper and kindling for their meagre fires and keeping chickens (eggs for themselves and for sale), and breeding cockerels (roosters) for sale for the island speciality, *pastitsada* (rooster cooked in tomato with pasta). Their domestic functions thus continue as a mixture of physical and financial need. The woman in the house – wife, mother, grandmother, widow – may have stopped spinning for a living, but she continues in rural Greece – and, I suspect, in the towns and cities – not unaware of her gender's entry into the public world, but not part of it.

In 1866, G.G. Pappadopoulos, in his essay "On Womanhood in Greece", believed that "a substantial part of the Greek resurgence is due to Greek woman [...] When her son is educated, the man is illuminated, but when the daughter is educated, the entire family is illuminated".[26] This pre-vision of the future emancipation of women through education would be a long time coming, but the entry of women into the *agorá* or public arena (depicted by women writers such as Evgenia Fakinou, Maro Douka, Alki Zei and Ioanna Karystiani) shows education to have been an essential part of emancipation, and, in parallel, the ability to be self-supporting by taking a place in the workforce.[27] Anna Karamanou (a former MEP) describes the "emergence" of modern Greek woman as "the great-est peaceful social evolution in the age-long history of Greece".[28]

Although more women have found their way into the labour market, this tends to be restricted to the lower and more menial levels: cleaning (domestic and public), child-minding, factories, very similar to the jobs achieved by upwardly mobile women in the nineteenth century. Despite the constitutional insistence on equal pay for equal work, women's pay is approximately three-quarters of men's in the same work.

Movement from the villages into the towns, the arrival in 1922 of 1.5 million Anatolian refugees, and simply awareness of urban behaviour, by physical contact or through television, have greatly diminished the power of local custom as an inhibiting factor in women's – and men's – lives. Their interaction today, apart from the perennial biological one, is conducted on a changing basis.

Traditionally, the woman was the principal οικονομολόγα – *ikonomologá* or "economist"; not only did she control the purse-strings, but inside the home she was dominant: decisions affecting the family's well-being were primarily hers, while her husband's responsibility lay in the way the house's "economy" was represent-ed in the community.

It is important to understand that the traditional role of wom-an in the home was not only material and physical, but also essen-tially *psychological* in all its aspects: the ordering of the household, the acculturation of children, the relationship of the house with the extended family and outer community are basic characteristics of the *woman as civiliser*. My signal towards society as the basis of politics will be obvious. Even in cooking, a woman exercises a cultural role that is one of the key concepts in Greekness.

When it is said that a woman is *tou spítou* – literally, "of the house" – it implies that she is "master in her own house", that there is a metaphorical transvestism between man and woman, where-by some of his masculinity is transferred to her and, I should add (since I frequently see men in the village gathering wild herbs for the stockpot), of her femininity to him. The dominance of women in the home may, of course, be total: she may reduce her husband to a caricature. I am reminded of a line in John B. Keane's drama of wits, *Sive*, in which the wife silences her husband with the words, "will you sit down and be said by me".[29] To "be said" rather than to have one's own narrative, is a lowly status, and, as Dubisch says, "a Greek man cannot achieve full adult status until he is married [...] It is through his connection to a woman that a man takes his place in society".[30]

But one cannot, and must not, extrapolate an example of either a Kerry village or an Aegean island to provide either Ireland or Greece with sexual stereotypes.

Marriage was a partnership, in which the husband and wife (distinguished as νοικοκύρης – *nikokyris* – and νοικοκυρά – *nikokyrá* – respectively) established the νοικοκυριό (*nikyrió*, household), the shared ground as fundamental to their common good. As Juliet du Boulay observes, the paradox of women's position in rural Greece rests on "the unequivocal association of woman both with symbolic, moral, and physical weakness and with the role of spiritual guardian of husband, house, and family".[31] There is, I think, some beauty in such a paradox: the "weakness", such as a male-oriented mind would see in the "fair sex", is in part a valid perception; the strength, as the pillar of the house, is equally valid. One might say "in my weakness is my strength".

Karamanou again:

> More women, as well as more men, are facing conflicting responsibilities both in their private and public lives. The challenge of modern society is how to ensure that these two spheres of life can achieve compatibility and complement each other.[32]

Du Boulay suggests that there might be a parallel between the perceived strengths and weaknesses of women with the idea of "appearance" and "reality": man appears to be strong and enjoys prestige outside the house, and woman exercises the reality of power within.

Any discrepancy between "appearance" and "reality" is compensated by the fact of *drama* and *performance*. Commitment in assuming, and belief in playing, a role are the means by which appearance, via make-believe, becomes reality and vice versa. It is the strategy adopted by many peoples, in many contexts, to make sense of their situation and condition. That is what drama *is*: the performance of self-as-other, the place of make-believe, of the irrational made credible – *credo quia absurdum* (for which I think there is no Greek original).

The persistent sense of the dramatic in ordinary folk is not merely fanciful: one does not need today to see a performance of Aeschylus to hear a villager say, "*I zoí íne théatro*" ("life is a theatre") because life is seen as a theatre or drama, with "performance" by men and women of their different functions as the drama, and the *agorá* as the *mise en scène*. It's part of the everyday ritual of metaphors, finding a fit between reality and one's visions.

Leaving aside the phenomenal part of women in modern Greek literature, the place and function of women as dramatic characters has reflected the changing attitudes to, and emergent strengths of, women outside the home. From Kalliroi Siganou-Parren's *The New Woman* (1907), with its clear reference to Ibsen's *A Doll's House*, to Loula Anagnostakis' *The Victory* (1978), women as principals in the dramatic *agorá* have become integral forces.

As du Boulay records, *i gynaiká synkrateí to spíti* (the woman holds the house together) and *chorís ti gynaiká to spíti den yinetaí* (without woman the house cannot exist).

When Salamone and Stanton refer to an "ongoing opposition between man and woman, child and elder, individual and community, and personal and community prosperity"[33] it might be more appropriate to think of "juxtaposition" rather than "opposition", since, despite the undoubted prevalence of the *agón* in many households, the essence of the household *oikonomía* is mutual survival and, where possible, prosperity.

And we would have to totally disbelieve the assertion by Robinette Kennedy that "men and women spend relatively little time with each other, know little about each other's domain, and have a great deal of animosity towards each other in general".[34] While this may have been true of *some* rural households, and possibly is still true in both city and country (as it is in Ireland), it is given the lie by the fact that it is in the intimate intercourse (and I don't mean sexual) between husband and wife – the meeting-point of their "domains" – that the *oikonomía* is achieved. Kennedy's further point, that "women see men [...] as tyrannical [...] women perceive men as the oppressors" is risible in the extreme: not even the most ardent, prejudiced and resentful feminist (with the possible exception of the late Betty Friedan) could subscribe to such a bald and preposterous statement by a professional psychologist such as Kennedy.

A Society "As If"

Having discussed in Chapter 3 Greece's simultaneous centrality and liminality in the Balkans and the Levant, we may look at Takis Theodoropoulos' opinion in a recent newspaper:

> Greece is kind of European, with kind of eastern roots and Balkan influence, and a kind of Mediterranean mentality. Greeks speak a language that sounds kind of Greek and, as a result, they kind of understand each other.[35]

Theodoropoulos is taking the same view of Greece as I do of myself in calling my house *Ipothesi*: he sees not only an approximation to a "real" state but also an "as if", an idea capable of flexibility, offering at the same time both affirmation and denial, because it exists in-between, as Greece always has. That it should be necessary at present to insist that the hurler should vacate the ditch and get onto the field, is indicative of the expectation of western-looking rational minds which demand "either/or" rather than "both/and". It's to look for reality where none, substantively, exists. It is a society and a state in search of metaphors for the *dénouement* of the drama of performances.

And metaphor makes its most powerful presence in the form of storytelling, from the simplest folk tale to the most sophisticated novel or drama. It makes connections in men's and women's minds which they might not ordinarily make.

All life is cyclic: birth, marriage, parenthood, death; seasonal: sowing and reaping; political: sowing a philosophy or ideology and reaping the harvest in votes and power. It becomes *ritual* and thus a drama.

The *hearth*, whether it is a peasant's cottage or the parliamentary chamber, is the focus of all these actions and counter-actions, the dispensing of wisdom, and the testing of convention. When one considers how closely the drama in Irish theatre is related to the "drama" of everyday life, my argument does not seem so far-fetched. The "drama" provided by the (disgusting) exchanges by senior bankers in the "Anglo" tapes, the "drama" of play-acting in the Dáil and Seanad, the match-making that persists in rural communities, the saturation of inner cities by the drug culture, is mirrored in the plays of J.M. Synge, John B. Keane, Brian Friel, the ANU theatre company, and on television by docudramas such as *Charlie* (2015, charting the rise and fall of C.J. Haughey). We will meet these in Greek cinema in Chapter 8.

Social Behaviour

The emphasis in Greek life has always been on *freedom*. The Greek word for "freedom", *eleuthería*, expresses the concept of both movement and behaviour, the right to self-determination. But how does one "act" or "perform" freedom? The ways in which one chooses to exercise freedom are political acts in the widest sense, and their symbolism is a factor in the way society is shaped. If there is a conflict of interests between the citizen and the state, the citizen's sense of freedom predominates. One example of defiance of the State – and, thus, by definition, of one's fellow citizens – is the failure of the smoking ban, first introduced in 2009 and revised in stricter format in 2010. As an editorial in *Kathimerini* newspaper observed, "smoking cigarettes is not simply the ritualized inhalation of nicotine, tar and other addictive substances, but a personal statement; not an admission of dependence but a declaration of personal liberty."[36] Where in Ireland the ban was immediately and almost universally accepted, in Greece the opposite has been the case. One restaurant in Athens actually had to advertise that it was a "non-smoking" establishment, so widespread was the defiance. That has changed slightly: the more upmarket venues (hotels, shops, restaurants – as distinct from tavernas), some offices and most public locations make smoking impossible; others still tolerate it. In the village, it would be unthinkable for the *kafeneío* to ban smokers. It has also resulted in outdoor heaters, which were previously non-existent in Greece.

It was clear at the outset that the ban was not being observed, and the minister of health appointed 800 "smoke-police" to enforce it, with fines of, for the smoker, from 50 to 100 euros, and, for the bar owner, from 500 to 10,000 euros.

As *Kathimerini* noted in an editorial, "If this law is flouted, it will simply lend credence to the widespread belief that people can do as they like because laws exist only on paper".[37]

Meanwhile, in April 2011, the then Prime Minister George Papandreou, was actually awarded the World Health Organization's "World No Tobacco Day" accolade, for his insistence on implementing the ban, even though at that point it was clearly unenforceable – an "as if" situation *par excellence*. Papandreou was praised for his "political courage", but courage is insufficient unless there is political clout to support it – a personal failing which led to his downfall six months later.

One reason for the disregard of the ban is that, for most of the year, it's possible to sit outside cafés, and therefore to smoke legally. When the weather becomes so inclement that even the hardiest smokers are driven indoors, the smoking continues, regardless, because it is merely relocating on a temporary basis a natural activity and a fundamental right.

In Athens, the anti-ban campaign was led by a bar owner who even formed a political party to contest elections. In answer to the charge that smokers imperil the health of non-smokers as well as their own, he said, "the authorities cannot tell us what to do. That's tampering with the electoral process."[38]

Even the health minister admitted that the smoking law could not be effectively implemented. This wasn't Greece's first attempt to confront the twin problems of smoking and passive smoking – it's the fourth since 2000.[39] The previous one, introduced in July 2009, failed completely, due mainly to the fact that there was no designated inspectorate to enforce the law. At first, cafés removed ashtrays from indoor tables and placed receptacles at the doors marked "please extinguish your cigarettes here". But, as regular customers retreated from the winter and refused to observe the law, the ashtrays reappeared and no notice was taken. One of the ideological points of the Irish smoking ban was to protect employees; in Greek cafés it was the waiters who flouted it first.

As one ordinary citizen said: "Why are we Greeks so troublesome? Why is it so hard for us to respect laws?" *AthensPlus* saw it as a test of the government's (that is, Papandreou's) ability to introduce change in other, perhaps more significant, aspects of society: "However unrelated this seems to the monumental effort of reforming the economy, social security and the labor market, the smoking ban could serve as a measure of how much Greeks are prepared to change."[40]

But, as a worldwide issue, smoking is as serious in Greece as elsewhere: 42 per cent of all Greeks smoke; 63 per cent of men, 39 per cent of women, 37 per cent of the 12-17 age group and 45 per cent of those aged 16-25. Overall, it's the highest smoking rate in the EU, annually consuming 32 billion cigarettes, with 20,000 deaths from smoke-related diseases at a health cost of €2 billion. The government called in the Harvard School of Public Health to train officials responsible for implementing the ban. Harvard says that if smoking among young people is not curbed, 350,000 of today's young people will die prematurely.

Which cuts no ice with dedicated smokers, who are bracing themselves for a further hike in tobacco tax: a packet of 23 cigarettes (yes, 23) costs €3.80 at present, hardly a deterrent to smokers in Ireland where 20 cigarettes cost €10.00.

It isn't an exaggeration to say that the smoking issue and that of national security emanate from the same root cause. A fresh outbreak of terrorism in 2010-11, accompanied by an outburst of illegal smoking, points to the concept that to interfere with personal freedom is an insult to democracy.

There can thus develop a significant gap between faith in the concept of democracy and suspicion of the democratic process: yet another mismatch between the ideal and the real.

I've heard it said that "Greeks love their country but they don't trust it". Perhaps this is a justification for my idea of "loving and mourning", but it doesn't matter as much as appreciating that there are in fact two Greeces: the "system", which has obviously failed, and "the people", who allowed the system to grow into a monster which, because they put their trust in politicians, they hardly recognise and bears little resemblance to what they dreamed of.

And, for the outsider, it helps to explain why we can be philhellenes and hellenosceptics at the same time. In a sense, the fact that Greeks live in a "fake" or "make-believe" world only epitomises the larger make-believe of Europe (but that is to anticipate Chapter 10).

Rural Depopulation

Irish readers need no introduction to the phenomenon of rural depopulation, seen as the death of the countryside, its villages and traditions, through migration to the towns, cities and suburbs, and emigration to the diaspora, mainly (in the case of Greeks) in North America and Australia.

One serious problem about the village, which is a characteristic common to both Greece and Ireland, is rural depopulation, which is far more threatening than the villager aping the townie in manners or fashion. A villager driving a 4x4 or a BMW is still a villager. But a village child who goes to college and discovers a wider world than his or her home environment can provide is no longer a village child but a young person in that wider world. In the village where I now live, most of the (very few) teenagers have declared their intention of leaving; if they do so, one of the two tavernas and one of the two shops will, most likely, close. And who can blame them? Why spend your life behind a shop counter selling cigarettes and sweets, or waitressing in your parents' café, when you could be in the metropolis, highly trained for a lucrative profession? Much though it is politically incorrect to say so, the trend today towards education – the training of the peasant mind into new avenues – points inexorably to the death of the village, as the peasant mind says farewell to its natural habitat and hinterland.

By 1963 the urban population of Greece was slightly larger than the rural, due almost entirely to the growth of Athens, which has seen fourteen new suburbs developing since 2000. A sprawling city which goes every which way but up, has turned what were once country villages, such as Kifissia, into dormitory suburbs and retail and business parks resembling Dublin's Liffey Valley, against which city-centre traders struggle to maintain not only their livelihood but a part of the inner city's social fabric.

The Plaka, as Peter Levi said, was already devalued in the 1970s. Today, it is no more than a glorified *souk*, a tourist trap where, however, it is still possible to find tavernas patronised by locals around the Plateia Filomousiki Etaireias. In Athens generally, the shops are the same high street outlets as in any European city, selling the same foreign-made souvenirs. I have even seen a model of a *komodo* dragon on sale: truly authentic! In the fast-changing built environment, it's disappointing to see so many neoclassical mansions abandoned and near derelict in the city centre.

The city has become the focus for protests which often develop into riots. The shooting dead of a fifteen-year-old boy, Alexis Grigoropoulos, by a policeman in the Athens suburb of Exarchia in late 2008 sparked riots which still take the form of protest marches on his anniversary (6 December) as a sign of citizens' distrust of the police. "Hoodies" have become a uniform for the disaffected, so much so that, identifying their wearers with law-breakers and possibly terrorists, the government attempted to ban them by law.

Increased mobility through car ownership means that the shopping centre is replacing the village shop: financial concentration makes local trade non-viable. Increasing administrative centralisation is another factor: a village diminishes as its vital organs atrophy – the post office, the school, the *kafeneío*. The village mind is affected by urbanised ways of thinking, with the consequent perception – whether real or imagined – of loss of traditional values.

In Greece, the options for school-leavers are very limited, with unemployment running at 55-60 per cent in the 18-25 age group. Will they or won't they get the points they need for their chosen college courses? If they do, there's a strong likelihood that their degree will mean living away from home for most of their working lives. In a small village, that creates its own dilemmas.[41]

The points system in Greece is very similar to that in Ireland. Out of a maximum of 20,000 points, you need 10,000 to be eligible for university, and at least 13,000 for the college and course of your choice. As in Ireland, the points requirement mounts in the more specialised subjects and according to availability of places in the individual colleges. A basic BA in computing or economics may confer little job potential (I know of one civil engineer working at a supermarket check-out).This may therefore point the graduate back home to take over the family business.

Rural Greece lost most of its schools over the past thirty years. Villages are even losing their focal point: the local bar. I can think of three in Corfu that have recently closed due to the deaths of their elderly owners. The village is not yet dead, but very silent. It is also losing not only its agricultural people, but their skills, thus endangering Greece's ability to feed itself.[42]

Does the shrinking village suffer from its failure to adapt? Does it deserve to die? Would the introduction of small industries, especially high-tech ones, reverse what is fast becoming a string of skeletal settlements, validated only by the passing tourist trade during the summer months, and invisible and dormant the rest of the year?

An even greater factor in this leave-taking is university (or technical college) education, which provides an exit to a "better" life – a professional career and wider horizons than the village can offer. One schoolboy in the village made a bazooka that fired a missile 300 yards. He's now at university studying robotics and weapon design. Luckily, he hasn't heard of the Daleks ("ex-ter-min-ate!") or he would have a one-stop destination for his twin talents. But he isn't coming back. His best friend isn't so bright, and stayed at home as an apprentice electrician. Another school-leaver went to study cosmetics with a view to working in the film or fashion industry as a make-up artist: another one gone. Win one, lose two. It's glib to say "the soul goes out of the village" but, haemorrhage or brain-drain, it's true nonetheless. Not much call for robotics round here.

That leaves two young men – and no girls – in a village which once boasted two schools (none now) and over ten *kafeneíon*s (two remain).

I saw the same problem in Connemara, where I lived for a few years in the early 2000s. In one village, two of the pubs and two of the three shops closed because the children did not want to take over their parents' business. One girl studied aeronautical engineering and now works for British Aerospace. Alcock and Brown's historic landing in Clifden in 1919 didn't encourage a local aeroplane industry. Nor did the long-defunct Marconi transatlantic signalling station stimulate any local initiative in communication technology. The exodus of the young is one of either choice or necessity; but it seems to be inexorable.

Family and village pride lose out to the attractions of better-paid cosmopolitan life. There is no jobs market at home, and few marriage options. There are no bank loans for start-up enterprises, and family savings have long been exhausted by the imperatives of austerity. "Cottage industry" doesn't exist.

Can you argue with "progress"? These young people are entitled to a first-generation university education and the opportunities it offers to take them away from the traditional, inward-looking, familiar world towards something new, challenging and exciting. No one has yet devised a programme that can reconcile this legitimate demand for self-improvement with the equally legitimate need of rural society to cohere and, to use Brian Friel's wonderful word, "resile".

Zissimos Lorenzatos did not oppose progress, but he was sceptical of the impact that education will have on this "real" Greece:

> Just because [...] Greece today is rapidly changing from the agricultural life to one of urbanization and industrialization, it does not follow that it must sell its soul to the devil or lose its mind altogether [...] Things will go right only when the educated people realize that there is no conflict between the village or island and their own education [...] and that it is not necessary to destroy the village or island [...] but that they should submit to it, learn from it, follow it, and fruitfully or creatively use it [...] Most educated people who are separated from the folk and from life, don't leave us much to hope for.[43]

The possible "death of the village" has in the last couple of years been contained, in a very small way, by young people, disillusioned with city life, returning to the ancestral village to start a small busi-

ness such as organic farming, which is a significant growth industry in a country, and cuisine, based on traditional home-grown
produce. But there seems to be no end to the inexorable sprawl
of suburban Athens, which today absorbs 35 per cent of the entire
population (and Thessaloniki a further 12 per cent).

Josiah Strong's nineteenth-century vision that "god created
men in a garden" and that the city was the result of the Fall, may
attract some who seek to revivify the countryside and its values,
but the attraction of the city for work, wealth, bright lights and
politics is irresistible.

It is time now to turn to the "reality" of the state structure and
the political parties which have, in their own ways, attempted to
turn "appearance" into "reality" – or should that be "realities" into
"appearance"?

5

STRUCTURES OF POWER
AND DISSENT

In the previous chapter, I looked at the strengths of the Greek people – their home- and family-based character, their temperament, the changing social profile with the new roles of women and the phenomenon of rural depopulation – and the weaknesses and problems emanating from the insistence on individual liberty. In this chapter and the next I turn to the way that state structures and the Greek character have come into conflict, and the way that those structures do not always reflect, or serve, the Greek mindset.

In many senses, Greece is an accidental democracy. Plato, whose views on democracy anticipated those of Machiavelli, might have approved of the conditional state which has evolved, firstly under Bavarian tutelage and later under self-management; a state the principal purpose of which was to bind together a sense of the nation (*éthnos*) – still under the influence of external powers – and only secondarily as a means of protecting individual citizens.

Athenian journalist John Psaropoulos once quipped that the reason for Greece having three "national days" – "Ochi Day" on 28 October, Independence Day on 25 March and, marking the junta's suppression of a student uprising, 17 November – was due to the fact that "It's a small country, it's had to become independent several times".[1] Each attempt at independence has proved to be in-con-clusive because it was insufficiently in-clusive.[2]

From 1844 onwards, when the Bavarian monarchy was forced to grant a constitution, Greece's successive constitutions (including those of 1864, 1911, 1925, 1948, 1968 and 1975) have served the purposes of their architects in creating the appearance of a democracy while reserving powers which, in a crisis, would conflict with the tenets of democracy: they are designer-documents, wearing on their sleeve not the fullest aspirations of all the people, but the options available for the time being.

Greece is reborn at each turn in its history in a different costume, reflecting the fashions of the time – the art of wearing the possible rather than the ultimate garment of nationhood. This discrepancy between appearance and reality, which we have met in the case of the family and the community, becomes a hallmark of a nation in which "ethnic" refuses to be translated into *éthnos*.

The Constitution

Immediately after the ousting of the Colonels, Greece returned to democracy with a Constitution (*Syntágma*) adopted by referendum in 1975 and last revised in 2008. It is the ultimate authority of the Greek state.

A relatively new society on the world stage such as Greece or, much more recently, Ireland, must acknowledge to its people the vulnerability and fragility of the state by a circumspect approach to statehood, which will be reflected in both the "positive" rights (involving action) and "negative" rights (impeding such action), and in how these are to be exercised, protected and controlled.

Any reader of John Kelly's *Fundamental Rights Under the Irish Constitution* will be familiar with this meeting-point, where the individual confronts the state on issues such as human rights and freedoms, or the ontology of the person vis-à-vis the greater good of the whole society. Through its analysis of case law, Kelly's study becomes a mirror of the evolution of expectations, assertions, confrontations, admissions and denials of those rights and freedoms, those concepts of the balance between individual and society.

There are, of course, textbooks on human rights in Greece, but none based on case law that examines what we might call an *agón* of the citizen and the State.[3] One factor in the comparative absence of individual case law is the "closed shop", which functions in similar fashion to the family unit. If a member of a closed profession encounters a legal or administrative problem affecting a personal right, that problem can be negotiated by the profession rather than the individual.[4]

In my opinion, this *lacuna* is due to the difficulty in making open what is too often closed: the mismatch between the individual and the state, and between the state and itself, which becomes painfully evident in the terrorism which is ever-present on the streets of Athens and other cities, but which draws strength from an undercurrent of self-doubt among Greeks as to what they have created beyond the fireside and the village *agorá*.

Adamantia Pollis points out that "the abrogation of civil and political rights [in the Civil War] was claimed to be justified on the grounds of the state of emergency facing Greece in the light of the insurgency of a communist-led movement".[5] She then refers to "the persistence of formalism and legalism and the absence of an underlying consensual democratic ethos" in the current Constitution. The juxtaposition of these two observations is instructive.

Predictably, the Greek Constitution lists the basic rights it protects. Not even an autocratic constitution would openly state that it did *not* protect the rights of citizens. However, as with all constitutions, the Greek and the Irish both acknowledge basic rights and hedge them with promises in the name of the general good or, much more significantly in the case of Greece, the security of the State.

The Foreword observes that the principal motivation of the 1975 Constitution was to raise the respect of the value of man. Reviews in 1986, 2001 and 2008 extended the protection of individual rights and bolstered the institutions of the welfare state.

The Constitution established the state as a "parliamentary republic", founded on "popular sovereignty", deriving all powers "from the People" (Articles 1-3). All Greeks are equal before the law: "all persons shall have the right to develop freely their personality and to participate in the social, economic and political life of the country, insofar as they do not infringe the rights of others or violate the Constitution" (5). Here one finds one of the roots of discord in society, since it is the activities of plutocrats and, in current parlance, kleptocrats, who have created a deep division between the "haves" and the "have nots", between the ultra-rich and the 30

117

per cent of citizens living below the poverty line. In the light of the economic crisis and consequent austerity measures, this division has been attributed also to politicians and bureaucrats, some of whom, it has been proven, have enriched themselves by taking massive bribes.

The Constitution recognises the rights of "all persons living within the Greek territory" – that is, including non-Greeks – to protection of "their life, honour and liberty irrespective of nationality, race or language and of religious or political beliefs" (5); and also guarantees freedom of religious conscience (13). The difficulty in this case is twofold: the rights of immigrants who "live" in Greece, however poorly or illegally, and the issue of sexual orientation, which is clearly excluded by this Article. In 2014, the minister of justice (in the outgoing government) stated his opposition to gay marriage: "We are a country that respects traditions and human nature... This government will not allow gay marriage"[6] – the two statements do not seem to coincide unless one accepts his view that homosexuality is "against nature". Greece has in fact been criticised by the European Court of Human Rights for lack of recognition of civil partnerships.

The State guarantees the right to information and participation in "the Information Society" (5a) (except where issues of national security or crime prevention arise); in this respect, the constitutional guarantee would seem, in explicitly referring to the Information Society, to be ahead of its Irish counterpart.

The *home* is recognised in the English-language version as "a sanctuary" and an "asylum" (9).[7] The family is "the cornerstone of the preservation and the advancement of the Nation, as well as marriage, motherhood and childhood" (21). Clearly, the drafters of the Greek Constitution did not fall into the same trap as the Irish, in identifying the wife/mother as a "support" to the State, "without which the common good cannot be achieved" and therefore discouraged wives working "to the neglect of their duties in the home" (Art. 41.2 of the Irish Constitution).

The position of women in Greek society in regard to marriage and motherhood is so crucial that perhaps it was self-evident that it did not need to be enshrined in the Constitution.

The Constitution also safeguards the right of assembly "peaceably and unarmed" (11), the right to work, equal pay for men and women (22), the right to form trades unions and to strike (23); the right to found and belong to political parties, provided these "serve the free functioning of democratic government" (29). The existence of the Golden Dawn fascist party, and the massive question mark over whether or not it is illegal (since it does not seem to advocate "democratic government") is a constitutional conundrum that perplexes both politicians and jurists: the fact that in 2014-15 almost all the MPs belonging to Golden Dawn had been indicted on charges of murder or incitement, that its leader was in jail awaiting trial, and that it unequivocally admires the Nazi ethos, all underline this constitutional dilemma.

The Constitution provides for "the protection of the natural and cultural environment" as "a duty of the State" (24). This emanates from the concept of a particular freedom: access to the coastline which, for a maritime nation, is a *sine qua non*. It has, however, caused serious clashes between the interests of tourism and those of development, and within the tourist industry itself. For example, the nesting-place of the loggerhead turtle (*Curetta curetta*) on a beach in the Ionian island of Zakynthos is endangered by the proposed development of a hotel adjoining the beach. Which is more important to the Greek "natural and cultural environment", the turtle or the tourist? In the past three years, the government has attempted to introduce legislation restricting the concept that Greek shores are public property, in order to facilitate development of marinas and resorts. The situation is grey: while that legislation has been withdrawn in the face of opposition, measures dictated by the economic crisis, including sale of national assets, have led to certain designated areas of coastline being taken into state ownership and then sold on to commercial developers.[8]

The Constitution provides for election to, and the conduct of, parliament. We conventionally employ the term "parliament" to refer to the legislature of any country, yet there is a significant nuance in the way each country designates its law-makers. Yes, of course we have "parliaments" – places of talking, of discussion – but the Irish Dáil, the Israeli Knesset and the US Congress are, literally, places where legislators gather – places of assembly. In Russia there's the *Duma* – a place of thinking. In many Arabic-speaking countries such as Iran, Saudi Arabia and Kuwait it's called a *Majlis*, a place of sitting, or of taking counsel.

In Greece, parliament is the *Voulí*, which at root means "will" (of the people). And it also means – or implies – a "Council of Elders". Maybe it's unique. As with all constitutional matters, the difficulty lies in whether it does, or does not, reflect the will of the Greek people.

If the *Voulí* is a "council of elders" it has shown itself on many occasions to be incapable of knowing its own mind or of recognising and interpreting the will of the people. Riots in the cities and discontent in the countryside are the symptoms of a disaffection with the two-party system of PASOK/New Democracy for the past forty years and the need for new avenues of government, for which Alexis Tsipras and Syriza have demonstrated an at least temporary possibility. It's worth a moment's thought for an exchange in Theo Angelopoulos' 1988 film *Alexander the Great*: "Who made the Constitution?" "The Nation." "Whoever made it can unmake it".

As we shall see in discussing bureaucratic reform, there is a mismatch between intention and action. In many social instances, the protections offered by the Constitution are not in fact available. In respect of environmental responsibility, for example, the State's obligations are empty words when we consider that there is no adequate environmental policy to sustain them; several of the (few) cases of environmental impact studies that have been made have been set aside by the courts. If the Constitution is concerned with "quality of life", its environmental provisions are negated by the lack of urban and rural planning, especially in relation to tourism.

The expansion of state machinery, in its bureaucracy and NGOs, with consequent increase in inefficiency, impedes the constitutional notion that the state exists to serve the citizen.

Thus while the post-junta Constitution is essential for a viable democratic society, the dramatic change in Greece's circumstances has, however, been subject to what Couloumbis, Kariotis and Bellou call "conceptual inertia".[9]

If it is a reasonable argument that "a people gets the government it deserves", and if, by extension, it can be argued that a people gets the *constitution* it deserves, then both constitution and government will always be subject to argument, interpretation and revision. The essential point is the effect of constitution and government on everyday life.

Church and State

At the time of the war of independence, Greek orthodoxy was one of the adhesives of resistance and rebellion: its command of allegiance identified it as one of the most powerful forces on men's minds and hearts. There was nothing intellectual about it, any more than there was a comprehension of the meaning of independence and sovereignty among the peasants: it was a devotion – but not a mindless one – to elements of religion such as Mariolatry and miraculous icons, which were integral to daily life. There was an almost complete mapping of faith onto social existence, so much so that to be Orthodox was to be Greek, and to be Greek meant to be Orthodox.

The centrality of the Greek church is underlined by the word *orthodox*: the word identifies not only the Church itself, but also the conformity to right, proper, correct (*orthós*) beliefs and doctrine (*doxasía*). So a Greek who behaves in an "orthodox" fashion is in social, intellectual and religious conformity. The faithful *are* the citizens and the Church *is* the State.

In 1987, more than 150 years after independence, it was claimed that "Greece cannot exist without Orthodoxy".[10] And on one occasion a poster was produced depicting an airforce fighter plane over Tinos on 15 August (the Feast of the Assumption or, in the Greek church, the Dormition), proclaiming it as "Day of Military Strength", thus emphasising the conventional wisdom that not only is the second most important date in the religious calendar (after Easter) identified with national pride, but also with Greek dominance in the Aegean.

When novelist George Theotokas described Greek Orthodoxy as the "national religion", he linked it to custom and tradition: "indissolubly woven with the contours and character of [the] people, the climate and fragrance of the country".[11] The pagan element in Greek society was indeed successfully married to Christianity through the imposition of festivals, such as Easter, onto previously pagan celebrations; it led to the dominance of the Greek character by the church's festivals. A Greek's name-day (the day of the saint after whom he is named) is of far greater significance, and a far greater occasion of celebration, than his actual birthday. In Corfu, where approximately half the male population are named "Spiro" after the island saint, Spiridon, work comes to an almost complete halt on 12 December.

It is almost certainly a coincidence that the flag of Greece should have been raised on 25 March, the Feast of the Annunciation, one of the key points in the Orthodox year. The coincidence was employed as a method of binding together faith and fatherland which resulted in the centrality of the Orthodox Church to the State.

Thus, 25 March signified a double annunciation: the Greek state and the son of God. As Jill Dubisch observes, there is a useful coalition between the word *epanástasis* (rebellion) and *anástasis* (Christ's resurrection).[12]

It would be as difficult to understand Greece without the Orthodox Church, or to envisage a Greece in which Orthodoxy was not the majority faith, as to imagine Ireland without the Roman Catholic (some would say *Irish* Catholic) Church – or, for that matter, Northern Ireland without Anglicanism or Presbyterianism. That it reflects conservative values is hardly surprising, but its influence on successive governments, both democratic and undemocratic, has been marked. As Yannis Palaiologos comments, the state allowed the Church "to set public standards and often public policy on any number of issues, almost always at the expense of those who were different".[13] It is significant that the minister of education is also responsible for religious affairs.

Mount Athos, a peninsula in the north which is regarded as the monastic centre of Greece, is, by virtue of the Constitution, "in accordance with its ancient privileged status, a self-governed part of the Greek state, whose sovereignty thereon shall remain intact" (Article 105).

The Orthodox Church is not, in fact, established as the "national" or "state" church; as was the case of the Roman Catholic Church in Ireland (until 1974), it is recognised as "the prevailing religion" (Article 3).

There are some signs that the Greek church is hedging its bets with regard to political developments. During the conflict between Venizelos and the royalists in the 1920s, the Church sided with the latter; in the Civil War, the Church was unequivocally on the monarchist side, although under the Nazi regime the Archbishop of Athens withheld co-operation as far as possible. During the military junta the Church appeared to be complaisant, and its titular head was appointed by the Colonels; its submission to the junta was based on the grounds that Greece "was returning to a moral regeneration based upon devotion to Greek nationalism, anti-communism and the Orthodox church".[14]

Today, the Church has openly associated with, and given blessings to, members of Golden Dawn, whose leader, Nikos Michalaliakos, has referred to the support he receives from certain (unnamed) bishops.

The pervasive influence of the Church, as the custodian of the Orthodox faith, inhibits the expression of anti-establishment opinions. Many supporters of left-wing parties, including the Prime Minister, Alexis Tsipras, acknowledge this influence because it is politically necessary to do so in order to maintain grass roots support. Tsipras wishes to end the Church-State nexus which is enshrined in the Constitution (thus also freeing the ministry of education from its remit in religious affairs), but before the 2015 election he courted the Ecumenical Patriarch in seeking common ground for electoral purposes (although he declined to take a religious oath when sworn in as Prime Minister). Left-wing voters may not be atheists, but they abhor the power and privileges of the Church as a virtual national institution and resent the unsuitable conduct of Church officials, whether in real estate deals or sexual matters. Very few have spoken openly of the sexual predations of parish priests and higher clergy, but the Corfiot writer Maria Strani-Potts, in her stories *The Cat of Portovecchio*, explores this area of conduct as well as the equally unspoken truths about

Civil War executions.[15] Greek bishops, like Irish bishops, have mistresses (one thinks immediately of the then Bishop of Kerry, Éamon Casey and his American *amour*, Annie Murphy, who bore his son).[16] This will be further illustrated in Chapter 8.

The Church pays no taxes, and owns very considerable tracts of land. This latter point became a major public scandal in 2008, when the Vatopedi monastery on Mount Athos was involved in real estate land-swap with the government, resulting in a reputedly massive profit for the monastery. In 2010, PASOK called for five former ministers (in the New Democracy government) to be indicted in connection with the scandal, but they were deemed immune from prosecution. The investigation of this alleged fraud, which was, to say the least, lacking in transparency, culminated in 2011 in the arrest of the abbot of Vatopedi but, amid judicial secrecy which has been attributed to the continuing influence of the Church at the highest levels, it was almost impossible to establish who had been indicted, on what charges or with what result. Altogether, thirteen people – including two monks, a notary and officials of the State Mortgage Company – eventually went on trial in 2015, while the government is seeking €234 million in compensation for its loss on the deal. A further three government ministers escaped prosecution due to a statutory limitation on their culpability.

The scandal caused widespread condemnation of both government and the Church, with one newspaper editorialising on "the holy trinity of Greek graft: cash, property and the Church".[17]

Local Government

The Constitution of Greece states that "The administration of the State shall be organized according to the principle of decentralization" (Article 101). However, recent changes have reduced the number of local authorities in favour of fiscal savings and efficiency. The "Kallikrates" reform, which came into operation in 2011, was named after one of the two architects of the Parthenon – an unusual choice of name, perhaps. I've heard it said that other historical figures named Kallikrates (the name literally means "beauty and strength") would have been equally unsuitable: one led Athens into submission to Rome; another, a Spartan, died in battle; a third, a sculptor, made models so small that they were barely visible. On either the micro- or macro-level the name was a dubious choice for a reform which decided that small was not, in fact, beautiful because it encouraged graft, inefficiency and financial wastage.

"Kallikrates" was introduced as a "New Architecture of Local Government: Devolved Administration", but it is difficult to see how a reduction of municipalities from 1,033 to 325, and of seventy-four regional units to thirteen, could be regarded as encouraging or facilitating devolution.[18] Instead, by distancing local communities from local authorities, it creates a mismatch between *community* and *authority*. Fiscal imperatives (the reform was introduced at the time Greece hit the financial doldrums) seem more likely: one justification was the projected saving of €1.2 billion per year. Announcing the scheme in 2010, Prime Minister George Papandreou stated that it was "a precondition for the country's exit from the crisis" and "a democratic revolution".[19] The two ambitions may run in parallel, but have little organic relationship.

Among the many place-seekers and heroes of patronage there are – or were – some commendable heads of local government: Yannis Boutaris, elected Mayor of Thessaloniki on an independent ticket in 2011, has proved to be as efficient, committed and effective as he was in his previous incarnations as a wine-maker and founder of a refuge for wild bears. Other mayors, including the incumbent in Corfu at the time of "Kallikrates", have been the opposite: uninterested in citizens' welfare, and capable only of autocratic mismanagement.

In Corfu, the reduction of municipalities from thirteen to a single unit (and this is similar in all islands except Crete and Euboea) made citizens apprehensive that decision-making at the centre would disadvantage them. The village where I live is only twenty-five miles from town, but local affairs were previously managed much more locally – almost literally in the village street, when it was possible to approach the mayor on a personal basis. "Kallikrates", as far as access to decision-making is concerned, is an example of Greece going "forward" with many aspects of Greekness left behind. But the reform has placed extra pressure at village level on the "chairman" or "president" of the village council who is now the focus for villagers' problems, of which the pot-holed roads, waste collection and the provision of a weekly local health clinic are the main causes of concern.

There was also an unspoken agenda in "Kallikrates" of modernising the "local" image of Greece which many tourists carry in their mental camera – of gnarled old men, telling their beads (*kombolói*) and sipping coffee or ouzo under the "tree of idleness" in the *agorá*, or fishermen tenderising octopus on a quayside or traditionally clad peasant women with wooden-saddled donkeys. Professionalisation of the locality and the region would, instead, project a Greece that was modern and forward-looking, rather than picturesque and retrospective. It hasn't succeeded because, however corrupt local politicians may have been, the ingrained dependence of both the bosses and their clients in the patronage game meant a degree of mutual trust and dependability which the new system has neither replaced nor reformed.

Political Dynasties

Almost all of Greece is a closed shop, and politics is no exception. The *politikós kósmos* is the term for the elite ranks, mostly middle-class professionals (lawyers, economists and professors), at the centre of power. In the twentieth century four family dynasties – Venizelos, Karamanlis, Mitsotakis and Papandreou – held most of the power.[20]

Members of these families were raised from the cradle to the culture of political leadership. One might say that each discovered at birth that he was a future Prime Minister: Sofokles Venizelos, son of Eleftherios, Prime Minister in 1944 (in exile), 1950 and 1950-51; Konstantinos Karamanlis, four times Prime Minister and twice president; his nephew Kostas Karamanlis, Prime Minister from 2004-09; Konstantinos Mitsotakis (great-nephew of Eleftherios Venizelos), Prime Minister from 1990-93 and father of two government ministers; George Papandreou I, three times Prime Minister; his son Andreas, twice Prime Minister; and his grandson, George II, Prime Minister from 2009-11.

The dynasties are in effect no different from the extended families in every part of Greek society: connected by kinship and common interest which set them on a prescribed path. If a Greek is always inescapably linked to his family, then these dynasties carry that sense of family obligation into the political arena: negotiating the village or the *Voulí* is the same destiny.

The fact that, under the military junta (1967-74), George I was held (and died) under house arrest, and that Andreas was forced into exile in the USA, raised veneration of the Papandreou family into sainthood. Sofka Zinovieff, a friend of the family, says "the Papandreou family is the nearest thing Greece has to the Kennedys".[21] This obscured the fact that the Papandreous, as defenders of democracy, were in fact creating a state that turned democracy on its head.

Andreas and George II were the victims of history: Andreas's marriage to an American, his exile and, as a consequence, his son's birth and upbringing outside Greece, made many Greeks suspicious of their *bona fides*. The left, in particular, branded young George as "American" rather than "Greek", and he is not helped by his less-than-perfect command of the Greek language.

Three generations of Papandreou family Prime Ministers: George (senior), left; Andreas, his son, right; George (junior), grandson, front. Young George looks bewildered, as if he were already looking for the exit.

George Papandreou II carried his birthright from the cradle to his political grave. Mark Dragoumis, a former government spokesman and later journalist, described him as "a nice person, full of good will" – which was certainly not the hallmark of a party leader – and, Dragoumis added, "extolling the virtues of dialogue for problems for which he had no solutions".[22] He was famous for over-consultation; as a child he woke up and asked too many non-family people how to change his nappy. To do what he tried to do – to bring down the house of PASOK – was tantamount to running away from home.

Having been ousted from PASOK, his father's own party, George II formed "Movement of Democratic Socialists", abbreviated to "The Movement" (*To Kínima*); with 2.5 per cent of the national vote, he failed to win any seats in parliament, and thus the Papandreou dynasty reached its natural end as a political force. George's brother, Nick (or Nikos) refers to politics as "the enemy to family. At some point love, no matter how strong, hides and cowers in the corner while politics, hot, naked and sweating, moves in like a Minotaur". In 1981 he saw his brother taking his seat in parliament and said, "I was a little jealous of him, but also relieved that it was him standing there and not me, that it was him locked for ever into my father's world, not me."[23]

Ireland, too, has seen such dynasties, with the de Valera/Ó Cuiv, Kenny, Lenihan and Cosgrave families among many.

Political Parties

In 1875, Emmanuel Royidis (whom we shall meet again in the next chapter) wrote of the typical political party at that time:

> A group of people able to read and to misspell, sound of limb but hating all work, who will serve under any leader and seek to make him prime minister by any means, so that he may grant them the wherewithal to live without having to dig.[24]

Not much change there, then.

Between 1974 (the end of the junta) and 2015, Greece was governed by a two-party system, with New Democracy (ND) and PASOK alternating in power. The return to democracy was led by Konstantinos Karamanlis of ND; PASOK, founded by Andreas Papandreou, was waiting in the wings and gained power in 1981 until 1990; ND returned to power under Konstantinos Mitsotakis for three years until defeated again by PASOK in 1993; Papandreou retired on health grounds in 1996 and was succeeded by Kostas Simitis. PASOK lost power to ND in 2004 but were returned, under George Papandreou II, in 2009, at which point the economic collapse threw the political situation into a chaos only commensurable with that of the 1930s and 1940s, leading to the first-ever left-wing government in Greece (Syriza in coalition with Independent Greeks, ANEL) in 2015.

The end of the ping-pong match between ND and PASOK was signalled not only by this crisis but also by citizens' growing disillusion with the "old reliables": neither party could be said to have any ideological or pragmatic solutions to the increasingly severe social conditions of the country, nor to show any discernible differences in their preferred strategies. As one journalist put it:

> The left-leaning Papandreou and the conservative Samaras are the yin and yang of modern Greece, heirs to historical divisions and symbols of interlocking currents of reform and tradition. An acquaintance from their college days suggests that even amid public animosities, the two remain bound together by shared private history.[25]

George Papandreou (front left) and Antonis Samaras (top right) as fellow-students at Amherst College, Massachusetts in the 1970s.

Papandreou and Samaras were, in fact, roommates at Amherst College, Massachusetts in the 1970s, and have remained "bound" by that.

One of the most significant aspects of party politics in Greece has been the fragmentation of parties in the wake of individual disappointments over preferment or, less often, on ideological grounds. In Ireland, the foundation of the Progressive Democrats (PDs) in 1985 was due in no small measure to the frustration of prominent members of Fianna Fáil with the leadership style of C.J. Haughey, but individuals saw the new party as a means of political preferment. The fact that it is almost inconceivable that single-party government could ever occur today in either Ireland or Greece[26] is a sign of a changing political landscape.[27]

In Greece, new parties are formed much more frequently: for example, in 2010 Dora Bakoyannis, a senior ND minister and scion of the Mitsotakis dynasty, resigned from the party to form her own "Democratic Alliance" (*Dimoktrátiki Symmachía*), ostensibly on a matter of principle; two years later she was reabsorbed into ND when she saw that her party had no chance of electoral success. (The small parties have almost no prospect of getting into parliament, and independent candidates none at all.)[28] Bakoyannis' chief rival in ND, Antonis Samaras, himself defected from ND in 1992 with the foundation of "Political Spring", spending eight years as a political outsider before being rehabilitated into ND, and leading it to power 2012-15.

There have been so many parties formed that merely to describe those established (and extinguished) since 2000 would use ink best employed elsewhere.[29] Only *Potámi* (River) merits mention because it was formed by intellectuals with no previous political experience; it succeeded, probably for that reason, in attracting sufficient votes to secure seventeen seats in 2015, the fourth largest party in the *Vouli* after Syriza, ND, and the fascists.

The factor which distinguishes Syriza and KKE on one side, and Golden Dawn on the other, from the centrist parties, is that they have ideological starting-points (which have never been an advantage in Greek politics), whereas the centrists have lacked any policies other than the pragmatic imperative of political survival.

PASOK

PASOK (Πανελλήνιο Σοσιαλιστικό Κίνημα – *Panellínio Socialistikó Kínima* or "PanHellenic Socialist Party") seemed to offer something new in the post-junta period: a socialist vision based on inclusiveness and radical reform. But, as with many previous governments (those of Venizelos particularly), Andreas Papandreou's pragmatism was rooted in the art of the possible and in harnessing goodwill through a more extensive system of patronage than Greece had ever experienced: PASOK *became* the state, embracing everyone in that system of mutual benefits. His populism was also his popularity, which he owed not only to his nepotism and cronyism but also to his charisma; coupled with his ruthless statecraft it made him comparable to C.J. Haughey in Irish politics: a highly visible man of and for the people who was, in parallel, covertly an elitist and a thug, summed up by Angelos Elefantis as "the myth of the Savior hand in hand with the myth of the People".[30]

How many Greek democratic politicians have believed that *"L'état c'est moi"*? The prospect of having millions of minions must appeal to all who have been tempted towards the gates of power. But a leader can only afford to be arrogant if he is also an attractive character offering to embrace everyone – kissing babies in an election campaign develops into kissing everyone all of the time. Andreas Papandreou did that with "grace" ... and favour. History is full of popular heroes who were loved by the very people whose death warrant they would happily sign in the morning.

The cult – or at least the successful predominance – of personality meant that the charismatic leaders were of more importance in the direction of Greek politics than party policies.

Antonis Karakousis sees political leaders as "deeply introverted and trapped by small games".[31] They could therefore be seen as the prisoners of a system which their forefathers created: the use of power at the service of minor preoccupations rather than the transcendence of the small-scale in favour of the bigger picture.

Even when major leaders – usually autocratic – have seized power, their vision has, with the possible exception of Venizelos, been a narrow one: the nation as the Greek people fuelled by the Greek values of orthodoxy and conformity. Dissent, as Neni Panourgiá so vehemently points out, brands one as an enemy of the people.

The modern Greek word *chárisma* means "talent, gift, endowment"; its classical meaning was "grace", either possessing, or bestowing, grace and favour – perhaps the starting-point for the idea of patronage by an attractive boss towards his favoured associates.

In founding PASOK after the fall of the junta, Andreas Papandreou had two imperatives: to heal the wounds caused by the Civil War and the junta, and to raise standards and conditions of living, especially in rural areas. A return to democracy, index-linked to a rosy future, was music to Greek ears.

Andreas' strategy was brilliant and unique in Greek political life: a "Contract with the People". He created nationwide grassroots *cumanns* (I am deliberately using the term for Fianna Fáil local branches) which made PASOK, and himself, synonymous with the state – paternalist and clientelist: a social transformation, including health care, social insurance, equal pay for women, eradication of privilege, with EU membership bringing agricultural subsidies.

PASOK's grassroots support depended almost entirely on votes-for-favours, like the Irish TD sorting out his or her constituents' difficulties by adroit representations. Greece went one better, allowing the system to become permeated by this mindset.

When young George II assumed leadership of PASOK, almost by divine right, he inherited the dichotomy between tradition and modernity. Within the party, there were reformers like himself who wanted to make PASOK more relevant to Greeks today, and the old guard, for whom the clientelist model was as sacred as the name Papandreou.

The Greek word for "truth" is *alíthia*, meaning "no forgetting". So "truth" requires memory, and memory, for Greeks, is even more painful than it is for the Irish. You cannot afford truth or memory if they stand in the way of expedience. PASOK, having condoned deliberate obfuscation and mis-statements on the country's economic situation (see the next chapter), became "a post-truth party".

Fascism

The rise of fascism in Greece (in common with many European countries) might seem incredible given Greece's recent history in the Second World War, the suppression of communism in the Civil War and its aftermath, and the means employed to sustain the junta in 1967-74. But it can also be seen as a reflection of Greece's need for stability, which some factions believe it is legitimate to protect by any means – a legitimacy which can be found within the Constitution itself.

Golden Dawn (GD – the translation of *Chrysí Avgí*) is the political wing of the far right which cannot rest because its defeat of communism and leftist politics in the Civil War has proved to be temporary; therefore the right needed a political counter-balance to the emergence of a radical left. But GD has shown that its "politics" is overtly fascist-Nazi by its adoption of a swastika-like emblem, the Hitler salute, denial of the holocaust and singing of the Nazi marching song "Horst Wessel Lied" (which is banned in today's Germany). Hitler-type harangues against Jews have reached the point where leader Nikos Michaloliakos lays the blame for the world economic crisis at the doors of an alleged international Jewish conspiracy, calling Jews "the absolute evil". Its deputy leader has been filmed teaching children to chant "Heil Hitler". Despite this, GD members deny that they are neo-Nazis, claiming instead that they are "nationalists", although in 2013 Michaioliakis announced "If they like they can call me a Nazi – the Nazis will pull Greece out of the state it is in".[32]

GD was founded in the 1980s; its original manifesto expressed admiration for Hitler and described Jews as "parasites of civilisation". Michaloliakos has a criminal record from the 1970s for supplying arms to far-right groups. GD is in direct political descent from the military junta of 1967-74, which it reveres. The phenomenal rise in its popularity, from 0.3 per cent in 2010 to eighteen MPs in 2012 (seventeen after the 2015 election) as the third largest party in parliament, is due in part to the economic and social crisis.

At one point, before the meteoric rise in the polls by Alexis Tsipras and Syriza, the two parties were neck-and-neck (on approximately 15 per cent). It was partly the direct involvement of GD in the murder in 2013 of communist rapper Pavlos Fyssas, and its implication in many other crimes, that put a stop to its increasing attraction. But, given its electoral success, GD is comparable to some of its European counterparts, such as the Party for

The Golden Dawn emblem (left) is one of several versions which combine elements of the "Greek key" design with the Nazi swastika. The swastika/ key design (right) is copied from the robe of a kore (Greek maiden, usually standing, pre-500 BC) in the Acropolis Museum, Athens.

Freedom in Holland and the Austrian Freedom Party (both of which have been in coalition governments), UKIP in Britain and the *Front National* in France. Ireland has no corresponding party, the only explicitly fascist grouping having been the "Blueshirts" under Eoin O'Duffy in the 1930s, which morphed into Fine Gael in 1933 with O'Duffy as leader. With six per cent of the total vote, a neo-blueshirt party in Ireland would hold ten Dáil seats.

The appeal of GD's policy of "Greece for the Greeks" is an attraction to a country struggling to maintain its viability and, more importantly, cohesion. However, the idea that one must have four Greek grandparents in order to be Greek is so far-fetched that one is entitled to think of the Aryan purity sought by Hitler as its nearest example in Europe: a policy which would, for example, see George Papandreou II declared non-Greek (his mother is American), and in Ireland would see historical figures such as Éamon de Valera equally disqualified, along with current politicians such as Leo Varadkar and former TD Moosajee Bhamjee.[33]

It's not all that long ago (1985) that the then Bishop of Limerick stated that you could not be Irish unless you were Gaelic, Catholic and nationalist. If a neo-blueshirt party had the power to adopt GD-style policies, it would also call for the expulsion of public figures like Paul McGrath, Simon Zebo, Kevin Sharkey and Seán óg Ó hAilpin.

In 2013 Michaloliakos referred to two Greek citizens, Giannis Antetokounpo and his brother Thanassis (sons of Nigerian immigrants), as "chimpanzees". Giannis is a rising star in basketball. Last year a member of the highly successful Greek national basketball team, Sophocles Schortsianitis (Greek father, Cameroon mother), was also denounced by another GD MP for being insufficiently Greek. "Greeks have never been black," the GD leader proclaimed.[34] He should read Martin Bernal's *Black Athena*, which argues that ancient Greece, probably including its genetic structure, derived much from Africa and the Middle East.

GD's vigilante groups in the cities pick on immigrants such as Afghans for beatings, to which the police turn a blind eye. For some time, GD operated a food kitchen for the needy, provided they could produce Greek identity papers – or a beating was likely to be administered.

Since 2010, as many as 900 migrants, mostly Pakistani, but also Roma gypsies, have allegedly been beaten up by GD vigilantes. "They play football with our heads," said one. One interviewee, an ordinary citizen, was of the view that GD is "doing what the politicians should be doing. There's a hole, and they fill it" – referring to this vigilante presence on the streets.

Given the affinity of the police and army with right wing movements in Greece throughout its history, it's not surprising to find that GD has the support, unofficially of course, of many in the police force; many police officers are members of GD, and a poll showed that a substantial minority supported their vigilantism.

A prominent left wing politician claimed that GD infiltration into the armed forces was also prevalent, and an inquiry in 2014 revealed that prosecutions of GD members for a range of offences have been delayed by sympathisers within the judicial system. Nevertheless, seventy-two GD supporters, including all its MPs, were indicted awaiting trial in 2015.

But racism is not GD's only policy. It also pursues anti-gay, anti-semitic and anti-Muslim policies and activities, encouraging arson attacks on synagogues and mosques,[35] in an effort to purify Greece of all non-Greek elements.

If we ignore (but how can we?) its more extreme xenophobia, homophobia and racism, it is less difficult to appreciate GD's rapid rise in popularity. An example from my village will illustrate people's ability either not to know of GD's antisocial policies or to ignore them. I am in conversation with my neighbour, Manolis:

"Why do you support Golden Dawn, Manolis?"

"Because they have some good policies for this country."

"Do you want me to leave the country?"

"Why should I?"

"Because the party you support has a policy of evicting all foreigners."

"But you are my neighbour!"

"That's not the point, but thank you anyway. Do you support the burning of mosques?"

"No..."

"Or the attack on the synagogue here in Corfu?"

"No, of course not!"

"But Golden Dawn do it!"

"Ah."

"Do you know that they want to cut your balls off because you're gay?"

"I didn't know that..."

It is perhaps ironic that the two extremes of the political spectrum – the fascists and the current government – share the anti-austerity platform; it is of course out of the question that GD could ever be invited to form a government (although its leader was able, in prison and using his mobile phone, to address a party rally *in absentia* at which he offered to do so), but it is indicative of the effects of the crisis that they should be sharing the same bed, figuratively, because voters see in them an alternative to the ineffective governments which permitted the crisis to occur.

In 2013, I wrote that "I would not be surprised or even shocked to see tanks rolling into Athens to signal the advent of a military junta. Greece is an accident waiting to happen."[36] I stressed that that was a far-fetched possibility, but that, in the unstable political and social environment of the time (and ever since), there was a palpable sense that citizens wanted a sign of leadership lacking in the then dominant parties.

A judicial investigator, attempting to assess the culpability of GD's MPs in relation to the Fyssas murder and membership of what is in effect an illegal organisation, has stated that the party's aim is "the dissolution of the democratic system of government". That system has been abused by successive governments to such an extent that its suspension would be welcome to many disillusioned Greeks.

The passivity of citizens, already exhausted by successive waves of austerity and degradation led by Brussels and Berlin, would reduce the likelihood of any meaningful opposition to military rule. Many Greeks, quite apart from the fascists, would agree that the prospect of stability and a dependable vision of the life to come is more important than democracy, and better than the life they currently lead.

The Left

By "Left" I mean a political entity in Greece which is qualitatively different from the political parties – even the "socialists" – which have been in power since 1821. Since that time, the Left, until 2015, was a political entity outside politics. "Left" indicates an alternative which, Neni Panourgiá would persuade us, was in fact "constituted by the Greek state"[37] – by which she means that, through its behaviour, the state has made inevitable a "Left" position outside the corridors of power, outside the conventional discourse, in opposition even to the "opposition" as it is understood in parliamentary terms.[38] Her subtitle, "the Greek Left and the Terror of the State" is nicely ambiguous: the Left is both a terror for the state to contemplate and an idea which is terrorised *by* the state. This idea Panourgiá nominates and personifies as a "dangerous citizen", "dangerous for the polis [...] a suspicious enemy [...] transcend[ing] the polis" who is nevertheless *within* the *pólis* and who "learns and produces a topography that is also a topology completely unimagined and unsuspected".[39]

That this alternative, "other" idea of society, excoriated by official Greece since 1821, should have attained power in 2015 is indeed a "terror of the state" if, by "state", we mean a centrist, essentially bourgeois society. While the "working class" was predominantly peasant, it was absorbed by the landlord-tenant system of patronage; as Greece, in its modernisation, grew an urban middle class, the natural conservatism of the bourgeoisie became the political norm; since at least the Second World War, it has been bolstered and supervised by extra-state powers intent on the diminution (at least) of radical socialism, taking measures such as the prison islands of the Aegean to suppress the Left: the list of "guests" on Makronisos, Amorgos and the other detention/correction centres reads like a Who's Who of the Greek Left.

Panourgiá's passionate commitment to this Left was born of her juvenile experience of the Polytechnic revolt of 1973; it is concomitant with that of Yanis Varoufakis (Greek's finance minister) as a seven-year-old seeing his communist father being abducted by the junta's secret police in 1968. She refers to the Left accounts of Greek history (such as Foivos Grigoriades' four-volume history of the Civil War, *To Andártiko*) as "attempts to put in writing, to bring up to the level of public discourse, indeed, to make public and discursive something that the whole of Greece was experiencing as private and unspeakable".[40] But it is not merely a state of mind engendered by oppression and suppression: it is, as I have been anxious to emphasise throughout this book, a natural and organic reaction to nature itself, to the harshness/austerity of existence, for millennia, of the vast majority of the population while subjected to oligarchs, foreign powers and autocrats.

Panourgiá states:

> I am most interested in "life": bare, naked, clothed, conceptualized, contested, taken, given, suspended, sustained. And I am interested in what surrounds life: humans who want to give it meaning, take its meaning, make worlds that this life inhabits, keep this life from expiring. And in the politics that surrounds this life and these humans: crude partisan, sophisticated intellectual, engaged, activist, philosophical. [...] And at what translates meaning: ritual, kin, law, the body (of the patient, of the condemned, of the student, of the desired).[41]

This may have political manifestations, but it is much deeper than that: a commitment to, and emanating from, the soil of life. The *latifundia/tsiflíki* are not only the *tópos* of power politics, they are, more fundamentally, as in Ireland, the landscape of fact, the contours of expression in survival strategies. I am deliberately evoking the lines of Brian Friel in his play *Translations*: "a civilisation can be imprisoned in a linguistic contour which no longer matches the landscape of fact".[42] In this case, it could be argued by the opponents of the Left (that is, almost everyone in power throughout Greek history) that its lexicon is outdated, imprisoned in history, that its memory of misery, while valid, is no longer relevant. In a sense, the wounds inflicted on the Left during the Civil War and its aftermath, and by the junta – especially the pain (in Greek, *martírio* which also means "bearing witness")[43] of the prison islands (which occupy many pages of Panourgiá's book) – only replicated the relentless effect of sun, wind and rain to which the peasants had always been prone. Like the Cromwellian banishment of Catholic priests to the death island of Inishbofin, the Left were being exiled for their faith, not their misdeeds; a faith emanating from the same landscape that bore fruit in the poetry of Seferis and Elytis, to which Kazantzakis in his novels and Theodorakis in his music bore witness in order to keep faith and to transcend experience.[44]

Panourgiá sees the downfall of the junta not as a release of democracy but as a conceptual failure: "everyone in Greece expected complete and total catharsis [but] it became apparent that neither the willingness nor the ability for such an undertaking was possible. This inability or unwillingness eroded any remaining sense of trust between the public and the state" which, she believes, was the opportunity for "November 17" (see below) to enter the political *agorá*.[45]

No one could question Panourgiá's commitment to the Left, yet her insistence, from her own experience, would persuade many on the "Right" that the state, in order to maintain stability, would be justified in restraining her ideology. This is the harsh fact of life which has confronted the Left in Greece throughout history – condemned to silence and exile. Perhaps it is more effectively promulgated through the music of poetry, song and dance, the articulation in art of an imagination which bears little, if any, relation to the normative procedures of the bourgeois society which has assumed the identity of the *pólis*. I find an echo of this in the introduction (by Cedric Whitman) to *Eighteen Texts* (above, p. 60), in which he evokes Homer: only a free man is a whole man; if that freedom is inhibited by tyranny, it "drives their words into the mind's refuge and their pens into dangerous utterance".[46] We shall meet this again in the cinema of Theo Angelopoulos: it is Panourgiá's "private and unspeakable" language with all the power of silence and the dignity of indignation.

Terrorism

Between 1909 and 1974 Greece experienced nine major and ten minor coups and counter-coups, three continental wars (the Balkan wars, and the First and Second World Wars), the Anatolian Catastrophe, a Civil War and three periods of dictatorship, the last being that of "the Colonels" from 1967 to 1974.[47] This is a society whose memories of such instability cause continuing unrest.

We have had intimations of political violence (post-Civil War) since at least 1963, when a socialist MP (Grigoris Lambrakis, who was also a veteran of the resistance and a champion athlete) was assassinated; his death led to the resignation of Prime Minister Konstantinos Karamanlis, and accusations of implication of right-wing army and police personnel in the killing. The film *Z* (1969), made by Costas-Gavras, based on the novel of the same title by Vassilis Vassilikos, brought to the attention of western audiences the ideas behind the facts. In Greek "Z" means "he lives" and signalled Lambrakis' legacy as a continuing presence in the Greek imagination. (The music for the film was written by Mikis Theodorakis.)

Not least of the causes of unrest is what Brian Friel, speaking of Irishness, described as the "paranoiac individualism" of the peasant mind:[48] putting oneself and family ahead of the greater good. To suspect and resist authority is a natural part of being Greek. So too, today it seems, is the phenomenon of terrorism. "Happy New Fear" proclaims a *graffito* in Corfu Town. Another reads, "Do some good – kill a cop".

There are more terrorist organisations in Greece than political parties – but only by a small margin. And they split, just as MPs defect from one party and form another. I have therefore included terrorism in this chapter because, in a sense, the many and disparate groups operating in Greece constitute an opposition which almost amounts to a "political party"; in many ways they resemble the fascist party, Golden Dawn, which has also committed murder and other acts of terrorism in pursuit of its ideals. And terrorism is the most visible sign of the "discontents" with which we are concerned.

Greece at present seems to have cornered the market in home-grown terrorism, with a plethora (a fine Greek word) of major gangs and splinter groups, apparently doing what comes naturally to angry people. It's what young Holmes, in the third series of *Sherlock*, calls "their version of golf".[49]

From 1975 until 2002, when its leaders were jailed, "November 17" (17N) was the premier group from which all others have descended – not necessarily with their parent's approval. The title marks the date in 1973 when students at Athens Polytechnic resisted the army, with many resultant deaths. "People of Greece, you're hearing the truth now. We are unarmed. Our only weapon is our faith in freedeom" were their last words. These killings, and the fact that they occurred during a protest against the military junta, became the lodestone of subsequent protests against authoritarian regimes, whether civil or military, or which seemed to their antagonists to be authoritarian and repressive. The word *antagonist* is our clue to the divisiveness which this has caused in Greek society, since it is an *agón* and an *antagón* – a struggle for and against.

17N's first "success" was the assassination in 1975 of the CIA boss in Athens, followed by that of the head of the Greek security forces; in the twenty-five years of its activity, it was responsible for twenty-three assassinations, including two US and one British military attachés, the proprietor/publisher of the conservative newspaper *Apogevmatini*, Pavlos Bakoyannis (a New Democracy MP and husband of Dora Bakoyannis-Mitsotakis), the Turkish press attaché, a shipowner, and a public prosecutor. Many of the others were the official drivers of the targets. It was a war against "imperialism and the local immoral grand bourgeois class".[50] 17N's personnel included an icon-painter and a bee-keeper, who became part of "Europe's most lethal group of terrorists".[51] It was like a small industry: one journalist described it as "a career", pointing to the $3.5 million netted from bank raids. "They lived off it for years and they lived well".[52]

The escape from prison (or, more accurately, while on "home leave") of its leader, Christodoulos Xiros, in January 2014 and his re-arrest one year later, was like an earthquake for the security forces. In a video he made after his escape, Xiros stated, "I've de-cided to fire the guerrilla shotgun against those who stole our lives and sold our dreams for profit".[53]

Since the demise of 17N in 2002, the chief terrorist groups have been, firstly, "Revolutionary Struggle" (RS), formed the following year, which mounted a rocket attack on the US Embassy in 2007 and the Athens Stock Exchange in 2009, and is believed to have been responsible for a bomb which killed the aide of the Citizen Protection Minister in 2010. In 2009, after a failed bomb attack, RS issued a statement: "we earnestly apologise to the Greek people for not managing to blow up Citibank".[54] It could be a line from a Woody Allen movie. Secondly, "Sect of Revolutionaries" who killed a counter-terrorist officer in 2008 and hit the Alter private television channel in 2009; their spokesman has said that "police are like doughnuts: better with a hole in the middle".[55]

Many compare themselves to Baader-Meinhof or the Red Brigade. Some terrorists are members of more than one group – like someone belonging to two golf clubs – and there are certainly many anarchists working on their own. In 2015, for example, it was reckoned that there is a strong descent from 17N to the "Conspiracy of the Cells of Fire".

Many journalists have been attacked, one of them fatally, on the grounds that they write sympathetically about the government. In 2009, John Psaropoulos, referring to two previous killings of journalists by 17N in the 1980s, played down the danger: "it hasn't really been a massacre".[56] He was wrong to dismiss the ongoing threat.

The "Sect of Revolutionaries" has been the main proponent of targetting the media, announcing, "We are entering an extremely dangerous period in which coercive state mechanisms and mass media are collaborating to shape a climate of social insecurity, to apply totalitarian controls over all of society".[57] "Sect" has also attacked foreign-owned banks and companies, such as McDonald's and Microsoft.[58]

The death of Alexandros Grigoropoulos (above, p. 111) led not merely to immediate protests but also to a climate of youth rejection of the state's security forces, and its sympathy with revolutionary organisations that offer to make that rejection militant. "Revolutionary Struggle" became the symbol of this militancy, but "December 6" was another group commemorating the date of Grigoropoulos' killing. RS have argued that their activities are a "political response to the death of Grigoropoulos, against the regime's uniformed thugs and riot squad murderers".[59] "We need to create a mass revolutionary movement so that this crisis can signal the death of the system".[60] November 17 and December 6 have joined other, official, national days in an alternative calendar of remembrance.

One member of RS, when arraigned, refused to recognise the court (this will stir Irish memories): "The organisation I belong to is the prosecutor and you are the defendants."[61] He is now serving a fifty-year jail sentence. The intention is "to overturn the criminal regime", thus neatly reversing the values and procedures of justice vis-à-vis freedom of belief and expression.

In 2014-15, the list of terrorist organisations known to be operating in Greece (some of them sharing the same personnel, or frequently changing their title)[62] include Revolutionary Sect[63] (with a subsidiary "Robbers in Black" who carry out the bank heists); Revolutionary Struggle; "Gangs of Conscience" (formed 2009); "Popular Will" (2009); the "February 12 Movement" (dating from the anti-austerity laws and subsequent riots of 2012); "Urban Guerilla War" (since 2012); "Circle of Outlaws" (aka "Nucleus of Lovers of Lawlessness", 2012); "Conspiracy of the Cells of Fire", also 2012, which has specialised in sending firebombs to embassies, the Court of Justice in the Hague, and French president Nicolas Sarkozy;[64] "Fighting Revolutionary Peoples Force" which killed two members of Golden Dawn in 2013 in retaliation for the GD killing of rapper Pavlos Fyssas; "Revolutionary Arc" (since 2013); "Group of Popular Fighters" who in 2013 hit the German Ambassador's residence, and in 2014 the Israeli Embassy and ND offices; and "Untamed Desires", which sounds more like the title of a porn movie.

On the tit-for-tat killing of the two GD members, Nikos Konstandaras commented: "it is hard to imagine many other countries – especially mature Western democracies – where the murder of two rank-and-file members of a relatively small political party could raise serious fears of political instability and national division. Yet this is how precarious things have become in Greece".[65] Between the lines, he was saying that Greece is *not* a mature Western democracy, nor is it stable, since this particular killing was provoked by a fascist murder of one of its opponents; Greece is once again seeking its independence.

In killing the GD members, "Fighting Revolutionary Peoples Forces" described GD as "an extension of state violence". It is easy to see how, in a disaffected mind, the concept of "state violence" (riot squads in particular) can be extended to a fascist group, one which has been acknowledged by unnamed police as "doing their job for them" in beating up immigrants on the Athens streets.

In such a conservative climate with, until recently, little articulation of radical views other than those of the terrorists, it has been regarded as a betrayal of the "regime" to criticise any part of the status quo; for being "politically incorrect" one could be branded as a nihilist or an anarchist.

The semantics can become confrontational. One might almost see it as an example of the mis-match between official *katharévousa* and real-life demotic. The "Villa Amalia", an Athenian squat, was closed by police in 2012 on the grounds that it was an "anarchist stronghold", whereas the occupants described it as a "cultural centre", offering free concerts and daycare for children. They denied any involvement in bomb-making, but one admitted that "we don't say we don't participate in violence". They disseminated anti-authoritarian leaflets in order to "overturn a status quo in which a powerful few influence the lives of many".[66]

The interpretation of emotive vocabulary, its inflection and grammar, is the borderland between passive and active thinking: many who would run a million kilometres from the idea that they are anarchists or squat-dwellers have termed the Greek social and political system a "kleptocracy" and an oligarchy. The literature is extensive.[67]

One can in fact readily comprehend those Marxist or even anarchist terrorists who aim to destroy a system dominated and manipulated by what they see as a conservative, bourgeois, elitist, oligarchic kleptocracy, controlling politics and the media (including ND's attempt to silence the national broadcaster as discussed in Chapter 6).

There is an unequal society in Greece which one cannot but deplore. I'm not referring to the urban-rural split, since the villages and small towns show plentiful evidence of prosperity and poor elderly widows are – well, poor elderly widows. It is the urban deprivation, the 25 per cent of the population out of work and the more than 50 per cent of young people who cannot find jobs, which persuades many compassionate onlookers that the system is failing: gross tax evasion, bribery at every level and the venality of politicians across the spectrum are the overt causes of inequality, but the fact that 20 per cent of Greek children and 30 per cent of the overall population live in extreme poverty is an unforgivable blemish on a state whose Constitution protects the welfare of all, and a state which wishes to be part of the Euroclub. In 2012, it was disclosed that the average lawyer spends more than 100 per cent of his/her *disclosed* income on mortgage repayments alone. This is hardly likely to reconcile a long-term unemployed "indignant" with the idea of bourgeois respectability.

It has to be said that, if we can ignore (but, again, how can we?) the fact that they are murderers and possibly psychotic, the leaders of the revolutionary terrorists are more charismatic, and show greater leadership potential, than the leaders of the political parties who in recent decades have been lacklustre, hesitant, apologetic, complacent in the shadow of the "great" figures of political history. This is no doubt the same in all contested democracies. The protagonists of revolution will have a ruthlessness and a rhetoric which becomes a character in its own right, whereas politicians, especially at a time of stability and prosperity, will more likely be passive, non-coercive seekers of the middle ground.

In a polarised society where the desperate poor see affluence unchecked or untaxed, it is not difficult to understand how the fiercely individualistic underdog will turn disillusion into acts of violence in Syntagma Square (as Lady Bracknell might have said): it seems to be only the degree of violence which differentiates the rioting protesters from the calculated murderer. Besides, says

Alexis Papachelas, "many a youth sees Molotov cocktails as an antidote to boredom".[68] And it's a short step from indignation to the pronouncement by "Cells of Fire": "the organisation consists of very angry young people who don't have anything to hope for".[69]

The "Indignants/*Aganachtisménoi*"

In Greece in mid-2011, such was the feeling of despair among ordinary people that a movement, similar to that of the *indignados* in Spain, came into existence, with the equivalent Greek name, *aganachtisménoi*. Not only were they indignant at the political and economic situation, but also without hope, faced with the alternatives of emigration or poverty. This peaceful and dignified protest occupied Syntagma Square, facing the Greek parliament, for many weeks, an expression of their quiet desperation. It was the most serious popular resistance to authority since the students' protests in 1973 during the military junta, and it marked a leap beyond, a turning point in Greek society and the lives of the individuals who constitute it.

On 15 June 2011, Jose Manuel Barroso, the President of the European Commission, chaired a meeting of EU commissioners which discussed what many foresaw as the collapse of the eurozone in the wake of an inevitable Greek default. At the same time, he received a letter from the *aganachtisménoi*, the Greek "Indignants", who at that stage had peacefully occupied Athens' Syntagma Square for the past three weeks. The letter was supported by the signatures of over 100,000 Greek citizens.

The Indignants never received a reply from Barroso, but they hardly expected to. As one of their facilitators explained to me, one would hope for the courtesy of a reply, but "even the mafia has certain rules they obey. The EU bureaucrats don't have any rules, moral or otherwise!" A letter in *The Irish Times* asked why the Greeks should be indignant, since they had effectively brought their troubles on themselves. The Indignants' letter to Barroso made it clear why that is not the case.

Written (anonymously) by a very senior Greek diplomat,[70] the letter expressed the wish of the Greek people "to be given the chance to decide what we consider best for our future". The means of doing so, it was argued, should be a referendum on the terms and legality of the bailout, and, in particular, on the Memorandum of Understanding between Greece and the IMF, which, it alleged, was unconstitutional and therefore contrary to natural justice as an illegal infringement of national sovereignty.

The tone of the letter, and the unequivocal suggestion that the Greek government has acted unconstitutionally and illegally, underlined the fact that tensions within Greek society had become so deep and so extensive as to bring into question the capacity of the state to remain coherent and cohesive. I refer not to the riots which accompanied crucial parliamentary votes at that time, since violent protests are a commonplace feature of Greek society. I mean the almost complete rupture between ordinary citizens and those in authority, whether politicians or bureaucrats.[71]

Cultural studies by, for example, Homi K. Bhabha have concentrated on the *gap* or *between-space* as the place where culture is enacted. On the macro-scale, this is what Bhabha calls "the *Heim* [home] of the national culture".[72] On the micro-scale, it is the place for the working out of individual identity which, in the case of the home and its *oikonomía*, is enacted between husband and wife and, in the village, between the household and the community.

It is when this between-space becomes unnegotiable that an estrangement occurs: in marriage, it might lead to separation and divorce; in the "national culture", it might provoke civil war and/or the cessation of the state as the *heim* or focus of an *ethnos*.

I've referred in the previous chapter to the transitus between *appearance* and *reality*. That transitus is a "gap", a between-space, across which the subjective must pass in order to create an objective metaphor: translating[73] the personal into the collective, the desires and expectations of the individual into the consensus of the "national culture". Without that metaphor, both citizen and state remain on the cusp of meaning – each valid in itself but unable to engage with the other. It leaves each on the border of the other, as Greece itself is, in both the Balkans and the Levant, an in-between *tópos*, an "as if".

It is worth noting Renée Hirschon's point that "the link or continuum between word and action, between statement of intention and commitment to act, is variable".[74] She is writing of more domestic matters, but as I have tried to emphasise, the process from the domestic to the universal means that such a *lacuna* between words and action, which has belittled aspirations for the education or health systems, has characterised the division between citizens and the state.

The anarchists would say that the people are estranged from the Constitution by reason of political and administrative atrophy, but the gap is more profound than that, and acts of terrorism will do nothing to reconcile them. Nor will destroying the state. Estrangement is not merely a mis-match between the people and those in whom they have placed their trust. It is also due to the processes of modernisation and the development of globalisation. These, it can be argued, are faults which can also be laid at the door of government(s), and thus make them responsible for people's estrangement from their Greekness.

6

A FAILED STATE?

"We are coming in to radically change the way that policies and administration are conducted in this country", Alexis Tsipras announced on 28 January 2015, two days after taking power. Nothing in the Constitution would need to be changed in order to effect this intention, but it requires a radical change not only in the attitude and performance of civil servants but also in the expectations of citizens: Greeks anticipate a system of bribery as of right.

You will recognise the title of this chapter as rhetorical; it must be clear that I do *not* regard Greece as in any way a failure, but my reservations about how it conducts its business demand that I examine "Greece Inc." for its faults. If, in previous chapters, I show how much I love Greece, this chapter is the place to mourn. The Greeks have not failed; the state has failed – it has failed the Greeks, and it has failed itself.

If people become like their pets, the opposite is also true: we tend to emulate our masters. So, in the light of bureaucrats looking after their own interests rather than those of the people, and especially in the light of the kleptocracy which has so far seen many former government ministers and civil servants indicted (but only one imprisoned) for accepting massive bribes, it is not surprising that ordinary folk should resort to tax evasion on one hand and bribery on the other.

Bribery and tax evasion are included here for the simple reason that they are integral elements in Greek society. Perhaps we should try to separate the inseparable twins "bribery and corruption": bribery is certainly a feature of everyday life in Greece, but corruption, if we mean unprofessional, tainted, secretive, amoral criminality, is of a different order. The Greek term *favlokratía* means "corrupt government", from *favlos*, unprincipled, unscrupulous, profligate. I don't feel "corrupt" because I bribed a bank manager, or because I aided a shopkeeper to avoid paying VAT (see below). No citizen in Greece – and, I suspect, Ireland – would feel guilty at having small amounts of undeclared income. Certainly we could easily establish a calibrated scale where a certain level of dishonesty or "bucking the system" at the "innocent" end developed into bribery and, eventually, at the "guilty" end, found the culprit in the dock on charges of accepting millions of euros for defrauding the public purse.

In the nineteenth century the satirical novelist Emmanuel Royidis saw bureaucrats as "Mercenaries [...] appoint[ed] to redundant public positions" who, at that time, "constitute[d] a most fearsome power, before which King, government, parliament and indeed the entire nation fell trembling to their knees".[1] Richard Clogg calls this "an attitude to public service that persisted well into the twentieth century"[2] – he might today have said "into the twenty-first century". Things haven't changed: it may be an exaggeration – but not a gross one – to say that these "mercenaries" held the entire country and the whole structure of the state to ransom, while the infiltration by the sense of dependency, of having given a hostage to fortune, results in a helplessness which weakens, if not entirely cripples, citizens' ability to think, and act, for themselves.

Alexandros Papadiamandis (1851-1911), the father of modern Greek fiction, also wrote, in 1892, of politicians "deceiving the common people with campaign promises, bribes and divisive techniques all leading to strife and corruption at a time when the nation was passing through one of its most crucial phases". *Plus ça change....*

John Psaropoulos refers to today's civil servants as a "milk-fed reserve of party appointees",[3] while Yannis Stournaras (later Minister of Finance)[4] referred to the state's "irrational control of the economy".[5] The pincer movement of cronyism and state control has stifled economic growth and defeated transparency.

According to the Constitution, civil servants are "the executors of the will of the State and shall serve the people" (Article 103.1). Entry to the civil service is by competitive examination "or by selection on [the] basis of predefined and objective criteria" (103.7). The latter clause has allowed appointment of persons who might not otherwise succeed in competitive examination, but whom the relevant minister can justify on the basis of his or her "criteria": namely, nepotism in its broadest sense. This in turn restricts the operation of Article 103.1 in that the ambitions and persuasions of the appointees do not necessarily dictate that they should "serve the people", if serving the interests of the minister is considered preferable.

While this Article also provides for "special situation procedures" underpinned by "guarantees of transparency and meritocracy", it is the lack of meritocratic criteria which has alienated so many who would otherwise have pursued a career in the public service. "Transparency" has a habit of becoming opaque.

Greece suffers from five inter-related systemic problems; they can be attributed in part to the pre-independence era under the Ottomans (as is clear from a nineteenth century novel such as Andreas Karkavitsas' *The Beggar* [*O Zitiávis*, 1890]), but mainly to the way in which the modern state developed. The problems – which we might call "diseases" – are: clientelism, bribery, tax evasion, the "closed shop" or "protected professions" and the intransigence of the public service.

Intransigence is related to the "conceptual inertia". Greece's systemic failure is attested by social and political scientists and economists who detect it, for example, in the health service, where poor reporting procedures blur the areas of responsibility. In education, administrative structures which were supposedly reformed by PASOK are in fact almost unchanged. Those who are most in need – the sick and the young – do not receive the service they deserve. At all stages in the public service, it is in the area of accountability that the system fails, with obfuscation and a professional blame-game making reform impossible to implement.

Calliope Spanou states unequivocally that "Greek public administration meets neither domestic expectations nor EU membership requirements", due to mutual influence between politicians and key personnel at all levels. She explains: "deficiencies that were meant to be eliminated were reproduced or allowed through the back door because they provided short-term benefits to governing parties."[6]

Successive governments have pledged themselves to reform, but in order to achieve it they have followed a pattern in replacing the resistant personnel at the top of the pyramid with their own trusties. Syriza proved to be no different in this regard. Reforms partially implemented by one government have been undone by its successor on the conservative-socialist swingometer. More significant still is the fact that at lower levels of the pyramid (Yannis Palaiologos calls it "the plumbing level")[7] "change" means "no change", aided by the opacity of horizontal transfer of responsibility between and within departments with overlapping functions.

Overall, as Manos Matsaganis points out, "what seems to be missing is a deeper understanding of the role of values in public policy, a closer examination of the motivations underpinning interest groups' opposition to reform, as well as an appreciation that rampant individualism is simply incompatible with the ethos of public service".[8]

Thus analysts such as the contributors to *From Stagnation to Forced Adjustment* list a litany of reforms introduced which, they have to acknowledge, look good on paper but mean little in execution. Couloumbis, Petropoulos and Psomiades point to the American designation of Greece as a "praetorian state", that is, "an imbalance between popular pressures for rapid political, economic, and social mobilization and unresponsive, brittle, and archaic institutions which cannot effectively channel, absorb and accommodate those pressures". This suggests an urgency which is always deferred to *ávrio* (the Greek for *mañana*). They postulate that "when pressures inevitably mount in praetorian states, and since civilian institutions are condemned to stasis, one should expect extra-parliamentary 'solutions' to be spearheaded by politically supported factions in the officer corps".[9] It is thus potentially a formula for a military coup, but also, one might add, the fuel for terrorist activity.

(i) Clientelism

Keith Legg links clientelism with external influence in Greek affairs: "the prevalence of patron-client relationships and the importance of foreign influence [...] define what is often termed 'Greek reality.'"[10] There is some justification for this view since the Bavarian monarchy brought with it a system which rewarded subservience with patronage for place-seekers: the Greek word for "a favour" is *rousféti* (from the Turkish *rusvet*, a bribe, indicating its historical place in the Greek system) and its use can be traced to the first years of the state; it is closely linked with a term more familiar to Irish readers, the *fakeláki* or "small (brown) envelope". The system was foreign to the Greek mind and spirit, but not the practice: it was, no doubt, a pragmatic attempt by the west to re-educate Greeks into a more efficient and responsive mindset, but it failed in so far as it could not prevent the continuance of existing patterns of association and patronage which formed one of the bases of the pre-independence war- and land-lords, an atmosphere of fear and dependence on one side, and of benign autocracy on the other. This patronage has its descendants in today's clientelism and cronyism. To appropriate Joyce, it seems history is to blame.

In 2011, the then deputy Prime Minister, Theodoros Pangalos, who was responsible for co-ordinating the reforms of the key ministries, acknowledged that what he called Greece's "original sin" of clientelism could be traced back to the founding of the Greek state in the 1830s. In a traditionally rural society, peasants became the "clients" of landowners and local government officials. Just as successive governments in the 1970s and 1980s "bought" votes through protectionism, so these historical "patrons" bought obedience and adherence from the land. In other words, Greek society is permeated by the idea of dependence, and has been so for the past 180 years.

In the nineteenth century, bureaucrats worked to their political masters. There was no perceived need for the civil service to see itself as the servant of the people or to enunciate any policy in relation to the administration. "The growth of bureaucracy was unrelated to necessity."[11] Nikos Konstandaras refers to "the prin-

153

ciple that political will can solve all problems" so that "the individual citizen does not have to deal with reality".[12] This leads to a denial of reality and an embrace of mere appearances, since the matter is being taken care of elsewhere, by beneficent patrons, to whom one's loyalty is therefore indentured. It's a form of collective make-believe.

Clientelism was the principal obstacle to the development of any ideological approach to administration; it was utterly pragmatic, and in some ways evolved from the family which, in its widespread ramifications of dependency, already brought a "Yianni'll fix it" mentality.

Nick Malkoutzis believes that there has been a natural progression, or expansion, from the hub of the family as the dominant social unit, outwards to the community, in continuously developing relationships, until the "family" is transposed into political parties, unions, and specific business interests. Politicians, in order to ensure cohesion, became patriarchs of their "families" through awarding positions and contracts – looking after our own. "The language became a language of exchanging favours, as the only way to survive."[13] One might almost call it *cosa nostra*, especially if one takes into account the custom of the *koumbáros* or "best man" at a wedding becoming almost a family member, and having an organic place in subsequent events such as baptisms where the *koumbáros* becomes the "godfather". Politicians have been exceptionally adroit at becoming godfathers, even by proxy, and even to the children of people with whom they have only a passing acquaintance.

Resistance to change is not merely a matter of self-interest within Greece: Yannis Palaiologos remarks that "the average Greek is very sceptical of western models of government" and quotes a senior official of the ministry of finance that he would not co-operate with the EU Task Force because "they represent the foreign occupiers".[14] While this may seem irrational, it is in fact deep-seated and, however unconstructive, has to be taken into account. Furthermore, Malkoutzis attributes the resistance of PASOK to EU and NATO membership in the 1980s to a rejection of foreign interference; this too should change, because "the recipe for change has been imposed from outside".

Greece was unique among European states in introducing universal male suffrage in 1844-48 (although women did not achieve equality until 1952), but the vote empowered Greeks to do nothing other than to support the vested interests in their accession to power. It did not encourage democracy in the sense that the people were the rulers of their own destiny, merely that they now had the right to preferment within whatever sphere of influence they found themselves.

In recent times, the chief architect of state paternalism was Andreas Papandreou, leader of PASOK, after he became Prime Minister in 1981; his intentions were diverted into the same stream of clientelism that had prevailed throughout Greek history. Thanos Veremis observes that Papandreou's wish to "promote recruitment on an ideological, not on a patronage basis" was undermined by senior members of the party who "chose to implement law so as to allocate state resources and services to their supporters".[15] Papandreou himself "often challenged certain principles of the constitutional regime by giving priority to the 'needs' of the people over the authority of institutions".

The origins of protectionism lie in the creation of a catch-all society led by Papandreou in the 1970s, in the wake of a series of right wing administrations. In principle, the elitism of the "Colonels" and their predecessors in the right wing governments of the 1930s would be replaced by an inclusiveness – a case of a rising tide lifting all boats.

Government bought political loyalty in exchange for privilege. This explains why the closed professions go right across the board, rather than being limited to white collar workers. Insofar as it had *filotomía* at its heart, it was a *mutual* self-esteem between client and patron.

It also explains why the accusation of cronyism can be levelled at the social and political system. The philosophy of "jobs for the boys" permeates not only the closed professions but, more seriously, the public service. Calliope Spanou points out that attempts to regulate the recruitment process in order to establish a meritoc-

racy was hampered by politicians who "bypass[ed] official procedures. Public employment represents a precious electoral resource
that is difficult to subject to impersonal rules".[16] Another abuse of
the system is the high number of officials who, in recent years,
have been found to have falsified their qualifications in order to
secure appointment. To open up the professions was one aspect
of the massive upheaval that Andreas Papandreou's son, George,
was attempting during his brief and disastrous premiership. He
found that to dissolve the mentality of clientelism was much more
challenging.

The prevalence of clientelism in Ireland has been the subject of
scrutiny and criticism by many, including Ireland's current president, Michael D. Higgins, when a sociologist and member of the
Dáil, but it has also been described more as a system of *brokerage*
than clientelism.[17]

Higgins' pioneering work makes it clear how strong are the
similarities between the Irish and the Greek practices. His description might easily be translated into Greek and make sense.
He disclosed that clientelism was both a cause and a result of
"comprehensive location" encouraged by the landlord-tenant relationship in the colonial era, which created a "residual tradition"
evident in the politician-constituent relationship. This "has led to
the privatisation of state activity" in securing "the collusion of the
bureaucracy, local and national" to the detriment of the legitimacy
of the state; "the effect [...] is to lower [...] the confidence of the
citizenry in the state" by creating reliance of constituents on the
adroitness of their elected representative. "Above all, clientelism is
exploitative in source and intent."[18]

While one could not suggest that Greece was "lawless", it has
developed under patronage in such a way that the Constitution
and its dependent laws are of less importance than their interpretation and implementation by way of directives and memoranda.

Clientelism has been described by Yannis Palaiologos as "an
acid corroding everything in Greek life, leaving the country in the
hands of well-connected mediocrities",[19] while an economics professor saw the closed shop as "segments of society grabbing a piece
of the economy for themselves".[20] Between clientelism and protec-

tionism, participation in the economy is truly restricted. They can be seen as twin strategies for an efficient style of stable government which nevertheless perpetuates a feudalism which we might nowadays call the class system. But while, under pressure from the EU, deregulation of professions must proceed, the eradication of patronage is a far less visible phenomenon and therefore far less amenable to change.

(ii) Bureaucracy

The most aggravating aspect of bureaucracy is not the paperwork involved in the simplest transaction, such as obtaining a tax number, but the impenetrability of the "service" one is entitled to expect, when bureaucrats refuse to respond to an inquiry if it is not in their interests to do so. Thanassos Cambanis reminds us that in insuring his moped in Greece "the government-mandated paperwork was more complicated than an American mortgage application".[21] Citizens often resent the fact that, until recently, the system of bonuses payable to public servants was mind-boggling. Most public servants received *fourteen* monthly salaries per year, one as a holiday bonus in August, the other at Christmas. More ludicrous (again, to western eyes) was the fact that train drivers received a bonus for each journey; bus drivers received a bonus for arriving at work on time *and* were paid for commuting time; some foresters are paid a bonus for working outdoors. Some of these are systemic, applying across the board, while others are specific to duties, such as secretaries who are paid extra for using computers, or, allegedly, officials of the culture ministry who are given a clothing allowance. In the case of public employees such as train drivers, their benefits can be attributed to the strength of their respective unions' bargaining power.

Sofka Zinovieff, visiting a civil service office, observed its inmates "drinking the ubiquitous *frappé* [...], smoking furiously, and playing patience on their computers. They were perhaps the bureaucrats known as 'chair-centaurs', who are supposedly so inseparable from their desks that they seem to be welded to their chairs".[22] The resistance to cutting 15,000 jobs in the public service (at the insistence of the Troika – the EU-IMF-ECB team investigating the

Greek economy) was understood by Poul Thomsen, leader of the IMF team in Greece: "It is somehow taboo to talk of laying off non-performing members", or that they should be replaced "by young and well educated people desperate to get a chance". He pointed out that "no collective dismissals have been approved for more than thirty years".[23]

There's an anecdote about the widespread view of a civil service position as a sinecure in the story of a man asking his local MP to find a place for his son: the MP offers him a choice between a job in a factory owned by his friend, or a placement on an EU-funded training scheme (not unlike FÁS in Ireland) which would lead to a good job. The father expostulates: "I asked for an *appointment* for the boy, not *work*."[24] "Serving time as a bureaucratic supernumerary"[25] has been an increasing feature of modern Greek society.

The conventional way to deal with awkward enquiries is to ignore them. I have encountered this three times: once in relation to an academic query to a university professor; the second when the relevant civil servant did not respond to any queries on state funding for translation of Greek writers; the third in relation to a set of CDs of Greek composers, the existence of which the relevant ministry (which published them) denies. More persistent researchers might be able to circumvent the obstacle of silence, by personal contacts – another example of achieving what one wants by means of who one knows.

The story of the CDs, and their existence/non-existence, is as follows:[26] they are like a lost city of the Incas – an El Dorado which is known to have existed but can no longer be located. In 2004 the cultural wing of the Athens Olympics produced a 12-CD set of "Works of Greek Composers" from the nineteenth and twentieth centuries: classical composers, whose works had almost never been recorded. These CDs were presented to visiting dignitaries, but a large number remained, reputedly stored in the basement of the Ministry of Culture, which commissioned the recordings (from an independent production company, now out of business).

Hearing about this from a colleague who had actually written parts of the accompanying booklet, I innocently enquired about their availability but was told that the ministry had no evidence whatever of their existence.

I took my enquiry to the Ministry of Information, which contacted the Ministry of Culture on my behalf. The official reply was "the ministry claim they have no knowledge of such a set of CDs". Could I please give them more information? Certainly. I sent a full list of contents, along with evidence that they *did* exist, since they were offered for sale on Amazon and eBay. More silence.

The booklet has a foreword by the then secretary-general of the Ministry of Culture. How could this have happened, if his underlings knew nothing about it? The most likely explanation is that no one in the ministry can be bothered to either look for the stored CDs or to dig out the file which surely must exist.

This is a unique resource. Very few recordings exist of works by these composers, some of whom, like Nikolaos Mantzaros (author of the national anthem) and Pavlos Karrer, created the school of Greek composition. These CDs are a national asset, providing a key to Greece's cultural heritage. There should be a copy in every school in the country. To neglect this is tantamount to secrecy and wilful disregard for education. But you can't distribute what doesn't exist.

(iii) Tax evasion

The problem of tax evasion runs throughout Greek society, and became a public debate in 2012 with the resignation of Diomidis Spinellis, whose task, as secretary-general of a special task-force inside the Ministry of Finance, was to identify tax evaders. Spinellis asserted not only that "there is a deficit of management" in the identification of evasion, but also revealed the "4-4-2" formula at the heart of the tax (evasion) system; any tax collected is divided: 40 per cent is rebated to the tax payer, 40 per cent is pocketed by the tax collector, and 20 per cent finds its way into the exchequer. Spinellis resigned in frustration at the impossibility of doing his job. The amount of unpaid tax increased from €38.7 billion in 2010 to €62.3 billion in 2013.

Spinellis was succeeded by Haris Theocharis, who in his turn resigned in 2014 due, in part, to government resistance in giving his office the necessary competences. They seemed powerless to ensure that tax systems they had introduced were not implemented by officials at local level. One must question the sincerity of their appointments if it was clear that nothing was to be achieved. When, in 2015, as part of Syriza's attempts to re-negotiate the bail-out, it was proposed that €300 to €400 million might be raised by measures dealing with tax evasion, it was clear that both sides – the Greek finance ministry and the IMF – knew that the idea, while worthwhile, was impracticable.

As Yannis Palaiologos comments, "if Kafka had been Greek, his masterpiece would probably have been entitled *The Tax Office*".[27] Palaiologos describes the frustration of tax clients as "existential despair".

Theocharis has spoken, privately, of the fact that on several occasions he was "advised" by senior politicians not to proceed against specific tax culprits.[28] Such blocking of tax pursuit is a common feature of the clientelist system, whereby each party to *cosa nostra* watches the backs of the others. In 2011, for example, the head of the tax division at the finance ministry resigned after it was revealed that he had blocked the collection of €15 million of fines imposed on fuel traders who had laundered their tax records.

Very few of the prominent people who have been named as tax dodgers have been penalised. Angela Gerekou (at that time a MP for Corfu) was forced to resign as junior minister for tourism and culture, when it was disclosed that her husband, singer Tolis Voskopoulos, owed over €500,000 in taxes. He received a three-year suspended sentence and was given the option of paying his taxes at the rate of five euros per day. At that rate, it will take him almost 300 years to pay what he owes.

Investigative journalist Cambanis stated in 2014 that, "In daily life, cheating, bribes and tax evasion are still a matter of course. Even anti-corruption officials reputedly accept bribes". But although his ancestors have lived on the Aegean island of Paros for many generations, Cambanis grew up in America and adopted a view of the matter which would be anathema to many Greeks: "You don't cheat, not because you might get caught but because it's wrong. You pay taxes because it's the law and the government provides security and services".[29]

Ordinary citizens have always hidden part of their income, from the time when, under the Ottomans, the money economy started to replace that of barter. The justification today is that if the super-rich do it, why can't we? And they would argue that the state does *not* provide adequate services or security, particularly for the less well-off. On which Cambanis comments, "the Greek system can feel like a Mexican standoff. Citizens won't obey the law until the government fulfils its duties. The government shirks its duties because it doesn't have enough revenue to govern responsibly". For example, the annual tax on the average-size swimming pool is €700; in the Athens area, less than 500 households pay this tax, even though aerial photos indicate that there are approximately 10,000 such pools. Cambanis believes that "the Greek elites mirror the predatory habits of the [Ottoman] sultanate, while the citizens act as if evading tax is a heroic act of revolt". But, as with other aspects of Greek society, it cannot all be blamed on life under the Ottomans. One might say, courtesy of Heineken, that the black market of evasion and bribery nourishes parts of the state which the civil service cannot reach. The black market in Greece is termed "the grey economy": according to OECD statistics, it accounted for 27 per cent of GDP, compared to 20 per cent in Italy, 16 per cent in Spain, and less than 12 per cent in the Netherlands.

One of the more curious incidents in the use of foreign bank accounts was the leaking in 2010, to the Greek minister of finance, of a list of over 2,000 Greeks with bank accounts with HSBC in Geneva amounting to billions of euros; the leak was authorised by the then French minister of finance, Christine Lagarde (now head of the IMF) and is known as the "Lagarde list". It was allegedly doctored by her Greek counterpart, Giorgos Papaconstantinou, in that he deleted the names of three of his relatives and sat on the list for two years. (In 2015, Papaconstantinou was convicted of removing the names of three relatives from the list and received a suspended one-year sentence.) Having a bank account in Switzerland is not in itself an offence, but some of the accounts amounted to €500 million, suggesting that some of the money was not acquired by straightforward means and might have been liable to tax in Greece.

In 2015, Leonidas Bobolas, one of those named on the "Lagarde List", reached a settlement with the tax authorities of almost €2 million, the amount which he was found to have in his HSBC account. Bobolas, as a member of a family which controls the Mega television channel and *Ethnos* newspaper (as well as having stakes in casinos and gold mines in Greece and Italy), was the first high-profile public debtor to be exposed; the tax authorities hoped that this would indicate their determination to eradicate plutocratic tax evasion.

Five years after the publication of the Greek names on the "Lagarde List", it emerged that in 2010 the same French source had also supplied the names of Irish citizens with accounts in the same HSBC bank, some of whom have since made tax settlements with the Revenue.

Kostas Vaxevanis, the journalist who leaked the names on the list, was charged with violating personal privacy and acquitted, but re-arrested on similar charges and again acquitted. Vaxevanis points to the fact that the media absented themselves from his trial and were silent on the matter, suggesting to him that "the public is deprived of real information, as television stations, newspapers and online news sites are controlled by the economic and political elite".[30]

Successive governments have vowed to establish a cadre of "incorruptible" tax inspectors, but public cynicism dismisses such a notion as mere wishful thinking. In 2015, a newly-elected MP for the Potámi party stated that when he was responsible for the office of tax collection, he received death threats and was told that "it would cost only €5,000 to break his legs".[31] Despite having a police escort, finding himself under political pressure for attempting to investigate "the well-connected", he resigned, seventeen months into a five-year contract. The choice between political castration and the other kind, as the Greeks would say. between Scylla and Charybdis, or in Ireland, a rock and a hard place, was an impossible one. (A similar situation arose in Ireland where the chief of the Criminal Asssets Bureau allegedly carried a pistol for personal protection, presumably against the drugs barons whose wealth he was investigating.)

Perhaps the most bizarre, as well as the most insulting, incident came when the then deputy Prime Minister Theodoros Pangalos announced that he would not be able to pay the €7,500 tax for which he has been assessed in respect of the fifty-four properties he owns, with a declared income of €614,000. Our hearts bled for him so much that in Corfu we joked about taking up a collection, until we found that the people of Rhodes had done just that. Imagine the outcry if an Irish Tánaiste made such an announcement, and you have the measure of Greek indignation.

(iv) Corruption

Natural resentment and frustration at bureaucratic red tape and inefficiency can easily be dispelled. But the venal and almost national institution of bribery – for that is what it is – by way of the small brown envelope (the *fakeláki*) is so inured and so intimately connected with the clientelist system that re-education of Mr and Mrs Citizen in the ways of freedom is necessary if they are to exit such a system and construct a better one.

When Evangelos Venizelos was Finance Minister, in 2011, he declared that "tax fraud is a national crime, a national plague". It is reasonable to state that almost all civil servants have the opportunity to take bribes at some level: petty, maybe, but rising to super levels. Every section of the administration, from the police to car-licensing to the health service, involves payment of some kind, under the counter, to ensure that the public servant does – or does not – do his job. And beside tax evasion we must also place fraud: for example, many citizens have recently been detected collecting pensions for relatives long dead.

The most ironic twist in this scenario is that, when people's incomes fell as a result of austerity, bribable civil servants had to accept smaller bribes, as the traditional sums were no longer affordable.

In 2014, the Ministry of Administrative Reform disclosed that in the previous four years a total of 5,260 civil servants had exported €1.5 billion to foreign accounts (an average of €71,000 per person per year, on average annual salaries of €25,000 to €30,000).

Bribery has to be considered from two aspects: bribery of civil servants from within the state (mostly by individual citizens but also by Greek companies) and bribery of influential ministers and senior civil servants by external interests.

The catalogue of briberies that have actually come to light in government and within the civil service is extensive. A few examples will give a flavour of their extent and magnitude.

In 2014, an act was passed (which will most likely be repealed by the Syriza government) granting retrospective immunity from prosecution to thousands of civil servants. (Former government ministers already enjoy such immunity.) While on one hand the government has been committed to the eradication of bribery, on another it has created rat-runs. Immunity for top-level appointees has been justified on the grounds that they would otherwise not take the jobs (somewhat like the over-scale salaries paid to some chief executives in Ireland). "These laws are not so much to cover scandal but to allow government to function" said one constitutional lawyer.[32]

Nevertheless, some scandals have unveiled unforgivable offences, with the successful prosecution of former defence minister Akis Tzochatzopoulos (who narrowly failed in his bid to become leader of PASOK) for accepting bribes amounting to *at least* €70 million, which he hid through Swiss bank accounts. Due to the magnitude of the defence budget, the position of minister of defence has therefore been the most lucrative in the cabinet: a popular joke used to be: "Why is Evangelos Venizelos so fat? Because he is minister of defence." Tsochatzopoulos was sentenced to twenty years' imprisonment for his part in the purchase of four German-made submarines at a cost of €1.6 billion. The submarine purchase was alleged to have cost its manufacturer, HDW Ferrostaal, €55 million in bribes. In 2015, thirty-two further suspects (politicians, businessmen, soldiers, bankers and arms traders) went on trial in connection with the submarine bribes.

As Nick Malkoutzis emphasises, corrupt Greeks took bribes, but corrupt Americans and Germans paid them. "It was a reminder that claims that Greeks are somehow more genetically conditioned to be corrupt are as racist as they sound."[33] (His reference to Americans relates to a fine of $70 million imposed on Johnson & Johnson by a US court for bribery in Greece.)

In 2014, a former mayor of Thessaloniki was sentenced to life imprisonment for embezzling €17 million of city funds (his sentence was subsequently reduced to twelve years); his accomplices, the city treasurer and secretary-general, were also convicted. The mayor enjoyed some personal glamour as he was a former champion sprinter. In this case, he didn't run fast enough, but in many others the culprits will never be traced.

But the most extensive scandal was the "Siemens affair" which came to light in 2010-11 when a parliamentary committee recommended that thirteen former ministers should be investigated for alleged venality: the purchase from Siemens of equipment for the state telecom, OTE, and security systems for the 2004 Olympics. However, as *Kathimerini* pointed out at the time, "the possibility of any of the politicians facing action is remote as the statute of limitations applies to any offences they may have committed".[34] Only one politician, a former minister of transport, admitted receiving a bribe, of €200,000, from Siemens, claiming that it was "a donation to his re-election campaign" and represented "only a fraction" of the €5 million paid to Greek officials.[35] The ex-minister admitted that some of the money was spent on his son's education at Harvard; his son now works for Siemens. He received a three-year suspended sentence and was fined €7,500.[36] A former aide to the Greek Prime Minister also admitted receiving a bribe, of €1 million, from Siemens "for the party" (i.e. PASOK); the party denied receiving the money. An agreement was reached between Greece and Siemens that the company would pay €90 million in settlement and invest a further €100 million in developing its Greek subsidiary.[37] Meanwhile, it was not until 2015 that sixty-four people were put on trial for giving and receiving bribes, including executives of Siemens Hellas, a former PASOK MP and several former OTE executives.

In a completely different area of bribery, two MPs of the Independent Greeks party (now in the coalition government) alleged that the then Prime Minister, Antonis Samaras, had attempted to buy their support in the crucial vote which eventually brought down his government: the sum on offer was €3 million. When I discussed this one evening with a Corfiot taverna-keeper I expostulated, "But that's a *huge* sum of money!" to which he replied with a cynical smile, "Not to Mr Samaras"; but a greater cynic than he suggested that "they were paid to say they had taken the bribe". *O tempora, o mores.*

Ministers have traditionally been immune from prosecution. In the two years 2012-2014, eighty-nine felony cases were brought against ministers, with immunity lifted in only one case. Immunity – or other means of evading prosecution – will come as no surprise to Irish readers, who are familiar with the corruption cases involving government ministers and senior public officials; the withdrawal of findings against a planning official, George Redmond, by a tribunal of enquiry evoked dismay and disbelief among ordinary citizens. Likewise, investigations by the same tribunal into alleged involvement in bribery in planning decisions by a former minister, Ray Burke, and a former Taoiseach, Bertie Ahern, came to nothing. Another minister, Liam Lawlor, was imprisoned three times by the tribunal for contempt of court, but was never convicted of any offence.[38]

Planning laws are perhaps the easiest to manipulate: in 2003 the assistant director of a regional authority's real estate department killed herself after facilitating a planning offence. Her suicide note hoped that by assuaging her guilt, others might act more responsibly.

The dedicatee of this book set up, after considerable bureaucratic delay, a photovoltaic project in Greece. He did not object to paying bribes to the relevant officials in order to obtain the necessary licences (the term is *grígorosimo*, for an "acceleration stamp"), but he was enfuriated by the succession of such bribes as he was passed from one civil servant to the next. "In Bulgaria," he said, "we set up the same projects with a single, up-front bribe; we knew at the outset how much it was going to cost."

Greece announced several years ago that opening a business would be facilitated by a one-stop-shop; it seems that different levels of civil servants have resisted this: they would have to compete with the Bulgarian one-stop-bribe-shop. In 2010, such facilities existed in Afghanistan, Peru and Rwanda, and Greece was ranked by the World Bank 125 out of 132 countries for the ability to facilitate new business. Unless you have *méson* – inside influence – you find yourself in a waiting-room equivalent to a long-term left-luggage office.

Many companies in Greece have relocated their financial headquarters outside the state. These include the Hellenic Bottling Company, the world's second largest distributor of Coca-Cola (and until recently Irish-controlled). Many others are leaving Greece due to the difficulty of negotiating red tape, describing the attitude of bureaucracy to foreign investment as "inhospitable". One industrialist who invested in Greece but took his company out of the country in the face of this "inhospitability" said "this country is held hostage by politicians, corruption and an elite clique that exploits the people".[39]

The bribery "system" operates in the private sector, too. It has been common practice for Greek companies, including Wind Hellas, to use Luxembourg and Liechtenstein as tax havens, similar to tax avoidance by Irish companies like Glanbia.[40]

On one occasion I was buying a quantity of stationery; the marked price totalled €120; the shopkeeper asked, "Do you want a receipt?" "No." "Then that's €95." I was getting a hefty discount, but I was conniving at his VAT avoidance. But how often, in Ireland, have we been asked, "Do you want a receipt?", and have taken the advantage of a cash transaction?

A more interesting instance of self-help in the private sector was my encounter when an ATM would not honour my cashcard. Inside the bank, the manager informed me that my account was "frozen". What did this mean? "Every five years you must re-submit your documentation. It's an EU rule." Knowing that this was untrue, I said, rather forcefully, "I have bank accounts in the UK and Ireland for the past forty-five years and it is *not* an EU rule. Whose rule *is* it?" To which he replied, with a polite smile, "It's a rule here." Sensing that what was necessary was a bribe, I slid a €50 note across the desk; it disappeared instantly beneath his paperwork. "Does that help?" "Sir, your account is now unfrozen ... for two years." On reflection, this somewhat unofficial variation on the theme of bank charges was reasonably cheap – only €25 per year. The manager had taken a 20 per cent cut in salary due to austerity and he was probably paying considerable sums for his children to attend crammer schools (discussed below) in order to increase their chances of a university place.

In 2003-4 the watchdog Transparency International listed Greece as the most corrupt of the (then) fifteen EU states, with one-in-ten Greeks (a very conservative estimate) admitting to bribery over the past year. Greece ranked 50th in the world list of 133 countries surveyed. But I hope I am not making a "special plea" if I say that while Greece may score high in any global analysis of corruption, I am sure that it would score equally high, if not higher, in measurements of acumen, intelligence and willingness to work, quite apart from its traditional reputation for hospitality.

(v) Closed Professions

The operation of closed professions, which include architects, civil engineers, hairdressers, opticians, real estate agents, speech therapists and bakers, was described by the director of IOBE (the government's think tank Foundation for Economic and Industrial Research, similar to Ireland's ESRI) as "the last Soviet-style economy in Europe". The director was at that time the ubiquitous Yannis Stournaras.[41]

The monopoly position of most professions in Greece is contrary to EU regulations, in that they effectively restrict membership to Greeks. Whereas any citizen of the EU should be allowed to work in Greece and, more significantly, open a professional business, this is not possible in most instances.

Since government attempts to conform met with successful opposition (the professions ignored the law) the insistence of the IMF/EU bailout for Greece on the deregulation of closed professions is another way of ensuring conformity. It is even uncertain how many of these closed professions there actually are. Some sources quote a figure of seventy, some 140. In 2011, the government introduced a single bill providing for the deregulation of pharmacists, architects, accountants and lawyers. When attempts were made to open up their profession, lawyers threatened, for their part, to shut down the courts, while accountants intended to block tax revenue, for example by refusing to process property transactions. Yet in 2013, Yannis Stournaras claimed that 70 per cent of the professions had been liberalised.[42]

Some examples of the prevailing situation will indicate the extent of the problem and of attempted solutions. No new licences for truckers were issued from 1986 onwards until 2010: there were 34,000 licences in existence, changing hands for as much as €300,000. With deregulation, these became virtually worthless, which explains the consequent truckers' highway-blocking strike. Young truckers, who may have paid as much as €300,000 to set up a trucking business, were left with an almost worthless piece of paper and a debt to either the bank or the family which they can never hope to repay.

Greek taxi drivers also protested at the creation of new licences, bringing Athens and other cities to a standstill, and seriously disrupting tourism through a blockade of ferry ports and Athens Airport. As with their trucking colleagues, the cost of a licence was drastically reduced. The situation in Ireland is similar in relation to the deregulation of taxi licences.

Pharmacists are among the most protected professions, requiring a qualification from a Greek college if you want to open a pharmacy in Greece; a licence to practice changes hands at around €300,000. In addition to the restriction on qualification, the number of pharmacies owned by one company is restricted (probably to prevent the opening of chain stores such as Boots in the UK and Ireland due to a reasonable fear of globalisation).[43] Pharmacists responded to deregulation with a series of two-day closures throughout 2012 and 2013.

Lawyers operate a particularly Byzantine form of protection, whereby bar associations are limited to geographical locations, and an attorney in one region may be prohibited from practicing in another. This intensely localised system epitomises the complaint by those trying to enter the professions: that it's who you know rather than your own innate merit that admits you to a lucrative and secure future. It also in effect restricts the entry to the profession to the sons and daughters of lawyers, and enforces a middle class culture among jurists.

In 2009, Adam Shatz, writing in the *London Review of Books*, stated quite bluntly that "Greeks know not to expect much from their state apart from graft and inefficiency".[44] It is perhaps too melodramatic to refer (as does an unnamed commentator) to the pervasiveness of evasion and bribery as a "value system of nihilism and antisocial behaviour" promulgated by "parents and schools".[45] "Nihilism" is hardly the appropriate term, and citizens would not see their actions as "antisocial" since, as I have already explained, it is the family that comes first and the rest of society only when the family's protection is assured.

To say this is tantamount to saying that all Greeks suffer from the incurable disease of recidivism borne of a slave mentality. It totally ignores the intelligence, entrepreneurship and creativity in every Greek. Greeks abroad have in general tended to be successful in a variety of occupations, some becoming very wealthy in the process. Perhaps this is due to the need, as immigrants (especially in the early years of entry to the USA) to prove themselves capable of doing well in an entrepreneurial society. The question has to be asked: why is such a talented, cultured, positive people served so badly by the Greek system which they, as voters, have put in place?

Education

The answer to that question lies partly in the educational system at secondary and tertiary levels, which absorbs those talented and intelligent young people. The answer also exemplifies the problem.

Article 16 of the Constitution states that "education constitutes a basic mission for the State and should aim at the moral, intellectual, professional and physical training of Greeks, the development of national and religious consciousness and at their formation as free and responsible citizens". The Constitution provides for "free education on all levels".

There are manifold disproofs of the adage that a people get the government/education that they deserve. Greece's education system is a prime example: the talent of young Greece is squandered by a system which betrays their ability to demonstrate their acumen and creativity, while rewarding those who joy-ride at the expense of the taxpayer and exit the system with a bar-code instead of fitness for modern society.

At this point you may well have exhausted your tolerance for history lessons, but I have to point out that one of the basic topics of the education system since the foundation of the state has been the question of *language*, when a debate immediately ensued over the status of *demotic*: did the Greek language actually spoken by most people – essentially the peasants – have any validity vis-à-vis the "posh" form of speech and writing of the more ancient Greeks?

The fact that the language debate has been "a conflict for the appropriation of the authority to form the national identity"[46] indicates its importance within the educational context – in fact, an educational form of civil war – especially since, as late as 1974-76, this conflict continued in the schools and universities.

Peter Mackridge, probably the leading world authority on the evolution of modern Greek, tells us that, until recently, "generations of Greeks were taught at school that the Greek language was unique in its expressive capabilities, but that spoken Modern Greek was a debased and corrupt version of it. This led many Greeks to be ashamed of the language they actually spoke"[47] – thus renewing the arguments since before independence on the relative values of *katharévousa* and demotic.

Universities were the strongest opponents of demotic. Modern Greek ("the language generally spoken") was not taught in primary schools until 1881, and not until 1909 in secondary schools, and then only *katharévousa*.[48] Modern Greek literature, whether written in *katharévousa* or demotic, was introduced to the secondary school curriculum in 1884.

A parliamentary committee in 1911 examined the fact that modern *katharévousa* was "the means for the expression of thought" while demotic was "the expression of emotion".[49] Under the 1925-26 dictatorship of Theodoros Pangalos (grandfather of the present-day politician of the same name), it was asserted that demotic was the language of communism, and its teaching was banned. The debate continued into the 1970s, and again took on a political complexion under the Colonels.

The Constitution of 1975 was written in *katharévousa* but made no mention of any official version of the language, but the subsequent law (no. 309) of 1976 stipulated that "Modern Greek" – meaning demotic – was the sole language of education, the "Panhellenic instrument of expression [...] without" – it should be noted – "regional and extreme forms".[50] The following year, demotic was adopted as the official language of administration, in which all documents and laws should therefore be written.

An issue not unlike – and not divorced from – that of the country's official language has been the control of textbooks. Education is a process of storytelling: the introduction of a narrative which will guide young citizens in their appreciation of their history and, therefore, of their future. As in Ireland, issues of what may, or may not (or should, or should not), be taught have been highlighted by the response to textbooks, especially in what is recognised worldwide as the "history wars".

In 1984, a textbook was accused of "undermin[ing] the foundations of Greek civilization", of being "unpatriotic" and "denying the national sentiment" for moving from the favoured ethnocentric approach to a broader-based method of creating awareness; it was replaced in 1989. Others were banned in 1990 and 1991.

One textbook, issued in 2006, was withdrawn on three counts: downplaying the role of the Church in the War of Independence; mis-representing the issues in the Cyprus situation; and fudging the background to Greek-Turkish relations (in favour of Turkey). Opposition was led by the Church, which asked, "how can you show the children an impure history?" and asserting, "we have history and tradition and it is a crime of extreme betrayal trying to abolish those things for which our fathers fought".[51] One politician said on television, "this book undermines our national heritage", and another referred to "the genocide of memory", while a teacher said, "the book completely deconstructed our history". The communists and the fascists also opposed the book, while Syriza supported it. It seems that Greece is not yet ready for the revisionism which has become a primary qualification for historians in Ireland.

It has even been alleged that the replacement of the junta in 1974 by democratic government had marginalised Greek values and jeopardised the Europeanisation of Greece by ignoring its national identity: "In order to become proper Europeans we must first become proper Greeks" – thus confirming the perennial agenda of Greece since independence.[52]

In 2013, I wrote that "the schools are a shambles and the universities are chaotic". That was, perhaps, too harsh a headline, but the somewhat primitive education system may have been adequate when Greece was backward and marginal, and had only a minor role in international affairs. Today, with the expansion in curricula, diversification and specialisation in university faculties, and the pressures of the marketplace, this isn't good enough for today's young people.[53]

Tsoucalas and Panagiotopoulou describe secondary and university education in Greece as "antechambers of a non-productive and leisurely public employment", where "knowledge is rarely coveted and expertise is unnecessary, if not totally useless".[54] While there are some highly recognised research departments (for example at the Aristotle University of Thessaloniki), the universities in which they are situated are judged (by the government's own commission on quality in higher education) to be bureaucratic and inefficient. Huge expenditure on third level education is not achieving the results it deserves.

School leavers deserve a university system which is transparent and offers both hope and opportunities. Most young Greeks, like their Irish counterparts, are not content with the old ways: they want to acquire skills and reach new horizons. The education system stands in their way.

Even when they graduate, however brilliant they may be, employment commensurate with qualifications is almost inconceivable. The best prospect is emigration, usually to Britain (40 per cent of emigrants), Germany (16 per cent), Italy (16 per cent) and North America (5 per cent). Emigration by graduates is lower than in Ireland or the Baltic states, but only 16 per cent of graduates working abroad would contemplate returning to Greece; 46 per cent of PhD-holders earned more than €60,000 abroad, more than twice their equivalent in Greece. The main subjects for emigrating graduates are economics and business studies, law, computer science, physics and chemistry.

But only affluent parents can afford to send their children abroad to university; the effect is what has been called a "two-speed" race for careers.

Of the "free" secondary school system, one newspaper, *Kathimerini*, said, "It's not free and it's not education". The annual budget for education, pre-austerity cuts, was €6 billion, or slightly more than 4 per cent of GDP. This is insufficient to enable schools to meet modern standards. The worst affront is the fact that teachers direct pupils to the crammers (the *frontistério*, technically a "tutorial college") where they themselves work out-of-hours. Teachers earned a pre-cuts average salary of €30,000, making the *frontistério* industry an essential extra cash-earner. There are an estimated 3,000 crammers, to which anxious parents are paying an annual total of €1.6 billion, or €200 per month per family. It's been described as a form of kleptocracy, but in fact it is mandatory if you want your son or daughter to get into university.

One result of the austerity measures was non-replacement of retiring workers: 23,000 teachers retired in 2011; the government could afford to replace only 3,500; the areas worst hit are teachers for the disabled and those with special needs.

In 2010, the then Prime Minister, George Papandreou, in yet another of his visionary pledges, promised to "fundamentally change the way Greek pupils learn and teachers teach". Attempts to honour that pledge by his, and the subsequent, government met with severe opposition from the teachers' unions, because they believe that the intended reforms wouldn't achieve any real improvements.

The most extensive reforms envisaged include revamping school teaching methods (at present largely learning-by-rote), coupled with abolition of the existing Greek "Leaving Cert" and the points system for university entrance. At present, 50 per cent is required in the Leaving Cert for university entrance, but 20-30 per cent of school leavers failed to reach this. Greek schools rank 28th out of 31 countries measured by the OECD for skills in literacy and maths. Nikos Konstandaras argues that the problem is not only economic and political, but *social*:

> The underlying cause is the absence of personal discipline. Getting into a university or technical college without any effort is not far removed from soccer hooliganism or cheating the tax office. When illiterates enter the university system they undermine the reputation of the entire system.[55]

The "liberation" of schoolchildren from the exam mentality, so as to facilitate broader thinking and more meaningful lives, remains an ideological issue intimately related to Greece's self-image and its possible metamorphosis in the light of modern experience.

Universities are not amenable to a system of control, despite continuing efforts to reform the system. Universities have to be autonomous and yet responsible. That balance has yet to be found in the Greek system, which, on this subject, is impenetrable to the rational mind.

There are nineteen universities in Greece, plus sixteen technical colleges, with a lecturer-student ratio of 31:1. Three Greek universities are ranked in the world's top 500, at 193, 226 and 338. Five more feature in the range 500-1,000. Greece ranks 118th in the world league for university efficiency.

As Prime Minister, George Papandreou made it clear that if the third level were not radically reformed, large numbers of young people would leave the country. In a poll of September 2010, 70 per cent of graduates said they wanted to work abroad; a survey confirmed this one year later, when 42 per cent said they were actively seeking to do so. Employment prospects, on the minimum monthly wage (which had dropped from €700 to €590), depend on who you know. The system consistently favours the well-connected over the talented.

It's long been realised by all political parties as essential that the schools system and the universities are reformed together. But the two problems seem to be intractable. Greece is still struggling to find its way in the world, trying to decide how to educate its young people.

One of the most significant facts about the university system is the *asylum* status enjoyed by campuses, which is both physical and conceptual. Its recent origins lie in the student revolt against the junta in 1973, in which an untold number of students (at least twenty-four) were killed by the security forces. Police are forbidden by a 1982 law to enter university campuses, except at the discretion of the rector (president). The intention of the regulation was to honour the revolt of 1973 by safeguarding freedom of speech and thought. No other European country provides this level of protection to universities.

With terrorists, illegal immigrants, drug dealers and party-affiliated student unions using the campuses – especially the University of Athens – as bases for political broadcasting and assaults on teaching staff, it is argued that universities abuse this freedom, which should be restricted in the interests of state security. One rector (of Thessaloniki University) who was knocked unconscious by students nevertheless believes that "the symbolic value of asylum should be prized and protected". The rector went on to ask: "Which university would dare let in the police, knowing it would have to face the wrath of the media and society the next day?" He had done so and, he says, "paid for it very dearly".[56] It was only the third time this had occurred anywhere in Greece since the 1982 law.

The law of 1982 has been seen by some as permissive, in that it introduced party politics to the universities. Whether or not that view is valid, it is certain that that "permissiveness" in the use and sale of drugs and on-campus broadcasting by terrorists/anarchists is a danger to the state, but it is argued that it is the university's responsibility to police its own internal affairs.

The central problem is: how to ensure that self-management is conducted in the public interest, without imposing external controls? It is not surprising that the job of minister of education has been described as "a political graveyard".

Broadcasting: The Story of ERT

Imagine Irish people waking one morning to find that RTÉ (Raidió Teilifís Éireann), the national broadcaster, had been taken off the air by an overnight government decree. The social and political repercussions would be far-reaching. That is precisely what happened in Greece in June 2013, when the national broadcaster, ERT (Ελληνική Ραδιοφωνία Τηλεόραση, *Ellinikí Radiofonía Tileórasi*) was suspended by order of premier Antonis Samaras. The silence of ERT was on a par with listeners' experience of the blackout on 21 April 1967 when the Colonels took control of the country's media.

Whatever one's opinion of the relative merits of specific programming, the concept of a national broadcaster as an objective source of information reflecting the "state of the nation" has been central to most emerging nations, both east and west. Naturally, there will always be arguments about the agenda of the nation, and the control of a national broadcaster, and these will always be more fiercely conducted in societies where opinion is more sharply divided. But the validity of the concept survived into the age of commercialisation and profit-motive in media ownership, and is still maintained as a national good.

The crucial point is that the state should guarantee an objective information service without seeking to influence it: a nice balance is needed to ensure this, which in many cases is achieved by an arm's length system where broadcasting, both public service and private, is regulated by a statutory body, as is the case in both Greece and Ireland.

The Samaras decree was fundamental to Greek society because it called into question not only whether or not the country wants public service broadcasting (PSB), but also the rectitude of the manner in which the decision was taken and, perhaps even more importantly, the government's announcement that ERT would be replaced by a new organisation as "a state company owned by the public sector and regulated by the state".

On one side are the basic arguments about accountability, especially where many ERT staff (as in so many areas of the public service) owed their positions to nepotism and clientelism, and where the cost of maintaining the service was appreciably higher than that of the private channels. The Troika was promised a reduction of 2,000 places in public service employment by the end of 2013: sacking almost that number in one ministerial decree was one way of effecting this in a single measure.

On the other, it was widely condemned both inside and outside Greece. The European Broadcasting Union stressed the need for public service media independent of government. The EBU director-general called the closedown "the worst kind of censorship": "just closing down an organization in a knee-jerk fashion is not only rash, it is unprofessional".[57]

The quality of both ERT television and the private channels is, to put it bluntly, poor-to-atrocious; the predominant television diet is game shows and sitcoms (some of them Greek-made soap operas, but many foreign – even Turkish) with minimal coverage of news and current affairs, at least by Irish or British standards. Only in current affairs is there anything that will alert the glassy-eyed dullard in the *kafeneío*. But that is not the point.

As government-controlled media, radio and television (as in Ireland) were not expected to be independent. The Constitution (Article 15.2) requires that the national broadcaster "shall aim at the objective and on equal terms transmission of information and news reports", but ERT in particular was criticised for its pro-government reportage and representation on current affairs programmes.

The state monopoly of broadcasting, in common with that of almost all emerging nation-states, was maintained until deregulation became inevitable with illegal media proliferation in the 1980s. ERT lost its monopoly in 1986, yet, as one authority states, deregulation "has been closely associated with politics rather than a well-organized plan according to the needs of the industry".[58]

Anyone with a knowledge of broadcasting budgets and staffing levels would recognise that, in the case of ERT, the proposed reduction of the workforce from 2,650 to one-third of that size, and a comparable budget reduction, would be untenable, if responsible quality programming were to be maintained on three TV channels and a nationwide network of local radio.

The European Commission, which denied that it had any part in the decision (although it coincided with a Troika visit to Athens), also supported the role of PSB as "an integral part of European democracy". To give Greeks a sense of Greekness at such a crucial time could be argued as one of the principal justifications for PSB.

And anyone, like myself, who is concerned for the status of orchestral music, would have deplored the fact that closure of ERT, and the consequent dismissal of the entire staff, entailed the demise of the broadcaster's two orchestras. A similar decision in Ireland would have meant the cessation of the RTÉ National Symphony Orchestra.[59]

Before the advent of broadcasting, the print media in Greece were, predictably, political. It is not surprising that newspapers should reflect the political leanings of their proprietors and editors. This has been the case in Greece since the nineteenth century. Newspapers and periodicals were at the forefront of social change and political upheavals. The titles of some indicated their allegiance or orientation: *Forward*, *Regeneration*, *Fatherland*, *Motherland* and *Romios*. Some were royalist, some liberal (such as *New Greece*). The press of the Left included *Radical* and *Free Greece*. The "quality" papers remain *Kathimerini* (leaning towards the right), *To Vima* and *Ta Nea* (liberal, owned by the Lambrakis family) and *Eleftherotypia* (on the left).

I was astonished when a Greek journalist expressed indignation at media ownership by vested commercial and political interests. He seemed oblivious of the fact that this is a ubiquitous pursuit in most societies. The Constitution provides (Article 14.9) that "the ownership status, the financial situation and the means of financing of information media must be made known as specified by law" and seeks to ensure "transparency and plurality in information". Concentrated ownership of "more than one information medium of the same type or of different types is prohibited", especially the electronic media.

In addition to the state broadcaster ERT (now NERIT) there have been, since the 1980s, eight privately-owned television channels; Skai is owned by a shipping magnate; Mega is controlled by an oil baron (who is also a major shareholder in Piraeus Bank) and by two newspaper proprietors. Mega has been operated as a loss-making enterprise in order "to exercise political and economic influence".[60]

Concentration of media ownership has long been the subject of international debate (for example, the International Commission for the Study of Communication Problems chaired by Ireland's Seán MacBride in 1980); students of this concentration will recall the statement (which amounted to a boast) by Tony O'Reilly that, "Since I own 35 per cent of the newspapers in Ireland I have close contact with the politicians." This, he alleged, facilitated the granting of oil exploration licences to one of his companies.[61]

As in the case of Tony O'Reilly in Ireland, agglomeration of media by commercially-oriented families has been a well-known feature in Greece. For example, Christos Lambrakis was described as "the dark centre of *diapléki*" – the conglomeration of media interests – "credited with making and breaking governments" and "the rainmaker of Greek politics" according to his obituary in *The Independent*; he owned 20 per cent of Greece's newspapers and a stake in television; his company described itself as "the largest and most influential company group in Greece".[62]

Kostas Vaxevanis, in his disclosure of the "Lagarde list", referred to "publishers, businessmen, shipowners, the entire system of power is shown to have transferred money abroad [...] Meanwhile in Greece, people are going through dumpsters for food".[63] The list also included the then speaker of Parliament (a former government minister). The connection between government, business and the media was exemplified in Ireland by the marriage of Fianna Fáil and the building industry in the 1960s through its fund-raising branch, TACA (from the Irish *tacaíocht* meaning "support", "security" and "guarantee").

As a last word, it should be noted that NERIT, the "new ERT" (which came on air showing a black-and-white oldie film), was on even more uncertain ground than ERT: the managing director was sacked two days after the first transmission, and his successor resigned four months later, citing political interference which threatened to boycott a speech by the rising star of the Left, Alexis Tsipras. For New Democracy to have closed ERT on grounds of "lack of transparency" seems perverse in such circumstances.

Tourism

Tourism is probably Greece's single most important export, both financially and in terms of the country's image. It earns 20 per cent of GDP from 20 million tourists (compared to Ireland's 7.6 million) and employs 20 per cent of the workforce – more than that at the height of the season. How it is presented, and how its mass and niche markets are exploited and developed, are thus major preoccupations for government. Yet successive governments have failed to control developments which damage, rather than enhance, the coastline and reduce the "charm" and "authenticity" of the islands by popularisation, commercialisation and indiscriminate flaunting of the "product".

Some islands – Santorini and Mykonos, for example – have been changed out of all recognition by tourist infrastructure and the commercialisation of their inhabitants. An example: in 1955 Gerald Durrell published *My Family and Other Animals*, an affectionate portrait of the island of Corfu where he had lived as a small boy in the years 1935-39, and where he had found the inspiration of his life's work in the conservation of endangered species. He, like his older brother, Lawrence, had referred to Corfu as "Paradise". But the publication of his book, and a BBC travelogue he made in 1966 (*The Garden of the Gods*), began a worldwide interest in Corfu as a destination for mass tourism. Durrell was so horrified at the extent of the development which attended this interest that he blamed himself. In the 1980s he returned and likened the island to "a ravishing creature who was mature and beautiful". Revisiting it after fifty years "was like paying a visit to the most beautiful woman in the world suffering from a terminal case of leprosy, commonly called tourism". He accused the Corfiots of "vandalism beyond belief".[64] That was almost thirty years ago. More recent developments would add vitriol to the leprosy.

The type of development which has affected Corfu so badly (in environmental terms) is endemic in Greece. Resort hotels have the same effect as air travel: they narrow the mind, but their exponential increase in Greece is a major contributor to the statistics, even though little tourist money is spent beyond the "factory gates" within which the fortnight's holiday is largely spent: brain-dead bednights.

Because I still have sufficient of the "tourist gaze" to see the landscape objectively, I can appreciate the typical holidaymaker's view: the beauty of land and sea, the character of the people, their customs, festivals and creativity are part of what endears Greece to me. Like Neni Panourgiá (quoted above, p. 138), I can experience "life" in all (well, almost all) its visceral affect in my western consciousness – life which is in danger of extinction by poor development and lack of co-ordinated planning. If there is an "other mind" of Europe, this is its "other land".

"Culture", in its widest sense, is Greece's chief attraction. "Culture" is not merely the artefacts of its temples, theatres, sculptures and fortresses, but the way of life of the people and the environment within which they pursue that life. But we must always remember that, however quaint an old man telling his worry-beads (*kombolói*) may be to the tourist, the beads have far more significance for him than for the home movie which the tourists show to neighbours on their return.

Tourism in Greece does, however, perform the same dubious function as in Ireland: it temporarily gives the "locals" a sense of their own worth. So much so that there is a very marked contrast between the behaviour (*performance*) of "locals" in summer and winter. As Hugh Brody reported on "Inishkillane" (a name invented for a village on the western Irish seaboard in County Clare):

> the drunkenness in which the tourist participates occurs during the brief summer holiday season. It is a drunkenness of elation and extroversion. In the winter months, however, this elation gives way to the opposite [...] What the tourists do most surely bring to these communities, however, is reassurance and approval [... they] affirm *their* esteem for the rural milieu and its ways [...] The presence of these outsiders, these representatives of the social and cultural forms which the country people so frequently unquestioningly assume to be superior to their own, thus gives a renewed confidence in their own society and culture.[65]

Brody's study has of course been superseded in one basic detail: access to the internet makes the tourist's world, its values and *mores*, much more accessible to even the humblest community. And he ignores the fact that the income which the tourist brings to the community is a highly valued source of self-esteem (provided, that is, that it is spent on "real" local people and not within the compound of the resort hotel). But the sense that modern Greek (or Irish) people are a vital ingredient in the tourist magnet, and that their "performance" is part of the overall scenario, is one reason why tourism is such a major component of Greece's GDP.

That is why a crassly inane decision on the promotion of Greece as a tourist magnet raised such protest, nationally and internationally, in 2014 when, at the World Tourism Market, Greece's Minister of Tourism, Olga Kefalogianni, unveiled the 2015 campaign of the National Tourism Organisation (EOT). Its central plank is an eleven-minute video, "Gods, Myths, Heroes", which has all the trappings of a sophisticated travelogue extolling Greece's mythology and bringing it into the twenty-first century.

But it raises a major question as to how a political decision was taken about exploiting Greece and its culture. At a time when Greece urgently needs a better international profile, promotion of non-controversial aspects such as the landscape is an obvious strategy, but "gods, myths and heroes", harking back once again to "the glory that *was* Greece", seems perverse, when Greece is demonstrably short on heroes and knee-deep in myth. It ignores almost all of its present-day virtues and assets, its vibrant *contemporary* culture, and casts the whole country in the light of a backward-looking, introspective people obsessed with, and offering to the world, nothing better than the make-believe of mythology rather than the positive merits present and active in the people today. As Vangelis Calotychos observes, "Greek literary studies can not live on mythical and classical allusion [...] alone".[66] Neither can tourism live on gods, myths and heroes, or sea, sand and sex, alone.

The video is narrated by an American, Don Morgan Nielsen, who purports to be a writer from New York who visited Greece for a month and stayed for a year. It doesn't take much rocket science to know that in fact Mr Nielsen, a former Olympic athlete, married a Greek wife in 1991 and has lived here ever since. Nor is he a writer. The video is thus a deceit, not a travelogue but a deception, creating its own myths.

Nielsen is part responsible for his scripted narration, which may fool some people but is, on balance, crassly clichéd and juvenile. I shrank in disbelief as I watched it and, when we reached the point where he describes the light in Greece as "luminous", I frankly lost the will to live.

But much more serious than the video's blemishes is its *raison d'être*. Minister Kefalogianni's speech explained that the strategy is to reconnect people – like Mr Nielsen – with the gods and myths with which we have been familiar from childhood. At every turn the video insists on the everyday relevance of these gods and myths. But in doing so it turns its back on the many other aspects of modern Greece that are – or could become – tourist attractions.

By affirming some aspects of Greek culture, it ignores others, especially the modernity of Greece. Yes, Greece has museums, but it isn't just one huge museum, a relic of the past.

Tourists certainly come to see the antiquities, but they don't expect to meet Achilles or Poseidon in the village street, as this video implies. Nielsen tells us, "we walk through the forest with Artemis by our side. The olive trees that dot the landscape are the gift of Athena". A nice thing to imagine, perhaps. But Greece and its tourism cannot live on fantasies, any more than the economy. It is hard to believe that any tourist with a modicum of intelligence would accept, as anything other than ridiculous fancy, the idea that these mythical creatures will be there to greet them on arrival. Yet one *can* experience an awesome sense of a presence in a site like Mycenae or Tiryns, if one is prepared to divest oneself of preconceptions rather than travel with them, which the film seems to encourage.

Tourists want sun, sea and sand. And the famous "luminous" light. But they also want to see folklore, examples of modern history, Greek achievement today.

One can understand EOT's desire to stress the ancient world (especially given the depressing state of the country, socially and economically). Ever since the foundation of the state, the connection with "the glory that was Greece", appealing to the eternal verities, has been an ongoing project of nationalism. EOT claims that the film highlights enduring Greekness in "natural beauty, special light" – luminous of course – "history, mythology and the universality of culture". And the film emphatically does not focus on history. But it could be seen as part of that nationalist attempt to return to former glory, denying much present-day reality. As a tourist strategy, it fails.

Greece needs a better profile. Loving Greece, Greek people and Greek culture, it saddens me that such an opportunity to advertise Greece abroad, and to add to that profile, has been squandered.

The cost, according to EOT, was €60,000. It would have been a snip at the price if it had had a wider appeal, more punch and more accuracy. A Greek journalist recently referred to Greece as "a country of riches led by impoverished minds".[67] And impoverished budgets. The riches of Greece are its people, not its myths. Those responsible for this promotion don't seem to know that.

Certainly, the film will attract visitors to the Parthenon, Olympia, Delphi – the old reliables – but they were coming anyway. Earlier, the minister announced ambitions to widen the tourist market with niche attractions, especially in the cultural sector. We've heard that from successive ministers, with no perceptible outcome. I have personally been involved in proposals to develop the niche for cultural tourism in Corfu, presented to the relevant minister (who happened to represent Corfu at the time), with absolutely no result.

Greece does not need to be represented by Taiwanese-made dreamcatchers and miniature pianos that play non-stop "Für Elise", which are to be found in tinseltown throughout the known (and probably unknown) world, when it has its own distinctive and wonderful crafts for all pockets: simple olive wood products, multiple wines and cheeses (for Mr Noonan), honey in a profusion of tastes, fine jewellery (traditional and contemporary) and superb authenticated reproductions of classical sculpture. If the tourist wants to see *performance* (other than dancing, plate-smashing waiters lying in wait for Shirley Valentine) they can go into the villages and watch life as it is performed everyday by ordinary folk.

The Acropolis Museum in Athens is a magnificent, spacious place in which Greeks take obvious pride and where tour groups of schoolchildren listen attentively to their instructors. The fine public relations stunt is to have an empty gallery, awaiting the return of the Parthenon (or "Elgin") marbles. Whether or not these were legally or illegally obtained by Britain, it is the moral entitlement of Greece that is at the centre of the ongoing dispute. (The situation is comparable to the "Lane Bequest" of Impressionist paintings which commutes between London and Dublin.)

There is, in fact, considerable scope for the combination of the traditional way of life with the means of attracting and satisfying tourism, without diminishing the values of that life or disappointing the tourists.

These have been examples of ways in which the state apparatus does not live up to its Greekness. To administer a country efficiently and compassionately, it is necessary to tap into creativity, to think laterally, to match resources to needs and, if they are outstripped by needs, to plan for the effective development of a more appropriate and viable portfolio of skills and materials, both traditional and innovative. In the next two chapters we will examine Greece's creativity in the art-forms, which demonstrate both the strengths of the creator, and the weaknesses in the social environment where she or he can offer remedial skills.

7

LITERATURE

Introduction

This chapter and the next are, of necessity, an extended essay on modern and contemporary culture rather than a comprehensive survey. I can do no more than skim, subjectively, over the surface, and my examples, from literature in particular, will be limited by the extent of my reading and the fact that I am obliged to read in translation. How could I present any comprehensive view of the gamut of literature, from Anagnostakis to Zei, from *Antigone* to *Zorba*?

It will be clear that I am writing of "culture" in its widest sense. Greek culture has been both the parent and the child of history. We must not lose sight of the invaluable assessment by F.S.L. Lyons, that "evidence of diversity" is to be found "in all the manifold circumstances of [...] life from the furniture of men's kitchens to the furniture of their minds".[1] I have already given some indication of the importance of those kitchens, and minds, in Chapter 4.

One of the most regrettable aspects of Greek writing is its scarcity in translation. When I asked a colleague who is thoroughly familiar with the spectrum of Greek writing, why most of the translations I have read are concerned with the *agón* of life – politics, betrayal, greed and disaster – and why there are no novels or poems celebrating girls, chocolate, dancing, sunshine, she replied, "Oh there are, but they don't get translated because only bad news travels well". So it's unlikely that we will find many translations that tell of men chasing girls (to use Manolis Anagnostakis' image) in the hope of "rearranging the trigonometry of their lips".[2]

As Roderick Beaton observes:

> The highest sales today are usually the prerogative of novels whose subject matter is recent Greek history [...Such novels] confront questions which run right through Greek literature in modern times: namely, the relation of the Greek present to the historical past, of modern writing to the Greek tradition, and of both to a dominant foreign culture or cultures.[3]

The word "translation" – in Greek, *metaphor* – means so much more in the context of Greek literature than making novels or stories available in foreign languages. "Translation" in this context means to carry across the ideas of the Greek mind, as expressed in literature, into a different mindset, to explain the Greekness of these narratives in a language which will immediately create in the reader a sense of otherness and difference, to create an *atmosphere* in which the readers are inducted into the narrative of people whose lives they might not otherwise understand. It is the *immediacy* of apprehension that is the translator's, as it is the narrator's, key skill.[4]

Why is modern Greek drama so little known outside Greece? The answer is the same: lack of translation. As to why modern Greek drama is so little known *inside* Greece...read Chapter 8. However, in order to present characteristic vignettes of cultural excellence and of social significance I have chosen the ruthless strategy of concentrating in this chapter on

- the *Karagiózis* shadow- or puppet-theatre and *rebétiko* music

- the stories of Alexandros Papadiamandis (1851-1911), the father of modern Greek fiction

- novels of war/*agón*.

And in Chapter 8 on

- the music of Mikis Theodorakis and Manos Hadjidakis

- the films of Theodoros Angelopoulos and Pantelis Voulgaris' *Deep Soul*.

Novels which I particularly enjoy, and am educated by, are those which take the most ordinary situations – a widow, a farmer, a foot-soldier, a child – and present them with dilemmas, challenges, questions in the form of myths, in which the writer creates a fable which, like those of Aesop (who may or may not have existed in the sixth century BC), have universal application: I find this from Papadiamandis' *The Murderess* (*I Fonissa*, 1903) to Menis Koumandareas' *Koula* (1978).[5]

The emphasis which I have placed on the homestead and the family as the primal unit of society is evident in the attachment to place – *tópos* – and its surrounding landscape (and the analogues of exile and absence) in which the dramas of love and hate, honesty and cheating, trust and betrayal, and above all the roles of memory and conscience are performed.

An entire literature of legends, folktales and superstitions has grown up around the supernatural. Its early study in fact helped to convince some critics that folklore and folk poetry were the natural origins of modern literature. In *The Celtic Twilight* (1893), Yeats insisted that Irish countryfolk have daily commerce with the "other world", stating unequivocally, "In Ireland this world and the other are not widely sundered".[6] This would appeal to many in Greece – the poets, such as Elytis, or historians and archaeologists – who see the maintenance of that commerce as an essential factor in maintaining Greekness itself. As Nicholas Gage (from Epirus) says, "the landscape of Greece [...] is haunted",[7] while Peter Levi records his discovery of mythology as "a clue to the landscape, something that revealed a secret about daily life".[8] Travelling in the Peloponnese, Nikos Kazantzakis recorded that "the mission of the Greek mind has always been to illumine [...] the warm, dark, rich subconscious [...], to make it conscious [...] to give form to the formless".[9]

Although they became increasingly scripted, the *Karagiózis* performances were still valued for the fact that they emanated from oral culture. The thematic and organic connection between this folklorism and surrealism, which inevitably became a feature of the avant-garde in the 1940s, is clear if you acknowledge the similarity in their basic tenets: suspension of logical belief, an imaginative response to the phenomena, the uncanny and the surrender to the unconscious. Metamorphosis is one of the most striking aspects of both, leading one to suppose that, like surrealism, the changing shapes and identities in primitive folklore are part of a "peasant aesthetic" where *aisthísis* is "the roots of perception".

The most prominent features of modern Greek culture are firstly, the examination of the cultural heritage and of its present-day influence; and, secondly, the usefulness of the arts as a reflection of, and commentary upon, modern life: its *mores*, its passions, its manifestations in politics, religion, economics.

Greek culture bears a direct relationship to the phases of history which I described all too briefly in Chapter 2: independence, modernisation/westernisation, dictatorial suppression and correction, civil war and more dictatorship. And today, economic austerity. The basic premise of Greekness, the fundamental identity of the individual and the family, is the motive power of art.

Here, as in politics, we are in the realm of discord. Just as there was – and is – an ongoing dispute about modern Greece's connectedness with its classical past, so too in the arts there are question marks over how significant today are the tragic dramas and the sculptures which are a major element in the heritage. There will always be an anxiety about authenticity and continuity, especially when "authentic" classical art is so different from "authentic" demotic culture, from which springs so much contemporary art. Language into literature is one of the hallmarks of such art.

> I woke with this marble head in my hands;
> it exhausts my elbow and I don't know where to put it down.[10]

With these lines from "Mythistorema" (1934), George Seferis summed up the dilemma of the modern Greek poet weighed down (literally) by the burden of the past. The "marble head", representing the untouchable and enigmatic lien of the past, reappears in Theo Angelopoulos' 1998 film *Landscape in the Mist* as a broken marble hand in the sky above Thessaloniki, as a symbol of antiquity and its challenging secrets, as a young couple seeks a new life; forever admonishing, compelling, and both offering and retracting hope. (The lines are also quoted in Angelopoulos' 1980 film *Alexander the Great*, in which the head itself appears at the end of the film, like an epigraph which is both *alpha* and *omega*.) Andrew Horton tells us that "Angelopoulos has verified that the spirit of his films absolutely reflects the spirit of this [Seferis'] poem".[11]

Some decry the "backward look", as Frank O'Connor called it in Ireland, and Seferis and Elytis in Greece, because it is obsessed with the past. Yet where else but the past does one come from? It's a rear view mirror, a recognition that there *may* be truths to be elicited: we find it in Seamus Heaney's "Tollund" poems, in Brendan Kennelly's "My Dark Fathers", in Patrick Kavanagh's *The Great Hunger*. I call it a rear view mirror since a driver must always use it to check what is coming up from behind; history has a habit of doing just that, and overtaking.

Much of this "backward look" was enabled by the realisation, in the nineteenth century, by poets like Dionysios Solomos (a Zakynthiot who spent most of his life in Corfu and authored the text of the national anthem) that the old tavern ballads and the epic poetry, such as the Cretan *Erotókritos*, were a "source book" and passport for their own entry into modern Greece. And it has fuelled much of the desire by writers to regard the demotic, the life of the peasant and the village (or, today, the small urban community), as the thesaurus of their imagination and their confrontation with reality.

Previously, poetry had been founded on the central element in Greek rural society, the demotic song, which, as Linos Politis says, "is [...] the means by which the people gave the most authoritative expression to its world and to its personality".[12] Thus the transition from song-based poetry to prose was a challenge to continue to give expression to that world and that personality through the medium of prose. The genre involved a tight focus on sites such as the house, the village and the island, and generated a magical realism within the "concrete" of the site.

The general tenor of Greek literature is subject to the hegemony of the past, in which the sense of polemical failure is deeply imbued. As Vangelis Hatziyannidis says in his novel *Four Walls* (2000), "Some people are proud of their past; others embarrassed by it; some people are indifferent to it, while for others, the past is so important that they spend more time planning it than they do planning the future".[13]

It will be no surprise to you that I find, in contemporary litera-ture and cinema, a critical questioning of society and its norms. You might expect that in turning from a troubled politics to the theme of culture we might be entering a peaceful zone of creation (*poiésis*, from which we receive *poetry*). That would be a miscon-ception. To the extent that all art (even abstract) is representation-al, it figures a state or condition of society and is a reflection on society, and is therefore subject to the same disputes as the shape of laws, the design of education, the conception of decency. Greek culture is the expression of all the emotions of Greek people in their joy, sadness, argumentativeness, bewilderment, resistance to stereotype and thus their individuality and love of freedom. His-tory is once more up for discussion.

That is not to say that there is no beauty. Of course there is. But even the most remote, abstract beauty is a contested icon in its many aspects.

Migrant, Immigrant and Minority Cultures

"Greece is uniform both as a land and as a spirit", a Greek Prime Minister once stated; he was supported by a later Prime Minister, Andreas Papandreou in the 1990s, who expressed his concern that the Muslim minority in Greece's northeast (the only minority of-ficially recognised in Greece) might endanger "our integrity". Al-exander Kazamias uses these remarks to underline his argument that, officially, Greece would like to be homogenous ethnically and religiously, a "Helleno-Christian nation".[14] The need to achieve this was one of the unifying strategies of the independence movement, but to ignore the various cultural strands which constitute the overall tapestry of "Greek" culture is perverse and politically, as well as culturally, dangerous. The silence accorded to such minor-ity cultures is akin to the experience of the Irish composer today, expressed by Raymond Deane as "the honour of non-existence".[15]

Many Greeks would indeed like to think that their culture is pure and unique, but, like their language and their racial mixtures, their culture is adulterated and made more complex and challeng-ing because it embodies and reproduces many immigrations, of which the Turkish and Albanian are only the most obvious. As a central staging-post for Balkan and Levant migrations, it couldn't be otherwise. And as a racial soup-mix it has bred a heterogeneous culture. As Lawrence Durrell pointed out, "Greece [...] cannot have a single real Greek left (in the racial sense) after so many hundreds of years of war and resettlement; the present racial stocks are the fruit of countless invasions".[16] And each invasion brings its own culture.

In recent decades other, more persistent arrivals have disturbed the idea of Greekness: the Pontic refugees (from ancient Greek settlements around the Black Sea) after the collapse of the Soviet Union, many of whom speak a dialect incomprehensible to "Greek-Greeks", are a major factor in Greece rethinking its claim to a monoculture. Ovid was an outsider in his Pontic exile: the Pontics are outsiders in Greece today, and are made to feel it, as portrayed in films such as *From the Edge of the City* (1998, directed by Constantinos Giannaris), but also celebrated in films such as Angelopoulos' *Voyage to Kythera* (1984). But other cultures, represented by racial migrations of non-Greek peoples, such as political refugees from the Middle East, have also disturbed the supposed heterogeneity of Greekness. At least ten per cent of people living in Greece today are non-Greek.

As a "minority culture", women – for so long relegated to domestic devoirs and excluded from public discourse – have become a forceful and articulate presence in literature and drama, but, as Stratos Constantinidis points out, for a long time they shared the fate of homosexuals, Jews and Pontics as a minority with no voice and no representation.[17]

The term "culture" is all-embracing when used in the anthropological sense of a whole society, a catch-all term for the ubiquity of humankind. All human life is there. Well, almost. There is, however, a tapestry of another version of the orthodox humankind: the cultures of migrants whose lifestyles are perhaps the only remaining chattels to have survived the journey. These are indeed marginal, tangential to the larger Greek picture, but they are the vital element, the battered cardboard suitcase which the migrant holds close to his heart, and which we see in Theo Angelopoulos' film *The Weeping Meadow*, which we hear in the *Rebétiko* songs, which we read in accounts of folk caught up in the deracination of the Anatolian Catastrophe. The title of Thea Halo's memoir *Not Even My Name* spells out the lives which (in this case Pontic) migrants leave behind.

Migrants, especially asylum-seekers, are a political hot potato, due mainly to the fact that Greece is one of the most penetrable points of entry to the European landmass. But they are also cold potato because Greece tends to turn its back on what it hopes is merely passing through. The lessons of 1922 have yet to be learned. The xenophobic behaviour of Golden Dawn towards immigrants is one vicious face of this blindness, but culturally Greek-Greeks would like to ignore not merely these recent epiphanies but also the Italian, Turkish and Albanian elements within them. The fact that a migrant is uninvited and probably illegal should not be a cultural problem. The "provocative indifference" of the authorities to illegal immigrants,[18] is thus complemented by a similar indifference to their cultures.

The transhumant shepherds, though diminishing in number, have little regard for the borders which increasingly restrict their lives – any more than the Sámi peoples of Lapland care for the four national frontiers which they seasonally traverse. But if it had not been for John Campbell's 1964 study of the Sarakatsani in Epirus their culture, too, might have been ignored by purists.

Even the suppression of "Left" culture under successive fascist regimes, and the banishment of poets and composers, amounts to a cultural version of a mindset which fears and therefore attacks the "other", while the return of those children, now adult, who were sent away during the Civil War, is another discordant note in the comfort of the preferred music.[19]

Karagiózis Theatre

In modern Greece, popular culture ranges from the still-vibrant *Karagiózis* theatre to the avant-garde cinema of Angelopoulos, whose cinematic lighting techniques owe something to those of *Karagiózis*.

The *Karagiózis* tradition has survived because, like modern-day productions of the classical tragedies, it has adapted to circumstances. The character of Karagiózis has been described (by a film critic) as "an ugly, long-nosed, bug-eyed [...], hunchbacked, poor and ragged Greek" but who nevertheless "triumphs over his opponents through cunning and trickery".[20] The traditional *Karagiózis* shadow- or puppet-theatre, like the "Punch and Judy" puppets, has strong resemblances to the *commedia dell'arte* of sixteenth century Italy in its set of stock characters; like the *commedia dell'arte*, *Karagiózis* spread widely, in this case throughout the lands of the Ottoman empire in which it originated, with the diminutive hero confronting invaders, cheats and bullies.

Karagiózis itself (I am referring to the generic title of the theatre, rather than to the eponymous hero) as an art form – and a very *laic* or roots-based art form – is, despite its centrality in Greek culture, in fact of Turkish origin: the central character, *Karagöz* in Turkish, means "dark-eyed". It was adopted by Greek people who changed its stock personnel so that they became representative of peasant society, and reflected their experience under oppressive rule and unscrupulous adventurers.

While Karagiózis is undeniably a crude, crooked, deceitful character, he is nevertheless accepted as being totally and honourably Greek by virtue of his fidelity to basic values. We are back once again in the typical, or stereotypical, household. Perhaps this tells us something about Greek psychology: that the not-so-beautiful and the not-so-honest man can rise above his base nature in order to fulfil a necessary and splendid destiny in the service of others who, like him, are powerless and, psychically perhaps, deformed.

As Lawrence Durrell, witnessing a performance in Corfu in the 1930s, commented, the Greek national character "is based on the idea of the impoverished and downtrodden little man (*kosmákis*) getting the better of the world around him by sheer cunning. Add to this the salt of a self-deprecating humour and you have the immortal Greek." Of Karagiózis he says, "the disturber of social justice, he never does anything to alienate the audience, and his political licence is almost absolute" – Durrell observes that even under the Metaxas dictatorship, *Karagiózis* was not banned.[21]

Karagiózis has been taken so deeply to the heart of Greek performance as to be termed "the national theatre of Greece".[22] It is, of course, not merely social but also political in that it allows for a spirit of defiance (Karagiózis, the diminutive folk hero, against the "Goliath" of the Ottomans) and in later times has been adapted to many socio-political situations. Karagiózis as "Goliath", "Quixote", "Jack-the-Giant-Killer" transcends his fundamental nature: he is the little man who becomes great by virtue of his humanity and courage, plus a large measure of cunning which is integral to the Greek social endeavour.

In addition to Karagiózis himself, its repertory includes *Hatziavatis* (the Sancho Panza to Karagiózis' Quixote), *Barba Yiorgos*, a rough-and-ready mountaineer, a *Jew* (stereotypically mean, resourceful and obsequious), the *Pasha*, representing the Turkish ruling class, *Veli Gekas*, a local policeman (sometimes Albanian), and *Aglaía*, Karagiozis's nagging wife.

Where Karagiózis is a rogue, Hatziavatis is honest and industrious; they are perfectly matched and play off one another. In 1831, Hatziavatis was even cast in the allegorical role of Kapodistrias, such was the political application of this popular art form in the year of Kapodistrias' assassination.

These are the same villagers and functionaries whom we meet in Karkavitsas' novel *The Beggar* and are valuable for the same reason: they catch the mood of basic Greek society at a fulcral or transitional point in history, as the traditional society morphed slowly into a more modern version. It carries with it the concepts of individuality, typecasting, base and noble feelings and actions: a crude but panoramic representation of life in the village, its emotions, tensions and ambitions.

Songs from the repertory entered popular folklore, just as people today might sing a number from a contemporary musical, while some of the characters' stock expressions and gestures were incorporated into everyday speech and behaviour. The word *karagiózilíki* means capering or clowning, and "*Ti karagiózilíki!*" means "what a performance!"; "*mi ginessi karagiózis*" means "don't make a fool of yourself" and if someone tries to trick you, you say "he tried to play Karagiózis with me!" Yet despite these somewhat derogatory characterisations, Karagiózis is still loved and treasured because he incorporates harmless fun and heroic energy.

Some characters from the Karagiózis shadow-theatre, as depicted on modern matchboxes. From left: Ο Χατξηαβάτης (Hatziavatis), Ο Αλή Πασάς (Ali Pasha), Ο Καραγκιόζης (Karagiózis), Η Αγλαία (Aglaía), Ο Εβραίος (the Jew – Ebraios).

In the nineteenth century the *Karagiózis* movement was a powerful factor in reinforcing peasant adherence to the basic qualities of Greekness rather than the westernising influences increasingly evident in manners, mind and morals. As a "political" animal with a wild streak of antinomianism, *Karagiózis* has been seen as a unifying force between city and mountain, the *klepht* and the citizen.[23] In 1901, *Karagiózis* was described by the newspaper *Estia* as "an entire Democracy [...] social fences collapse [...] a new populism, a new socialism".[24]

Durrell summed it up as

> on this little dazzling screen you have the whole laic mystery of Greece which has been so long dormant in the mountains and islands – in the groves and valleys of the archipelago. You have the spirit and the unconquerable adaptability of the Greek who has penetrated with the leaven of his mercuric irony and humour into every quarter of the globe.[25]

This value was later transmuted into a number of similar situations, so that *Karagiózis* continued to uphold the peasant traditions and, more importantly, realities. In the 1800s this was particularly sensitive and, partly to ensure that performances were not politically subversive, partly to prohibit obscenity (like Punch, Karagiózis was, shall we say, priapically endowed) *Karagiózis* came under government regulations which made the local police responsible for its surveillance.

Karagiózis came to be regarded as subversive precisely because it featured the little man triumphing over adversity and has even been described as "agit prop". In this respect it has extensive similarities with another Turko-Greek import, the *Rebétiko* music from Anatolia.

It's impossible to establish definitively how many versions of the *Karagiózis* texts there have been, but it is estimated that the 280 extant represent perhaps twice as many. They often incorporated themes from contemporary melodramas of the Greco-Turkish and Balkan wars. Modernisation of scripts has gone as far as "Karagiózis to the Moon". The scripts were always subject to modification to suit local circumstances. In Corfu in 2002, when the Durrell School presented performances by the legendary Evgenio Spatharis (son of the even more legendary Sotiris Spatharis), the *maestro* tailored his performance to the fact that the show was sponsored by Coca-Cola, the purveyor of *Amitá* orange juice, incorporating frequent references to *Amitá* as a nourishing and stimulating beverage – a 45-minute commercial worth every *lepta* of the sponsor's investment.

Today, one can buy *Karagiózis* puppet kits; in the 1970s and 1980s ERT (the national broadcaster) carried a television series and even today the most popular brand of safety matches depicts characters from the repertory.

Rebétiko Music

The origin of the music genre of *rebétiko* is claimed by two factions: one insists that it is Anatolian in character and culture and came to Greece after the Catastrophe; the other, that it was a Greek genre, flourishing in the cities of Piraeus, Thessaloniki and Volos (ports which were a natural location for urban disenchantment). The compromise is that it existed in both Greece and Greek Anatolia, but the advent of a disproportionate number of musicians in the 1920s led to an exponential growth in its presence in all major cities.

On one major point, all are agreed: that *rebétiko* is the music (songs and dances) of the underdog, the dispossessed, the downtrodden and that the music is therefore characterised by songs of loss and resistance – from which it derives its continuing political strength.

The ρεμπέτης (*rebétis*) is an "outcast", and *rebétikos* is the behaviour of the *rebétis*. The word has other connotations: *rebeskés* are rascals, and *rébelos* is an idler. All of these meanings can be read into the corpus of *rebétiko* culture.

The genre can be traced to the mid-1800s and was exclusively the music of "those who lived outside the accepted standards of society and who showed contempt for the establishment in all its forms". The *rebétes* – the singers – was an argot term for "persons embodying various kinds of subcultural attitudes and behaviour",[26] while the *mángas* (a term of Turkish-Albanian origin), the hard man of the underworld, had all the characteristics of the mountain *klepht*. The *mángas* was an habitué of the Psirri area of central Athens, now gentrified but until recently a no-go area of malcontents where groups of *Kontsavakídes* (soulmates of the *mánges*) held court.

Resistance to authority was therefore one of its hallmarks, as were the "jail songs" of those who had unsuccessfully defied the law. Gail Holst has written that "it is this quality of flair, this posture of defiance in the face of poverty, repression and even death, which seems to me the most attractive feature of *mangas* society".[27] It has been said that "the womb of *rebétiko* was the jail and the hashhouse",[28] where improvisation was the norm. It has a cousin in the underground nature of Irish traditional music after 1690 which "provid[ed] a fertile ground for revolt, a corrosive subversive idiom".[29]

The singer (*rebétis*) has been defined as "the suffering, wronged, hunted man", "a man who had a sorrow and threw it out".[30] *Rebétiko* was the expression of those who had loved and lost, who had dreamed and woken up to reality, but all of whom had the indomitable will to survive.

Rebétiko therefore had all the characteristics of the Greek spirit, as far as readiness for the *agón* was concerned: a voice from the bottom of the heap, semi-outlaw status, rejection of outside influence and, with the Anatolian influx, the memory of exile.

It is little wonder that *rebétiko* was banned under the Metaxas regime, the Nazis, during the civil war and under the Colonels. As Nick Papandreou observes, "a man carrying a bouzouki in the late 1940s stood a strong chance of being stopped by the police and questioned about his habits".[31]

The Smyrniot variety was more oriental in sound, with a chromatic scale that facilitated half- and quarter-tones. It was this "oriental" tone which purists later decried, in attempting to deny that *rebétiko* could be of Turkish origin in a culture ridding itself of vestiges of foreign rule and working to a nationalist agenda. Yet, like *karagiózis*, its Turkish origin continues to manifest itself, not least in the long memories of those who hanker after their Anatolian roots.

Rebétiko was in fact born in Smyrna, a mixture, as is so much in modern Greek culture, of Greek and Turkish, plus Armenian, Jewish and Bulgarian: a mosaic of musics, melded fortuitously into one cultural form.

Like the traditional musics of many other colonised peoples – for example Ireland – *rebétiko* accommodated itself to the imperialism of the colonisers. Anatolian *rebétes* sang in both Greek and Turkish, an in-betweenness enjoyed by those who were neither. The Turkish instruments such as the *oud* (a form of lute), the *kanun* and the *santoúri* (forms of zither or cembalo) became the vehicle of *rebétiko*.

The songs of love and loss (the same category in which the patriotic songs of the Irishman Thomas Moore are found)[32] are informed by a particular argot of the *rebétes*, which includes the street-slang of the *mángas*.

Rebétiko was also associated with hashish – indeed, in "orthodox" *rebétiko* circles the two complement one another – and the locale also featured gaming-houses and brothels. Stolen goods were part of its currency.

It has been argued that *rebétiko* was close to drugs in that its songs "offer an escape into another sphere of feeling, perceiving and relating, a respite from life's normal toughness".[33] This, too, seems a natural handmaiden to the singer whose experience of toughness (austerity) was to be transcended through song into an "other" sphere, the mode of thinking which underlay the mode of behaviour of the *mángas*.

What seemed to be anti-social in "respectable" society was the norm within the underworld, and therefore carried with it its own loyalties, obligations and sense of honour (among thieves).

Like the *Karagiózis* tradition, *rebétiko* originated in an oral culture. It was only with the opening of the commercial recording era in the 1920s that its "compositions" began to lose their idiosyncrasy and spontaneity and to become stylised, with the addition of the piano and what is now seen as a "typical" Greek instrument, the *bouzouki*, but at that time regarded as of doubtful authenticity. Greeks even began to speak of "going to the *bouzoukía*" rather than to a *rebétiko* session.

Yona Stamatis opens her 2011 doctoral thesis with the quotation from Pavlos Vassiliou, "*Rebétiko* is the truest expression of the Greek people".[34] If other artists (Vassiliou is a master *rebétis*) have sought the essence of the Greek people (I'm thinking of Seferis, Elytis and Theodorakis, whom we shall see later in this chapter and in the next) *rebétiko* can clearly argue its way into the Greekness or *ellinikótita* by which the national spirit is measured. But how this accommodation was to be arrived at, in the stormy process of establishing a consciousness of national identity, was predictably contested. How does one domesticate a wildcat? The history of the development of *rebétiko*, from its rawness in the taverns of Smyrna, Piraeus and Volos, to acceptance in the house of Greek music, finds Theodorakis at its centre.

In *Epitáphios*, Theodorakis, in Nick Papandreou's words, "succeeded in linking the old and dying world of the *rebétes* to the new world of politics". This was tantamount to the outlaw being officially unofficial, receiving some kind of ambiguous pardon. As an underworld culture, it found, with Theodorakis, "an overtly political character".[35] Perhaps the fact that his mother came from Smyrna had something to do with it.

The film *Rembetiko* (1984, directed by Costas Ferris) shows the genre from its Anatolian origins to the poverty and social ostracism the refugees encountered in mainland Greece. From the 1919 ill-founded anticipation of victory over the Turks, comes joy and self-congratultion; from the 1922 catastrophe comes exile, poverty, squalor, prostitution which could just as well be the setting for *From the Edge of the City* depicting the Pontine Greeks. The refugees bring only their music, and cling to it as their cultural imprint – apart from the music, they have nothing: for the exiles, it is now the vehicle for grief and despair, in a cyclic experience: to grieve is to sing is to grieve.

Rebétiko thus had a therapeutic function: the music of the underdog was both a statement of buried identity and an attempt to transcend it.

The heyday of *rebétiko* was also the day of its decline, as it became popular with the bourgeoisie and encapsulated in a performance style – and in performance spaces – accessible to the middle classes: a gentrification of a style which, at its roots, rejected respectability. Only in very few establishments, such as Pavlos Vassiliou's *Rebetiki Istoría* in Athens, is the old-style still to be heard. It is, today, "public, respectable entertainment"[36] of the kind offered to tourists and shunned by purists (as in the Irish traditional music fraternity). Vassiliou's "defensive musical nationalism" is a form of separation which defies official Greekness as much as it shuns "commodification and Europeanization".[37] Today, with "social" performance and recordings of *rebétiko* widely available, there is a nostalgia for the earliest extant recordings from the 1900s "as sacred cultural treasures".[38]

In the view of Yona Stamatis, *rebétiko* has been "a pawn in national identity debates throughout the twentieth century". It is typical of the loyalties of Greeks to their separate, originary traditions, that *rebétiko* could be at one and the same time "emblematic of an ideal Greekness" and a "corruptive force".[39] If it were not so, one might well suspect that a homogeneity of Greek culture had been imposed by a new regime of art-police. That *rebétiko* as an evolving art form is dead does not diminish its continuing presence in Greek cultural life. *Rebétiko* has achieved such a point of respectability that it was played at the opening ceremony of the 2004 Olympic Games.

Myth and History

The eighteenth century poet and novelist Novalis said that "novels arise out of the shortcomings of history". Many treatises might take that statement and run with it: the relationship of fact and fiction, the *lacunae* of memory, the need for invention. But in the case of Greece the statement directs us towards the ontology of the novel itself; is it fact or is it fiction? To Novalis we might add the contemporary English poet Hugo Williams who admits that "writing is the disguise of ignorance",[40] his point being that, in the absence of fact or realities, the writer *invents* (in the sense of *finds* or *dis-covers*) other truths.

And we might even go a step further and add Nikos Kazantzakis, who recorded that "my heart scream[s] because I am not creating art".[41] Perhaps he meant that the mere act of creation was the inescapable function of the writer, or perhaps something deeper: that by writing one bears witness to one's experience: *testimonio*, or in both classical and modern Greek *martiría*.[42] This can take on a very serious political dimension.

The difficulty, for non-Greeks, arises from the word for "novel": *mythistórima*, a meeting-point of myth and history or, put another way, the attempt to interpret myth (which may be history) and history (which may be myth). Roderick Beaton notes that in inventing the term Adamantios Korais identified "the combination of history with myth, of timeless story-pattern with linear, time-bound narrative".[43] This mixed marriage of the timeless with the linear is at the heart of the dilemma of how to interpret and project Greekness for western minds.

Beaton tells us that the earliest Greek works of the modern era (from 1834) were based "on the belief of direct continuity from antiquity", which was also the founding discipline of the emergent nation-state. But, as will be obvious, novelists (and short-story writers) could not be expected to subscribe indefinitely to such a myth. Engagement with the reality of the developing state, as in other art forms, necessitated the use of imagination in the creation of "myth-histories" which were forward- as well as backward-looking, imaginative zones in which possible worlds were examined and either embraced or discarded. Thus the sensitive writer put down markers on both history and future, on what was possible in relation to what was permissible. The literary imagination became a place of questioning, of loving and disavowal.

If Greek writers had not created "myth-histories" which engaged with history past and present, they would have placed themselves outside the national project of defining and refining Greekness. As I have written elsewhere, modern Greek writing is an experiment in living.[44] The experiment involves measuring the imagination and its desires against the social and political realities. Since, as I have continuously made clear, the Greek spirit demands the freedom of dissent, it is therefore likely that a writer, whose imagination (as in the conscience of his "real" life) is disturbed by dictatorships or other threats to imaginative freedom, will move from the centre to the left. In 1984 Declan Kiberd saw that there was not yet any study explaining why Irish literature was left-wing.[45] It would be difficult for any study of Greek literature *not* to engage in such an explanation. In Greece, entire generations of writers have asserted their right to comment adversely on adversity by means of realist, allegorical or elliptical novels, stories and poems – the same strategy adopted by writers under other, similarly oppressive, regimes.[46]

Perhaps the most refreshing aspect of both Greek and Irish literature (and film) is their attention to the lives, aspirations, anxieties, comedies and tragedies of ordinary folk rather than the "grand lines" depicting the progress of victory. It is these little people, often far removed from the centres of power, or buried deep beneath the weight of national politics, whose lives, when recorded, illustrate the larger picture: history, in literature, is large writ small.

The poet Nikos Gatsos (1911-92) said to Peter Levi "Talent is nothing. We have hundreds of them. What we need is something else".[47] The "something else" is the means of expression, underpinned by talent but deriving its relevance and energy from a meeting of culture and society. It has become the consuming passion and quest of modern Greek artists: to conceive of "something else" which is more than mere talent and can live within the millennia of Greek creativity.

Since Gatsos said that (in the 1960s) there has been a renewal of the arts in which that engagement has been increasingly evident and increasingly profound – in the cinema of Angelopoulos, in the stories of Ersi Sotiropoulos,[48] in the music of Mikis Theodorakis, and in the resurgence of *rebétiko*.

To say that the Greeks are creators – poets – is, as Gatsos said, a commonplace; to say that their creativity is often stifled by procedure is almost as true (we have seen evidence of it in the silence of writers under the junta). It is inhibited, for example, by economic conditions, and results in the same kind of protest as austerity produces in Syntagma Square.

Whereas the general popular sympathy with the left has been traditionally censored, suppressed and marginalised, in the arts, the role of dissent and satire seems almost to constitute their *raison d'être*.

In the case of the arts it is perhaps less strident and less overt, but in February 2014 the then Minister of Culture was booed off-stage (in a protest organised by the "Mavili Collective")[49] at a conference on "Financing Creativity"; the protesters said "the Greek state is increasingly abandoning its support of contemporary culture" – a criticism that arts organisations have recently made in the Irish context, too. The minister was derided when he stated "culture is not only our national identity but also our national pride".[50] As I have described in Chapter 6, the use of culture as a tool of "national pride" was disastrously demonstrated in the 2014 tourism promotion.

There is a forked path for Greek writers, leading in one direction to nostalgia and a celebration of the primitive, and in the other to a confrontation with the forces which threaten this primitive spirit and the harsh reality of political turmoil which is never far from the surface of the Greek mind. The literal meaning of *nostalgia* – the pain (*algos*) of the journey home (*nostos*) – makes it clear that to revisit (and to revive) the pristine, and to attempt to find therein a refreshing spirit (the chief characteristics of Seferis and Elytis) is a dangerous, possibly self-deluding, path. But the other route, towards confrontation, is also dangerous and possibly self-destructive, such as we see in the internal exile of poets such as Yannis Ritsos under authoritarian regimes.

Although my natural inclination is towards the novel and the short story, the issue of poetry is equally pressing in Greece, not least because two of Greece's most prominent twentieth century writers (and its Nobel laureates) were poets. Together and separately, Seferis and Elytis shaped the conscience of modern Greek aesthetics.

Seferis was an exile from paradise. Greece to him, as to many Smyrniots, was an "other" country, yet as a career diplomat he found himself re-presenting the political reality internationally. As a poet, he embraced a regained paradise in his glorification of the "spirit of place", so much so that, in my atheistic view, he was in danger of identifying "god" with *tópos*, with deifying Greece itself in a supreme effort to synthesise the old and the new, the perduring and the incursive.

Politically, as a diplomat, he could have no politics other than those of his masters, but, as we have seen, his anti-junta broadcast aligned him with the Left (above, p. 60). In fact the more one deciphers the texts of the so-called "Left", the more inclined one is to detect an insistence that only in the privacy of the house, only by sitting at the hearth (*estía*) could Greece be rescued from foreign *diktats*; that the stability insisted on by the "right" or the "fascists" must be opposed with the story, the *mythistórima*, of the individual, bringing always back to the roots, the radical, the argument as to who Greeks really are, and in what Greekness consists. As a diplomat, the truths of geopolitics would be reinforced whatever inner truths were already in Seferis' DNA: you cannot (or should not?) wear *fustanella* when presenting your credentials to the Queen of England.[51]

Naturally, this argument involved – and still involves – a debate between tradition and modernisation, between western ways of thinking and "the other mind". The kernel of the difficulty, for the western mind, is to appreciate and accommodate the intense importance of landscape as a residuary of truth and permanence. For city dwellers in particular, the idea that one can achieve, or simply perceive, serenity in a landscape, in a primeval *tópos* such as, in Ireland, Roundstone Bog or the rugged character of the Aran islands, or in Greece the "unspoilt" islands of the Aegean, sometimes becomes risible, and certainly unimaginable. But even Greek city-dwellers – for example, in the endless drab and desultory suburbs of Athens – retain an allegiance to their native village or island of origin.

For Seferis, this was paramount. He tried to build a religion out of it, even though he was, by experience, a cosmopolitan. His experience in the World War and Civil War had expanded his view that such tragedies could be avoided by resort to places in which they had no currency.

It is dangerous to assume that poets' appeals to the radical identity of Greece are necessarily narcissistic and escapist. When Elytis said, "Western modernist models are sensitive only to the ways of logic and surface reality, and thus unreceptive to the mystic voice and metaphysical force that [...] passes behind and through things",[52] he could be accused of fudging the issue of modernity and the *realpolitik* that affected poetry as much as any other part of society. But such a criticism would ignore the fact that poets like Elytis and Seferis were striving to find in this "mystic voice" a possible route to a new society, which would reflect Greekness in all its aspects and prioritise it above western notions of identity.

I think many westerners, unwilling to explore the "other mind", reject, and perhaps laugh at, terms such as "mystic voice", which they perceive as hopelessly old-fashioned. I myself disclaim any interest in a "mysticism" which has any theology as its origin, but am willing to accept, and immerse myself in, any secret which we might not otherwise discover. I am willing to put my trust in poetry, not in gods. (To put it another way, I would not believe in any god who would have me as its creation.) This does not prevent me from experiencing the "spirit of place", maybe in an olive grove, on a mountain-side, in a cove, especially if the experience is augmented, as I once heard it on a hillside near Delphi, by a shepherd playing on the pan-pipes.

Elytis also wrote: "I and my generation have attempted to find the true face of Greece. This was necessary because [...it] had been represented as Europeans saw Greece."[53] Philip Sherrard comments that Elytis, with the help of surrealist techniques, freed his imagination "from the need to pay attention to the logical and pragmatic way of looking at things by which the modern western mentality was dominated".[54] For Elytis, "the true poet [...] makes the invisible visible".[55]

Sherrard says the same (and more) in his own response to Greece, which was prompted in his case by his encounter with Elytis. "The world of the imagination – the world of incorporeal images – is a world in its own right [...] It is the imaginative reality of things that takes precedence over their material and outward appearance." The "dualism between the world of the senses and what is called the supernatural world" is overcome by "revealing to us the numinous or the mystical aspect of things".

For Seferis, the selfhood of the Greek "is a part of the greater nature which is Hellenic".[56] He conceived of "Hellenic Hellenism" as distinct from the Hellenism perceived by the outsider. Hellenic Hellenism was the irreducible and inalienable core of Greekness. "This particular Hellenism will only show its face when the Greece of today has acquired its own real intellectual character and features". (It is significant that Seferis wrote this in 1938, during the Metaxas dictatorship.)

Kazantzakis would agree, decrying the European view of Hellenism "with its worship of logic and the belly, with its miserable knowledge and its expedient little certainties".[57] His criticism of western superficiality is part of the reaction among many writers to the "Americanisation" of Greece through political influence and post-war financial aid. They looked back to an idea of pre-Turkish and pre-Nazi Hellenism which might be affirmative. Vangelis Calotychos points to Elytis' *Axion Esti* (1959) as "the last *magnum opus* of Greek poetry"[58] which espoused the "Byzantine and Orthodox vision" as the antidote to the unpalatable aspects of modernism.

Despite the acknowledged progress in material terms, Zissimos Lorenzatos viewed and judged the island life as the embodiment of the "real" Greece. In an echo of all those who have written of a *deus loci*, or a "spirit of place", Lorenzatos insisted, as did Papadiamandis before him, that there are "certain inner laws operative within the man who is native to a place" and that these are non-negotiable in any organically healthy society. They make man "one with the terrestrial, the chthonic and the heavenly simultaneously", a cyclic phenomenon which "determines the meaning of life".[59] He writes of "the farmer and the fisherman [...] the alpha and omega of this land and its true aristocracy". Little doubt as to where his loyalties and perceptions were rooted.

And we should not be deaf to his shrewd judgements on the Greece of his own time which apply so aptly to our own, when he speaks sarcastically of "miracle cures with which to treat an entire nation". Could he have foreseen the present Greek dilemma? If he had been shown Greece today, would he have said "I told you so"? When he refers (in 1979) to "the whole series of disasters with which our country has paid and is paying for its fallacies or its other willful, costly and unnecessary follies", was he simply setting the scene for today's confusion and despair? This seems to be particularly true of the ever-widening chasm between the culture of the cities and that of their hinterland, from which, in Lorenzatos' terms, essential Greekness is derived. And (even though he was speaking of Russian influence on the Greece of 1979) it is frighteningly true of a Greece which, today, is "given over wholeheartedly to foreign patrons".

If Lorenzatos is conservative and cynical, he nevertheless expresses a truth about Greece ancient and modern when he quotes a Turkish proverb, "the Greek's wisdom comes after the event".

Kazantzakis finds a "god" in the natural world – in men, women, children, the sea, the wind, in a desolate mountain, in sheep and shepherds, in storms and sunshine, in the sense of the erotic – and, as such, "god" is a cleansing, purifying force, the essence of Greece: "the almighty soul of Romiosini"[60] which gives order to his "inner chaos". While, again, I step back from such a faith, I totally respect it when Kazantzakis, in company with Seferis and Elytis, says, "Everything in the azure air – stones and trees and people – breathed in god-given serenity, like symbols".[61] Perhaps I can accept the symbols without the entity they are supposed to represent. And I would find it easier to accept a *pantheon* (meaning *all the gods*) that included Demeter (the corn-goddess), Selene (goddess of the moon), Dionysus (wine and ecstasy), Hecate (wealth and good luck), than any monotheistic system. But I would not be so keen on Hades, and I have never thought highly of Zeus.[62] After all, as the short stories of Papadiamandis show us, monotheism is only grafted as a veneer onto the pagan virtues and vices which, subhumously, reside in the unploughed fields.

The most prominent characteristic of Kazantzakis was his un-compromising nature. His title "Freedom or Death" sums it up: if one cannot be free, and articulate one's freedom, then one would be better dead.

At the age of thirty-one (in 1924), he wrote his "Apology" (in answer to his arrest on charges of subversive behaviour). One does not need to be a Marxist or an anarchist to see that Kazantzakis was an unredeemable socialist, analysing a system that had ob-tained in Greece for a century and which was unsuited to both the new European inclinations or a changing landscape of social thought. His portrayal of society, especially in the light of the Civil War, engendered both resistance and disillusion which he retained until his death in 1957. He wrote in 1924, "what class is going to succeed the bourgeois system? I have the adamantine conviction that it will be the working class: workers, farmers, people produc-tive in the spirit". Dream on. But he also imagined that "in Greece [...] we have remained extraordinarily backward. There is probably very little time left to adapt ourselves to an international rhythm quicker than the rhythm of Greek necessity." (He might have added, "we have no word to express the same sense of urgency as *mañana*.") Reality caused him, as both a novelist and a polemicist, to temper his vision of the desired revolution: "My aim has been to make as many people contemplate more profoundly the histori-cal moment we are experiencing and prepare themselves for the rebirth of their individual and social life: a psychological rebirth first of all, of course; and then a spiritual and social one; and finally (in time) an economic and political one".[63]

We must remember that he was writing in the immediate af-termath of the Anatolian Catastrophe, when the violent end of the *Megáli Idéa* enrolled all Greeks in a re-imagining and re-defining of their national identity, reflected, in poetry, in the emergence of a new generation of socially conscious poets and novelists such as Seferis, Elytis and Gatsos.

Twenty years later (1946), Kazantzakis was still asking "can literature, art or theoretical thought influence the present movement of history? Or do they merely mirror existing conditions?"[64] At that time he was regarded as one of the leading intellectuals in literature. It has been suggested that he might have seen himself as a latter-day Kapodistrias on whom, as we have seen, he wrote an allegorical play. Theodorakis would also come to represent the same icon of hope and protest. Is it a coincidence that they were both Cretans, from the same island as Venizelos?

Kazantzakis was an ambitious man, who matched his desire to emulate the world's great novelists with his messianic role in stirring the conscience of Greece. Like Seferis, he was passionately intrigued by the landscape, as reflected in his "Travels in Greece" which were confined to the Peloponnese and, like Seferis, this led to a spirituality which was not inconsistent with his socialism.

His relevance to world literature came late: he was sixty-three when *Zorba* (the original title was *The Life and Times of Alexis Zorba*) was published, and he followed it with six further novels, of which *The Fratricides* (1949) is the most acerbic, even cruel, and *Freedom or Death* (1949-51) the most allegorical and didactic.[65]

With both Seferis and Elytis we have to understand that they cherished, but did not worship, a pre-modern Greekness which, when the "specifics" of everyday life had inevitably changed the demography and behaviour of Greek people, "the rocks remain" – to borrow Gavin Maxwell's term. Their *agón* was with the entry of the "nation-state" into the pre-modern, and with two areas of conflict: firstly, between pre-modern and modern, and secondly between Greekness and the world.

For example, Yiorgos (or George) Theotokas believed that Greeks should "throw our byzantine and balkan traditions into the sea and find a new way".[66] This was especially necessary after the death of the *Megáli Idéa* and the consequent realisation that the quest for a national identity necessitated another route towards meaning and consensus.

Yiorgos Chouliaras observes that in recent decades "differences of dress, food, the built environment, furnishings, everyday behaviors, and, in general, various attributes of cultural distinction have been losing specificity".[66] The cardinal point is that, nevertheless, writing has *not* lost specificity; it has remained subject to the same influences which have characterised it throughout the nineteenth and twentieth centuries, in its questioning of Greek identity and destiny, its exploration of modernism, and its insistence on speaking the truth as the writer sees it. In this, it has been a commentary on not only the "everyday behaviors" of Greek society but also its *mores*, its political persuasions and its assertion of freedom(s).

Chouliaras believes that a distinct, unambiguous culture "entered its swan-song phase some time ago". While acknowledging his argument that "the maintenance of a 'traditional' culture is conceivable only in cultural theme parks", and his further argument that, in terms of popular culture and the consumption of cultural commodities, the products available are increasingly non-Greek (for example, television shows such as soap operas), it is difficult to follow him to the conclusion that Greek culture must adapt and renew itself in order to survive. His point is damaged, I think, by his observation that "mainstream national culture" is identified by what enjoys "popular and official acceptance" and that the mainstream tends to accommodate the marginal. The lessons of postwar literature suggest that many writers have remained marginal, lacking "official acceptance" during times of political suppression, while the role of writers, filmmakers and visual artists as commentators obliges them to stand outside the mainstream, and to define their own norms, either in association with, or in conflict with, dominant society. It is this capacity for dissent which shows the artist as an integrated member of the "*Ochi*" community rather than a willing communicant in popular culture. It is in the contested identities, themes and *topoi* that art thrives in any community, and from these it derives both its strength and its purpose.

Perhaps Chouliaras demonstrates most clearly his view of "official acceptance" in his wry observation that "a cultural history of those buried at public expense ever since the creation of the modern Greek state would tell us more than any speculation about

what has been official and mainstream and what has been marginal".

Alexandros Papadiamandis

It is a small step, both imaginatively and intellectually, from Seferis's insistence on the "spirit of place" to the deep-seated Greek
belief in the supernatural. Whether or not one believes that "gods"
are immanent in the landscape, Greeks certainly believe in a power which is more than natural, and which defies linear reason. We
may call it "supernatural", but it inheres in a folklore which persists
in manifesting itself to the present day. Votive offerings, designed
for example to bring pregnancy to barren women, are less visible
than when I first visited Greece fifty years ago, but the belief in
their efficacy is undiluted.

There is little discernible difference between the peasants' belief in the supernatural, as described by Karkavitsas in *The Beggar*,
and that which maintains a presence in contemporary novels such
as Yiorgi Yatromanolakis' *The Spiritual Meadow* (1974) or *The
History of a Vendetta* (1982). *The Spiritual Meadow*, in which a
man witnesses his past and future life in the dream-like context of
Greek history and culture during a period of twenty-four hours,
is one of the most compelling treatments of this suspension of
time and also of place. Yeats bears repetition here: "this world and
the other are not widely sundered". As Juliet du Boulay explains,
"the Hellenic world of the dead [...] is overwhelmingly present in
the villagers' consciousness in the period immediately following
a death"[68] while Philip Sherrard believed that there are parallel
worlds in which knowledge of reality commute between them by
accessing images that are extra-sensory. The state after death is not
"the next world" or an "afterworld" but an "other" world present in,
and parallel with, the world of the living.

Between Karkavitsas and Yatromanolakis we have the monumental work of Papadiamandis, whose world-view can be summed
up as: sky, sea, land and the inexplicable. In this, as I have written
elsewhere, he has an Irish parallel in the short stories of Aran by
Liam O'Flaherty.[69]

"Before the ridge of Serifos, as the sun rises, the guns of all the great world theories fall silent," wrote Elytis. "The mind is overcome by a few waves and some rocks; absurd perhaps but nevertheless sufficient to reveal man in his true dimensions."[70] The same might be said of man, land and sea in Skíathos, the home, both real and imagined, of Alexandros Papadiamandis (1851-1911).

Papadiamandis was the son of an Orthodox priest, and was imbued by both the spirit of Greek Christianity and the year-round cycle of observance and celebration to which it gave rise. At one point he went to Mount Athos (in whose "shadow", or *ískios*, his own island lay) with the intention of becoming a monk, but instead went to Athens for further education. Thereafter, determined to be a writer, he lived in comparative poverty, shackled to the city by the need to earn a journalistic living, but with his mind populated by the peasants and priests of Skíathos, where he returned three years before his death and in which he sees, with Homeric eyes, the sea's intimate relationship with the garden toiled by man: man, sea and earth in symbiosis constitute the "boundless garden".

Papadiamandis earned his living as a translator for Greek newspapers, and as such he is regarded by Roderick Beaton as "Greece's first fully professional writer".[71] He was admired by Cavafy and Seferis and by Elytis, who bracketed him with Solomos as the two turning points of modern Greek literature. David Weinberg says Papadiamandis is "perhaps the quintessential Greek writer".[72] His bread-and-butter was translations of stories by modern French, Russian and English authors for over twenty newspapers and periodicals, for which he also occasionally translated novels including Bram Stoker's *Dracula*, Sinkiewicz's *Quo Vadis?*, Hall Caine's *The Manxman* and Dostoyevsky's *Crime and Punishment*. Ibsen and Zola had a very considerable impact on Greek writers in the nineteenth and early twentieth centuries, in matters of transparency and realism, pointing away from allusion to the classical *pantheon* and towards a more open, honest and searching, hard-hitting and plain-speaking literature. In the nineteenth century, in addition to literary journals such as *Estia* (hearth), newspapers featured poems and short stories (and serialised novels). It was Papadiamandis's problem to accommodate this realism into the "magical realism" of his native Skíathos.

The fact that Papadiamandis' writing largely followed the "festal" or *eortástiko* cycle is not simply a genuflection to the religious year, but an acknowledgement of social reality and of the newspaper editor's seasonal demands. His novella *The Murderess* (*I Fonissa*, 1903), one of four late works, stands on its own in his *oeuvre*; Dmitri Tziovas calls it "one of the key texts of Greek fiction".[73]

A Greek postage stamp commemorates the centenary of Papadiamandis' death in 1911

Papadiamandis' most intimate world may have been the diminutive universe of his native island; his deepest affect may have been the church year within which he came to consciousness of both himself and the surrounding world. But the decades in which he flourished as a writer were crucial in so many European crucibles, and nowhere more so than in the transformation of Greek society in political, financial and ideological terms. Papadiamandis would have had very mixed feelings if he had heard Karamanlis declaring, "We belong to the West". The cusp between two eras is an exciting and dangerous place wherein to live, and especially to write.

It is today very dangerous to think that any writer could define the modern Greek experience, yet sometimes the imaginative writer can touch "realities" that are not available to historians and social scientists. If the question of Greek identity – and destiny – is intricately involved with that of language and its uses, then Papadiamandis's work can easily be seen in a political light. Matters of style become issues of intention. Beaton observes that a writer who once looked over the shoulder of the folklorist "now looks over the shoulder of the social historian or even of the political activist".[74] Yet while Papadiamandis was, in Beaton's words, "sceptical towards innovation deriving from Europeanized, urban institutions", and has been criticised for that, he straddled two worlds and continues to do so.

Of course modern Greek society is quite different in most of its outward manifestations from that of the period 1890-1910. But the countryside is, in many respects, the same. The society of which Papadiamandis wrote in "Civilisation in the Village" (1891) remains not only beneath the surface but in its everyday transactions. "Real" life is a drama – an enactment of hopes, fears, greed, such as Chekhov made the stuff of his stories and plays.

Papadiamandis has been compared with Dostoyevsky, particularly for the spiritual quality of his writing; with Hardy, for his bucolic realities; and with Chekhov, which to me is the most valuable link, since it was Chekhov who famously said that he wrote by looking out of the window, where he saw his characters passing by in pursuit of their everyday lives. As David Ricks observes, Papadiamandis "can use language to bring about a festival on the page".[75] Conversely, sometimes nothing seems to "happen" in a Papadiamandis short story, but it is usually here that he is at his most profound, writing in the opposite direction to the western tradition in order to evoke some larger truth. One may look out of the window, but sometimes it breaks your heart. As Papadiamandis wrote in "Fey Folk" (1892), "the smaller the village, the bigger the evil".[76] We would do well to bear that in mind when looking at the "villages" of Greek politics, including the *Voulí*.

Lorenzatos says Papadiamandis is "singing to you of things unuttered, confessing things unconfessed, disclosing what lies concealed".[77] Those whose reading sensibilities are attuned to the "western" narrative mode are frequently deranged by less amenable formats. The Irish short stories of Frank O'Connor or William Trevor, for example, have the same discomforting quality. They are read as if they were written in a language other than that which is ostensibly on the page. It is in the cracks between words that "things" are confessed, and this is why Papadiamandis is so rewarding to read. The reader is drawn into the story and becomes a participant in the confessional. This is Papadiamandis' continuing legacy and his excitement as a writer.

Perhaps the principal characteristic of Papadiamandis's work is *ithografía* – the depiction of manners and customs. The depiction, however, cannot be separated from what he calls the "boundless garden" – the landscape within which the behaviour, physical and psychological, occurs. If all art speaks in analogies, then Papadiamandis's art is an analogue in the same way as a wave has a correspondence to both itself and the rock on which it breaks, a connection with something that is "other" and yet the same.

But is it "art"? Is it a "true" depiction of "reality" or, as David Weinberg argues, "a literary distillation which creates a world, a universe with which we can identify, with which we can empathize, and with which we can sense with verity the essence of a culture and a people"?[78] If so, our acceptance rests on an illusion, an artifice only made possible by a writer who has complete control of his language. As Papadiamandis quoted from Hesiod in a footnote to "Black Scarf Rock", writers of fiction "know how to speak many false things as though they were true, but we know, when we will, to utter true things".[79]

The island is both the locus and the focus – the real place known intimately by Papadiamandis and the centre of a world where man and woman examine and resolve the viscera of their minds. Landscape and character: character as a "function" of landscape. Yet Papadiamandis's iconic people – priest, fisherman, widow, orphan, innkeeper – are not only intensely local but also symptomatic of the destiny of Greece in the late 1880s and early 1890s when these stories were written.

The danger of sentimentalising Papadiamandis lies not in his elegy for a vanished world but in imagining that it continues to march alongside the world that has, ostensibly, replaced it. Yet the haunting quality of his work – and I mean this in a positive sense – is the fact that it evokes a world which *per*sists because it *sub*sists. Certainly, as Anestis Keselopoulos says, it has to do with "the profound and beautiful truth of ordinary lives",[80] but also with their profound and ugly truths, or, to put it oppositely, their profound and beautiful lies.

Papadiamandis's attention to landscape and character is both an affirmation of nature – those sunrises, waves, rocks, church bells – and a questioning of nature. If his is a "religious" mind, owing so much to Orthodox spirituality, it also acknowledges the pagan man and woman on whom a new orthodoxy has been laid.

(As Lorenzatos noted, despite the "fathomless depths of the Or-thodox faith", "we shall always remain pre-Christian.")[81] *Paganus* – as, literally, a village quality – can only persist if the village itself continues. In the view of many – and this is the crux of the argu-ment about Papadiamandis as a writer of Orthodoxy – his work embraces paganism *within* Orthodoxy. The village epitomises the persisting "sanctity of place" in David Ricks's words. To recognise this inevitably means acknowledgement of the essence of pagan-ism, a *deus loci*. We are in *Golden Bough* territory: "Numen inest!" In Papadiamandis, transcendence is earthèd.

As Anestis Keselopoulos says, Papadiamandis "offers his read-ers [...] a vibrant life in the Church, and substantial relationships with other people and with God". Yet the Orthodox presence in the Greek mind was – and is – an everyday fact, and it is highly debat-able whether that, alone, is a reason for our wanting to read him today, or, indeed, whether that is *the* central feature of his writing. Greek people today are deeply *spiritual* without necessarily be-ing *religious*. I agree with Julian Evans, who sees Papadiamandis as "simultaneously pantheistic and Orthodox"[82] – that is, able to accommodate the pagan and its later overlays, the rustic and the urban, in one optic. As Papadiamandis writes in "At Saint Anas-tasa's" (1892), "The ordinary folk had long felt a pious impulse to make up for the many temples and altars it had once possessed, by multiplying country chapels in every vale and on every moun-tain. They forgot the old gods, but substituted their new saints".[83] Skíathos is undeniably a religious landscape, both physically and figuratively, and the spiritual quality of Papadiamandis's writing is not in doubt, but I think that "magical realism" – which of course deals intimately with the supernatural – is a finer key to Papadia-mandis' current relevance.

Elytis, writing of the "magic", or "spell", of Papadiamandis, says that "everything takes on the nature of a mystery, of a supernatu-ral occurrence, almost without disturbing the daily succession of events". We could call this a "psycho-narrative" which combines realism with nostalgia, a revisiting of places where the psyche is possessed.

Psycho-narratives such as *The Murderess* are crucial not only to the emergence of modern Greek writing but also to our understanding of a *transitus* in modern Greek society. In more than one sense, therefore, Papadiamandis' languages are *mihti*. They – or it – are/is in an in-between state. One might think of it as a folk opera by Smetana or Janáček, entitled "Love" or "In the Village" or "Her Mind", in which different and disparate voices can be heard simultaneously, singing of and with different passions and emotions within an overall context which has yet to be defined.

Papadiamandis seems to stand outside literary history and, almost unarguably, outside Greek society – an exile from Skíathos and a stranger in Athens. Is that the sole reason for his readability today: the "unfashionable" rebel who wanted to conform to some orthodoxy, or the conformist who saw many reasons to rebel?

Recently, a film entitled *Nostos* explicitly acknowledged Papadiamandis' stories as its inspiration, and theatre director Mirka Yemetzaki has staged a Papadiamandis story in "The Departing Daughter" (2006) because his work continues to resonate, at least within the artistic experience.

If it were merely a matter of piety, then the celebration of an outmoded figure, however important, would be worthwhile but not necessarily relevant. But the abruptness with which the reader, coming to Papadiamandis for the first time, is confronted with a writer who continues to disturb us, to illuminate our darker places, and to speak of phenomena which remain present in the Greek psyche as well as in the landscape, is what alerts us to Papadiamandis's continuing importance as both an inspiration and a signpost. Theofanis Stavrou has identified Papadiamandis as "a symbol of major political and cultural issues confronting the modern Greek state and society".[85] That is as true of Papadiamandis today as it was of the writer of the period 1890-1910; whether that says more of the writer or of our times is of course debatable.

War and the Novel[86]

It is no exaggeration to say that consciousness of war, and the consequences of war, permeate the literature of modern Greece. A passage from *The Heroic Age* by Stratis Haviaras (1984) exemplifies this preoccupation:

> His body was probably like the trunk of an ancient olive tree, a trunk with many rings and much history: here the 1896 disaster, and here the First Great War, and after that the Asia Minor catastrophe. Here the Italian attack, and here the German and Bulgarian atrocities, and here the Resistance, and more Resistance, and more and more Resistance: terror, the civil strife, the islands of detention and the death camps. Year by year our glorious history, the whole history, and throughout the years the starving and the dispossessed, the disabled and the thoroughly dead – unnamed and unclaimed forever.[87]

Although the example is an extreme one, it underlines, in a graphic way, the fact that modern Greek history can be recited as a series of disasters, of which the Anatolian Catastrophe has been the most severe. *The Heroic Age* is set in the Greek Civil War, and concerns a group of young boys and girls who have lost their homes and have been swept up in the internecine struggle for a new Greece which they barely comprehend, and which forces them to live as adults and to survive by their wits.

It is noticeable that the speaker does *not* mention in his catalogue of warfare the *successes* of Greece in the Balkan wars of 1912-13, which expanded its frontiers to the north, west and east, at Turkey's expense. It is as if the reference to "the starving and dispossessed" and the "unnamed and unclaimed" transcends any positive aspect of Greece's international affairs – as if those terms describe a population which persists in the imagination of the author as an entity to be "named and reclaimed", to be nourished and repossessed. Such irredentism of the Greek psyche is a keynote of its literary imagination.

At first sight, this appears to sit uncomfortably beside the conventional view of Greek rural society as an idyllic, timeless, arcadian epic in which nothing happens except in a periodic, cyclic fashion of constant but extremely slow repetition. The later novels of Yatromanolakis, for example *History of a Vendetta* and *A Report of a Murder*, which, rather obviously, introduce the concept of violence, also make it clear that strife, in some form, is a constant in the Greek experience. An *agón*, or contest, may be the struggle of a man with himself, or with another.

But if we recall the commonplace, that war takes place after the possibilities of diplomacy have been exhausted, we can postulate that there is a calibrated scale of activity, starting with the expression of an opinion, moving to the discussion or denial of that opinion, until we reach the stages of violence which embrace two people, or two families, or a township, or two tribes or nations, in all-out violent destruction. If we think of the Greek word for war – *pólemos* – as the outcome of a series of *polemics*, this calibration becomes very persuasive.

If, as Anthony Stevens tells us, "conflict is endemic to the human condition", then it is *more* endemic to the Greeks than to most other peoples; not surprising, perhaps, when we remember that "endemic" is itself the Greek word for "that which pertains to a people", that which is innate or inborn.

Furthermore, as Stevens reminds us, "Wherever human communities exist, conflict is generated both *within* them and *between* them at all levels of intimacy – conflict between husbands and wives, parents and children, brothers and sisters, teachers and pupils, workers and bosses, leaders and followers".[88]

Therefore if, in Stevens's highly illuminating words, "conflict is cooperation's shadow", it is hardly surprising that conflict will appear in even the most tender and sensitive love story – as it does, for example, in Alki Zei's story *Achilles' Fiancée* (1987, trans. 1991), with the deeply divisive figure of Marxism as its central character as well as its hinterland.

It would of course be absurd to suggest that all modern Greek poems, short stories and novels are oriented towards war. There are many love stories and poetic idylls in both poetry and prose. As younger Greek writers are living in a time when Greece itself is removed from most – but not all – war experiences, it is easier for them to turn their attention to topics evident in modern Greek society which are not – at least on the surface – concerned with violent strife. As Roderick Beaton has noted, "the new Greek novel of the 1980s is grounded in the fictional techniques of allusion, parody, the *rapprochement* between realism and the fantastic, and between realistic story-telling and Modernist experiments".[89] And many of these explore states of mind which, on the surface at least, have nothing to do with war (see Further Reading).

As the translators of Theotokas's novel *Argo* (1923) emphasised, one of the results of the Anatolian Catastrophe among Greek writers was "the urge to achieve the greatest possible measure of mental and spiritual liberty"; "freedom from all dogmatism; the need to attain absolute sincerity in life, in thought, in art, and to lift this quality of sincerity to the plane of a supreme moral value [... and...] the fusion of Greek traditions with the flower of the genius of modern Europe".[90] (It is remarkable that Theotokas' novel appeared in the immediate aftermath of the Anatolian Catastrophe.)

I will briefly discuss three novels which take us from the subliminal to the explicit in terms of their treatment of war, and from the time of the Anatolian Catastrophe to the dictatorship by the army colonels after their coup in 1967. These are firstly, *The Third Wedding* by Costas Taktsis (1962); secondly, *Aeolia* by Ilias Venezis (originally *Aeolian Earth*, 1943); and thirdly, *Fool's Gold* by Maro Douka (1979).

The German writer on war, Karl von Clausewitz, said that war depended on three human faculties: violence, imagination and reason, by which he meant that *violence* was the expression of the people, that *imagination* was the remit of the army, and that *reason* was the responsibility of the government. I would like to give these three words a different orientation, which does not stray too far from Clausewitz's meaning.

War has no *reason*, other than the opposed interests of the entrenched protagonists. It is therefore an illogical, or irrational, reason, such as Virginia Woolf's "insane truth".[91] War is, in fact, a form of magical realism which has a surreal quality both for the participants and the spectators. Its realism consists in the fact that it is happening – armies advance, people are killed. But it is *unreal* in the sense that, however natural the aggressive instinct may be in us, individually and collectively, war is extremely difficult to understand except in metaphysical terms.

Violence is evident not only in war or other forms of strife but also within love – the power of love can be violent, impassioned. The following extracts from *The Third Wedding* by Costas Taktsis, in which a mother speaks about, and addresses, her daughter, illustrate this:

> I can't stand her another moment! Dear God, why did you send me such a burden to bear? What have I done to deserve such punishment? How long must I put up with her, see her horrid face, hear her voice, how long, Oh Lord, how long? Surely there must be some misguided Christian who'd want to take her? Somebody to take this monstrous freak of nature off my hands, this souvenir her father left to avenge himself? The devil take those who stopped me having the abortion! [...] "God made you ugly", I tell her, "but at least you could dress up a bit more. You never know, you might fool somebody!" [...] "Go on. Get dressed. And do what you damn well like. But I'm giving you one last warning: if you aggravate me again like you did today [...] there'll be murder done in this house. I'll chop you into little pieces like mince-meat!"[92]

To "chop you into little pieces" is a convention of marital violence, but it is seldom that it occurs in mother-daughter relationships; its violence is redolent of the butchery which we more readily associate with warfare.

While the monologal nature of the novel is preoccupied with inter-personal and intra-personal relations, the background is the long historical perspective of Greek history: the individuals and couples whose lives are recounted, live within the war environment. As critic (and novelist) Kay Cicelis noted, "the diary of a middle class woman succeeds in becoming for me also the Book of War, the Book of the German Occupation, the Book of the Civil War, even the Book of the Greek Situation."[93]

The book is permeated by two types of aggression: that on the macro scale between Greeks and Turks, between royalists and Venizelists, between right-wing and communism, and that on the micro scale between husband and wife, mother and daughter. But the emotional climate of the book persuades me that the style of address quoted above between mother and daughter is contained within the ambit of *love*, and that no mother could so despise her child as to actually intend or mean the abuse which she heaps on her. War is love/love is war.

To turn to Clausewitz's third keyword, *imagination*: imagination is of course at the core of literature. War, like democracy and peace, rests on a belief system, just as communism and fascism do – or, to connect it with magical realism, a *dis*-belief system. It is only in the minds of a madman that war can be regarded as *constructive*, but we must recall not only the expansion of the Third Reich but also the appalling episode of the *Megáli Idéa*. In other words, war is almost always destructive, and this has an impact on the *imaginative* element of the *agón*, in the sense that the imagination has at its back a consciousness of destruction and *loss*, and the literature that results from the imaginative activity is therefore imbued with that consciousness.

Ilias Venezis's *Aeolia* exemplifies this. The reader's mind is saturated from the opening pages ("The Discovery of the World") with the sacred atmosphere which binds men to the soil, and the ensuing political and military crisis invades and dissipates that atmosphere, replacing it with that of darkness and despair. As a refugee, escaping from the Turkish advance, one character attributes brutality to the nature of man: "Surrounded by the throng of hunted people seeking refuge by the sea, she sensed that this was it, that the demon, their dark instinct, was roused, and she tried to comprehend it."[94]

Another child asks:

> "What is war, Uncle Joseph?"
> Lena imagined it to be a dragon, bigger even than the forty dragons which had imprisoned the little princess in the fairy tale. It must be something like that. But this terrible dragon did not prey only on princesses, it prayed [*sic*] on the whole of mankind, who fled in terror to escape it.
> "What is war, Uncle Joseph?"
> "My little one, why do you want to know?" replied the old man. "Wait until you are bigger..."

224

Lena came to find Artemis and me to discover the truth. Since the grown-ups could not enlighten her, perhaps we might.

"Do you know what war is?"

Something stirred in the depths of our childhood memories.

"Do you remember...?" said Artemis. "Do you remember that time when we first heard the jackals?..."

Yes, that was the first time we had heard that terrible word. For the first time we had watched our men rushing with fierce cries and drums to drive off the jackals when hunger had drawn them to the edge of our farm. "War", they had called it that....

And now, we told Lena, we must leave our land.

"We must".

That must be war.[95]

There is no magical realism in *Aeolia*, only the harsh reality of the sadness which becomes a way of life for the children of the tale, as it would twenty years later under the pen of Dido Sotiriou in *Farewell Anatolia* (1962) and many others which have displacement as their focus. The unhoused mind is both a vulnerable and a dangerous mind.

Unhousedness is also at the heart of Maro Douka's *Fool's Gold*. The narrator's life is displaced as, in the opening pages, the Colonels' coup of 1967 is announced:

My father, thunderstruck, was demanding to know: but when? This is madness! Impossible. When at last he replaced the receiver... he broke the news to us: Dictatorship.... I had been hearing talk of dictatorship for years. Coups and juntas and clandestine organisations were things that people talked about, but on a purely theoretical basis. Rather like footnotes to a glorious past... I watched them in silence. My mother was staring transfixed, as though at some terrible memory.[96]

The juxtaposition of the words "past" and "memory" suggest that, while the coup had not been a physical reality up that point in the narrator's consciousness, it existed atavistically in the consciousness of her family.

The account of the narrator's involvement in left-wing political organisations during the colonels' regime is in fact a flashback from 1974, when the regime collapsed, partly due to the resistance by students at the Athens Polytechnic in 1973. The narrator tells us:

> Not long after Christmas, in 1974, a girl I used to know came up to me: did I want to join the political group she belonged to, and if so, would I please fill in a questionnaire. Her group didn't interest me at all, but I was curious. There was a certain fascination in trying to sort out the hows and whys. What's more, I was used to it. Ever since I'd joined the Left, in the way of things at that time, I'd been constantly having to account for myself. To the point that even when nobody else bothered to cross-examine me I'd put myself in the dock, it had become second nature to me.[97]

The questionnaire provokes the memoir that follows:

> What is my name. My date and place of birth. Where do I live and with whom. What do my parents do. My resistance record (covert or other activities). Trade union or similar affiliations. My family's politics. Why and how did I join the Left. Record of police harassment. My intended profession. Books I have read. Strengths and weaknesses (my own estimation). What help do I expect from the group. My attitude to this particular group, and reasons for wanting to join.[98]

On the final page of the novel, she answers the questionnaire, although she has illuminated her answers by writing the book:

> OK, my name is Myrsini Panayotou. I was born in Paris on the 25th of July, 1949. I live at 10 Sinopis Street, by myself. My father doesn't do anything, my mother is dead. During the dictatorship I took part in the resistance, first of all in the Rigas Pherraios group. Leaflets and other printed matter. Later on I was in various covert groups, whose names I may not reveal. At present, no, I am not a member of any

group. My family, my father that is, is a socialist, or so he says. I have no idea how I first came to join the Left. I suppose because of my first boyfriend, Paul. I have been harassed by the Security Police and continue to be harassed to this day. Intended profession I have none, I may give more time to dancing, though the years have passed me by. I have read a great many books, but very few specifically related to Marxism. Only the *Eighteenth Brumaire of Louis Bonaparte, the Communist Manifesto, State and Revolution* and five or six shorter books. As for my strengths and weaknesses I can make no comment. So when all's said and done, sometimes I feel like a god, and sometimes the merest creature.[99]

The idea that dancing may no longer be appropriate suggests that the *joys* of life and the celebration of those joys has been usurped by political strife and the continuing notion of a police state – an unwritten and invisible form of violence which is present in many other recent Greek works of fiction.

There is a deeply divisive set of ideologies operating at both the explicit and the subliminal levels in the Greek "imagination", to which the record of warfare from at least the long War of Independence from 1821 up to the Civil War and the 1967-74 dictatorship, has contributed significantly. And furthermore, that Greece's role in the new Europe, especially in relation to the Balkans, Turkey and Cyprus, is intimately related to the past and to the chronic events therein. These episodes have all marked Greek consciousness in a way that makes it impossible not to carry forward a knowledge, and an acknowledgement, of war into its literature.

8

Drama, Film and Music

Drama

More urgently, overtly and provocatively than in novels or poetry, drama, in public presentation, makes statements which its audiences can measure against expectations, hopes and history. As recently as 2011, the Greek National Theatre was in a similar situation to Ireland's Abbey: trying to re-establish its *raison d'être* as a reflection, and part, of national identity. "Today, more than ever, it is important to see what is left of the Greek, the Byzantine and the post-revolutionary spirit and how these elements are assimilated by contemporary culture," said its artistic director, Yiannis Houvardos.[1] He sees the theatre as playing a part in fighting "financial and psychological strangulation" by becoming "a cultural lighthouse for the nation". The 2011-13 programme offered a dramatisation of the *Odyssey* as part of an exploration of the "essence and dynamics" of Greece's cultural heritage, in "a journey back to our political, social and financial history, a mirror of our ethics but also a reverse mirror of the way that foreigners saw us and continue to see us." In addition to the Greek repertoire, the programme included international works inspired by Greece, such as Eugene O'Neill's *Mourning Becomes Electra* and Shakespeare's *Pericles*, adaptations of Greek literature and new commissions "touching upon burning issues of our time" (they specifically referred to immigration). History would be explored through dramatisations of the Anatolian Catastrophe and readings from *Z*. Modern works would include Kambanellis' *The Court of Miracles* (1957) and Loula Anagnostakis' *The Victory* (1978), both of which are critically regarded as major presences on the Greek stage.

This exploration had already taken place since the 1950s. In writing *The Court of Miracles*, Iakovos Kambanellis said, "my ambition in theatre is to discover the Greek as a contemporary man. I want to discover the characteristics of the people of my own place and time through the temporary expression of their relationship with the present social reality".[2] This was also the ambition of many composers, filmmakers and visual artists. Kambanellis' play was not unlike Andreas Franghias' novel *The Courtyard* in using the strategy of four walls to focus on individual emotion and interaction.

Immediately after the Civil War, Margarita Lyberakis's *The Other Alexander* (written as a novel 1950, and staged as a play in 1957) expressed the social fissures, as the death of an old order encouraged divisions of opinion and intention regarding the new. This approach became increasingly urgent with what seemed the unabated rise of right-wing politics, so much so that one critic stated, "the theatre has become indistinguishable from a political rostrum".[3]

By the 1970s, anxiety about the limited number of new Greek plays being staged was still prevalent. It was in the work of experimental, fringe groups that examination of the classics, and new ways of approaching social problems, were attempted. Part of this alternative to the mainstream was the *Momogería* form of masquerade imported by the Pontic Greeks – a survival of a cabaret that can be traced back to Roman and Byzantine times.

The post-war dramatists who eschewed their own classical dramas looked to European and American contemporaries for ideas in an era of survival and reconstruction. Brechtian alienation techniques which were presented by Petros Markaris (better known as the creator of the detective "Inspector Charitos" and as a collaborator with Theo Angelopoulos) in his play of social protest *The Story of Ali Redzo* (1971). At the Art Theatre (which began in 1942), Carolos Coun deliberately staged contemporary foreign plays in order to stimulate native writers.

The post-war desolation experienced in the work of Sartre, Beckett, Ionesco and Pirandello found a Greek echo in Loula Anagnostakis' 1976 statement: "Madness is the ultimate liberation of the soul".[4]

A 1977 production (that is, three years after the fall of the junta) by the Athens University Drama Club, "The Arta Bridge", used the traditional poem and myth of bridge-building as a metaphor (rather appropriate in the case of a bridge) for the "building" of the new state and the sacrifice to be made (in the original, the architect is forced to immure his wife alive in the foundations of the bridge to ensure stability).

Lawrence Durrell claimed that in the *plaka* of Athens you can meet a modern-day Aristophanes or Agamemnon or Clytaemnestra, and I believe the residual power of the Greek dramas is in their tragic or satiric modes which are continuing presences in the *agorá* of the Greek mind. Aliki Bacopoulou-Halls stresses that, after critical examination of the classics, "what has possibly remained from that distant past are the archetypal myths [...] and the primordial Aristophanic spirit. It is a spirit which seems to rail at the evils of this world while it thoroughly enjoys life on this almost barren and sun-scorched spot".[5] The continual revisiting of Sophocles, Euripides and Aeschylus by nineteenth and twentieth century Greek dramatists is due to their continuing relevance not only for Greeks but for all who recognise human weakness and want to see it presented in an oblique or allegorical way. As Stratos Constantinidis argues:

> A modern Greek play that dramatized the tragic story of Oedipus could only finish a distant third to Sophocles's *Oedipus the Tyrant*. The available evidence shows that the majority of modern Greek dramatists, directors, designers, and actors did not follow in the steps of their ancestors. When they turned their backs on the Greek classics which were revered as major, universal, seminal, and eternal prototypes, the critics had little mercy. Modern Greek plays were regarded as minor, local, marginal, ephemeral, parochial imitations of "European" models.[6]

It is generally agreed that the basic elements of Greek drama – especially the tragedies – can be found in contemporary society and that adaptations are therefore relevant on the modern stage. Figures like Oedipus or Medea have become archetypal instances of our most basic fears and instincts, and the *agón* between Antigone and Creon a lesson in the struggle of conscience with law. (I saw a teeshirt in Athens which read "Oidipus – the original mother-fucker", which sums it all up.)

A 2010 production of Aristophanes' *The Acharians* at Epidaurus projected the play into the present day, with expressions of distaste for "chicken thieves, wannabes, criminals, tax dodgers, pissant MPs, managers of the big debt business, those responsible for the death of the country". During the play, a photo of the assassinated Grigorios Lambrakis (the character portrayed in *Z*) holding a banner proclaiming "Hellas", was greeted with a standing ovation.[7]

Since so much of modern drama suggests the same fears and care for freedoms, we should hardly hesitate in looking at their earliest manifestations in newer, more accessible, versions. In notes for *Mourning Becomes Electra*, O'Neill asked himself, "is it possible to get a modern psychological approximation of the Greek sense of fate [...] which an intelligent audience of today, possessed by no belief in gods or supernatural retribution, could accept and be moved by?"[8]

Classical Greek theatre maintains its place in the repertoire, and also inspires modern productions elsewhere: George Steiner's study *Antigones* traces the play's modern epiphanies throughout the western world; he quotes Plato and Montaigne to the effect that we are "only the interpreters of interpretations" (*erminéon erminis*). In Ireland alone we saw five versions of the play in the period 1984-86; that by Aidan Carl Matthews was preceded by a reading of the then pending Criminal Justice Bill,[9] which was widely considered to be unnecessarily oppressive. Other Greek dramas on the modern Irish stage have been Seamus Heaney's *The Cure at Troy* (a version of Sophocles' *Philoctetes*), Brendan Kennelly's *Medea* and *The Trojan Women* (Euripides), published with his version of *Antigone* as *When Then is Now*; and Monica Carr's *By the Bog of Cats* (*Medea*). Kennelly refers to "the terrifying freedom of their dramatic explorations [...] Distance became immediacy when I embarked on *The Trojan Women*. The ancient city of Troy became a 20th-century Irish village, and Trojan citywomen became Irish villagewomen [...] These ancient plays are *then* illuminating *now.*"[10]

But it has also been argued that it is possible to overrate their relevance to modern society. While I think it would be difficult to dismiss *Antigone* from our consciousness, it may well be said that if there are "eternal verities" in the tragedies, or a continuing cause for merriment in the comedies (just as the English stage celebrates Shakespeare today), there is a need for contemporary drama which, on the evidence of most critics, is lacking in the contemporary Greek repertoire, for example in the National Theatre or the Athens Art Theatre.

The notable absence of contemporary Greek plays from the repertoire has been explained by a director of the Athens Art Theatre as an ignorance of what was available. Drama itself has not featured prominently in any survey of Greek literature, whereas poetry and fiction claim the principal interest. Those playwrights who preferred to explore other avenues were ill-received by critics and conservative audiences accustomed to the emphasis on continuity in culture as in other matters.

A negative view of such revivals in Britain was expressed very recently by Catharine Nixey, who regards as "utter nonsense" the relevance to modern society of plays such as *Elektra* and *Antigone* which, she thought, would evoke tired descriptions such as "visceral" or exerting "an atavistic power".[11] Nixey notes that "in the past 30-odd years, Greek tragedies have been put on more than at any time since classical antiquity". She totally disputes that the plays "speak to us", preferring instead to suggest that "we respond with unquestioning awe". They contain little meaning, she says. She even goes so far as to question whether Athenians themselves in the fifth century BC were really impressed by these plays.

The article, however, defeats itself with the headline (which may not be Nixey's own): "It's tragic to pretend we all like classical drama". We do not attend such drama to be "entertained" and we do not necessarily "like" it.

"What shall I do?" (the question posed by Sophocles' Philoctetes, which is the crux of the play) is a perennial dilemma. As Rush Rehm observes, "we can do anything we like but refuse to answer it".[12] This is a form of response to the writer who puts his or her *testimonio*, or *martiría* before us; it creates responsibility in the audience and thus a sense of co-authorship or at least connivance, in both text and performance.

Rehm draws attention to racism in the USA which suggests parallels with Aeschylus' *Suppliant Women*, "particularly in the current epidemic of dispossessed and fugitive peoples"[13] – a phenomenon which troubles Greece greatly today. To "say something" about this is a role of the playwright today, just as it was for Aeschylus, and for the same reason: it questions the meaning and efficacy of the *pólis*.

This is a play which, Rehm reminds us, refers to "our own political reality: lying speech, manipulation, criminality, the power of special interests, the lack of oversight, human stupidity and exhaustion, an overworked population with no time for self-government."[14] It seems that all human – and inhuman – life is there; and it also tells us that nothing is new.

In the 1930s and 1940s Angelos Sikelianos and Kazantzakis (the latter more notable as a novelist) had preached a drama of faith and hope, reconstruction and harmony. But the post-war generation has not shown such optimism. One critic, Aliki Bacopoulou-Halls, sees modern Greek drama as an existentialist exploration of the absurd – not unlike Samuel Beckett's – in which playwrights seek new possibilities without fear or hope. (On a recent visit to Athens I noted two theatres playing Beckett, *Endgame* and *Waiting for Godot*, another presenting Brecht's *Caucasian Chalk Circle* and a fourth with Durrenmatt's *The Visit – Der Besuch der alten Dame*.)

The drama is primarily one of *protest* which, it need hardly be said, does not recommend itself to the conventional bourgeois audience. The authors in question, including Kambanellis (1921-2011, a survivor of Mauthausen), Stratis Karras (1934-92), Loula Anagnostaki (b. *circa* 1935) and Pavlos Matesis (1933-2013, also a notable novelist), were children of the World War, the Civil War and the junta (under which experimental drama was discouraged if not completely prohibited). Their characters are fatigued, hopeless, disillusioned and alienated.[15] Stratos Constantinidis sees this as a "trajectory of protest [...] from potent, self-assertive action to diffidence and inertia".[16]

But there is also a black satire on offer: the one-man performance of Costas Varnalis' satire, *The True Apology of Socrates* (1977) might have an Irish pre-echo in Conor Cruise O'Brien's *King Herod Explains* (1969), in that it attempts to lay open and question received wisdom as to certain canonic elements in our collective psyche. Other expressions of resistance were made in Iakovos Kambanellis' *Our Grand Circus* of 1973, which juxtaposed the events of history with the contemporaneous experience of the junta, while more recently *National Anthem*, played in a warehouse in the old Athenian gangland district of Psirri, denounced the national anthem after a succession of cabaret numbers. Psirri, despite gentrification, remains a night-spot for fringe theatre of the irreverent and iconoclastic genre, where as many as 120 experimental groups are said to perform.

Film

Coming in ignorance to Greek film (other than Costas-Gavras' *Z* and Cacoyannis' *Zorba*[17] – a somewhat bizarre alphabetical pairing), I immediately found myself witnessing an entirely foreign genre, quite unlike most films from Ireland, the UK or America in their approach to cinematography, characterisation and narrative. The films with which most westerners would be familiar – and they are, in their own genre, very fine and entertaining films – include *The Magus* (1968, from the novel by John Fowles), *Shirley Valentine* (1989, screenplay by Willy Russell), *My Big Fat Greek Wedding* (2002) and *Driving Aphrodite* (2009), both written by, and starring, Nia Vardalos, and the BBC television series *Who Pays the Ferryman?* (1977), plus two films starring Melina Mercouri and directed by her husband Jules Dassin, *Never on Sunday* (1960) and *Topkapi* (1964).

I was struck by the beauty of the more "serious", heavy-duty films: the striving for intelligence, exploration, connections, using the techniques of the cinema as we find in so much Greek literature: a "cut-and-paste" episodic presentation to the reader-viewer which can be very bewildering until one is immersed in the de-realisation and accepts it as a sort of fantasy or dream-world in which it's the viewer's responsibility to find his/her own way towards meaning and cohesion.

Greek cinema is severe. It is unnerving in its exploration of history, myth, memory and, of course, Greekness, and universal in its tenderness. When it decides to be satirical or outrageous, its humour veers between black and gold. Angelopoulos' *The Weeping Meadow* (2004) and *The Dust of Time* (2009) exhibit the former; Yorgos Lanthimos' *Dogtooth* (2009) and Athena Rachel Sangari's *Attenberg* (2010) the latter. These films are profoundly exilic and alienating.

In a nutshell, as Katerina Zacharia puts it: "Greek filmmakers had a clear agenda between 1970 and 1976: to subvert the ideology of dictatorship, create a new cinematic language, resist the Americanization of Greece, and provide a more composite and sophisticated picture of modern Greek culture."[18]

As with any art form, Greek filmmakers have examined their cultural heritage, especially in relation to modern cultural identity and the need of the state to hold together a consensus on Greekness in a highly volatile and disparate population. Some have celebrated this heritage, others have rejected it; many more have employed it as a *point d'interrogation* as to what Greekness, whether classical or modern, may be in terms of portraying how Greeks behave as Greeks and as citizens of the world.

In doing so, *ellipsis* and *palimpsest* have become major strategies, requiring viewers to sift through layers of history, layers of memory, in order to construct their own identity, or to affirm the identity offered by the filmmaker's imaginative use of fact and fiction.

Not only has Greece adopted the western genre of cinema as a way of explaining itself to the world, but it has also realised that film can be used as a medium for understanding Greece's relations with the Balkans and the Levant.

Apart from films made entirely for the purpose of entertainment, the Greek cinema has been a forum for debate. Its modern roots lie in the wars of 1940-49 and the junta 1967-74. Documentaries on film and television continue to relate the key periods of Greek history, such as *Smyrna: The Destruction of a Cosmopolitan City* (2012) and *From Both Sides of the Aegean* (2013, the latter referring to the exchange of populations after the Catastrophe), both directed by Maria Elias and Alexander Kitoeff. *Makronisos: Exile Island* (2009) by Elias Giannakakis and Evi Karabatsou showed the experiences of internal prisoners-of-war during the Civil War, on one of the cruellest of the punishment islands, where as many as 100,000 partisans were sent for "re-education". (Other islands were used for internment, both in the Civil War and under the junta, including Amorgos, and Gyaros where, among others, the poet Yannis Ritsos wrote *Epitáphios*, which became "the anthem of the Left".)[19]

Films such as *Z* (1969) directed by Costas-Gavros[20] from the book by Vassilis Vassilikos, in which Yves Montand played the role of Grigoris Lambrakis, a left-wing politician assassinated by a right-wing faction shortly before the junta came to power, is one tip of many icebergs,[21] with the most consistent and significant being the work of Angelopoulos, from *Days of '36*, to the biting allegory of *Alexander the Great* (1980), *The Weeping Meadow* (ranging from the Anatolian Catastrophe to the Civil War) and his best-known outside Greece, *Eternity and a Day* (1998).[22]

Theodoros Angelopoulos (1935-2012)

Due in part to the fact that his career began during the junta, Angelopoulos, in order to evade censorship, adopted two strategies which have made his films so idiosyncratic: the use of allegory and the fractured, episodic structure in which there is no immediately discernible narrative, no story with a statement that could be construed as offensive or derogatory. Family histories intrapolate the larger social history. In *The Weeping Meadow* the most moving scenes are those of migrants, refugees and exiles from history, whom we meet also in Salman Rushdie's *Shame* and Eavan Boland's poetry (*Outside History* and *The Journey*)[23] – but we can find in their displacement an allegory for the alienation of humanity from concepts of home, stability, assurance, love.

Angelopoulos was by no means a pessimist, but his vision of a Greek spirit was tempered by realism. Perhaps he, too, loved and mourned. When, in *Ulysses' Gaze* (1995), a character declares "Greece is dying, we are dying as a people, we have come full circle", Angelopoulos was, I believe, displaying the black, fatalistic side of classic tragedy that embraced Charon and Hades, but hoping that that character would be refuted by a revolution in history. (The character continues: "So many thousands of years among broken stones and statues. But if Greece is to die, she'd better do it quickly! Because the agony lasts too long and makes too much noise".) Angelopoulos said that he was preoccupied with "the eternal return", the setting out on a project, encountering themes which remind him always that they are obsessions, ghosts to be confronted, and trying to achieve resolution, only to find himself once more at the starting-point of a new attempt to engage with these phenomena. A continual story-telling, an *orobouros*, in my end is my beginning.

The continual re-visiting of themes was due partly to the film-maker's conception/inception of a film. "The point of departure may be an image, a meeting, a journey, an old story that emerges and seeks to become an image"[24] – that is, seeks the filmmaker who will create a filmic image capable of sustaining the first message throughout the drama.

Due to the impossibility of "official acceptance" of his films, Angelopoulos resorted to allegory, to overcome "the fear of intervention – the fear that our artistic expression would be corrupted".[25] (He also joked that the lookout man, on the alert for military police, was more important during shooting than the film's director.) He stated that his method was "the result of political choice. I sought a secret language. The allusions of history. Suppression. Elliptical speech as aesthetic principle", and thus "a film in which all the important things seem to be taking place off-camera".[26]

When he referred to "elliptical speech" and "important things taking place off-camera", he was not only referring to the evasions necessitated by circumstances, but to a filmic genre of concealment as much as display, in which we intuit fatalities without overtly witnessing them, thus accommodating them more deeply within our own consciousness.

Watching an Angelopoulos film, the viewer has to supply the "off-camera" parts of the narrative in order to find the cohesion of the storyline. There is no Chorus (as in classical drama) to announce off-stage events: the viewer *is* the Chorus. The technical aspect of his filmmaking is an integral part of this process of disorientation. Not only are his narratives allegorical or elliptical, but his cinematography is also oblique, dream-like. They are often shot in a pale light of suggestion rather than fully lit fact, as if the director has placed a gauze over the lens, like a veil over memory, and the disruptions in narrative are like a major act of pixilation or *pointillisme* in that the fragments individually are both more, and less, than the storyboard.

Part of the disorientation is the movement between timeframes, bringing together and thrusting apart key episodes in the characters' experience. One long scene (a single, ten-minute take) in *The Travelling Players* begins in 1952 and ends in 1939. This slow movement back and forth in time is a reflection on the fickleness of memory both public (history) and private (the diary of each man's mind).

Andrew Horton calls the films "an attempt to see clearly through the dark window of Greek history [...] so that we experience [...] how individuals and their destinies are absolutely woven into and from the fabric of their culture and their times."[27] Angelopoulos had seen "politics as a faith" but in the light of his experience as a citizen he now saw it as a profession. "Serving people is a job, not an ideology. I come from a generation where we thought we were going to change the world. Back around 2000 was when it felt like the dream was over."[28]

Despite the presence of the marble head/hand in two of his films (above, pp. 190-91), Angelopoulos was determined not to be a victim to history: "we live in a culture that has inherited these myths and we must destroy them at all costs. I don't accept destiny or the idea of fate".[29] To escape that destiny/fate, it must be re-embraced in every film, re-examined before it can be rejected. *Alexander the Great* (unlike its namesake by Oliver Stone) is a modern-day brigand (*klepht*), the classical hero of Greekness fast-forwarded into the year 1900, holding English aristocrats hostage (and eventually executing them) and demanding redistribution of property: he "tried to get back what was rightfully ours from the landowners and the money-lenders".

If Greek cinema is severe, Angelopoulos' is the severest. It's been frequently remarked that to sit down to watch one of his films one needs stamina and intense concentration (*The Travelling Players* runs for three hours and forty minutes). David Jenkins commented that "possibly his grandiose mythical parables require such concentration, willingness and openness from their audience that they could never be consumed as simple entertainment."[30]

For both their content and their longitude the films have been both acclaimed and criticised in Greece for the same reason: his portrayal of painful and secret affairs; even when he is showing us the beauties of innocence and ignorance, he is unrelenting in his pursuit of the powers that will destroy them.

Angelopoulos has been concerned with *borders*. He concentrates especially on Greece's northern and eastern borders with Albania, Macedonia, Bulgaria and Turkey, perhaps because they are in themselves metaphors for Greece's uncertainty, its failure to draw its identity fully around itself, its vulnerability to events just beyond its reach. Perhaps these borders are also intended to tell us something about the changing nature and values of power, as evolving circumstances (shifting borders and balances) necessitate difficult choices in politics and morals. A country must have borders in order to be defined, on the map at least, but it also needs to be flexible in the self-definition which takes place in the cartography of the mind. Flexible, porous borders permit possibilities which a closed frontier cannot admit.

In *Ulysses' Gaze*, for example, the central character travels between Greece, Albania, Macedonia, Bulgaria, Romania, Belgrade and Sarajevo; he is unsure of where he is, or with whom, at any one time, a time-traveller and a space-traveller in a world without clocks or maps. Angelopoulos has been called "the magic realist of the Balkans" and in this non-journey through the Balkans he clarifies, by means of obscurity, their imperfectly understood intellectual, cultural and emotional geography. And it is also a self-mockery, since Angelopoulos has said "there comes a moment when the filmmaker begins to doubt his own capacity to see things, when he no longer knows if his gaze is right and innocent".[31]

Angelopoulos (as also in *Landscape in the Mist* and *Voyage to Kythera*) was not the only filmmaker to present us with the dilemma of borders: the border between the mindset of Athens and that of the Pontic Greeks; the eternal borders between Greece and Turkey; the "lost" Greeks across the borders in southern Albania, Macedonia and Bulgaria; are all portrayed in contemporary cinema. In Sotiris Goritsa's *From the Snow* (1993, based on Sotiris Dimitriou's stories) and *Balkanizater* (1997), Giorgos Zafeiris' *Ephemeral Town* (2000), Yannis Enconomidis' *Matchbox* (2003) and Constantine Giannaris' *Hostage* (2007) all explore the physical, metaphysical and metaphorical borders between nations, tribes, individuals, tongues, beliefs and cultures which are so often less than fertile and impediments to love and comprehension, symbols of hyphenated identities and meanings.

At the time of his death, in a road accident, Angelopoulos was working on the final part of a trilogy, the successor to *The Weeping Meadow* and *The Dust of Time*. It was to be called *The Other Sea*, and brought the trilogy into the present day. It was to be "about the lack of a dream at the moment ... a general lack of values".[32] Of *Dogtooth* and *Attenberg* Angelopoulos said, "I hope that this new generation will lead to a true Nouvelle Vague".[33] "They've created a new language and they have something to say".[34] It's as if he had faith in the new filmmakers to overcome the disillusion that he himself had sensed since 2000.

The effect – on this solo viewer at least – at the end of (almost) all Angelopoulos' films is, despite the unexplained darkness and a vortical sense of powerlessness, a counterbalancing sense of light and joy. I would not use the word "hope" because I think Angelopoulos himself had decided that in the light of the history he was depicting – a filmic *mythistórima* if you like – "hope" was a useless word. Much more important was the pursuit of the many possibilities radiating from, colliding with, transforming, the starting-point: the image, the message, the song. Because he uses light so effectively, and introduces humour into even the most sordid and frightening episodes, his films leave one with a sense of satisfaction, a road well travelled, even though, for the filmmaker himself, the journey must start all over again. The title of his uncompleted final film, *The Other Sea*, suggests that there would never have been landfall, a point of disembarkation that was more than merely temporary, a way-station on the road to god knows where.

It would be hard to imagine Ken Loach being able, even in the 1980s, to make his film *The Wind that Shakes the Barley* (2006) but that is what veteran Greek filmmaker Pantelis Voulgaris did in *Psyhi Vathia* ("Deep Soul", 2009), sixty years after the Civil War ended.

Voulgaris adopted the same strategy as Loach in *The Wind that Shakes the Barley*, pitting two adolescent brothers against one another on opposite sides, which in a nutshell were the "National" forces of the *de facto* government and the "Democratic", largely communist, survivors of the anti-German guerilla resistance. The brothers represent "both sides of the face of the same drama".

Voulgaris has made nineteen movies, many of them (like the films of Ken Loach) with overt political dimensions displaying his "leftist" persuasions (he is married to the novelist and screenwriter Ioanna Karystiani, who was considered as a candidate for the Greek presidency by the left-wing government in 2015). Critical apprehension on the appearance of *Deep Soul* was concerned with whether the director had given the film any bias in favour of the communists. But his avowed intention was "to finally reconcile the bloodiest pages of our modern history". To do so, he showed each side as represented by one of the brothers, and placed them in one of the bloodiest locations of the war, in the Grammos mountains in western Macedonia: as Voulgaris puts it, "the last act of our nation's drama". Even the landscape – beautifully filmed – becomes a character in the drama of division and remembrance.

That Voulgaris is making a statement is clear from his opening captions, listing the numbers of casualties:

- Balkan Wars   12,000

- Anatolian Campaign   37,000

- Greco-Italian War   15,000

- Civil War   70,000[35]

While Voulgaris shows, with palpable empathy, the dying morale of the losers, he also demonstrates the moral and emotional dilemmas of the victors. At one point a grandfather, asking to reclaim the body of his only grandson, remarks, "This is not a war. This is a disgrace. Greeks fighting one another", to which Voulgaris provides the antidote of the military tribunal at which it is stated that the purpose of the state is "to provide the country with pure Greeks". It seems that if you oppose the politics of the current regime, you cannot be a "pure" Greek.

Voulgaris makes it clear that there are grey areas between the two sides, not so much in their ideology but in their emotional landscapes. The EAM frontline keeps asking when the Soviets will send support – ignorant that both Stalin and Tito had turned their backs on Greece. Neither brother can speak of why he is where he is, perhaps because he does not know. There is less of "us" and "them", of *agón* and *antagón,* than of an internal debate within the self. Certainties have been left behind. The final line, spoken by one of the disheartened losers is, "Did we win?" when it is clear that no one has won.

The American general supporting the official army in 1949 provides it with bombers, to drop napalm on the Grammos mountains, the last stronghold of the resistance, effectively bringing the war to an end. He states, "Grammos has been chosen for the world premiere" – of a form of warfare that would only come graphically to world attention in the US bombing of Korea and Vietnam.[36]

There have been other films in which the Civil War features to some extent – Angelopoulos' *Travelling Players* (1975), Nicholas Gage's *Eleni* (1985, directed by Peter Yates) and Giorgos Stampoulopoulos' *Pandora* (2006) – but none in which the war itself is the central character. This was a huge act of faith, by the director, in the role of trauma as a healing agent.

Angelopoulos' *The Weeping Meadow*, which can be taken as its director's commentary on the uncertainties and instabilities of Greece from the Anatolian Catastrophe to the Civil War, ends with a mother's dismay as she realises that her two sons have killed each other; she emphasises the mutuality of love, identity and destiny in her words, "You were him and you were you". Two sides of the mirror; one mind split by history.

But there is, you will be relieved to know, a serious Greek cinema which is not overtly connected to conflict of the political kind. However, it is not exactly light viewing. *Dogtooth* (2009), a psychological picture of a dysfunctional family, replicates some of the inhibitions inherently maintained in the Greek household, exaggerated to a frightening extent.[37] For the sake of brevity, this and *Attenberg*, two psychological thrillers, must stand for a range of work that challenges viewers on an alternative front to that of political battlelines, but they are an *agón* nonetheless.

Agorá, a documentary on the Greek economic crisis, was made in 2014 by Yorgos Avgeropulos, who explained that the *agorá* "was the heart of democracy. [It] has lost its initial sense and it has come to denote solely the place of commercial transactions", seeing the crisis as "an economical vortex that devours human lives".[38] The film is a clever juxtaposition of Greece's current economic malaise with the decline in traditional meanings and values.

There is also a satirical cinema, which occasionally runs the risk of forgoing "official acceptance". One such film, based on actual circumstances, was *The Saint of Agios Preveza* (1981). The bishop in question was not alone among his colleagues in availing of a mistress (unlike the priests, Greek Orthodox bishops are by definition unmarried) but he was caught and, well, exposed. The woman was the wife of another priest, who was also the bishop's chauffeur, owing his job to his complaisance in this affair. The bishop survived an ecclesiastical trial for "scandalising the conscience of the Christian faithful".

The film, directed by Dimitris Kollatos, was based on a play of the same name by Spiros Karatzaféres.[39] In addition to his sexual affair, the bishop, Stelianos Kornaroswas, also implicated in shady financial dealings, a preview of the scandals which would hit the church in the 2000s. He had previously been a junta-serving priest on the internment island of Makronisos.

Not only did the film capture the imagination and amusement of Greek viewers, but it provoked an elderly Corfiot sculptor, Aristeidis Metallinos, to make a bas-relief of the bishop with his mistress, he waving his penis at her while they engage in telephonic intercourse.[40]

The film was temporarily banned, allegedly due to the influence of the church, and the director was frequently in court on charges of impropriety.

The caption reads: "I'm waiting for you, I'm ready, nude my darling, I'm going to fuck you." (Reproduced courtesy of Angeliki Metallinos; photo by RobGroove Photography www.RobGroove.com)

Nothing quite so explicit can be found in Irish cinema, although Bob Quinn's *Budawanny* (1987), which was expanded into *The Bishop's Story* (1994), shows a bishop, his "housekeeper" and their child, a fact of episcopal life which became a reality in the revelation in 1992 that Bishop Eamon Casey, of Galway had, while bishop of Kerry, fathered a child in 1974. No one made a film about it.

An exhibition, *No Country for Young Men*, curated by Katarina Gregos, at the Centre for Fine Arts in Brussels in 2014, by young artists both resident in, and expatriate from, Greece, offers itself as a powerful example of the arts becoming explicitly political while at the same time resolutely doing what art should do: expressing the artist's own imaginative response to the world in uncompromising honesty and, dare I say, poetry.

The exhibition's title is, one assumes, a deliberate reference to W.B. Yeats' poem "Sailing to Byzantium", which opens with the lines, "That is no country for old men. The young / In one another's arms, birds in the trees – Those dying generations…" (equally, one assumes that the title is not a reference to the neo-western 2007 movie *No Country for Old Men*). The title, and the subtitle "Contemporary Greek Art in Time of Crisis", indicates the intention to show that Greece is an inhospitable place not merely for young artists but for all citizens.

"What are the prospects for the future in a country where 64 per cent of the under-25s have no work? How can we make the leap into the future from the ruins of Greece's glorious past?"[41] The exhibition made specific reference to the problem with titles like "Study for a Riot", "ADAPT – Apparatus for Defence Against Police Terror", and an ironic approach to the Greek heritage, "Parthenon Rising – Leave Your Myth in Greece", questioning the extra-tourist value of the site.

Not to be entirely negative, the exhibition showed "a sense of urgency, vitality, affectivity and emotive power". In the words of its curator, it aimed to "complicate" the otherwise evident effects of austerity (riots, strikes, the rise of fascism, street poverty) by examining how the crisis had affected people, institutions, landscape and artistic production. It combated imaginative poverty with realist presentations of how the artists saw their world.

Gregos referred, intriguingly, to statistics as "an abstraction", while clearly making the case that art was *not* abstract, that the work on show "transcend[ed] stereotypical media representations and provide[d] a wide-ranging, affective, insightful and critical view of what is happening in the country right now", reflecting "the social and economic reality" and "the dramatic transformations that have occurred". I find her use of two words, "affective" and "transformations", especially significant, since the art works have an affective impact on the viewer's consciousness and the artists all seem to believe that a transformation is possible.

The exhibition also "look[ed] beyond the gloom, to more imaginative, poetic, humorous or allegorical responses", offering "an opportunity to address our flaws, and shortcomings, to consider our collective responsibility […] to re-think and reinvent the country, and to imagine things differently" with the crisis making it possible "to reshape the country's future".[42]

No Country for Young Men – so titled despite the fact that 30 per cent of the artists were women – offered a broad spectrum of artistic-aesthetic responses to the crisis, in painting, prints, sculpture, video, photo-journalism and performance art; it was an indication that the perennial political role of art also has economic and moral repercussions in not only highlighting social problems (such as the collapse of the welfare state and loss of national sovereignty, consumer greed, and the shooting of Alexis Grigoropoulos) but also offering possible routes to a new scenario. It's an echo of Brian Friel's assertion, back in 1972, that "I see no reason why Ireland should not be ruled by its poets and dramatists".[43]

In emphasising that this was not a "national" exhibition, Gregos pointed out that the artists were selected "because of the relevance of their work at a very crucial historical and political moment for Greece, and for Europe as a whole" – not least because it was taking place in the European "hub", Brussels.

The thirty-five artists (and two collectives) ranged in age (with the exception of one 80-year-old) from 30 to 62, with an average age of 35-40; twenty-three were living and working in Athens, while the remaining twelve were in Germany, France, Belgium, Holland, Austria, the UK and New York.

The two collectives were "Guerilla Optimists", existing in Athens since 2004, and "Depression Era", formed in Athens in 2012 as a response to the crisis. The name "Guerilla Optimists" suggests (if taken in relation to their terrorist counterparts) that the members "engage in ephemeral actions in Athens". Pre-dating the crisis, it was formed because "national optimism was clearly ungrounded". Optimism is "an engine to get you out of bed and face the day", armed with "nothing but an absurd sense of humour and a belief that social conventions are malleable".[44] Their exhibit, "Dreamers: Public Dreaming in Omonia Square", is part of an agit-prop project "on public dreaming", in an experiment "with altering the psycho-acoustic field within the troubled Omonia Square" – a part of central Athens traditionally associated with illegal migrants, prostitution and drug-taking.

"Depression Era" – its name is also explicit – "suggests that there has been a loss of faith in the future, and understands that entropy, disaster and uncertainty are states of mind".[45] I'm bound to say that, as in poetry and prose, there are artists working on ideas about girls, chocolate and dancing (some of which was reflected, albeit in a macabre way, in this exhibition), but it is clear from the collective and individual statements of the artists in *No Country for Young Men* that there is a cerebral sense of social responsibility and at least a wish/hope that art can contribute to, if not influence, a new sense of direction which absolutely prohibits art from being abstract(ed). It is noteworthy, too, that not one of the artists referred to the issue of *national identity*, as if the pressing problems they encounter in their work have pushed identity to the sidelines as an irrelevancy.

Some ask "when will there be light at the end of the tunnel?" Others ignore such a foolish question and simply portray the current condition, leaving it to the spectator to decide whether the art points forward, back, up or down.

I have chosen a single image, not least because it has a direct relevance to one of Ireland's most international dramatists, Samuel Beckett: the artist, Nikos Navridis, finds "something affectionate, soothing and therapeutic in the words": "Try again. Fail again. Fail better."[46]

Nikos Navridis (b.1958), Again? No! *– neon light piece, incorporating reformulated words from Samuel Beckett's* Worstward Ho! *(Reproduced by kind permission of the artist)*

Music

Music is one of the great success stories of modern Greece. Composers of "classical" music have enjoyed more success and recognition on the international concert platform than film or drama on their respective "stages". At least four Greek composers of the

twentieth century have achieved this recognition: Mikis Theodorakis (b. 1925), Manos Hadjidakis (1925-1994), Iannis Xenakis
(1922-2001) and Nikos Skalkottas (1904-1949), the first three of
whom are Cretan.

My expertise as a critic is in the field of "classical" music. Although I deplore the walls which "classical" and "traditional" musicians have built between each other, my knowledge of, and ability to appreciate, traditional, "pop" and other genres of music are
extremely limited. So I have to exclude from my discussion such
popular Greek artists as the singers Nana Mouskouri, Vicky Leandros and Demis Roussos, and concentrate on the importance to
Greece of the question of "national identity" in music, which, you
will not be surprised to learn, is crucial to Greek society and culture. In these pages I shall concentrate on the friendship, rivalry
and contrasts of Theodorakis and Hadjidakis, calling heavily on the
work of Nikos Papandreou in his book *ΜΙΚΗΣ & ΜΑΝΟΣ: ιστορία
δύο συνθετών* (*Mikis and Manos: A Tale of Two Composers*).

The founding fathers of Greek music were from the Ionian
islands, and the principal composer, Nikolaos Mantzaros (1795-
1872), provided the music for the Greek anthem, a setting of the
"Hymn to Liberty" by Dionysios Solomos (another Ionian). The
provenance is important since it indicates the Italian influence of
the Romantic school of poetry and music, which provided such an
impetus towards ideas of "Liberty".

Epitáphios is Theodorakis' setting of the poem by Yiannis Ritsos (1909-1990), a communist whose work inspired the resistance
fighters; he was interned on prison islands for four years from
1949 and again in 1967 by the junta and his work, like the music of
Theodorakis, was banned. *Epitáphios*, written in 1936, on the eve
of the Metaxas dictatorship, became, in its musical setting from
1960, "the anthem of the Left".[47] Theodorakis said that in that work
"I succeeded in composing a piece of music which the people had
already heard, but only in their imagination".[48] This became the
hallmark of Theodorakis' skill as a composer and of the immediate
effect of his music: its ability to speak directly to Greek people of
their own, known, experience. And it helps us to appreciate how

Theodorakis himself has come to be regarded as the composer of "alternative" anthems which offer different routes to Liberty.

The principal difficulty in composing "classical" music to please Greek audiences was to adhere to a nationalist agenda in both respects: to emulate the styles of western music, which signified Greece's entry into Europe, while creating a "Greek" sound, thus, if it were possible, achieving continuity in both. Apart from a "Greek sound", the national agenda was followed by compositions – cantatas and operas in particular – based on events and personalities in the war of independence and subsequent milestones in the path to Greek freedom and self-expression.[49]

Music is a dangerous vehicle of expression, especially in the context of a society rooted in folk traditions which is experiencing the impact of the modern: dangerous because the attempt to be "modern" or, in this case, "European", may fail, thus relegating the society to backwardness in the view of modernisers; and dangerous also because in that attempt, the folk traditions may be damaged. This anxiety has been evident in many post-colonial situations such as Ireland, Finland, Norway and throughout central Europe. It is not so much the anxiety of influence as the anxiety of betrayal.

How to be Greek in music and yet accommodate western "classical" genres (or, *vice versa*, how to accommodate Greekness to those genres) has exercised the pens and consciences of Greek composers since the emergence of a "national school" in the nineteenth century. It bears a very strong similarity to the same dilemma in Ireland, where at the same period the debate centred on whether or not there *should* be a "national school" and, if so, what was meant by "national". In Greece, the pre-existence, in the Ionian islands, of an Italianate classical tradition pre-empted that debate, yet the Ionian music, from which sprang the foundation of Greek "classical" music, was regarded as non-Greek by the nationalists and therefore excluded from the agenda.

Manolis Kalomiris saw his symphonies as part of his "struggle to accomplish my mission: the creation of national music" – in which he saw the elements of folk music and "our past, our desires, our imagination and stories [...] the tradition of the Greek nation".[50] These symphonies have been seen/heard as the musical complement to the *Megáli Idéa*.[51] As Katarina Levidou observes, "music [...] was put at the service of building those cultural borders [...] in order to justify and defend [...] political borders".[52] A nationalistic insistence on the demotic folk tradition would find a natural home in the spirit of resistance, but the irony lies in the fact that that resistance would also become the home of the Left, in opposition to the gentrification of Greek through *katharévousa* and the purging of demotic.

Nikos Skalkottas who, in his own music, demonstrated an ambivalence most clearly (especially in his *36 Greek Dances for Orchestra*) said that "by using Greek themes, one could write music that would not be Greek at all, just as one could write Greek music without using any Greek themes".[53] Skalkottas was initially persuaded by his teacher, Schönberg, to believe that traditional music and classical were mutually incompatible – a belief belied by Hungarians such as Béla Bartók and Zoltán Kodály. But the *Greek Dances* were one of his attempts to circumvent this problem through experimentation. The problem remained one of using folk-tunes and being a modern composer at the same time.[54]

Skalkottas referred to "the noble origin of our folk-song, and its aristocratic tendency infus[ing] us with a breath of civilization"; in order to understand it, it is necessary "to gain a deeper intellectual knowledge" of the "national lyricism".[55] This seems to be hyperbole, and it also suggests a continuing confusion of ambiguity in the composer's mind. If the "national lyricism" is so potent, it should be visceral, rather than intellectual, in its affect. Skalkottas' dilemma is a microcosm of the debate between traditionalism and modernism, asking "how are we going to elaborate on them [folk themes] without distorting their real nature, beautiful content and strong character?"[56]

The Music of Mikis Theodorakis and Manos Hadjidakis

As we saw in the case of *rebétiko*, it is possible for a tradition to accommodate aspects of other genres and to undergo change; as with the language debate, one pleases everyone except the purists on either side. Nikos Papandreou writes that Theodorakis' direct contact with both *agón* and folklore "did much to free him of his obsession with classical composition",[57] but Theodorakis' continual revisiting of both folk music and classical was like that of Seán Ó Riada in Ireland – a never-ending attempt to bring the two into fertile congruence.

Theodorakis has, like Papadiamandis as a writer fifty years before, combined the Byzantine choral music (with which he was familiar as a child) with demotic (*rebétiko*) and the western classical style. At the age of ten he had composed a Passion and he later wrote a version of the liturgy of St John Chrysostom and a Requiem. The influence of these three styles can be seen in his subsequent work, whether symphonic, choral or dramatic.

Theodorakis stands head and shoulders above his compatriots as a national hero in respect of his world reputation as a composer of a particular genre: his innumerable compositions on themes of freedom and resistance, and versions of songs and poems by writers who have been punished for their beliefs.

To use a universal cliché, he is the *artiste engagé*, the equivalent, in culture, of a political leader almost entirely aligned to the Left. Having been banned by the Colonels, Theodorakis was "associate[ed] by default as the official musician of the resistance".[58] He wrote that "Greece needed art which sprang from the popular struggle and from living, modern Greek poetry".[59]

He was a member of EAM in the Second World War and organised its theatre group "Free Artists" which toured surreptitiously to villages occupied by the partisans.

After the assassination of Grigoris Lambrakis in 1963, Theodorakis not only composed the music for the Costas-Gavras film *Z* but founded the "Lambrakis Democratic Youth" organisation.

His settings of Seferis included one which was sung at the poet's funeral in 1971: the occasion constituted "a spontaneous (and rare) public demonstration against the regime of the Colonels".[60] The relevance of a Theodorakis song in memory of a poet who had defied the junta will be obvious.

Theodorakis has given inspiration to "freedom fighters" outside Greece: it is reported that in 2007 the Afghan Northern Alliance against the Taliban broadcast Theodorakis songs, while in

2014 Kurdish nationalists claimed inspiration from the music of *Z* in their fight against Islamic State (ISIS).

One has only to look at his *oeuvre* to realise the extent of his involvement with politics and literature. Some of the most notable compositions in which Theodorakis bore witness to the indignities, sufferings and injustices inflicted on the Left include his "18 Short Songs of the Bitter Motherland", mostly written by Yannis Ritsos in captivity on the island of Leros in 1968 after he had received a request from Theodorakis for a work which he could set to music. Of necessity, the work was recorded outside Greece in 1973.

Theodorakis emphasises that the word *symphony* "is a Greek word" and therefore that he has "the right to give it the meaning that I consider to be appropriate [...] For me, symphony is a wall-painting". He sees music as "a tragedy in which all persons would have to sing" (*tragoudia* being the Greek word for *song*, from which we derive "tragedy").[61] This helps to explain why most of his five symphonies[62] are choral, the seventh, "Spring" (1983), being settings of Ritsos, while the fourth symphony is a setting of two choral odes, Aeschylus' *Eumenides* and Euripides' *Phoenician Women*. His ballets *Antigone* (1959) and *Antigone in Jail* (1972) were banned by the junta (along with all his music).[63] It is alleged that policemen would stand beside an unsuspecting person whom they intended to arrest, sing a few bars of a Theodorakis song, and then make the arrest for the crime of listening to banned music.[64]

His cantata *Mauthausen* (1965) is the setting of the story of deathcamp survivor, the playwright Iakovos Kambanellis. *State of Siege* (1968) was written directly out of his own experience in prison, when his woman neighbour wrote a poem which "wounded me. Gave me comfort. Delivered me. It was the voice of all of us. It was our anger. Our bitterness. And our strength".[65]

Axion Esti (1960) is as important in the evolution of Greek music as its original poem by Elytis was in that of literature. At its conclusion, Greekness is defined in terms of symbols in which the natural world and its femininity are celebrated. In this work, Theodorakis was again responding to the "agenda" of establishing irreducible Greekness in the context of Greece's increasing Europeanisation. His judgement on the poem is at one with Seferis and with the Left's *agón*. "Its profound Hellenism places it in the forefront of our people's struggle for completeness from a historical and ethical standpoint".[66]

One strategy employed by Theodorakis to bring Greece and Europe together was the *bouzouki*, which immediately evoked the *rebétes* player (above, pp. 199-200). In *Epitáphios* his choice of Manolis Chiotis, the outstanding player of his time, was akin to Irish composer Shaun Davey's introduction to the symphony orchestra of the uillean pipes, played by Liam O'Flynn. This orchestration was a deliberate decision by Theodorakis to make his music accessible to an international audience (since the work was issued on the Columbia label) and at the same time to the national audience to whom the "resistance" of *rebétiko* would be instantly and viscerally appealing. A strong male voice underpinned this "*mangas*" aspect of the music.

The almost simultaneous recording of the setting of *Epitáphios* by Hadjidakis was, by contrast, more western-oriented, featuring the voice of Nana Mouskouri and a symphony orchestra.

For his inclusion of *rebétiko* in the work, Theodorakis was criticised by those who considered this low-life aspect of Anatolia to be demeaning to the "pure" Greece which the conservative classes and their politicians wanted to establish as the norm. The word "sacrilege" was used to describe his juxtaposition of Ritsos and *rebétiko*.

Theodorakis himself has acknowledged that "no member of the upper class could have ever listened" to his version of *Epitáphios*.[67] (It was, in fact, the popularity of Hadjidakis' version that drew attention to Theodorakis' among the middle classes.)

Nikos Papandreou wryly observes that the differences in the two settings "echoed two different visions of modern Greece – visions which continue to divide the country to this day".[68] Papandreou tells us that the two recordings sparked off a debate "analyzing the definition of 'Greekness' and aesthetic sensibility in Greek music. Does Greece belong to the East or to the West? Does Manos' lyricism respect Ritsos' poetry more than Mikis? Is Mikis' version authentically Greek?"[69] Theodorakis was seen as the "vocal agitator for the forces of change and progress", while Hadjidakis' "silence on political issues [...] was interpreted as evidence that he was on the side of the privileged and the elite of Greece". "Thus", Papandreou continues, "music became an expression of political sympathies [...] Until very recently, one could infer the political sensibilities of most Greeks through their record collection".[70]

This, as Papandreou points out, was "the most radical and powerful music modern Greece had ever heard" and "signalled the beginning of a rivalry between the two composers [...] into which they were drawn unwillingly".[71] They had, in fact, been friends, and, when Theodorakis was on the run in 1947, Hadjidakis sheltered him (although Theodorakis was eventually recaptured and sent to the prison islands of Makronisos and Ikaria). But their later "rivalry" served to highlight the difference between Theodorakis, an imprisoned artist closely identified with the Left, and Hadjidakis, a more establishment figure, who held positions in the Athens State Orchestra (director-general), the National Opera (deputy director-general), and the National Radio (director of music). He had won an Oscar for his music for *Never on a Sunday* starring Melina Mercouri, and, ironically, he was largely responsible for the revival – albeit in a purified form – of *rebétiko*.

Sofka Zinovieff remarks that "it was no coincidence" that Theodorakis and Hadjidakis "used the oriental, modal tunes of the rembetika as an inspiration and form for their work". Although she may be mistaken in thinking that both composers embarked on *rebétiko* as a compositional strategy, her observation that "music was a way of surviving in a country which was almost destroyed"[72] is apposite.

While embodying the spirit of resistance, all Theodorakis' works celebrate the sensuous, and express his distaste for coldness and indifference. *Passion* is both a spiritual experience and a sensuous immersion in nature. For example, his second symphony "Song of the Earth" (1981), with its obvious reference to Mahler's *Das Lied von der Erde*, not only articulates the composer's passionate embrace of the natural world but also acknowledges the darkness and uncertainty which threaten it.

Like Angelopoulos, Theodorakis has become disillusioned with the fate of Greekness. Nikos Papandreou paraphrases him: "where can you find Greekness (romiosyni!) in the modern villas mushrooming up in the suburbs of Athens? In the corruption of politics? The old passion that ignited his music," Papandreou tells us, "is lying somewhere in an abandoned trash can".[73] But, also chiming with Angelopoulos, Theodorakis says, "there is a ray of hope in my work because I was never able to accept a tragic end".[74]

9

CRISIS

Introduction

Suddenly, in 2010, a peripheral country in southeast Europe, with a tiny purse compared to the treasuries of Europe, known almost exclusively for its antiquities, its ancient wisdom and its eternal sunshine, moved centre-stage, as its budgets and their misman-agement overtook the attractions of a holiday destination. Antiq-uity was now in direct confrontation with modernisation; wisdom seemed to have been abandoned in recklessness; and gloom, rather than sunshine, was the order of the day.

Worse still, it seemed that Greek mismanagement and lack of financial savvy had not only endangered the welfare of eleven mil-lion Greeks – previously visible only as taverna-keepers and bou-zouki-players – but had undermined the foundations of the entire ten-year-old eurozone, as the possible catalyst of a domino effect which might be as serious for the global economy as the collapse of the Twin Towers or the Baring and Lehman Brothers banks.

Yannis Palaiologos, in *The 13th Labour of Hercules*, has coined the term "Great Crisis": in Greek it might be *"Megáli Krísi"*. If Greece began with a *Megáli Idéa*, it is danger of ending with a *Megáli Krisi*.

How could this possibly have happened? To quote Sophocles, "There is no evil greater for humans than fate imposed by neces-sity".[1] Greece, known for its classic drama, was now at the cen-tre of a dra(ch)ma of equally tragic character and import. It does not take a megabrain to assimilate the facts of a financial crisis, but it requires lateral thinking to see the crisis as a symptom of a deeper one. As President Papoulias warned in 2011, the crisis "is not just a question of numbers but a deeply political issue and an even deeper cultural one".[2] No one seems to have heeded his well-founded warning. This is the conceptual area which the European "statesmen" with responsibility for economic affairs were, apparently, incapable of appreciating. Economists, statisticians, strategists and their spin-doctors are not, professionally, qualified to address concepts beyond their sphere of expertise.

In *Understanding the Greek Crisis: From Boom to Bust*, two Greek economists, Michael Mitsopoulos and Theodore Pelagidis (both of whom had been financial advisers to the minister of finance), reached the height of economic irrelevance; they believe that, by means of 114 charts and comparative tables, they can "understand" the Greek crisis. The tables do, indeed, present a picture which *explains* much of the crisis, but they do *not* understand it. Admittedly, the authors' thesis hits the exact spot in their opening statement: Greece achieved "strong economic performance" (the "boom" of their title) but showed "very poor performance and pathologies on many other fronts".[3] Massive public debt, low competitiveness, an "underperforming educational system" and "high levels of corruption" were not exactly well-kept secrets for Mitsopoulos and Pelagidis to uncover. To call the Greek crisis "a rather straightforward textbook case of modern economics and political economy" is so naïve as to cause one to wonder how many other unique economies can be subjected to such explanation.

As is well-known and well-publicised, Greece has always been ungovernable. As Irish readers will readily appreciate, when your country is occupied by a dominant neighbour, you resort to evasion, secrecy, and bribery – this way of life permeates the DNA. Under its own domestic regime, Greece, from the 1830s up to today, was able to live comfortably with this DNA, haphazardly but according to its own rhythms. But Greece under external *diktats* which effectively control the economy, foreign relations and most of civil society, is a different country. It's one thing to live with your own defects at your own pace, and quite another to have those defects exposed by external auditors who demand their eradication.

The divided society that has always been Greece is today divided by those external forces, and the age-old capacity in the DNA for resistance becomes resurgent and more explicit than ever before.

As Palaiologos makes clear in *The 13th Labour of Hercules* (which *does* succeed in understanding the crisis, by case studies exposing the inertia, indifference and inefficiency of the public service), Greeks cling to the past and to closed societies because they resist change. They prefer to be mediocrities in a closed society (I am paraphrasing) rather than to let in the world. Yet, in the sense of nineteenth century Balkan nationalism, what Palaiologos detects as a "central malaise" is due not only to incompetence but also to wanting to remain Greeks rather than becoming, without reservation, "Europeans" – an as yet imperfect concept that yearns for completeness as its justification.

In these final chapters you may find that I am even more opinionated – and in Greece's favour – than previously. This chapter is limited in that, firstly, it is likely to go out-of-date as the facts of Greece's economic crisis are overtaken by more facts, more crises; and, secondly, to elaborate the complexity would use several trees to explore a collapse which, as in Ireland, can be reduced to a few words: ineptitude, greed, ignorance and indifference.

Thirdly, and in my opinion more significantly, it is not the nuts and bolts of the economy or the lies that were told by means of statistics and politically naïve rhetoric which can explain the crisis. Any competent draughtsman can write a timeline for the negotiations and the shenanigans that went on within the corridors of power. It is the wanton disregard, on the part of Greece's leaders, for the dignity and self-esteem – *filotimía* – of the people and the almost complete insouciance of the external powers to the needs of those people rather than those of economic models. Europe did not care, and Greece's leaders had become sufficiently Europeanised not to care either.

You might also expect that I would try to draw lessons from the preceding chapters to show how the crisis is embedded in history and/or culture (Papadiamandis and Angelopoulos *do* in fact shed light on the crisis-waiting-to-happen, but I'll refrain). In one sense, yes, the past and the culture it shows us are the seedbed of the problem; in another sense, one can look on it as a telephone directory in which one can find a reference to any aspect; not even the politicians are ex-directory. In a third sense, it is more than dangerous to attempt to appeal to history as an escape valve or a source of exculpation: history is *not* to blame, even though it may show where the blame lies. Like corporal punishment at school, it hurts history more than history hurts its pupils.

Like the general reader, my limited knowledge of the international financial markets prevents me from discussing "sovereign debt", "bond issue" or "haircuts". As if there were a banker with the skills of a Vidal Sassoon to cure Madame's itchy scalp without deranging her coiffure. I understand that Greece is indebted, to the point of bankruptcy, and that this debt is owed partly to lenders who invested in "Greece Inc." in the expectation of a profit. It is the debt owed to entities outside Greece – many of them invisible puppet-masters – that has caused the crisis.

Almost all the topics addressed in previous chapters – people, history, culture – have, with the exception of the problems discussed in Chapters 5 and 6, demonstrated the Greeks' capacity for survival. The problems of clientelism and the culture of dependence imperil that capacity, but not the instinct that drives it. The more one delves into the causes of the economic crisis, the more one realises that its systemic origins make it incurable. Most Greeks do not have a solution; only the most radical, who occupy the moral low ground of fascism and terrorism, believe they have the answer: the dismantling of the state. In such circumstances, politicians, strategists, economists, philosophers, financiers and bureaucrats are, to paraphrase W.B. Yeats, "helpless before the contents of their own minds".[4]

Of one fact I am absolutely certain: the man-in-the-street and the man-in-the-olive-grove are innocent of the macro-crisis. The people I see everyday in the village are ordinary folk who are dismayed and bewildered by their present circumstances – rising prices, cuts in their pensions – and disenchanted with the political parties that must take responsibility for the situation. Their support for Syriza in the January 2015 election was an indication that they voted for "hope" (the election motto of Syriza was *i elpída erchetaí* – "hope is on the way") rather than for any policy, because the distrust of governments and their policies has caused the greatest rift between the people and the state since the junta of 1967-74. (One thinks cynically of the much-quoted line by Seamus Heaney, "When hope and history rhyme",[5] and wonder at the piety of the thought in the Greek context.) What I opine in commentary on the crisis is therefore coloured by my automatic exoneration of the *kosmáki* from the blame-game.

The situation in Greece since the 2010 debacle has been a double-edged sword. It has, like the anticipation of death, focused people's minds on their trouble and made them realize that, in addition to the imperative to find a "life after death", the crisis was not merely economic but indicative of systemic failure. But the other edge of the sword has been the realisation that the system which they had allowed to be put in place, mainly at the behest of extremely persuasive politicians, had in fact not only caused the near-total collapse of their society but also been of their own making, since its genesis lay in their own desperate gullibility and their nonchalance about the larger matters of state.

As Kostas Tsapogas put it in 2012, Greeks had a "continuous disconnect from reality", an "unlimited sense of entitlement" which led to "denial of reality". Since the most recent example of geopolitical interference – the USA's support for the 1967-74 junta – Greeks had been bitter about such interference which, Tsapogas believed, had "greatly inflated [...] Mediterranean cavalier attitudes towards civil responsibility".[6]

While his linking of history to the current crisis is persuasive, we might add that populism (in the shape of the swollen public service) and lack of civic responsibility (for example, in tax evasion) were not the cause of the crash.

The high affairs of government, and their mismanagement, were certainly symptomatic of a malaise throughout Greek society. The pursuit of power by demagogues in New Democracy and PASOK was permitted and indeed made possible by the malaise at all levels of society. Unlike Ireland, where fingers could be legitimately and correctly pointed at key individuals and key institutions, in Greece transparency had always been impossible due to the opaque nature of society and its structures.

But the "disconnect[ion] from reality" is symptomatic of a much more profound difficulty for Greeks in perceiving and accommodating the western mind, just as, conversely, the western mind is generally incapable of understanding its "other".

If we look at the crisis from an exclusively domestic angle (the *oikonomía*), one of the most deranging aspects of the entire scenario, and of Greece's response to it, is that no one is prepared to take the blame, or even to admit that he or she knew it was imminent. Prime ministers, ministers of finance, civil servants, state economists and statisticians were reprehensible in their silence before the event, and in their disingenuousness after it. But the same can be said of all those who were living beyond their means: we are back again to the fireside, the husband and wife who over-borrowed in order to finance their children's extra-school lessons at the *frontistério*, or who simply spent money which they did not have; they were just as responsible for creating, from the roots up, the situation which, across the whole country, amounted to a national scandal which the politicians could not control but succeeded in denying.

Where have we heard this before? Ireland of course. No Irish person can afford to throw a stone at the Greeks for irresponsible spending, although there have been plenty of ignorant anti-Greek comments.

There are two attitudes to the impressions evoked by the overall crisis: one is typified by a reader's response to one of my *Irish Times* columns: "The Greeks want taxpayers in the rest of Europe including Ireland to pay the bill for twenty years of reckless spending, corruption and massive tax evasion." Another was expressed by a letter which argued:

> Greece is drowning in the platitudes of its 'friends' about remaining in the euro zone while simultaneously being emasculated by the insistence of these same 'friends' that it continue with 'reforms'... The whole debacle is now embarrassing. It is deeply damaging to Europe. It is also deeply humiliating for a people whose culture shaped European civilisation. Greece is haemorrhaging people, capital and

morale... Markets which, as Joseph Stiglitz has documented, were complicit in the failings of Greece's public finances, will make lots more money.[7]

As in all polarised positions, the "truth" lies in both, in neither,
and in the middle. Nick Malkoutzis sums up the reaction to the
original revelations of the crisis as:

> It's only when you're broke that people become experts on
> what you should or should not have spent your money on.
> It also gives them license to address you with all kinds of
> epithets. So, Greeks were labeled corrupt en masse with no
> regard for the fact that the serious graft was carried out by
> a small group of politicians, public officials and business-
> men, and that much of it took place with the help of for-
> eigners from countries that today preach to Greece about
> how it should follow the righteous path.[8]

The negotiations between the government and the EU have
been marked consistently by media commentators with headlines
such as "Greece Talks are Rooted in Unreality"; "'Til Debt Do Us
Part"; "Fiscal Figures are Hostage to Politics"; "Prescription for
Chaos in Europe"; "The Euro Has no Clothes"; "It's All in Vain" and
"Ousting Greece Will Not Bring Catharsis". While such commentaries have not been entirely negative, their authors have brought
a jaundiced eye and experience to the subject: clearly, the problem
would neither go away nor submit itself to facile solution.

The crisis has caused many, especially from the European
north, to take a "dim view" of Greece and the Greeks, as if suddenly the blanket charm of its touristic attractions had been stripped
away to reveal a people and a system indentured to graft, deceit,
inefficiency and incompetence.

It has also made many aware of the values enduring in Greece
despite this crisis. It has helped Greeks themselves to identify some,
if not all, of the causes of their malaise. The shock to the average
citizen, apprenticed to the mindset of "Yianni'll fix it", that PASOK
and the clientelist system were largely responsible, after raising his
boat, for sinking it again, could not have been more abrupt.

As Alexis Papachelas put it: "who will have courage to finally explain to the people just how much needs to change in order for Greece to become a normal country[?]"⁹ But what does "normal" mean? And who measures one "norm" against another? If that cannot be agreed, if the two mindsets cannot be brought into confluence on this point, there is no way forward: Greece becomes bankrupt and the architects of the eurozone are branded as inefficient and unrealistic planners.

The warning signs had been there since 2007, with a "real estate bubble", encouraged by the "lend, lend, lend" attitude of the banking sector, which in Ireland saw property prices rocketing, to be followed by massive collapses on the macro-scale for developers like Seán Quinn, and on the domestic front by many householders going into negative equity. The bankruptcy of Lehman Brothers, one of the USA's largest banks, not only punctured this worldwide bubble but precipitated a financial crisis throughout the world's banking and financial market systems.

Simultaneously, it was discovered that Greece's economy was in terminal decline; it owed €300 billion, a huge multiple of its GDP, and the highest "sovereign debt" in history. This in turn endangered the fragility of the eurozone which had not, up to that point, been challenged by any such factor. Greece's misfortune was that its crisis emerged at the same time as the larger picture took on its darkest colours.

Arthur Beesley, Economics Editor of *The Irish Times*, suggested that the question of whether or not Greece should be saved from extinction was comparable to the decision in the USA not to save Lehman Brothers, the collapse of which made the Greek, and even the European, segment look like relatively small potatoes.¹⁰ The question of saving Greece from itself was only secondary; saving Europe, and especially the banking sector, came first.

A considerable factor in its decision was the possibility that if the EU did not act to rescue Greece, Russian capital might be made available – geopolitics again, as if Russian entry into the Greek economy were the descendant of a Russian fleet passing through the Dardanelles. A central fact is that if Greece had not been a member of the eurozone, it would not have been saved; but, conversely, if it had not been in the eurozone, would it have needed to be saved? One is drawn to the conclusion that the EU panic would have occurred in the Irish, or the Portuguese, context rather than the Greek: if the Greek crisis did not exist, it would have been necessary to invent it.

As far back as mid-2011, an *Irish Times* editorial pointed out that the EU could either allow a Greek default "or take on some of its debts [...] The EU is being shaken to its foundations by this crisis".[11] That recognition of the choice – or lack of it – was not shared by hard-liners who insisted that Greece must not shirk its responsibilities. This increased exponentially after the complaisant New Democracy government was replaced by Syriza, whose policy, ever since the beginning of the crisis, was to rescind, or at least renegotiate, the bailout memorandum.

It was made startlingly clear by the European Central Bank that the banks were more important than the state, to such an extent that Jean-Claude Trichet, its president, pressurised the Irish government, in the same way that the IMF would threaten Greece, to adopt fiscal measures to restore the banking sector at the expense of the citizen, and to submit to a bailout. The Irish government was brought to its knees by ultra-national *force majeure* before it approached the question of financial support via a bailout.

It took an economic crisis of almost unparalleled magnitude and severity (on the Greek scale) to open up the inequities and weaknesses of the Greek system. If it did nothing else, it clarified issues which had remained largely unspoken – indeed, hidden – within the national conscience for many decades.

I say "almost" because, as early as February 2010, Vassilis Vassilikos (the author of *Z* and a former diplomat) suggested that the crisis "is actually a small problem by historic standards".[12] If history is not to blame, a historical perspective does show us that Greece, in the words of Kenneth Rogoff (a former economist with the IMF) is "a serial defaulter, worse than any Latin American country",[13] with a sovereign default most years since 1830, of which five have been near-catastrophic. That's another way of saying that Greece has been permanently in debt since its foundation, and its creditors were, and remain, the powers that founded it and maintained it.

Nevertheless, in 2011, at the World Economic Forum in Davos, Prime Minister George Papandreou admitted that "debt is not the problem, debt is just a symptom". The root cause was "poor governance".[14] This was the poisoned chalice of his father's legacy from which he had pledged himself to drink in order to deracinate that legacy. One wonders whether, even if he had survived the chalice, he would have succeeded in bringing Greece through the crisis.

When the *Voulí* debated a particularly harsh set of austerity measures, *The Irish Times* pointed out that "a continent holds its breath for a vote in the parliament of a small peripheral country".[15] This was not a case of the tail wagging the dog. The "peripheral country" had certainly moved centre-stage, but even so, Greece was not in a position to do more than lie down and beg for Bonio.

On the macro scale, in which even the entire EU and its common currency appears rather small, Greece is seen as a test case for a financial phenomenon much wider than the euro: there is a worldwide economic crisis which only radical correction, in the USA, Japan and the UK, for example, can overcome, while China sits on the sidelines waiting its time, which is now. The global economy has been called "an attack on the European principles of democracy, social justice and solidarity".[16]

It was in defence of, and in an appeal to, that sense of solidarity that Prime Minister Papandreou in 2011 wrote to Jean Claude Junker, President of the Eurogroup, arguing that a collective European approach to the Greek problem was necessary to prevent "new and possibly global calamities due to a contagion of doubt that will engulf our common union". He argued that only in this way could Greece secure its basic needs: "debt sustainability, access to [financial] markets and means to restart growth".[17] The fact that Greece has secured none of these points to the failure of Europe to act collectively to the Greek situation, as distinct from the overall European problem.

Statistics and Greek Statistics

Distrust of the Greek government by the EU and IMF has been based largely on the fact there were two major instances of false statistics being supplied to the EU. The first case was to support

Greece's admission to the eurozone in 2001; the government admitted, three years later, that the relevant statistics, relating to the country's budget deficit, had been falsified. The second case related to the state of the economy in 2009, when an actual budget deficit of 12.7 per cent was concealed (it was officially given as 3.5 per cent). The chief economist at the London-based Centre for European Reform called it "the most egregious example of budgetary data that we have ever seen in the EU".[18] It led to the cliché that there are "lies, damned lies, and Greek statistics", and to a common belief that Greeks were to be neither believed nor trusted.

The former head of the National Statistical Service, Manolis Kontopirakis, passed the buck to the Finance Ministry, claiming that he and his agency were forced by politicians to provide inaccurate statistics to the EU. Kontopirakis was disingenuous in fudging the issue: if he believed his agency should be independent of influence (as he subsequently asserted), why did he allow a political presence at crucial decision-making meetings? Everyone lied.

Brussels was supposed to check the statistics *and* the budget deficit forecasts. Clearly, it didn't do so. A major question must be asked, of which neither the asking nor the answer exonerates Greece: if Greece admitted to falsifying statistics in order to enter the eurozone, how could the EU subsequently accept further Greek statistics? The answer, in fact, is that because the eurozone was so vulnerable to a "Grexit" (or a "Grexodus"), Greece has to be kept inside the tent whatever the cost.

By 2010 the ubiquitous Yiannis Stournaras, who was at that time an economic adviser to the government, said that the national statistics were only the surface of a much deeper problem of inefficiency in the public sector, which meant that "nearly 1,000 public bodies do not publish annual accounts".[19]

One of the basic difficulties in assessing the income, expenditure and debt of the Greek exchequer is that its accounting procedures are not directly comparable to the "norms" of the international accountancy profession. This is only partly due to the imperative to hide one's assets from the inspector, whether Ottoman or EU. It is also due to a different way of seeing the world. The demand that Greece adopt "modern professional accounting procedures" would be better shod if it took on board the fact that, as in every other "cultural" aspect of the state, it is dealing with an "other mind" – one not necessarily amenable to the norms of the international abacus.

It's possible that Greek statistical methods simply were not commensurate with those of Europe as a whole.[20] But even if the statistical inaccuracies were the result of deliberate obfuscation and deception, their systemic nature can be traced back to the difficulties in establishing facts under Ottoman surveillance: not only were the peasants and their landlords "agin the government" and therefore predisposed to concealment, but there was also a completely natural difficulty in establishing the areas to be assessed, their ownership and their value. Today, for example, EU subsidies on olive over-production are over-paid because there is so much genuine (and non-genuine) confusion over the ownership and productivity of any particular grove.

Austerity and the Troika

The word "austerity" has figured earlier in this book. To say that Greeks today are affected by "austerity" is to say that they are re-experiencing – and of course in far more severe form – conditions that they have always known: first, the austerity of the landscape, climate and geography; second, the facts of history imposing a subsistence existence on the vast majority of the people; and third, the economic conditions under which its "independence" has been conducted.

If any body outside Greece was responsible for the imposition of austerity measures, as a means of correcting budgetary imbalances, it was the International Monetary Fund, the major partner in the "Troika" of the EU, the European Central Bank, and the IMF. The grounds on which the IMF's decisions were based have always been disputed, but three years after austerity began it was revealed (by the *Wall Street Journal*) that from the outset there had been disagreement within the IMF as to the purpose of the bailout.

The chief cause of dissension (voiced mainly by non-European delegates) was that there seemed to be only one solution on the table, and that its principal purpose was not to save Greece but to save the eurozone.

It was not merely the invasive and unsympathetic method of analysing the Greek system that enraged Greeks. It was the language of un-diplomacy, and the body language and personal unconcealed contempt in particular of Poul Thomsen, the IMF leader of the Troika. One can do business without being offensive, as Ajai Chopra (ranking number 2 to Thomsen in the IMF European department) demonstrated so ably when conducting a parallel investigation in Ireland.

After three years of IMF austerity, Viviane Reding, Vice-President of the European Commission, was honest enough to say, "European citizens do not trust the troika and they are right." She went on to present a fair case for its (temporary) presence: "We are grateful for the IMF's contribution to the various stabilization programmes in Europe, but this set-up has now run its course. The time for the troika is over."[21]

Thomsen's arrogant manner was symptomatic of this hidden agenda: to safeguard the eurozone, even if it entailed ruining the Greek economy. Greece would be used as a stick with which to beat other recalcitrant states such as Ireland, Spain and Portugal (the three other "PIGS"). By election time in Greece in 2014-15, it had become clear that "the IMF does not care about the political climate in Greece", that "all it cares about are the numbers and the goals".[22]

When Thomsen was asked, in 2013, whether he was "concerned about a social or political backlash" to fiscal measures, he evaded the question, merely saying that the "understood" that these caused difficulties, and that "horizontal measures should be avoided, focusing instead on areas where inefficiencies or excess spending remain", targeting carefully to protect the most vulnerable.[23] This, however, has failed: swingeing cuts in the health and social welfare budgets, and rising taxes, have damaged, rather than protected, the most vulnerable, while the mega-rich stay mega-rich and, it seems, untouchable. Cutting jobs in the public sector by mass dismissal rather than targeted severance and natural wastage may be more speedy, and it may rid the system of some of its passengers, but those passengers have families to support, who do not seem to have been taken into consideration.

The IMF/ECB/EU Troika demanded (forgive the pun) *perestroïka* – the Russian word for the complete restructuring of society introduced by Soviet leader Mikhail Gorbachev in the 1980s, along with *glasnost* (transparency). George Papandreou, the former Prime Minister and leader of PASOK, promised *perestroïka* in Greece, but it is the opaqueness, rather than transparency, of the Greek system that bedevils any demonstrable advance. And in the eyes of many, especially following Angela Merkel's statement that defaulting countries should be denied control over their own budgets, this puts Greece back where it was before 1821, when it began its fight for independence.

Following on from the issue of *filotimía* is that of "obligation": if one is in debt, one is beholden to the creditor; this creates a bond, and, in Greek society, it is only in the most extreme circumstances that one's self-esteem can accept such a dependence. Internally, as we have seen, the clientelist system created bonds of the extended family, but to be bound outside the family, community or tribe is an obligation – in fact, a dishonour – of another order.

Austerity meant less money in the pocket, and therefore less discretionary spending; higher VAT rates and emergency taxes on property and incomes to pay the unemployed added to the downturn. The result: widespread closure of retail outlets, exacerbated by the low-price wars between supermarket chains, which are largely foreign-owned. In 2011 alone it was estimated that nationally 120,000 shops would close, with a loss of €8 billion to the exchequer. Between 2008 and 2014 more than 200,000 small and medium-sized enterprises closed (a quarter of the total), 27 per cent of foodstores (butchers, grocers, bakers) and 20 per cent of minimarkets closed, with supermarket chains picking up most of the business. In downtown Athens, approximately one in five premises is vacant. A total of 280,000 people were put out of work in the first year of the crisis, and unemployment benefit (of less than €500 per month) is paid only for the first year. In 2010, 1,500 companies moved out of Greece; by 2012 the figure had reached 6,000, many of them relocating in a much tax-friendlier Bulgaria.

Old people used up their savings to support their out-of-work children and grandchildren, or those who could no longer pay their way after 25 per cent salary cuts, and a reduction in the minimum wage from €780 per month to €680 and eventually €580. (Those entering employment for the first time received 80 per cent of the minimum wage.) The comparable figure in Ireland was €1,461; in Spain €756 and in Portugal €589. Many employees have not been paid for several months, and those who lost their jobs have no chance of claiming redundancy payments.

Some public sector salaries were cut by 40 per cent. Pointing to the rise in public sector employment (from 12 per cent of the national workforce in 2000 to 20 per cent by 2011) was no justification for imposing such hardship on civil servants who, however inept or nepotic they might be, were hardly deserving, as a class, of wholesale dismissal.

By early 2012 it was established that more than 20 per cent of all Greeks were "at risk of poverty or social exclusion" – reckoning the poverty threshold at €7,000 per annum per person or €15,000 for a couple with two children. The figure increased to 35 per cent by 2013; the only European country with a higher at-risk sector was Bulgaria, on 48 per cent. Paying utility bills was the biggest single problem, with malnutrition becoming evident as shoppers could not afford a balanced diet of meat, vegetables and dairy products. Management companies of apartment blocks, inhibited by the rising cost of home-heating oil, shut the communal boilers. It was entirely sensible, if also rhetorical, for incoming Prime Minister Alexis Tsipras to refer to the crisis as "humanitarian", and having been caused by "the big wounds" of the bailout.[24]

While layoffs in the public sector were well publicised by the unions, the fact that over one million people lost their jobs in the private sector (due to the collapse of the retail market and of self-employed businessmen) went largely unnoticed, until one realised the extent of boarded-up shops in the high street. An unpalatable fact was that, by 2013, 120,000 professional young people had emigrated.

Youth unemployment in particular is causing tensions in which the financial dimension is less than the sense of being unwanted, unappreciated, unemployable, unable to contribute their skills and gifts to the common welfare. Society seems to be saying, "Let history repeat itself: emigrate".

The *Guardian* wryly called the Troika's package "tough love".[25]

Among my personal contacts in this position are pensioners whose income has been cut by up to 50 per cent, and journalists who worked either for a paper that closed (such as *Athens News*) or is so financially precarious (like *Eleutherotypia*) that salaries are permanently at risk. Kostas Tsapogas (whom I don't know) was foreign editor of *Eleutherotypia* until mid-2011 (when it temporarily suspended publication), with five months back-pay unpaid.

As the crisis deepened, the prevailing negative feeling was expressed as, "Nobody has a future". It led to suicides, with the *British Medical Journal* reporting in 2015 that the 30 per cent rise in suicides between 2011 and 2015 was directly due to austerity-induced depression. The most spectacular was that of a 77-year-old pharmacist (he shot himself in the head outside the Greek parliament) in 2012. His daughter described it as a "political act", while one observer, speaking on television, called it "political murder" on the part of government. Whatever his politics, there was no doubting his sincerity – his decision was the final, dignified act of protest against a system that had completely alienated him. It resonated through every Greek mind. Also in 2012, a television image showed a husband and wife on the ledge of the office building where they both worked, threatening to jump because they had both been sacked. It brought home to millions just how desperate an ordinary citizen can become when driven by fear or the very reality of losing these basics: home, family, respectability. Their (luckily averted) suicide was symptomatic of the increasing despair experienced by thousands of citizens, especially in the major cities.

Poverty is not ignoble. Odysseas Elytis saw its "ethical meaning" and "its own specific gravity".[26] At the most basic level it makes possible the survival of those against whom the elements seem to be hostile – not least the villagers of the smaller islands. Their fortitude in the face of adversity also has a spiritual dimension: their ability to live within poverty and to embrace, rather than resist, it. Elytis thought that this accounted for the "furrowed but always proud faces of the peasants". I mention it at this point because the "grace and strength of the Greek people"[27] is akin to the Italian idea of *sprezzatura* – grace under pressure. It is there in the down-and-out class which is now no longer composed of peasants but is a classless community struggling with one – but only one – of the worst social climates in their history.

Kostas Tsapogas may come from the professional middle class which one would expect to be more resourceful than the down-and-outs, more adept at survival, but he records that "like an overwhelming number of Greeks who are struggling just to get enough food, to keep their homes warm and to maintain a semblance of normalcy, we [he and his wife] are fighting to keep our dignity intact and avoid the depression that is enveloping our country."[28]

George Papandreou might have agreed with those who saw no future for themselves or their families, since, unless austerity laws were passed, Greece itself would have no future. But, as the son and brother of economists, he was lacking political *nous* if he believed, as he said he did, that the programme would introduce a five-year budget plan to "close this chapter of uncertainty".[29] If it did that, it opened yet another door to uncertainty. Four years later, we were no nearer knowing what the situation is.

One headline (in the *New York Times*) summed up the juxtaposition of the economic and social crises: "Amid the echoes of an economic crisis, the sounds of Greek society being torn." The article read: "Austerity is fraying the bonds of civility [...] Greece is unravelling [...] Every day the unbelievable becomes commonplace".[30]

In late 2011, on the eve of yet another bailout, Papandreou decided to hold a national referendum on the issue. He was three years premature. The 2014-15 election was precisely such a referendum, as Greeks voted for a party with no previous connection to the crisis or the political dynasties. Papandreou had, in fact, inadvertently donated to Syriza his 2011 slogan: "Let us allow the people to have the last word, let them decide on the country's fate".[32] It remained true as Greece was once more divided by the referendum which did, in fact, take place, in July 2015.

The economic consequences were obvious: a downward spiral of recession. By 2015 the "point of no return" had been reached: Greece could no longer meet its repayments to the IMF and other creditors, and the people could no longer afford to live. Which was the greater evil?

In a country whose GDP contracted by over 25 per cent between 2008 and 2013, it is totally unrealistic to expect anything other than spiralling recession, since the means are not there to inaugurate any kind of renascence.

In 2011, a year after the first rescue package was put in place, the question began to be asked, what is the *social* impact of the bailout? The numbers destined for long-term unemployment, when added to the growing number of homeless, the queues at soup kitchens and hostels, placed such a question higher in the minds of many than the purely (or impurely) financial ones, especially as NGOs which support the most needy with food and shelter were themselves in danger of closure.

Soup kitchens which were set up to aid migrants – "flotsam of human misery from central Asia" as *Irish Times* journalist Peter Murtagh saw them[33] – were now feeding "the new poor", whose average age had shrunk from 60 to 47 years. "I've lost my dignity" is a key refrain. *Filotimía* is the principal victim of austerity. If it is true that suicides have increased as a direct result of austerity, then it is a man's loss of dignity rather than his home or his savings that pushes him over the edge.

With the Athens municipal centre for homeless providing 1,500-1,700 beds per night, and, by 2013, the church operating 190 soup kitchens in Athens, these questions were still not penetrating the IMF mindset or, it seems, that of domestic politicians.

Whenever the time came for Greece to justify a new tranche of the bailout (and there were eight between mid-2010 and late 2012), parliament debated harsher austerity measures, the Troika continued to insist on more evidence of progress on promised reforms, and the media deepened our sense of crisis – society on the edge of collapse, the concept of democracy at stake, Greece further humiliated in the eyes of the world. And at every stage, the disbursement of the next tranche depended on clarifying residual uncertainties regarding Greece's capacity to implement reforms and to present satisfactory accounts.

And it was all true. The continual jumping through hoops became a circus repertoire which was only exacerbated by the change of government in 2015. When Syriza, of necessity, adopted the same strategies as its predecessors – albeit with an ideological face which immediately distanced it from ND and PASOK – it was proving the cyclic nature of political and economic reality: what goes round, comes round.

Whoever governs Greece would do well to consult W.B. Yeats's poem "The Circus Animals' Desertion", written in the disillusion of his last years, in which he reviews the "circus animals" of his career, creatures who sometimes danced to his tune, at others deserted him. He asks himself, "What can I but enumerate old themes" and concludes finally that "I must lie down where all the ladders start / In the foul rag and bone shop of the heart".[34]

The Euro-flaw

The major flaw in the design of the eurozone was that a monetary union without a fiscal union (with common accounting procedures and common tax rates) is in danger of collapse from the outset. Ireland and Luxembourg, with their attractive corporate tax rates and loopholes, have been thorns in the standardisation and Europeanisation of the EU's administrative system. Greece has posed its own differences.

The impetus towards the eurozone as a strategy of political cohesion has been the principal motivation of the centrist states, Germany especially. However much it made sense for them (and Britain decided not to join them) its application to the smaller and peripheral states had been arguable *ab initio*.

George Soros, the billionaire entrepreneur of Hungarian origin, criticised the "hidden weakness" of the euro in the lack of a common treasury; this had been exacerbated by the deteriorating political cohesion of the EU. Soros saw the inevitability of a "prolonged recession" of the eurozone, with "incalculable political consequences" which "could endanger the political cohesion" of the EU.[35] Meanwhile, criticism came from Irish MEP Marian Harkin, who called the euro "a currency still not fit for purpose".[36]

In 2014, months before he became a player in the Syriza bid for election, Yanis Varoufakis had called the eurozone "a one-legged giant".[37] Ashoka Mody, a professor at Princeton and a former IMF official, backs this up by saying that the inclusion of Greece, Spain and Portugal on Italy's coat-tails was the sign that "economic good sense in the euro's construction had been abandoned in the name of peace and friendship"[38] – although he really meant "in the name of desperately needed cohesion".

The entry of Bulgaria and Romania to the EU in 2007, and of Croatia in 2013, has caused doubts as to the wisdom of premature admission to an already unstable political and economic entity, with still undefined status in the eyes of the world. But the relentless drive, powered by Angela Merkel and her ambitions for Germany, seems to override any safety precautions. One Croatian farmer saw her country's future as "a province of Germany or Austria. I'm not sure that we have any chance".[39]

In 2015, the former chief economist of the European Central Bank said that he had seen the eurozone as premature and ill-conceived, and at that stage he doubted if all the members would remain inside. This was as close as he dared to saying that a "Grexit" would be neither petulant nor shameful. Moreover, operation of the eurozone is governed by regulations which have been described by senior economists as "impenetrable", their obscurity making them a mystery to the citizens of Europe to whose economies they apply.

From as far back as 2011, a Greek default was regarded as inevitable, even among senior politicians such as (we learn from WikiLeaks) Angela Merkel. Varoufakis was, therefore, for once not bluffing when he said it in 2015 to a Europe which pretended to be shocked by his statement.

For Greeks, their farewell to the drachma was sung with mixed feelings: even today, a majority favour remaining in the eurozone, chiefly because they have been warned of the dangers of a Grexit. But many support a return to the drachma. The eurozone suffers from the fact that as a uni-currency it cannot be devalued; an independent Greek currency would enable devaluation and thus save the country from the worst effects of a Grexit and a default on its debts.

Vassilis Vassilikos (quoted above) also pointed out that most Greeks regarded the euro not as a threat to national sovereignty but as a protection against "the headwinds of the international economic crisis". And he accepted that it offered an opportunity to create "a new world of economic development" to replace the outworn system. But the "burden if any needs to be fair and just";[40] in other words, if you tax the little man – the *kosmáki* – and reduce his salary, you must be seen to act equally towards Mr Big, and that, as the EU continues to point out, has not happened.

The IMF Error

It has been argued (by Antonis Karakousis) that in 2008 the IMF was too preoccupied with the US banking crisis to realise the significance of the Greek situation, and that they had even insisted that Lehman Brothers was "reliable, robust and protected from all dangers" just before its collapse. After the American debacle, the IMF saw a new role for itself in Europe, using Greece as a guinea pig; due to George Papandreou's indecision and inability to apprehend the dangers, the IMF entered and took charge of Greece.[41] Together with EU officials and the ECB, it constituted the "Troika" which has been the IMF surveillance mechanism, deciding on Greece's economic future and judging its performance of the imposed reform programme.

The basic flaw in the austerity package was the failure to realise that, since Greece does not have the elasticity of a modern, industrialised economy, with a sophisticated interface of imports and exports, it is not a "developed country" and therefore its exchequer would atrophy as taxes imploded and incomes collapsed. You cannot revive an economy in recessionary free-fall. Yet, knowing the conditions and structures of the Greek economy and economic history, the IMF and its Troika partners nevertheless insisted on a textbook austerity package which they later admitted was ill-conceived.

This was not merely a financial problem: as the chief economist of the Nomura Research Institute (an international consultancy) said, it was like "administering the standard treatment for one disease to a patient suffering from an entirely different disease which they knew nothing about," thus imperilling the political stability of the EU.[42] Following the referendum of 2015, economists worldwide condemned Angela Merkel in the same terms, arguing that German and EU medicine "has bled the patient, not cured the disease" (*Irish Times*, 7 July 2015).

Christine Lagarde, incoming head of the IMF, not only admitted that the IMF's decisions regarding Greece were, with hindsight, the wrong ones (taken under her predecessor, Dominique Strauss-Kahn), but also mistakes had been made in respect of the rescue package for the Irish banks. "Decisions were made on the spur of the moment under a climate of extreme crisis".[43] Many would say that this amounted to panic, and that panic suggested amateurism rather than a thoroughly professional judgement based on mature experience and comprehensive information. That the EU and the IMF could have got it so wrong on the issues of statistics and austerity in 2001, 2007 and 2010 can, of course, be attributed to the fact that they were dealing, unknowingly, with an "other mind", but that is no excuse: in warfare you must know your enemy, and the same goes for peacetime. As *The Irish Times* observed, there was not only a difference "between northern Europe's rule-based Germans and southern Europe's pragmatic Greeks", but "Greece occupies a different political reality from its EU partners".[44]

A comparison with Ireland is very instructive: as a letter in *The Irish Times* pointed out in 2015, "what Greece is asking is that the portion of its debt that relates to the private banking sector should be Europeanised because forcing the Greek taxpayer to borrow money it cannot afford to repay [...] is stupid, both morally and economically, not to mention inefficient".[45] Meanwhile, in early March 2015, as Greece entered crucial negotiations about the terms of future payments of the bailout, finance minister Yanis Varoufakis pointed out that "clever people in Brussels, in Frankfurt and in Berlin knew back in May 2010 that Greece would never pay back its debts. In this position, to give the most bankrupt of any state the biggest credit in history, like third-class corrupt bankers, was a crime against humanity".[46]

More serious than the IMF getting its sums wrong is that it failed to take into account the dysfunctional public service, which at present is quite unsuited, and resistant, to reform. If the system itself cannot be reformed, it is incapable of implementing the reforms demanded by the Troika. Funding dependent on a reform programme would therefore always be in danger of being withheld.

Members of the EU Task Force, sent to Greece not as a hit-squad but as a team of technical advisers (on issues such as reform of tax, public administration, the judiciary or on issues such as policy on migrants),[47] have told me that they understand why Greeks have two ears: so that the advice can go in one ear and out the other. That's rather unfair, but it is undoubtedly the case that the task force's advice is pointless in many respects because the system (which they are there to help reform) is incapable of absorbing and implementing it due, as always, to the impenetrability of the administration, the passing of files from one office to another, and the inbuilt resistance (that word again!) to change. The idea floated by the German finance minister that he would send 500 inspectors to sort out tax evasion was greeted not with hostility (another German invasion) but with hilarity.

In 2013, the *New York Times* had editorialised that austerity had "choked off investment and squandered human resources" and that "further sacrifices [would not] revive Greece's economy or make its debt burden more sustainable", but "the more implausible austerity becomes as an economic remedy, the more unchallengeable it seems to be as a political mantra".[48]

A year later, the former head of the IMF, Dominique Strauss-Kahn, admitted that the austerity programme was "unbearable" and that the Troika should have applied "less pressure and more growth". Greece was suffering "the terrible consequences" of the wrong policies.[49] In 2013, one Athens journalist stated his opinion that "the troika seems to have no plan, no real understanding of either the Greek economy, nor of the workings of the state, faulty as it may be. It's a bean-counter's game for them, but for the people involved it's poker with their lives as chips".[50]

George Soros also said in 2015 that the likelihood of a Grexit was 50-50; he anticipated that "efforts to save Greece might go down the drain"; Greece was in a "lose-lose game" and its problem had been wrongly approached from the start.[51]

History may not be to blame, but it can teach us how to avoid mistakes: one lesson to be learned and applied is that, on the eve of the Treaty of Versailles (1919) at which severe penalties were inflicted on Germany for its role in the war, the British economist J.M. Keynes had warned that there was a choice between "crushing Germany" and "not crushing Germany". "If Germany is to be milked, she must not first be ruined".[52] As we know, the consequences of the reparations were Germany's financial ruin and the advent of Adolf Hitler. Today, many see the punitive measures against Greece as ruinous, and the milking parlour as a place of execution.

Besides, to impose, as a desperate alternative, the vicious terms of a rescue package for Greece, Ireland and Portugal was, as *The Irish Times* opined in 2011, "in effect a form of collective European economic governance".[53]

Protests

The "indignants" (above, pp. 146-47) were the quiet face of resistance: their occupation of Syntagma Square was visible and dignified. Protests which led to riots and loss of life were the most overt, visible and violent.

Many protests have begun peacefully and ended in violence. It needs only slight provocation, and the degree of provocation lessens as frustration and temper grow in the face of hopelessness. Molotov cocktails and paving slabs on one side, baton charges and tear gas on the other. As Nick Malkoutzis observes, "When there are riot police in full gear standing in front of the Finance Ministry to protect it from disabled protesters riding wheelchairs and using walking frames, you can be pretty sure your country is heading in a worrying direction."[54]

Blockades of the parliament building and the ministries, shop windows smashed and looted, cars and waste bins torched, Afghans and Pakistanis beaten up on the streets. Three bank employees died when their bank was fire-bombed during a protest march in May 2010. A man in the crowd tells a journalist: "It is good that people take to the streets. They have taken away our rights. We have kids and loans to pay".[55] Even the police unions and the judges have gone on strike.

The polarisation of the country into pro- and anti- bailout has not only been extremely divisive but has obscured the fact that, regardless of external involvement, the country urgently needs systemic reform, and a repair of structural fissures, not all of which can be blamed on PASOK or the culture of clientelism. However much one may want to side with the traditionalists in protecting the inestimable quality of life endowed by the social heritage, it is impossible to see Greece surviving in the global marketplace ("a viable political unit in the planetary age")[56] as either a tourist venue, an importer or an exporter, without some accommodations with that marketplace: modernisation is not all bad; tradition is not all good.

Polarisation intensified to the point of mutual vilification at the end of 2014, when it seemed inevitable that Syriza would win the upcoming election. More threatening than any internal debate, however, was the blatant attempt by various EU-led factions to influence the outcome by denouncing the Syriza government before it had even gone to the polls or been elected.

One ordinary man told a passing journalist: "We are heading towards a scenario of civil war, but it's only natural when the rich are against the poor, when the extreme right wing fights the extreme left wing". Prime Minister Antonis Samaras tried, unsuccessfully, to use this argument in his bid for re-election in 2014-15, warning of the extremes of fascist Golden Dawn and communist Syriza as the enemies, while he promoted himself as the only one to defend the middle ground.

Passing the Buck

The blame game isn't a Greek phenomenon, but it is rife. In the opinion of political journalist Nikos Konstandaras, there was never any question of Greeks passing the buck and claiming that their "feelings of humiliation and incompetence" were attributable to "evil foreigners who had been waiting for an opportunity to terrify us with bankruptcy". Konstandaras attributes blame to the clientelism which had created an incompetent public sector "which destroys all ambition and productivity".[57]

Angela Merkel's personal attitude towards Greece has been seen as vindictive in making no allowances, and influencing other EU leaders to oppose a Grexit. But in 2013 she, too, passed the buck when she accused her predecessor, Gerhard Schroeder, of wrongly supporting Greece's admission to the eurozone. The present crisis was due to him, not her. In 2014, another German ex-Chancellor, Helmut Kohl, also blamed Schroeder for premature admission of Greece, calling for Europe to support Greece. His government, of course, was not a party to Greece's entry to the eurozone. Of course not.

When it came in 2015 to the question of a parliamentary enquiry into the background to the initial bailout, Syriza and its coalition partner proposed that the period under review should be 2010-14 – the time of the immediate crisis; PASOK wanted the period extended to the years 2004-2009, since those were the years of the New Democracy government, while ND proposed taking the enquiry back as far as 1981, so as to include PASOK even further in the blame game. Any outside observer could be forgiven for wondering which was the pot and which the kettle, so anxious were each to emphasise the blackness of the other.

But the most blatant, self-serving and disingenuous case of passing the buck was former Prime Minister Costas Simitis, in his extensive (350 pages) apologia, *The European Debt Crisis: The Greek Case* (2014). The best way to tell a lie is to tell it openly, just as one should wear one's secret where no one suspects it – on one's sleeve. Simitis proves, in this book, that he is a consummate liar (aka politician) because he never tells the truth but succeeds in persuading the gullible that it *is* the truth. And he is not a Cretan.

His narrative of the crisis is disingenuous in that he was the leader of one of the parties (PASOK) which supervised the crisis, and was Prime Minister from 1996-2004, one of the longest serving in recent history. At every point where it is possible for the author, and the party, to muddy the facts, he does so, but even more interesting is his disloyalty to the party itself and to his successor, George Papandreou. Simitis does not attempt to explain his government's actions; as a diversionary tactic he points to the previous (ND) government under Konstantinos Mitsotakis (1990-93), the

ND government which replaced him (under Constantine Karamanlis, 2004-09), the PASOK government under Papandreou (2009-11) and the ND-PASOK coalition 2011-15 under Antonis Samaras as the guilty parties – governments which mishandled the negotiations with the EU, supplied false statistics, and misled the people.

Reading his cosmetic, sanitised account of his own conduct of the premiership, one looks in vain for the slightest expression of responsibility or remorse. Not even a *mea minima culpa*. Everyone was to blame except Simitis. He might have recalled the Cretan proverb, "Can anyone be innocent, as long as someone else is at fault?" There is no sense of loyalty on his part towards his party, his colleagues or the idea of the Greek state which he was supposed to serve. Any unbiased reader, with no preconceptions or prior knowledge, would quickly form the view held by so many outsiders that Greece is a nation of cheats, incapable of rational thought, always adept at passing the buck and exonerating themselves. That reader would find it difficult to be charitable towards Greece or the Greeks because a respected political leader is so clearly incapable of resolute action, honest advocacy or responsible truth-telling. How could Greece maintain as head of state for eight years a man who excels at self-serving rather than serving the people?

I am surprised that Simitis identifies "the gulf in competitiveness between the Core and the Periphery" as the "principal defect of the Eurozone",[58] when it has been definitively shown that its principal defect, from its inception, was its lack of an adequate structure. Simitis does, however, suggest that the EU itself was incapable of solving a crisis due to political indecision and cowardice; but this is only to bolster his case that the EU mistreated Greece, a fact that is scarcely heavy ammunition in his exoneration of C. Simitis. Merkel and Sarkozy are the perpetrators, not the Greek government led by Mr Simitis.

Simitis turned Papandreou's ill-fated call for a referendum on the debt crisis into an attack on Papandreou's political cunning. It would have been more honest if he had said that Papandreou was simply not cunning enough to pull off the stunt Simitis attributes to him: "to isolate himself from the political costs of further reform" if he could not also gain re-election by means of the referendum.[59] He gives no credit to Papandreou for trying to change the political system instituted by his father, nor does he recognise that the systemic faults continued during his own period as premier, about which he did nothing.

The book, ultimately, is a litany of facts for which Simitis takes no responsibility, and for which he blames all other politicians. If one did not know who the author was, it would be impossible to deduce that he had been Prime Minister during eight of the most crucial years in modern Greek history.

2015

Syriza's victory in 2015 changed everything and it changed nothing.[60] As the first-ever Left government in Greek history, it marked a seismic shift in voters' attitude to the political options. As a government faced with the impossible task of carrying through reforms which it knew were impossible, its leaders were fated to become as susceptible to obfuscation and ambiguity as all politicians.

Syriza campaigned on a programme of which the foundation was the rejection not of the terms of the bailout but of the bailout itself (the "Memorandum of Understanding" between Greece and the EU). Rescission of the austerity measures followed from this. On this, as any strategist (including the man in the olive grove) could tell, they had to retreat. But this was not the first time that governments had tried to renegotiate the bailout. The New Democracy coalition tried it in 2012 and were slapped. Politicians who, in opposition, had denounced the bailout became, in government, its sponsors. As Nick Malkoutzis put it at the time, "they had not had a change of heart, they [had] simply traded roles."[61] The non-negotiable *diktat* of Brussels, heavily influenced by Germany and, to its shame, Ireland, was *pacta sunt servanda*: if you make an agreement, you honour it, regardless of the fact that it was your predecessors who inadvisedly made the agreement and regardless of the fact that no parliament can bind its successor.

Martin Wolf of the *Financial Times* observed that *pacta sunt servanda* was "the attitude that sustained debtors' prisons". He went on to say that "creating the euro zone is the second-worst monetary idea its members are likely to have", but that "breaking up is the worst".[62] It is Greece, not PASOK or ND or Syriza, which would default, and the blame for the collapse of the euro would be laid at its door.

From this lesson we can understand how important it was for Syriza to appear, at least, to rid the country of the bailout and to be seen to do so, so as *not* to accept any aspect of it.

The chief victim of all this was Alexis Tsipras, because he was elected on a programme he thought he might pull off (with the help of Yanis Varoufakis' gamesmanship) but which he, and everyone else, knew he couldn't. Different from almost all his predecessors in political breeding, grooming and performance, Tsipras ran the risk, as do all politicians, of behaving exactly like all the others. If George Papandreou I had been recognised as the creator of a monster, he would have died a fallen idol, rather than the national hero pushed into an early grave by the first wave of post-war fascism. Tsipras also ran (and at the time of writing, still runs) the risk of seeing his plinth collapse before his statue is placed upon it. Even to say that Syriza "as a relatively new party" has been "tainted [...] in the same way as other elements of the political establishment",[63] is to acknowledge firstly, that all other politicians *are* tainted and, secondly, that Syriza would, inevitably, *become* tainted.

Even after the referendum of July 2015, which definitively rejected EU demands for increased austerity, there is considerable doubt as to Greece's viability, as an economic state, either within or without the eurozone, so depleted have its resources and its morale become by the effects of the crisis. The fact that Greece won a battle but seems to have lost a war (with the likelihood of continuing austerity and indignity and further international humiliation) indicates that geopolitics, globalisation and Merkelisation are stronger than ideology or the will of the Greek people. The alternative to submission is to walk away: a Grexit, whether graceful or not, and a return to the drachma, would mean an already bankrupt country becoming more bankrupt and internationally vilified by politicians and financial institutions, but nevertheless set on a path of self-determination which might or might not be self-destructive. Rather to die at one's own hand than that of another, perhaps.

10

GREECE, IRELAND AND THE EUROPEAN UNION

The real "crisis" is not economic. The problem is "Europe". It is exacerbated by a curious linguistic conundrum: the letters "eu" are the prefix for Greek hopefulness and positive thinking: *eu*phoric, *eu*phemism, *eu*cratic and *eu*logy speak of good things, and even *eu*genics suggests the way to breed a better type of person. None of this chimes with the current Greek experience; in fact, Greeks might greet this eu-turn in linguistics with laughter, if they still had the capacity to laugh.

Economics – as the modern economists understand the term – are marginal to the European crisis of identity. The intimate relationship within the household was never money-centred; balancing the family budget is of course a priority, but the essential glue in the household is the sense of purpose and identity: the location of *filotimía* within the partnership of the family and extended family, where the balance between honour and the risks to honour supersede any idea of finance. The Greek household – like any other – predates the money economy and its priorities have not been overtaken by monetarism or even by globalistion. Extrapolate *filotimía* to the European or global level and you have the essentials of good housekeeping.

If survival is the basic imperative, and if one lives a subsistence existence, then any deficit means potential disaster in the form of famine. That's what Greece faces today. If you cannot *be* yourself, and *know* yourself, then whether you're in debt or have drachmas in the bank, is of no consequence.

The economic argument about fiscal rectitude ignores two factors, one of which is the domestic *oikonomía*. The second and the more vital factor affecting any society's wellbeing is its *cultural identity*, the essential "Greekness" or "Irishness" or "Frenchness" which distinguishes each culture from its neighbours and defies homogenisation. To homogenise tax rates across the EU may be a eurocrat's harmless dream, compared to the homogenisation of people's minds: perceptions, beliefs, behaviours, excitements, passions, sadnesses. To "integrate" cultural perceptions and practices will result in a one-party or one-mind state which punishes deviancy and, out of fear of the "other", presents a united front against that "other".

It is proving difficult to maintain the cohesion of the nineteen states of the twenty-eight-member EU which use the euro and which are bound by that single currency. It is impossible to bind them together culturally, by a single understanding of what it means to be European: an aesthetic and conceptual equivalent of the standardised "eurocumber" which, along with the homogenous apples, strawberries, tomatoes, carrots and twenty-six other fruits and vegetables, was attempted from 1988 until it was abandoned in 2009.[1] The idea of the "authentic" is becoming increasingly local; as a former president of the EU Commission, Jacques Delors, once commented, "You don't fall in love with a market"[2] – especially if the market vendors stock only standardised produce.

As Stratos Constantinidis remarks, "the expected unity of European culture will occur when there is a reciprocal cultural exchange in which each member nation-state internalizes the culture of the other nation-states [...] But who controls the 'gospel' of European cultural unification?" He asks, "how to educate the citizens of the various nation-states to see themselves as Eurocitizens (not as nationals) without transforming the united nation-states of Europe into one 'nation."[3]

If a workable formula could be found (and not a meaningless concoction of empty words) which would genuinely and positively respect identities and *all* their constituent elements, then citizens in Greece, Ireland and other states which are troubled by integration would perhaps be more willing to contemplate, if not to accept, the concept of a European unity which is less than a union but more than a concateNation.

Bullying

For the ordinary Greek citizen, the most shocking and offensive aspect of the run-up to the 2015 election was that, in the face of an anticipated Syriza victory, individual politicians and officials in Europe attempted to coerce public opinion into voting for the *status quo*, by scare-mongering tactics suggesting that a Syriza government would mean disaster. Voters ignored these tactics because they were already familiar with disaster: austerity had reduced them to pawns in a global game of money-power. Any as yet untried option would be preferable to the failed solutions which were also the cause of the problem they purported to solve. More disaster does not seem too terrible if you are without hope or resources – the man in the soup queue wearing a crumpled Armani suit.[4]

The bullying of the Greek voters was blatant. In December-January of 2014-15, Jean-Claude Juncker, the chief of the European Commission, made it clear that "I wouldn't like extreme forces to come into power". The tone was admonitory: "the Greeks know very well what *a wrong election result* would mean for Greece and the eurozone". When questioned, Juncker said that he wanted Greece "*to be ruled* by people who have an eye and a heart for the many little people" but "who also understand the necessity of European processes" (my emphases).[5] When he claimed that this was not his personal opinion, he was making it obvious that it was the EU's view of the Greek situation. And Juncker was also reported as saying that he would like to see "familiar faces" in government,[6] by which he presumably meant a continuation of the ND-PASOK coalition which had shown such deference to the EU.

Two inconsistent facts stand out from Juncker's statements: firstly, that the Greeks should be "ruled" and secondly, that while concern for the *kosmáki* is important, the "European processes" were more important. You cannot "rule" if you respect the *kosmáki*, and observance of any external considerations must come second to the welfare of the citizen; demonstrably, ND and PASOK had failed to honour this commitment to their electorate.

At the same time, Pierre Moscovici, the EU's commissioner for Economic Affairs, "indicated that Brussels had 'its preferences' in which government it wants to deal with", even though he said, in the same breath, that "he did not want to interfere in Greek politics".[7] So, in interfering, he was going against his own better judgement? After the election, the leader of the junior coalition partner, Panos Kammenos, drew parallels between today's negotiations with Brussels and the resistance to the Turks by nineteenth century Souliots (from Souli in northwest Greece) who blew themselves up rather than succumb to foreign power.

These were unelected officials of the EU. But many elected leaders, including Ireland's Enda Kenny, baulked at impartiality towards Syriza: Kenny made it clear in January 2015 that "while the forthcoming elections are a matter for the Greeks themselves", he hoped voters would "choose an option which keeps them in the euro zone".[8] Since Syriza had consistently stated that it had no intention of a Grexit, it's unclear whom else Kenny can have had in mind: obviously he was subscribing to the eurospeak, dominated by Merkel and Schäuble in Berlin, that Syriza *would* seek a Grexit once in power. Like Juncker and Moscovici, he wasn't interfering in another country's elections. Oh no.

And in playing Ireland off against Greece, undiplomatically and unwisely, eurospeak became offensive. Christine Lagarde told *The Irish Times* that "I trust the wisdom of the Irish people to see what is in the best interest of the country".[9] By implication, she was suggesting that she did *not* trust the wisdom of the Greek people to do likewise. Some even saw the need to "save" Greece from the supposed communism of Syriza as comparable with Churchill's decisive steps in 1945-46 to ensure that the communist partisans who had helped him to win the war should then be crushed, in order to safeguard Greece in his geopolitical strategy. Germany's Wolfgang Schäuble stated clearly that attempting renegotiation was "a waste of time", and that the Greek people were suffering for the mistakes of their political leaders.[10]

The bullying (or snide innuendo) was not limited to politicians: in the *New York Times* journalist Landon Thomas Jr. referred to the about-to-be-elected Tsipras as "the leader of an unruly band of left-of-center political parties", and described the Syriza alternative economic plan as "a grand bargain of sorts", even suggesting that a Syriza win was not a foregone conclusion (which it was).[11]

After Syriza's election, and the formation of the coalition government, Noel Whelan observed that "the centre-right governments in charge of most of Europe have no interest in seeing this new left-wing Greek government succeed".[12] That this antagonism towards a government might prove anathema to the austerity mindset stemmed largely from the fact that the centre-right leaders depended for their existence on voters who were annoyed, and even outraged, by further financial aid to Greece. Juncker himself said, "we all know what to do, but we don't know how to get re-elected once we have done it".[13] As Whelan remarks, "the economic case against giving the Greek government what it wants may be very strong but the political imperative against doing so is stronger still".

To read Arthur Beesley's chilling account of how European finance ministers stepped back from supporting Greece suggests that arms (and probably other parts of the anatomy) were twisted to induce a hypocritical reversal of intentions. The Slovak minister said, "he had no intention of losing another election by accepting write-downs on loans to Athens".[14] Portugal, Spain and the Baltic states followed suit.

The Slovak Prime Minister, Robert Fico, then expanded on his country's refusal to support Greece by saying:

> It would be impossible to explain to the public that 'poor' Slovakia should compensate Greece. To explain to people that we have to give money to Greece for their salaries and pensions? Impossible. Impossible. No one in Europe wants to pay money to Greece.

Mr Fico, a centre-left leader who faced re-election in 2016, said his views were shared by many EU member states, and that Syriza was slowly realising that its "beautiful plans", drawn up while in opposition, are now meeting opposition from other cash-strapped eurozone countries.[15] This hectoring of the Greek voters by senior European figures intensified in the week preceding the referendum of 5 July 2015, so much so that Greek politicians referred to foreign intervention in internal affairs as "blackmail" and "terrorism". Economics laureate Paul Krugman referred to "a truly vile campaign, an attempt to scare the Greek public into getting rid of their government. It was a shameful moment in modern European history" (*New York Times*, 5 July 2015).

Faced with an ill-concealed intention to bring Greece to its knees, if not lower, the new government, despite its acknowledgement of the need for compromise, continued to insist that it is the master of its destiny and had a mandate to fulfil. That, of course, is a montage (if not a *trompe l'oeil*) of rhetoric and naïve belief. "We are no longer going to be following a script that was given to us by external agencies," declared finance minister Yanis Varoufakis.[16] If Angela Merkel had ever confronted Alexis Tsipras with the line "will you sit down and be said by me!" (above, p. 103), this was the antidote. On the day of the July referendum, Tsipras reiterated that "no-one can ignore the message of determination of a people taking its destiny in its own hands".

Tsipras had begun his rebuff before the pre-election bullying – a case of getting his retaliation in first – stating that "our historic responsibility is to open the way for an alternative policy in Europe, transforming a eurozone country from the subject of neoliberal experiment to a model for social protection and growth".[17]

After the election, Syriza immediately reiterated its intention of rejecting the Troika as the instrument of the bailout and, as Varoufakis put it, "an anti-Eropean spirit [...] built on shaky foundations".[18] He challenged the terms of the bailout, but achieved only a change in its terminology. Rejecting the term "Troika", he insisted on "institutions"; where Greece is a party to discussions, it's now the "Brussels Group". The "bailout", which Syriza pledged to rescind, became "the current agreement". "Privatisation" or selling off state propoerty has become "making rational use of existing public assets".

Varoufakis referred to these new negotiating terms as "constructive ambiguity". It means that no one can be quite sure of what the other side is saying. If you are committed to the Left, in a predominantly conservative environment, the best strategy is, "Whatever you say, say nothing". As a result – and whether or not it was intended as part of Varoufakis' gamesmanship[19] – the "ambiguity" became an integral part of his discussions with EU leaders, so much so that Malta's finance minister said, "There is a huge gap between [what] Varoufakis and the institutions are saying about what is really going on. It is clear nobody is speaking the same language".[20]

The EU, in the person of the German finance minister Wolfgang Schäuble, made it clear that Varoufakis' change of terminology meant nothing. But to the man responsible for his country's economic survival, to translate the prevailing terminology into language acceptable to the underdog, and chiming with the self-respect of the electorate, was imperative. Tsipras followed this by asserting that Syriza wanted "a return to the founding values of Europe" based on "an alliance of rationality", avoiding a north-south split.[21]

On a practical level, Syriza's demands for a debt write-down were greeted by a mixture of derision, contempt and cynicism in Brussels and Berlin, as Tsipras and Varoufakis had anticipated. Yet, as noted above, Greek default on at least some of its debt is inevitable and acknowledged as such by the EU. It was only in order to play their parts in the political drama that critics of a left-wing government spoke their prescribed lines.

Nation-states and Sovereignty

At the time of Greek independence, Leopold von Ranke, in his essay "The Great Powers" (1833), wrote that Europe had reached a point where the Great Powers had shown that powers, rather than nations, were the safeguard of independent states, religion and law and that the union of all depends on the independence of each. (He only gradually, in extreme old age, came to accept the idea of a German "empire".) He drew an analogy with literature, believing that a "world literature" depended on the vitality of individual literatures.

However, as another great nineteenth century historian and Irish MP, John (Lord) Acton, countered, power tends to corrupt and absolute power corrupts absolutely. In that case, the idea (which we can see in Ranke) of "unity in diversity" becomes obscene, debased and mendacious when used to persuade people that they have more to gain by identifying with a common culture than by maintaining their difference. The appeasing catch-all slogan is, at best, high-octane bovine effluent, at worst an arrogant condescension to the "smaller" and more diverse cultures, designed to fool the greatest number of people for as long as possible. It is diversity which actually created Europe – more interesting in its differences than in its conformity and orthodoxy. "Diversity" has been caustically defined by a British MEP and eurosceptic as "people who look different but think the same way. Diversity applies to race, sex, disability, and sexual orientation. It emphatically does not apply to opinion."[22]

I have been accused many times of elevating the nation-state as a *desideratum* above the EU. This is a misrepresentation of my belief that *people*, rather than the outmoded nation-state, have lost their sense of autonomy, and today find it difficult to articulate their identity. Under fascism and, in eastern Europe, communism, this entailed a resort to the *samizdat* and the allegory. In "peace time" it is just as difficult to communicate one's frustration and outrage.

There is a radical difference between the *people* and the *state*, which Greek terminology, for pragmatic political reasons, confused by using *ethnos* as "the nation" rather than "the people", and thus making it possible for "nation" to elide into "state". It served its purpose in providing a focal point for the underdogs to exert their need for independence. Ireland's cry was "A nation once again" (the slogan of the nineteenth century Young Ireland movement) when it had never been a nation in the first place.

Since the first (1871) and second (1990) unifications of Germany, the idea of independent nation-states has been so eroded that the concept of the nation-state itself has become questionable, both on the micro-scale (with worldwide separatist exits of splinter groups), and on the macro-scale with amalgamations of interests in economic, legal and social matters in institutions like the EU, which increasingly takes on the character of a state in itself.

The great misfortune was that the nation-states emerged at the same time as the money economy. Together, they were a collision of the romantic and the pragmatic, which gave neither any advantage and has resulted in the stalemate we see today as far as governance and decision-making are concerned. Jeremy Rifkin suggests that "nation-states are too geographically constrained [...] They are exclusive, not inclusive, governing institutions. They were never conceived of as vehicles to manage global risks and threats."[23] But does this therefore mean that the global economy necessitates global political institutions?

A smaller country can never hope to withstand external pressure from a larger one, but can it withhold its identity from subjugation or extinction? Yiorgos Chouliaras has argued that "Greek culture has the capacity to renew itself in the context of a new Europe". But he also asks, "how different groups of people are to live together without being crippled by pernicious antagonisms".[24] Of course no one could insist that all dramas take on the same character – a standardisation of the Greek, English, French, Irish theatre traditions into a eurodrama akin to the eurocumber. But it *is* possible to see these individual traditions being subsumed under the weight of the "soap opera" or *telenovela* which does have that power to homogenise the human condition and to make it accessible to viewers by means of local subtitles to a universal script.

With so many newly independent states, such as those of the former USSR and those which were welded together in imperialistic gestures of farewell (such as Nigeria), the idea of a "nation-state" falls at the hurdle of "what is a nation?"

"Sovereignty" is also rapidly becoming outmoded, as the "nation" travels simultaneously in the opposite direction. Even if a European union reduces and even subsumes the autonomy of individual states, its own "sovereignty" is in question in the global context. As Patrick Smyth wrote in *The Irish Times*, "in a globalised, interdependent world the nature of 'sovereignty' has changed profoundly – it is as complex, overlapping and multilay-ered as that related, also absurd, concept of 'identity'."[25] In Greece, if one adds an extra layer of geopolitical bullying, it becomes clear that even before the EU and its interventionist policies, the country was never truly sovereign. Today, "sovereign" has only one "cur-rency" – sovereign debt.

Any reader of Iain Banks' novel *The Business* will readily agree that globalisation of capital is more dangerous for "sovereign" states than any concentration of political powers.[26]

It may seem bizarre that, having so emphatically described Greece's subservience to external influences throughout its his-tory, I should advocate the principles of autonomy and self-de-termination. Why defy reality in order merely to promulgate an unrealisable concept? The problem is reducible to *narrative*: who writes the script, and who speaks it? We like to believe that in art the creator can sing his joys and sadness, even in defiance of dis-tasteful and unwelcome authoritarianism; for a people to sing their narrative as they sing their national anthem (and Greece's anthem remains the "Hymn to Liberty") is the vital component – perhaps the only one remaining to them – in their assertion of identity.

But does the "reality" presuppose the denial of identity? That it may not determine its own destiny within the constraints of geopolitics and globalism? That it may not articulate that sense of identity, however troubled it may be, in literature, in film, in music which, as I hope I have shown, is truly troubled and has always been exercised by the differing claims of east, west and *here*?

Some, including Ireland's President Higgins, have seen the EU as "enhancing" Irish sovereignty by "opening up new horizons" and bringing "a new maturity to our relations with our former colonial power".[27] In Greece, it is true that new *economic* horizons were indicated by EU and eurozone membership, but Greeks' sense of Greekness has not been "enhanced" and its relations with its for-mer colonial master have never been mature.

In 1977, the then President of Greece, Constantine Tsatsos (formerly a professor of the philosophy of law), argued for Greece's inclusion in Europe (it was admitted four years later) on cultural and political as well as economic grounds. He stressed that Greece would strengthen Europe, but also issued the *caveat* that the difference between Greece and northwest Europe was "a difference in time". He linked it to other southern states – Portugal, Spain, Italy – all of which, he argued, would have to either catch up quickly or be left behind: their inherent assets would not be enough to sustain them in an age of technological change and wealth creation.[28] How right he was. But whether or not the time-warp of which he warned has now been bridged, and it is now the hour for Greece to capitulate to the mindset of neoliberal Europe, is the crux of today's national and international debate.

It is an obvious fact, which political rhetoric unsuccessfully obfuscates, that the price of *enosis* is a reduction of freedom and an acceptance of limits. Greece's borders are not merely physical. It matters not whether the society which submits to *enosis* (and even desires it) is corrupt and inefficient and mendacious and backward (as so many see Greece) or stable, solvent, honest and industrious, as we are persuaded is the case in the UK, France, Germany, Austria and Holland (all of them previous colonial powers). The crucial question is whether or not the new restrictions outweigh the benefits, whether those benefits are a sufficient carrot to justify the stick that will be applied by the new powers, whether the "soul" of the people can live with, and within, the indignity of denial, suppression and ignorance.

When the Ukraine agreed to political and economic association with the EU, its president, Petro Poroshenko, remarked that "no nation has ever paid such a high price to become Europeans".[29] He was referring to the tragic loss of life in violent protests *against* Europeanisation and *pro* maintaining links with Russia. The physical violence should not blind us to the fact that a high price is paid in every situation where a poor country, hungry and desperate for survival and expansion, throws in its lot with those who offer salvation. It may not throw away the key to its own future or identity, but it puts itself behind bars.

The opposing argument, emphasising the conditions under which sovereignty is surrendered, was made by Costas Douzinas, Greek-born professor of law at London University:

> The violent impoverishment of large masses, the extensive privatisation of services and utilities through the radical reduction of the state sector, and the extensive dependency on foreign markets for servicing the debt amount to a loss of sovereignty compared to a state under foreign occupation, to an extensive re-arrangement of national assets in favour of capital and a serious European legitimation crisis.[30]

If it had not been for the money-economy, Greece's current predicament would have been a far less complex one of another kind of indebtedness to the overlord – a moral indebtedness which is mutual and therefore negotiable.

A Leadership Deficit

Today, I see Europe falling apart, rather than cohering and integrated, due to *cultural* and *moral* factors. Not only are Europe and the nation-state both falling apart, but they are moving away from each other at a destructive rate. A former Italian Prime Minister, Mario Monti, warned his colleagues of the "dramatically declining" public support for the EU,[31] while Jean-Claude Juncker foresaw the possibility of a "social revolution".[32] The election of Syriza pointed very directly to such a revolution, against which Europe's centrist politicians immediately closed ranks.

Irish journalist Paddy Woodworth referred to "the moral failure of our political system";[33] Ireland's President Higgins advised that many Europeans "feel more and more disconnected" and urged the EU to be aware of "the social consequences of its actions" and to widen its "limited moral base".[34] The fatuous fall-guy of Greek politics, Theodore Pangalos, said that the EU was "lacking inspirational leadership", while a Greek journalist wrote, "Few of the 27 EU leaders are paragons of virtue – any group that has Silvio Berlusconi as one of its most prominent decision-makers can hardly claim the moral high ground".[35]

It wasn't original. Václav Havel said as much in the 1980s; Edmund Husserl said it in 1935. Writing of the Indian experience of independence, Salman Rushdie (in *Midnight's Children*) described its "collective failure of imagination" so that "we simply could not think our way out of our pasts".[36] In another post-colonial society, Nigeria, Chinua Achebe wrote (in *The Trouble with Nigeria*) of "a failure of leadership".[37] The principal failure lies in the inability of any statesman to write a narrative that could satisfy both reality and aspiration.

The consequence is the condition of *anomie* – a hopeless lack of purpose and sense of direction. In a sense, there is no point in blaming the political leaders, because they didn't cause the situation and, despite their obsession with finance, they don't have the answers. Berlusconi, Putin, Cameron, Hollande and Merkel: a plutocrat, a spy, an old Etonian, a serial monogamist and a plodder – to these people we entrust the destiny of our continent, yet none of them is capable of *leading*, and they are very dangerous bullies because of their blindness, their apathy, towards the destiny of Europe.

If, as so many wise men – and Mr Pangalos – have said, Europe no longer has any visionaries, and if, by contrast, every country seems to have short-sighted visionaries pointing to unknown horizons, then there is, at present, no solution other than submission to a greater power. This was the fate of Alexander's empire, the Roman empire and the British empire. Romano Prodi, speaking as president of the EU Commission in 1999, couldn't have been more wrong when he alleged, "For the first time since the fall of the Roman Empire we have the opportunity to unite Europe".[38]

In 2013, the ambassadors to Greece of the ten states which joined the EU in 2003-4 (Czech Republic, Slovakia, Hungary, Slovenia, Poland, Malta, Estonia, Latvia, Lithuania and Cyprus), co-signed a letter to the Athens newspapers stressing the significance of "the vital strategic goal" of unifying Europe in the aftermath of World War II, and the economic benefits of an open market. These are almost all countries still staggering from the effects of Soviet domination, with Cyprus becoming the only EU member state to have been illegally occupied since 1974 by a neighbouring force (Turkey). They called the accession "a symbol of the heritage of democracy". It is precisely this form of double-think which imperils open dialogue about what "Europe" is, what direction it is taking, to whom the benefits accrue and who takes responsibility.

What is "Europe"?

What can Poroshenko have meant by "becoming Europeans"? Ukraine seems to have the same choice as Turkey: to join "Europe" and thus become something that it isn't. At one stage (2002) former French president Giscard d'Estaing argued that "accepting Turkey would be the end of the European Union",[39] while from the Turkish side comes the question, "what is the point of changing our methods of governance if we are refused entry into this Christian club of Europe?"[40] (Christian? What happened to "give all you have to the poor"?)

One argument against Turkey's entry is that it is not European. The Turks would hardly adopt the Karamanlis argument that "We belong to the West": yet Greece (and, it can be argued, most of the Balkan states, to say nothing of Ukraine) is not European in the cultural sense, however far one may stretch physical limits. Moreover, so much "Greek" culture is, as we've seen in the case of both *Karagiózis* and *rebétiko*, Turkish in origin. Again, we have to acknowledge that Greece belongs to both east and west, and its strategic importance in that regard, even on a metaphysical level, makes it an uneasy member of either. Greece falls between the two; its dilemma is both for Greeks to solve and for others to observe.

There is a huge question mark over the entire ontology of the state and its relations with the EU's decision-makers. What began as a six-member "economic community" (EEC), excluding Britain and therefore, of necessity, Ireland, has become a twenty-eight-member nightmare. Not only is the euro in danger, but the entire fabric of a union which seems to be ungovernable except by *diktat*.

I doubt that anyone ever considered that the original treaties (on coal and steel co-operation) would become the all-embracing entity which many, today, would like it to be. Nor do I think anyone, at the inception of that co-operative spirit, intended that it would become anything more than a strategy, firstly, for preventing another war in Europe and, secondly, for rebuilding Europe's finances.

European integrationists should have learned that "Maastricht", "Nice", and "Lisbon" may be beautiful and meaningful places on the European landscape, but, as points on the route-map towards European integration, they have given their names to ugly and largely meaningless forms of words. Europe is more divided than united for one basic reason: it consists of irreducible units of culture, of people, of behaviour. This is not always articulated because it is politically incorrect to do so. The EU has been likened to "geese fly[ing] in formation", but the same authors acknowledge that the EU includes not only geese but "some eagles, some sparrows, even some chickens that cannot actually fly".[41] This disparity is anathema (a fine Greek word) to the breeders of the eurocumber. As Rifkin points out, "Europe is a kaleidoscope of cultural diversity [...] a hundred different nationalities who speak eighty-seven different languages and dialects [...] one of the most culturally diverse areas of the world".[42] We are back to de Gaulle and cheese.

This European problem is larger than any authority, any wisdom, any personality can solve. You cannot force people to adopt a way of life that is not their own, any more than you can tell a hill farmer how to raise sheep or an olive grower how to harvest his crop. You can advise, you can intimidate, you can withdraw the intervention subsidy, but you cannot force. But *force majeure*, as the insurance companies call it, seems to be what Europeans are facing, due to the anxiety of certain Eurocrats and the core megapowers to inflict a unity on the diverse cultures and peoples of Europe.

The major problem, which the Lisbon Treaty or any other set of windy words is quite incapable of solving, is the fact that Europe hasn't worked out what "Europe" means, culturally, socially, even spiritually. Obeying the fiscal imperatives has created a system which, in cultural terms, excludes more than it includes, in a form of internal exile. The new Europe has, literally, gone too far.

Apart from amnesiacs, those who lose their identity but cling to their memories become homeless people, orphans or foster-children of their own selves, hostages to fortune. If the loss of an individual's identity is to be regretted, is it not sensible that the loss of identity of an entire community, or an ethnic group, should not also be deplored? To be exiled from one's past and, with it, one's hold upon the future, is to enter a black hole of the self. This was the Greek dilemma since the "birth of the nation", brought to a painful conclusion in the present crisis. In Seamus Heaney's words, "Lost / Unhappy and at home".[43]

The EU, discarding the idea of "community" in favour of "union", has enveloped countries which, organically and systemically, do not find a natural home within this conglomerate. Greece's history and destiny are inexorably bound up with the other Balkan countries: Bulgaria, FYROM and Albania directly on its northern frontiers; further north Croatia, Slovenia, Bosnia, Serbia, Hungary; and, to the east, Cyprus and the old enemy, Turkey. Leaving Turkey aside, these are all countries with which Greece has far more in common than with any of the northern and western members of the EU.

But is Greece truly part of Europe? Greece's accession to the EU in 1981 had two effects: it signalled the inevitability of the other Balkan states (Bulgaria, Romania and the constituents of former Yugoslavia) eventually joining the EU, and it created the crisis of conscience, of territory and of diplomacy which we see today in the potential membership of Turkey, Albania and what is still called "FYROM" – the nameless Macedonia, once the heartland of Hellenism.

"Europe" becomes a problematic term. The Balkans, once behind the "Iron Curtain", are today *within* Europe. The southeast of Europe is volatile and vulnerable, and of immense significance for the way pan-European politics will be played out.

In *Europe as Empire* (2006), Jan Zielanka discusses the seemingly endless expansion of Europe in terms of a "neo-medieval empire"; it is not a "superstate" but "a polycentric polity penetrating rather than controlling its environment". Zielanka sees the enlargement of 2004, with the accession of ten new member states, as "dramatically and irreversibly transform[ing] the nature of the Union".[44] He expected that "new states are likely to be admitted on geopolitical grounds [...] despite their poor record in implementing the letter and spirit of [the body of EU laws] and despite an ever greater public resistance in current member states".[45]

European expansion has its risible side: as Daniel Hannan complains, "EU institutions have become more and more lavish. There are uniformed ushers in every corridor, chauffeurs to ferry MEPs back and forth, thousands of personal assistants and thou-

sands more permanent staff". Less risible but more revealing, perhaps, is his observation that "the monstrous scale" of the Brussels
headquarters requires "fifteen minutes to walk somewhere under
the same ceiling"[46] – suggesting to the cynic that this is a strategy
to exhaust those who seek to negotiate the corridors of power – a
form of Brusselosis.

Germany and Europe

In 1942, senior German officials (bankers, academics, most of them
economists), gave a series of lectures in Berlin which envisaged the
transformation, following the anticipated German victory, of the
European economy and, as a result, of its social structures. Strategies included a massive investment in infrastructure, sweeping
agricultural reform, industrialisation of southeast Europe, and a
rationalisation of fiscal conditions among the member states.[47]

Not only continental Europe was involved, but also Russia
which, at that time, had a massive food surplus which would be
used to supply net importers of foodstuffs. German military might
would prevail and create the conditions for economic peace and
growth. Britain, of course, would be excoriated and cut adrift.

One remarkable feature of these lectures is that the entity to
be summoned into existence would be known as the "European
Economic Community" (EEC) – a body which of course did not
actually come into existence until 1957 and is now the EU. The
guiding principle would be a "coalition of the countries of Europe",
"a community sharing one destiny", founded on economic integration, and a "unity of political order". To create such a unity would
be "an act of European self-determination immune to Europhobic
influences" – by which it meant the British attitude. Germany's
role was "to recreate a natural situation whereby Europe's natural
focus is the centre of the continent".

How this unity would also be capable of demonstrating "respect for the independence of the nations concerned" is difficult
to imagine, since those nations would be bound together by ir-
refragable economic treaties and their independence would be
subject to "the destruction of these monocultures: Europe has to
be dragged out of its romanticized backwardness".

The smaller nations, especially those of the east and south, would be satellite clients of this centrist system. They "must never remain in any doubt that they are dependent on their neighbours ... The spirit of the individual economies may not be allowed to go against the spirit of neighbourly co-operation". In terms of citizenship, we would see "the subjugation of the individual to the primacy of the economy" which is "the ultimate goal": "there will be victims here and there but the end result will benefit all the peoples of Europe".

Curiously, the one feature of today's eurozone which the German economists of 1942 did not consider necessary was the establishment of a single currency, since the Reichsmark would be the controlling currency to which all other currencies would be subservient.

It is not far-fetched to suggest that many persuasive figures in Germany today, including Chancellor Angela Merkel and her finance minister Wolfgang Schäuble, though they have entirely different motivations and could not be described as "neo-Nazi", have a similar vision of a united Europe, with Germany overseeing and guaranteeing the fate of the euro.

And a further remarkable feature of these lectures, and the economic vision they proposed, is not so much that the same blueprint seems to exist today, but that seventy years ago they so accurately predicted key factors in today's economic and social scenario, such as the Maastricht and Lisbon treaties, the British "eurosceptics", and the near contempt with which the European centre regards the peripheral newcomers to the EU.

An *Irish Times* reader responded to my rhetorical reference to the "Merkelisation" of Europe by asking, "It would be interesting to do a poll on what people understand by 'Merkelisation'". I see Merkel as cautious, conservative, scientifically orientated, wary of big ideas or grand schemes. She proceeds carefully and scientifically: trained as a physicist, she tests every option, discarding those that promise no outcome, until she finds the correct solution. In a 2012 profile, she was described as "overly pragmatic rather than visionary, dedicated to forging a future for her old continent in the new, globalized world" in "her quest to reshape her country and her continent", by overcoming "financial and monetary disorder". The fact that her idea of "more Europe", in the words of the journalist, "masks a deep lack of agreement between the continent's bickering nations on what their common future could be" seems not to trouble Merkel's agenda. She sees her work "like a mathematical challenge – how to corral both extremes of opinion in the same tent".[48]

Greek street poster depicting Angela Merkel wearing a swastika medal and armband

Pragmatic rather than a visionary, with a personal "quest", suggests to me a plodder who will determinedly pursue her goals irrespective of the wishes or opinions – or cultures – of others. Her unlikely *entente* with French president Sarkozy was a temporary union of the Teutonic Tortoise with the French Ferret, but only as long as it suited Merkel's experiment at the time in the science lab of her mind. Her ultimate purpose, as the Luxembourg foreign minister saw it in 2013, was German "hegemony in the eurozone".[49]

Greece and Ireland

In Chapter 1, I suggested both contrasts and similarities between Greece and Ireland. Here, I want to extend my argument, based on my disenchantment with the European scenario, to suggest that the most significant fact linking Greece and Ireland is that recent history has shown that neither country (nor indeed the UK) should be part of the EU: that Greece and Ireland, for very similar reasons, are not truly European, either geographically or culturally, and that the characteristics which set them apart from any European "norm" which may be on offer are not amenable to either homogenisation or submission.

Both countries are multi-cultural; therefore in theory they should be amenable to being accommodated within the multi-cultural and multi-ethnic composition of the EU, and the EU itself should be capable of expansion to at least its geographical limits, whatever they may be. But three factors militate (and I use that word deliberately) against harmonisation: the first is the appalling rift between the Muslim and non-Muslim worlds and minds, which is based on mutual fear when it might be overcome by mutual respect for the sense of honour which each embodies. The second is the globalisation of the money economy which concentrates real power beyond culture and politics, in the plutocracies, kleptocracies and oligarchies of anonymous capitalism. The third is the unfashionable argument that different peoples have different identities which can be harmonised but not homogenised. I call this "unfashionable" because it is now difficult to argue the case of irreducible "Greekness" or "Irishness" in the face of cosmopolitanism and mass-mediafication which rolls over these cultures.

Greece and the Greeks embody certain characteristics which I have been concerned to demonstrate in this book, which cannot become "European" without *agón*, without a reduction of identity that threatens the core. Ireland, too. There are so many – like critical readers of my column – who are able to say "I am Greek and European", "I am Irish and European", but there are many more who cannot accept what is being done in the interests of Europeanisation because they are unable to reconcile the process with their sense of Greekness or Irishness. The long histories of unified states such as Britain, France, Spain, Portugal, Holland, Sweden and Denmark (all of which had extensive imperial histories) points to a more solid and certain sense of national identity which can embrace cosmopolitanism through the experience of those histories. Greece and Ireland can not.

Before the crisis, Ireland had been a "poster boy", where the Hellenic Hound was intent, as a former finance minister said, on making Greece "the Ireland of the South" and – somewhat of a mixed metaphor – "the Florida of Europe".[50] And Greece became, after Ireland, the second best success story of Europe, in terms of short-term economic growth. After the crash(es), despite the common plight of the two countries, politicians were at pains to argue that "Greece is not Ireland" (finance minister Papaconstantinou in Greece) and "Ireland is not Greece" (TD Tommy Broughan in Ireland). This is in reference to the causes of the crisis in each country and the methods of dealing with them, and to the dissimilarities between their respective economies.

But in so many, more important ways, Greece *is* Ireland, and Ireland *is* Greece. In fact, the two countries could not be more similar. Over-spend, over-indulge, exaggerate, be over-confident. Each on the rim of a fragile Europe and an even more fragile eurozone, each proud of its independence from the age-old dominant neighbour, proud of its historic contribution to European culture. Nevertheless, both states are deeply ambivalent about their role in Europe and about the loss of sovereignty to supervening powers, the loss of that hard-won independence and identity. Susannah Verney, from contemporary research, suggests that Greek voters initially supported Eurosceptic parties because these also opposed domestic policies (and not necessarily because they were opposed to the EU), but that since 2013 Eurosceptic support has become linked directly to rejection of the bailout conditions. She furthermore suggests that this upsurge in public opinion is "comparable only to that which occurred as a result of the dictatorship of 1967-1974".[51]

And citizens in both countries are saying, "Don't punish us, the ordinary man and woman in the street, punish those responsible for these appalling debts" – in Greece they are called "the kleptocrats", who have been ripping off the plain people of Greece and walking away from the debts: not so much the banks as those in positions of social, administrative and clerical authority.

Since Ireland concluded its bailout, there has been a constant emphasis on Irish success compared with Greek failure. One of the most notable contributors to what amounts to an unwarranted superiority complex has been Michael Noonan, the Irish finance minister, whose disparaging and ignorant remarks we met before, and who, since the Syriza victory in 2015, continued to underline

Ireland's new-found status as a "good boy", leaving behind the other "PIGS", while undermining Greece's own attempts to exit the morass of debt. Angela Merkel, too, made reference to Ireland as an example that Greece should emulate in devising acceptable reforms.

Ireland was once again in the uncomfortable position of being flaunted as the "poster boy" of Europe: its "efficient public administration, a modern open economy and not much culture of protest"[52] made it immeasurably more successful and admirable than Greece.

The change in government in Greece in 2015 evoked a large number of letters to *The Irish Times* in support of Greece's request for a debt conference (similar to that held in 1953 to structure Germany's post-war reparations) and recognising the fact that in Ireland, too, the priority of saving the banks had caused, and continues to cause, hardship to taxpayers who were in no way party to the errors and deceptions which caused the crisis.

Commentators in both countries remark on their respective ungovernability. Fintan O'Toole's observation could do duty for both countries: "A very significant part of the population has ceased to feel that the state is theirs, that it tries its best to treat them with care and dignity [...] People feel that they live in a political world whose 'reality' excludes them".[53] Again and again we see the same commentaries highlighting the lack of viability and credibility of countries which permit such differences between rich and poor, between their own citizens and the opinions of outside forces. Whether it's the case in other EU countries is beyond the scope of this book, but it's clear that at least two countries have endangered, and will continue to endanger, the future of this monster union. *Enosis* means something rather different to the Greeks than European "union".

Psychologically, Greece and the Greek people cannot sink any further without complete civil unrest. The sooner the many eurosceptics among the Greeks find a powerful voice and lead Greece away, first from the euro and then from the EU, the better.

It's not very honourable to renege on one's debts, but the situation for every man, woman and child indentured to poverty is so intolerable that default and exit seem the only possibility. The problem is one of self-determination. With its sovereignty now completely suspended by its acceptance of the bailout memorandum, Greece cannot look itself in the face. In order to regain self-esteem, it's essential that it turns its back on those elements in Europe which are exacting this level of punishment. Like many divorces, Greece's exit from the EU would be messy and acrimonious, but it is in a place where it doesn't belong.

Personally, I would favour Greece returning to the drachma, and Ireland re-adopting the punt, France the franc, Italy the lira. Not merely because these are symbols of national identity but because they are *active* symbols of faith: a drachma in the hand is worth two euros; it may be devalued, but it has innate, tangible worth. One could be very glib and say that a country without its own currency is a country missing a part of its culture. The glibness is a cliché and, like all clichés, is true.

Why I am No Longer a European

So here are my *apologia* and my *credo*. I became a committed European almost by accident. An Englishman living in Ireland has many rivers to cross and fences to jump in order to establish any equilibrium. This focussed my attention on the two islands until, quite serendipitously, I became aware of the mainland: in 1978 I was invited to join a team of advisers ("consultants") to the Council of Europe's "Twenty-One Towns Project: *Votre Ville, Votre Vie*",[54] the purpose of which was to compare cultural development programmes in towns throughout western Europe and to arrive at a view of how *different* cultural problems and projects were pursued by *different* methods according to the local cultural and procedural norms.[55] In some, the problems to be solved were quite basic (providing leisure facilities in a new town), in others more complex (accommodating anti-establishment youth culture).

The common denominator was local recognition of a socio-cultural need and the means to satisfy it. Every case we inspected required that we bring no baggage of preconceptions. The major lesson we learned, which is of such relevance today in the light of the "PIGS", is that there is a profound north-south difference in

ways of combining work and leisure, ways of undertaking administrative tasks and approaching problem-solving, and ways of defining "culture". The two contrasting approaches were the top-down
(*dirigiste*) and the grass-roots. In some cases, what seemed to the
outsider to be absurdly simple was, in fact, a major dilemma requiring widespread community consultation, while in other cases
citizens expressed dismay at top-down provision of cultural facilities which did not meet their real needs.

Some of my most affective experiences, which are still deeply
imprinted, came from this project: observing the cultural transmission of wisdom and memory from older to younger people; the
schwellenangst (literally, fear of crossing thresholds) among young
Germans in a bourgeois cultural environment; the mayor of a tiny
Portuguese village, presenting an assembly of the elderly village
band, and saying, humbly but proudly "this is our culture".

The Council was predicated on cultural imperatives and on human rights and freedoms, of which Churchill saw "freedom from
fear" as the greatest. It represented a careful balance between the
victors and vanquished in the Second World War. Immediately,
discord split the search for a "cultural charter", which was to be
the first plank of European unity. It failed, due mostly to political
manoeuvring.

There had always been suspicion, misunderstanding and ignorance in the "old" Europe, especially between north and south,
between the bureaucrats who planned the lives of others and those
who placed more importance on living life. And all the time there
was tension within cultures – *schwellenangst* – fear of crossing the
thresholds of each others' ideas and beliefs and value-systems.

I believed in the Council of Europe, largely because I knew
little about it beyond its cultural section; and that it was the largest collection of democratic states in the world (this was before
the collapse of the Berlin Wall). It was instructive to find that at
joint meetings with the non-democratic states of the eastern bloc
the two "sides" (hosted by UNESCO) were polarised in a physical
seating layout which emphasised the cultural and ideological differences. I have been involved, in that environment, in writing a
cultural charter which had to be negotiated, phrase by phrase, be-

tween the two sides, whittling down ideas to pragmatic sentences that said little and pleased no one; energies and aspirations fumigated by the need for political correctness between ideologically opposed power blocks.

The same compromise and intentional ambiguity is to be found in the Maastricht Treaty, where one clause refers to the "respect [for] national and regional diversity" while another indicates the need to "bring the common cultural heritage to the fore".

It was at once challenging and depressing to find that "culture" was a negotiated commodity. Today, I see that anti-democratic mindset, which we associated with the communist states, replicated to a large extent in the workings of the top-down EU.

The visionaries of post-war Europe, of whom Jean Monnet is the most celebrated, were well-meaning optimists desperate to reestablish Europe as a house of peace rather than discord. That their visions should have been diverted into entirely economic forms of union is part of the EU's current problem: its inability to understand the cultural dimension of the diversity it is trying to unify, or on whom it is trying to impose common characteristics that defy classification. Monnet was reacting against the dismissive gibe of Charles de Gaulle: "As for Europe, it doesn't exist. It's France and Germany. The rest are just vegetables."[56] But Monnet also acknowledged that "Europe has never existed; one has genuinely to create Europe".[57] In the minds (or eyes) of some politicians, that vision has not been dimmed: Wim Kok, a former Prime Minister of the Netherlands, wrote that the vision was still valid, "the reunification of Europe's peoples in a constitutional framework that encourages them to work in peace and stability".[58] Counter to that is Daniel Hannan's wishful thinking, that "the European Union will eventually be [brought down] by irreconcilable differences among people who [speak] different languages. How long must we wait for that happy outcome?" he asks, but ruefully admits that "plenty of powerful interest groups are making a handy living out of the EU".[59]

My commitment to, and faith in, Europe was entirely cultural. I had no knowledge of, or interest in, political or economic affairs, except an awareness of the increasing power of the EEC (as it then was) and a concomitant reduction in national sovereignties. One of my most humbling moments came halfway up a Connemara mountainside when, in pursuit of my core-periphery exploration, I asked a sheep farmer what it meant to be remote. "*Remote?*" He looked at me with utter contempt. "Remote from *what*? *I* am not *remote*. Brussels is remote from me. *This* is the centre." In other words, *terroir*, the immanence of identity, is the thesaurus and the safeguard of how we perceive the world.

When I wrote a column in *The Irish Times* on "Why I am no longer a European", it provoked more readers' comments than all my other columns combined. The following is a selection of the pro- and anti- arguments. (I have omitted writers' names, as these are often pseudonyms or fun-names, e.g. "Dessie Derrata", "Conan Drumm" or "Zach Lee Wright".)

> The article reflects a general disillusionment regarding the EU on the part of many of its citizens. The early promise and ideals, inspired by some truly remarkable leaders, have been ground into dust. Our leaders treat us with total contempt, and we view them in like measure. As originally envisaged, a Europe of the Regions would have introduced a mechanism for resolving many of our tribal disputes and introduced true democracy at all levels of administration. Instead we have morphed into Stalinist central control which no longer listens or cares.

> We are held together by the euro, this is how the average joe on the street connects with the great euro project, I was only ever supportive of the European Economic Community, this to me made common sense and provide a simple basic structure to the benefit of all nations. Now we have a political beast that wishes to expand its borders.

> Europe will never be one nation, it can't, it's too culturally diverse, but it can be what we were promised so many decades ago, a place which co-operates to make everyone's lives better and helps each other and enhances our freedoms. Unfortunately Europe and those at the centre have become ever powerful and that has put self-determination further away from the little guy.

The author pointed out that none of the changes implemented in Europe over the past 20 years (if not longer) came about as a result of a desire for change among the general population. The European "elite" is driving the whole thing, and hardly even explaining the changes to the general populace, much less gaining their support for the changes being implemented. This has to change.

The political culture of the EU – in spite of the lip service paid to the principle of subsidiarity – is akin to that of imperial Europe before the outbreak of WW1 a century ago. Brussels is the imperial Vienna of our times and we know how that house of cards collapsed. The problem with the EU is that the more it has grown the more unrepresentative it has become, and the more consolidated and opaque it has become as a vector for ideological change in the political economy and social spheres of its member states.

Like so many literary critics Richard Pine has no grasp of economics and totally misreads the developments since the 2008 busts and banking crisis. Romanticized idyllic notions of local communities are one thing, but economics underpin their existence. Angela Merkel and the Germans were in fact extremely reluctant to involve themselves in the affairs of other countries. Intervention and fiscal rectitude only occurred because Greece, Portugal, Ireland, Spain, mis-managed their own economies and finances and the EU had to step in with a bail-out. Other countries who managed their affairs properly, the Finns, Danes, Austrians came through the global crisis pretty much unscathed. If there had been no EU bail out things would have got a whole lot worse, the money to pay doctors, nurses, teachers, benefits etc. would have run out. An inevitable part of a bail out is that countries have to change their ways, and stop doing the things that led to the bust. The Greek Gov't was spending vastly more than it was raising in taxes, and that could not be perpetuated with the EU endlessly covering the difference.

I have been working as a consultant to countries preparing for accession to the EU for 20 years and I have also come to the same conclusions as Richard Pine. The EU has lost its soul which originally attracted me to the ideals of enlargement; in the enforcement of austerity we see a Bureaucracy that is disconnected from any sense of humanity, personal pride or national consciousness.

Rather curious that Mr Pine fails to acknowledge that Europe's past was the primary motivating factor in the formation of the EEC and expansion into the present EU. Rather he limits himself to implying that the EU is some distinct superpower that is as determined to hold its sway and possession over "client" states in much the same way as the old European empires. No, Mr Pine seems to be hiding a narrow view of Europe and its role in the world under a cloak of "Culturalism". Many of us have an increasing sense of our role as Europeans and this sense of Europeanism does not rely at all on artists and writers. Indeed one might ask what if anything the high priests and priestesses of the Irish cultural world are doing to form positive opinions of ourselves as Irish and European? They mainly seem to limit themselves to moaning and groaning about grants to the Arts worlds and about protecting their tax exemptions.

My former colleague (in RTÉ), the late Desmond Fisher, wrote to me:

> I think all the initial vision of Robert Schumann and Jean Monnet has evaporated and the EU bosses are proving more and more the truth of Acton's dictum about the corrupting consequences of power. The former Irish minister for finance who arranged the recent bailout admitted bluntly that he was bullied into accepting the arrangements.[60]

One reader pointed out, "Those of us who voted 'no', to no effect, in successive referendums could see the writing on the wall, although there may have been widely divergent reasons for our doing so." Ireland's rejection of the first "Nice Treaty" in 2001 and of the first "Lisbon Treaty" in 2008 were signals that citizens would not accept the imposition of apparently innocuous documents that in fact enlarged centrist control over their lives.

Others wrote:

> Stay in Corfu Richard, you're better off with homemade petrol bombs, and occasional riots. Don't forget the coups, the communist rule and the military juntas either. Or the odd war here or there with your closest neighbour.

> [*After reading this, I scoured the history books, fearing that I had missed something, but failed to find any reference to "communist rule" at any time, other than the provisional, guerrilla, government during the civil war, about which I am sure the reader knew little or nothing.*]

> I hope this piece helps bring about the vibrant debate Ireland needs. Though I don't agree with all of it, Mr Pine is entirely right in his comparison of Greece and Ireland. As Padraig Pearse said: "*Tir gan teanga is tir gan anam*" [a land without a tongue is a land without a soul], but worse than that, a country without an identity is completely soulless and dysfunctional.

And my favourite, "Do people get paid by *The Irish Times* for this sort of rubbish?"

AFTERWORD

As I come to the end of this saga of a personal odyssey, I must hope that what I have written is a fair transaction between myself and the place in which I have come to live.

I was continually discovering and rediscovering Ireland. After fifteen years of living in Greece and discovering some of it, that is beginning to happen to me here: rediscovery or, to put it another way, finding a new aspect to what I thought I had already discovered. A continuous process of revisiting what one once knew, and finds different. Like rewinding a film, watching it again, and noticing the changes. Re-new-ing.

If, as I thoroughly believe, one travels in order to discover oneself, to establish a "home", then the place to which we travel must offer us some accommodation, some recompense, some sense of belonging, even though we know in our innermost thoughts and in our hearts that we can never, in fact, "belong". My reflections have therefore been unrepentantly personal, and intimately associated with my life in Greece.

Those who believe that the journey will, by and of itself, bring some kind of completion, deceive themselves. All one can expect is that before the end we can clear up as many misunderstandings as possible, answer as many questions as possible, reach some kind of *stasis* before our bodies impose their own. We are still left with the fact that arrival in a new place deprives us of any civility we may have carried with us. The poet Ovid, exiled to the Black Sea, complained *"barbarus hic ego sum quia non intelligor illis"*: "I am regarded as a barbarian in this place because no one understands me." All his civility had fallen away in the face of the civility of others.

314

Is it then possible, as Lawrence Durrell believed, that Greece "offers you the discovery of your self"? Elytis wrote, "It is a lie that there is no golden fleece. Each one of us is the golden fleece of his own true self".[1] The problem, if there is one, is to know this and to find the self without putting an inflated value upon it. It is, after all, only you.

One cannot divest oneself of a westernised education, however much that involved, in my case, a (somewhat Victorian) introduction to classical Greek drama. Meeting the east, when one comes from the west, is challenging, exciting and perilous (a bit like sex, really). Many Greeks of the diaspora, George Papandreou the younger included, had that same experience. But it is not so much the baggage one brings to the cusp, but how one unpacks and then re-packs it that shapes one's responses to the cusp, the *limen*, or in Greek the *katófli*. And that point, in so many instances, is all we have: our cuspiness.

To step outside one's known world – whether it was a safe and accommodating world or a harsh and threatening one – is to become an exile. For the writer, life is permanently exilic, so that the journey away from "home" is always known. It is not necessary for the writer to go consciously into exile, because he is already there. Seferis (an exile from Smyrna) located many of his poems in an imaginary place, where displacement is the concomitant, the other side, of "home". As a Greek-American writer recently observed, "one search[es] endlessly for roots discovered only through displacement".[2]

A writer lives always at the border: he can never go back, and the next step is a permanent adventure into the unknown. He lives between the written and the unwritten, the one a source of dissatisfaction, the other a source of wonder, apprehension and fear.

So the exile learns to be at home *in* exile. Thenceforth, he is at home only with and to himself. All else is else-where. *Ipothesi* indicates "home-as-if". Greece, like me, is on a journey, but is it in danger of becoming an exile from itself? Is it likely to lose itself in its attempt to embrace a new destiny? The old destiny – the lessons of history – remains a powerful affective presence in Greece's deliberations with itself about the need for modernisation – another *ipothesi*.

This book has been determined by the "backward glance", to use Frank O'Connor's expression: it's a view of history, and how that history has shaped present-day Greece, just as Irish history has made Ireland what it is today. And therefore, it's an *interpretation* of history and, thus, of Greekness.

Yanis Varoufakis challenges the idea that we "live in a tyranny of consequences"[3] – that is, that we can blame history for current ills. At best, he might convince all of Europe that it is the prisoner of history and that, therefore, the only redemption is a revolution to abolish history *and to start again*.

This is one of several recurring motifs you have met in this book. Geopolitics tells us that the Greek people have always been cast between the powers of east and west; the Balkans have been – and will continue to be – the fulcrum of east-west tensions. Greece, in ancient history and today, is so placed geographically that it cannot but be subject to supervening powers. So much of Greece's history, both fortunate and less fortunate, has been a condition for which the people themselves cannot be held responsible. No political leader has ever demonstrated the stature necessary to enable Greece to transcend these conditions.

This is not to exonerate the Greek people from having allowed an incomplete and inadequate system to evolve, or from having put their faith and trust in unsatisfactory leaders (all peoples do that), but simply to underline that it is in their everyday culture that their strength lies. The modern tourists see this at every turn: a character which complements the landscape they have come to admire and enjoy.

Czeslaw Milosz said in his Nobel lecture, "It is possible that there is no other memory than the memory of wounds" (which he attributes to the Old Testament "tribulations of Israel"). That may have been exaggerated for rhetorical effect on the day, but the Greek term *mnisikakía*, the "remembrance of wrongs", is a question not only of wounds, but of honour, *filotimía*, damaged by everything but poetry.

The criticism which any interpretation such as mine will incur will concentrate mostly on its author being a foreign resident. One of the most frequent readers' criticisms of my "Letter from Greece" is, "He is an expatriate living in Greece and therefore unable to integrate; it leaves him on the fringe of understanding what is really going on". Certainly, as I have stressed throughout this book, my western "Irish" eyes inevitably see Greece not as Greeks see their country. (It's worth noting that most of these criticisms come from Greeks living outside Greece, many of whom, like the American Irish, harbour inviolate visions of a fatherland/motherland which is beyond reproach and outside history.)

It is only a short step from that point of view to the chauvinistic idea that only Greeks can comment on Greek affairs. *Of course* I am "on the fringe" and I could *never* expect to integrate, to become "more Greek than the Greeks".

That criticism of me is sometimes followed by, "He is one of those who say 'Greece would be wonderful if it weren't for the Greeks'"; that, however, is a gross slander. I love Greece. The people *are* Greece. Therefore I could not possibly have that opinion.

I do experience exasperation and frustration, of course, but that is the daily experience of so many Greeks, too; and would I not be exasperated and frustrated by bureaucracy if I lived in Ireland? I was in Ireland when the Anglo-Irish Bank tapes were released by the *Irish Independent* in 2013: the exchanges between senior executives of the bank who were taking €7 billion of Irish citizens' money, knowing the bank to be bank-rupt, elicited one popular response: outrage!

Q: What's the Greek for "get the fucking money!" (the words of Anglo-Irish Bank chief executive David Drumm).

A: "*Mazi te fagáme*" (the words of Theodoros Pangalos, deputy Prime Minister of Greece, explaining the disappearance of EU funds: "together, we swallowed them").

The jump from desperate grabbing of funds to stay financially afloat (Ireland) to ostentatious and shameless guzzling (Greece) is merely a step.

Greece and Ireland both have classical histories of world significance. They share an experience of foreign domination and the fight for freedom. Disputes about identity and self-determination are never far from the minds of either. They have undergone the embarrassment of their respective economic collapses. They have both, severely and very publicly, been exposed as homes of clientelism, bribery and corruption.

But... In *Journey to the Morea* Kazantzakis concluded, "Mountains, fertile valleys, cities, villages, men, conversations, all crowd impatiently back into the mind, begging to be ordered in a total, to be organized, to find some meaning".[4] For Kazantzakis, for Philip Sherrard, for Peter Levi, for me, the search continues, the circle can never be closed; we have the parts, but we lose the "total"; we find meaning and it disappears. That is what love is.

I must ask myself again how one weighs Greece in the balance of beauty/ugliness, good/bad, sensible/crazy: where on the fulcrum does Greece really lie? If one ignores the mess of politics and public life, what may one encounter which is different from almost every other society? I refuse to emulate those like Don Morgan Nielsen (above, pp. 183-84) who extol merely the "glories of Greece", its myths and heroes. That kind of idolatry is false and disingenuous.

- Greece is a safe place to put one's trust if one wishes for fulfilment among ordinary folk.

- Greece is a dangerous place to put one's trust if one seeks the reassurance of public life.

- Greece is beautiful/Greece is ugly.

- Greece is rational/Greece is illogical.

- Greece is opportunity/Greece is loss.

These are simultaneous equations between which it is foolish to try to choose; or to distinguish that which adds up from that which doesn't. Under every beautiful stone there may be worms.

There is a great truth in C.M. Woodhouse's view that Greeks are both "naïve and subtle in their understanding".[5] That is, they see clearly and at the same time they see the complexity, and thus they know how to approach difficulty: with passion and stealth or, as Joyce might say, cunning and silence. A character in John Fowles' *The Magus* refers to his native Greece as "the most beautiful and the most cruel country in the world [...] It makes you suffer. Then you learn".[6] This is true for Seferis, too, for he wrote, "Wherever I travel in Greece wounds me".[7] But it was the kind of wound that lovers can inflict: beauty wounds, passions wound, and yet we persist in loving.

It would be far too easy and simplistic to say that Greece is diminished as a viable nation-state by the divisive politics which have characterised its history in the past 200 years. And to do so would also be disingenuous. In fact, at the risk of going entirely in the opposite direction, I believe that the capacity of Greek people both individually and collectively for debate and conflict is an admirable characteristic which enhances, rather than detracts from, Greece's viability. The general election of 2015, while representing the divide between largely bourgeois parties and a radical left, nevertheless indicated that capacity for debate which is at the heart of any quest for self-knowledge, self-definition, self-respect and, thereby, self-government. So too did the subsequent referendum, which was intended to decide Greece's economic fate and so much more.

I have no desire to be exploded by a terrorist bomb; it would interfere with my plans for burial; but I acknowledge that the authority of the state will continue to be questioned and challenged and resisted by groups such as the former "November 17" and today's "Revolutionary Struggle" and political parties such as KKE and Golden Dawn, which have been doing so ever since 1821.

In fact, Greece is all the more interesting and challenging because of this – it isn't Switzerland – and all the more worthwhile to live here, even as an outsider (the *xénos*) and a friend (the *fílos*).

Loving and mourning: Roy Foster and I are not alone. The *amenés*, the love-song, is always melancholy, singing its *meráki*, its yearning. As Nick Malkoutzis has said, Greeks are "torn between love for their country and hate for what it has become". But these are the *kosmáki* "who have been unable to prevent Greece's demise", "who are invisible to the outside world".[8] Yeats wrote of "love of country" and "love of the Unseen Life".[9] Too often we find ourselves living in the sadnesses between these two contours.

Yes, "loving or mourning" should be "loving *and* mourning" – the "both/and" rather than the "either/or". One cannot live in Greece for any length of time (and this may also be true for the casual visitor) without realising that, whatever attractions it may have, there are countervailing disattractions. The trick, if one needs one, in order to make life bearable, to protect the rational westerner from exasperation, is to distinguish between the beauties of the landscape, the people, the language and the culture on one side and the political corruption and chicanery, the denial of reality, on the other: embrace the one and find it possible not to blame the people or the culture for the seismic faults in the system. I cannot regard my neighbours, mostly old men and widows – Antigone, Ismene, Sofokles and Perikles – as villains in this drama.

When I had almost completed this book, Denise Harvey generously made available to me a proof copy of the late Philip Sherrard's correspondence with Elytis, prefaced by Sherrard's essay "The Other Mind of Europe". This immediately strengthened my belief that Sherrard's example, which had already influenced much of what I had written, is seminal in explaining east to west, in establishing the identity and value of the "other" which has been a recurring theme in this book.

In his essay, Sherrard speaks (in the third person) of his own encounter with Greece, "ways of thought and feeling, ways of understanding and response, quite other than his own and those of the world from which he had emerged, and which seemed to come from an altogether deeper and richer stratum of human life and experience than anything he had up till then encountered". Sherrard speaks of finding himself "on the threshold of some completely unexpected, undreamt of, revelation" which "at the time felt familiar, as if I had known it, but in some other, vanished, banished, eclipsed, life".[10]

In my own case, as I have stressed in Chapter 1, my years of encounter with the Irish mind had already prepared me for this "deeper and richer stratum" and, as I hope I have shown, the Greek and Irish "ways" are very similar to each other and very dissimilar to most of "Europe".

My western eyes show me that what I saw in Ireland in terms of physical beauty is matched and, perhaps, excelled by that of Greece; and that the problems of Greek society in this global world are present also in Ireland: the emptiness of politics, the corruption high and low. But is this not true of almost all modern states? And many of those can offer nothing like the charms of either Greece or Ireland. If W.B. Yeats could imagine an "indomitable Irishry", I see myself living amid an indomitable Greekness: like Yeats, I say this as an act of faith and admiration, and as a claim for a certain type of humanity that suits me, on whatever side of the *agón* I find myself. These are two great countries – greater than much of the land-mass that lies between them. I rest my case. And I find my-self... at least *I think* I do. *Credo quia absurdum.*

Home: as I said earlier, it all comes down to where one will be buried, the journey into the future indefinite. The last gasp is also the last cusp.

I suppose death is the final exile. And where will that exile be spent? At least I know the answer to that: when I die, I will be buried in the British cemetery – one of the most beautiful places in Corfu Town, and even today very tranquil, as a burial place should be. My daughters have already chosen the spot. Start digging, I say. I will not, in the proverbial sense, be "pushing up daisies", but help-ing to maintain its carpet of rare orchids. Come and see me there. Καλό ταξίδι, καλή υποδοχή. But please tread softly, because you tread on my ... orchids.

Appendix

WHAT THE GREEKS DID FOR US

The title of this appendix owes something to the great Irish classical scholar and *philhellene*, J.P. Mahaffy (1839-1919), who gave a series of lectures in Boston entitled "What Have the Greeks Done for Modern Civilization" (1910), in which he referred to the "striking evidence" of the "permanence of the Greek language" – a point which, as we saw in Chapter 2, the founders of the modern state were anxious to emphasise. Mahaffy observed:

> The earliest Attic prose differs from the Attic prose of to-day so little as to afford us an unique example of persistency [...] Herodotus, if you [...] put a Greek newspaper of to-day into his hands would at first find the type novel, but would presently recognise in it his own alphabet. He would [...] in a day or two read it quite fluently. So far as my knowledge goes, you will find nothing like this in Europe.[1]

As Lawrence Durrell observed thirty years later, "the profoundest words in Greek carry overtones unmatched by their equivalent in any European language".[2]

It is rare, nowadays, to find classical Greek (or Latin) being taught in secondary schools, and Greek Studies are threatened in many universities. So it is also rare today that one finds awareness of the classical Greek language in its ubiquitous presence in modern English.

I once met a supercilious Englishman in Dublin who pointed to a phone kiosk and said very patronisingly, "The Irish can't even find their own word for a telephone – they have to take one from us". I had to explain that both parts of the word are Greek in origin – *tele* meaning "from afar" and "phone", from *foni*, meaning "sound": sound from afar, just as "telegraph" and "telescope" are words the Greeks have given us. But *not* "television". As some wit once observed, nothing good ever came of combining a Greek word with a Latin one – which is why "television" and "automobile" have been such abject failures in the marketplace.

"Psyche" is also a multi-prevalent word from the Greek (we saw it in *Psyhi Vathia* – deep soul). "Soul" gives rise to "psychiatry" (literally, doctor of the soul), "psychotherapy" (literally, serving the soul and thus healing it), "psychedelic" (making things clear in the soul).

Many readers will recall the character in *My Big Fat Greek Wedding* who asserts, "Give me a word – any word – and I'll show you how the root of that word is Greek" and it is as dangerous to hold this belief as it is to design the front of your house to resemble the Parthenon. Richard Clogg points out that under the Metaxas regime ultra-chauvinism of this kind insisted, insanely, that "Human civilization was wholly fashioned by our race [...] Civilization is an exclusively Greek creation".[3]

But in the 1950s, Xenophon Zolotas, the director of the Bank of Greece and later Prime Minister, gave two speeches in Washington in which he spoke nothing but words derived from Greek, with the aim of drawing attention to the financial needs of postwar Greece. One began, "It is Zeus' anathema on our epoch for the dynamism of our economies and the heresy of our economic methods and policies that we should agonise the Scylla of numismatic plethora and the Charybdis of economic anaemia".[4]

One of the pleasures of living in Greece is to encounter the English spoken by Greeks, to whom English grammar and syntax, in particular, are a challenge. "Greeklish" flourishes in both town and village: my neighbour Alekos has fallen out with his cousin, who is somewhat of a shady individual. Alekos solemnly informs me, "My cousin is not trustful" – by which of course he means "trustworthy". One villager who lives and works in Corfu Town dutifully comes home at the weekend: "Every Saturday, I sleep with my mother". And at the pharmacy, the assistant handling my medication struggles bravely with the word "prescription" before asking "Have you a persecution?" But nothing compares with the statements of Lawrence Durrell's Cypriot students (in *Bitter Lemons*): "I am orphan and have never been enjoyed" and the rhapsodic, "As all people are dreamed, so am I".[5]

A: agony (*agón*, which we have met frequently in this book, is a contest, hence "antagonism", "protagonist"). Many words beginning with "a" indicate "without": amnesia (without memory), anarchy (without rule), apathy (without feeling), anodyne (without pain). More A-words: Angel ("angelos" was a messenger), anthropology, apocalypse, apostasy, apothecary (originally, someone in charge of a storehouse – *apothíki* is still in daily use meaning "storage"); aristocracy, arithmetic, axiom, axis. Auto (self): almost all words starting with "auto" such as "autobiography", "automaton", "autograph", "authentic".

B: bacteria; barbarian (meaning non-Greek, from the "bar-bar" noise they make); bathysphere; bibliography, bibliophile (*biblos* being the word for "book", hence "Bible").

C: cancer, carcinoma, catalepsy, catastrophe, catharsis, charisma (we met it in discussing clientelism), charity, chiropodist, chromatic, chronology, chrysanthemum ("golden flower"), cosmos (world: and from this we get cosmology, cosmonaut, microcosm); critic (originally, a judge), cryogenics ("cryo" means icy-cold; remember Austin Powers?); cybernetics (literally, "steering"), cycle, cyclone.

D: decathlon (and, for that matter, triathlon and pentathlon), democracy (anything beginning with *demos* meaning people, such as "demotic" or "demography"), dendrology (the science of trees), despot, diabetes, diaphragm, diaphanous, dichotomy, dipsomania, dogma, draconian (after the Athenian dictator, Draco).

E: economics (again, needs no introduction at this stage), ectoplasm, electron, encephalograph (*kephali* = head), ephemeral, epiphany, ethics, exodus (the road out), euphemism, "eureka!" meaning "I've found it!".

F: fire, fragment, frenetic (originally meaning "attacking the mind"). Not many "F" words come to us from Greek.

G: gastric, genesis, genetics, geometry.

H: haemorrhoids (meaning "bleeding"), heliocentric (*helios* being the sun), hepatitis, hero, herpes, hexagon (also pentagon, octagon); hologram, anything beginning with "hydro-" (water); homily (which today means "speech"), hypnosis (from *hypno*, "I sleep") hypochondria, hypodermic, hypothesis, hysteria (anything to do with the womb, e.g. hysterectomy).

I: idiom, iota (the name of the letter "I" in the Greek alphabet).

K: kallipygous (having attractive buttocks), kallisthenics (*kalo* meaning anything beautiful), kilo, kinetic energy, kleptomania.

L: leukaemia, lithograph (literally, writing on stone).

M: mania (madness), mastectomy, megalomania (*megalos* = big; strange that there isn't a "micromania" – thinking small); melanoma, metamorphosis, metaphor (which the Romans "took over" as "translation"), microscope, monogamy (and anything ending with *gamos*, meaning marriage, including polygamy), monolithic.

N: nostalgia (the pain *algos* of the homeward journey, *nostos*; from *algos* we also derive "neuralgia").

O: onomatopeia (the making of words from the sound they make, *onoma* being "name"). Orchid: the Greek word for "testicle": if you dig up an orchid, its bulbous root will make this obvious; it explains why Miss Blandish had none. Orgasm, orgy, orphan, orthodox, oxygen, oxymoron, ozone.

P: paediatrician, paedophile, pathology (most words using *path-* as a prefix or *-path* as a suffix, such as "psychopath" or "pathetic"), patronymic, pederast, pharmacy, Philadelphia (brotherly love), philately (love of postage stamps: although the Greeks didn't do it themselves, they gave us the words), philanthropy (love of one's fellow men, hard to find these days), philosophy (love of wisdom), phobia, photograph (literally, writing with light, a beautiful concept), photosynthesis, pleonasm, poet/poetry (a poet is a "maker"), polemics, politics, pseudo-, practice, prototype, pyromania.

R: rhapsody (originally, a recitation of poetry), rhetoric, rhythm.

S: sponge, sporadic (from the Sporades islands in the Aegean Sea, including Rhodes, which are all over the place), sphincter, static, synchronise, synergy, sympathy, symmetry, symphony.

T: taxi, meaning a form of vehicle, comes from Greek *tachi* meaning "fast", and is the modern word for the postal service – *tachidromeio*, indicating "the fast road". Taxidermy, thermos ("heat", hence "thermometer"), thesaurus (originally, a treasure house), topography, tragedy (literally, "a goat's song" – read Dermot Healy's wonderful novel of that title).

X: xenophobia.

Z: zoology, the study of life.

To conclude: it's safest not to plunge into the vocabulary unless you are very sure-tongued. Many words sound similar or even identical on the foreign ear. If you ask in a bar for a Margarita, you're likely to get a bunch of daisies. Don't say *kalamári* if you really mean *kaliméra*: one means "good day", the other means "squid". Don't ask for a *kideía* if you're looking for the key. You've just asked for a funeral. Try *kleidí* instead. And (work this one out for yourself) don't make the mistake of my friend who went into a DIY store in search of wood adhesive and told the assistant he wanted to glue two dogs together.

ENDNOTES

Preface

1. Another term, *Romiosyni*, is also applied to "Greekness" – and is the title of a series of publications initiated by the late Philip Sherrard and published by the Greek-based Denise Harvey – but it is in danger of confusing the discussion due to its suggestion of "Rome". We'll stay with "Greekness".

2. In Greek, the word *demokratía* means both "republic" and "democracy". Under the monarchy (abolished in 1974) the king was titled "King of the Hellenes".

3. P. Levi, *The Hill of Kronos*, p. 12.

4. N. Gage, *Hellas*, p. 24.

5. T.S. Eliot, "The Cocktail Party", in *Complete Poems and Plays*, p. 288.

6. H. Arendt, *The Life of the Mind*, vol. 1, p. 191.

7. P. Sherrard, "The Other Mind of Europe", pp. 39, 41.

8. L. Durrell, *Prospero's Cell*, p. 11.

Chapter 1 – Greece and Ireland: A Personal Perspective

1. Her father, the founder of *Kathimerini*, had previously closed down the paper during the German occupation of Greece.

2. T.S. Eliot, "Little Gidding" in *Four Quartets*.

3. E. Burke, "Appeal from the New to the Old Whigs" (1791), *Works and Correspondence*, vol. IV, p. 489; he was writing of the British Constitution (which in itself cannot be found anywhere because it is not a codified, or monolithic, document).

4. P. Sherrard, "Odysseas Elytis and the Discovery of Greece", *Journal of Modern Greek Studies* 1/2 (1983).

5. Like all statistics, the end figure depends on which organisation conducts the survey; figures for poverty (and definitions of poverty itself) range from 20 per cent to 27 per cent. Their severity remains unquestioned.

6. We must note that the interpretation, and application, of the term "fascist" to Greece is debatable: Richard Clogg, for example, calls it "a label that cannot be made to stick, unless the term 'fascist' is used in a wholly indiscriminate way, as a general term of abuse, that has now become the fashion"; the observation is all the more surprising since Clogg was writing during the military junta of 1967-74 which, he acknowledged, "manifests a number of characteristics in common

with regimes that have been accepted as fascist": R. Clogg, "The Ideology of the 'Revolution of 21 April 1967'", in R. Clogg and G. Yannopoulos, *Greece Under Military Rule*, p. 51.

7. W.B. Yeats, "Easter 1916": "Too long a sacrifice / Can make a stone of the heart", *Poems*, pp. 180-82.

8. D. Kiberd, "Inventing Irelands", *Crane Bag* 8/1, 1984.

9. Y. Chouliaras, "Modern Greek Culture", *Journal of Modern Hellenism* vol. 3 (1986).

10. V. Hatziyannidis, *Four Walls*, p. 36.

11. A. Karakousis, "From the truth to the other choice", *To Vima*, 7 December 2014.

12. *Sunday Tribune*, 16 November 1986.

13. Patrick West, "See Ireland and Live", *Times Literary Supplement*, 3 November 2001.

14. O. Elytis, *Axion Esti*.

15. Frank McNally, "An Irishman's Diary", *Irish Times*, 28 January 2013.

16. The following is based on my *Irish Times* column of 6 October 2012.

17. The following is based on my *Irish Times* column of 9 May 2012.

18. Quoted by Seamus Deane in *Crane Bag* 8/1 (1984).

19. R. Kipling, "Ballad of East and West", 1892.

20. Even though it was, somewhat surprisingly, an American, Edgar Allan Poe who wrote that in the first years of Greek independence.

21. Of whom 300 are women and 175 men, many of the women living in Greece having married Greeks (official figures).

22. If the statistics for Ireland bear any comparison with those for the UK, the proportion of Greeks to Cypriot Greeks is 1:3 (reflecting the movement of Greeks from Cyprus in the aftermath of the *enosis* crisis of the 1950s and the 1974 invasion of Cyprus by Turkey).

23. L. Durrell, "The Poetic Obsession of Dublin", *Travel and Leisure*, Autumn 1972.

24. P. Levi, *Hill of Kronos*, p. 129.

25. Despite an investment of €9 million in building the non-functioning airstrips.

26. I'm cheating: EasyJet was established by Stelio Hadji-Ioannou, a Greek Cypriot based in London.

27. Marcel Detienne and Jean-Pierre Vernant, *Cunning Intelligence in Greek Culture and Society*; I am indebted to Brewster Chamberlin for drawing my attention to this book, originally published as *Les ruses de l'intelligence: La mètis des Grecs* (1978).

Chapter 2 – Brief History Lessons

1. *Megáli Idéa* is usually translated as "Great Idea" but I prefer to see the "idea" as a "project" or "proposal"; I have always resisted the term "Great Idea" because it suggests a sarcastic question: "What's the big idea?" The *idea* was not only a state

of mind but also a specific, irredentist target: the reconnection of the new state with Greeks in other lands. The classical Greek word *idéa* meant "the look or appearance of a thing as opposed to its reality". One can perhaps see how this was transmuted into the modern meaning of an *opinion* – something not necessarily verifiable or open to definition.

2. Th. Cambanis, *Boston Globe*, 22 August 2014.

3. Foreword to A.R. and M. Burn, *The Living Past of Greece*.

4. In 2014 a Canadian consortium, intent on mining gold in the Halkidiki peninsula (in the Greek part of historical Macedonia), met with vigorous local protest against the possible environmental impact.

5. *Pólis*, meaning "a city", also means, by extension, "civil". A "civilised" person is a *politisménos*. In modern Greek, a civil engineer is a *politikós michanikós* – literally, a political mechanic. A civilian is a *politikós*; a statesman is a *politikós ándros* – a "political man". So "political" has a number of applications.

6. N. Kazantzakis, *Travels in Greece*, pp. 166-168.

7. L. Durrell, *Key to Modern Poetry*, p. 31.

8. Nothing to do with the religious "Society of Friends" – the Quakers.

9. Campbell and Sherrard, *Modern Greece*, p. 58. For an assessment of the status of the *klephts*, see John Koliopoulos, *Brigands with a Cause* (1987).

10. We use the term "ethnic" (from Greek *ethnos*) to delineate cultural and racial characteristics, rather than political, yet in modern Greek *ethnikós* equates with "national", as in *Ethnikí Trápeza tis Elládos* – National Bank of Greece.

11. See Campbell and Sherrard, pp. 69-70; Koliopoulos and Veremis, p. 12; Doumanis, p. 175.

12. Quoted in G. Zaharopoulos, "The Monarchy and Politics in Modern Greece" in J. Koumoulides (ed.), *Greece in Transition*, p. 190.

13. In the era of the Second World War and the build-up to the junta, public opinion was openly critical of the fact that King Paul was married to a German princess, who, as a Nazi sympathiser, scored exceptionally low ratings in the popularity stakes and in fact did much to diminish the standing of the monarchy under her husband and her son, Constantine II.

14. T. Gallant, *Modern Greece*, p. 9.

15. S. Constantinidis, *Modern Greek Theatre: A Quest for Hellenism*, p. 19.

16. Otto was *Vasilefs tis Elládos* [Βασιλεύς της Ελλάδος]; George was *Vasilefs tón Ellínon* [Βασιλεύς των Ελλήνων].

17. "Dodecanese" meaning "twelve islands" from *dodéka* (twelve) and *nisi* (islands). There were, in fact, more than twelve, but Rhodes, Patmos, Leros, Kos, and Kalymnos were the principal. Kastelorizo, the smallest, will be encountered in Chapter 3.

18. Kolettis was prime minister of Greece 1834-35 and 1844-47.

19. Quoted in R. Clogg, *A Concise History of Greece*, p. 47.

20. M. Llewellyn Smith, *Ionian Vision*, p. 1.

21. From the Greek *epta* meaning "seven" and *nisi* meaning "islands".

22. N. Stamatopoulos, *Old Corfu*, p. 40.

23. Douglas Dakin, "The Formation of the Greek State" in J. Koumoulides (ed.), *Greece in Transition*, p. 26.

24. Nugent was the younger son of the Marquess of Buckingham, and succeeded his mother (an Irish baroness in her own right) to the Nugent title. He subsequently became MP for Aylesbury 1847-50.

25. Young was a baronet; after his débâcle in Corfu he subsequently became Governor of New South Wales and then Governor General of Canada in 1868. He was created Baron Lisgar of Lisgar and Bailieborough in 1870. Edward Lear regarded Young's "court" as "wholly a dilettante affair" and that Young had a "vacillating manner and softness": Philip Sherrard (ed.), *Edward Lear: The Corfu Years*, p. 142.

26. C.M. Woodhouse, *The Philhellenes*, p. 144.

27. Quoted in R.N. Lawrence, *Charles Napier*, p. 65.

28. *Letters of Oscar Wilde*, p. 36.

29 W.B. Yeats, *Autobiography*, p. 90.

30. Between 1890 and 1910, 350,000 Greeks emigrated – almost all males – equating to almost one-seventh of the entire population.

31. P. Mansel, *Levant*, p. 187.

32. M. Llewellyn Smith, op. cit., p. 36.2

33. Quoted in ibid., pp. 46-7.

34. In 1919 Lloyd George and the French leader Georges Clemenceau had agreed that Greek troops should occupy Smyrna, but failed to back up this expectation with any military support.

35. M. Llewellyn Smith, op.cit., p. 29.

36. Quoted by P. Mansel, op.cit., p. 209.

37. L. Durrell, preface to I. Venezis, *Aeolia*.

38. Like the junta that came after him, Metaxas was adept at media management: he used film, radio, outdoor advertising and even bus tickets to establish himself in the Greek consciousness: "On the 4th of August Greece was saved by Ioannis Metaxas". He called himself "The First Peasant" and "The First Worker" and, as such, his face was printed onto light bulbs.

39. The Italian occupation of Kephalonia, one of the Ionian islands, is told in Louis de Bernières's novel *Captain Corelli's Mandolin* and in the subsequent film (2001) by John Madden, starring Nicolas Cage and Penélope Cruz.

40. In addition to Mark Mazower's *Inside Hitler's Greece*, see also a fictionalised account by Edmund Keeley, *Wine for Remembrance*. Mark Mazower has, in particular, documented the destruction of the village of Komeno, with the mass killing of 317 men, women and children on 16 August 1943, in which Waldheim was involved. Komeno was one of an estimated 1700 such villages destroyed; another was Distomo, where the story of eye-witnesses to the massacre of 218 people, including children, and pregnant women who were disembowelled, has provoked demands that Germany should apologise for the slaughter. There is

little question of money being repaid: it is a "moral obligation" (*Kathimerini*, 10 April 2015).

41. With the exceptional case of the Ionian island of Zakynthos, where the bishop arranged for "Christian passports" for many Jews who were then hidden on the island. In addition to this humanitarian act, it is also recorded that the bishop, when required by a German commandant to supply a list of all Jews in Zakynthos, gave only his own name and that of the mayor: "If you harm these people I will go with them and share their fate": Tassoula Eptakili, *Kathimerini*, 17 July 2014. A merchant's seventeenth-century mansion (of the Cobici family) in Corfu Town was bequeathed by its Jewish owner to the bishop of Zakynthos in recognition of his actions, and remained until recently in church ownership. In 2013 a film project was announced by the Greek America Foundation to make a documentary of the Jewish experience on Zakynthos.

42. Figures based on Red Cross calculations, quoted in M. Mazower, *Inside Hitler's Greece*, pp. 32-41.

43. C.M. Woodhouse, op. cit., p. 226.

44. In 1950, guerilla activity continued, with killings and woundings of many army personnel.

45. I am guilty of gross simplification, since there were many republicans who were not communists and did not support EAM, just as there were non-communists in EAM. To explain the split between left and right in detail would occupy many a volume: see in particular Woodhouse, *The Struggle for Greece 1941-49*, Sarafis (ed.) *Greece: From Resistance to Civil War* and Edgar O'Ballance, *The Greek Civil War 1944-49*.

46. P. Mackridge, op. cit., p. 310.

47. N. Svoronos, "Introduction" to M. Sarafis (ed.), *From Resistance to Civil War*, p. 12.

48. The agreement was explicitly set out in Churchill's history of the war, in which he said to Stalin: "Let us settle our affairs about the Balkans [...] How would it do for you to have 90 per cent predominance in Rumania, for us to have 90 per cent of the say in Greece, and go fifty-fifty about Yugoslavia?", to which Stalin "took his blue pencil and made a large tick" on the makeshift document which Churchill pushed in front of him. "It was all settled in no more time than it takes to set down": W.S. Churchill, *The Second World War, Triumph and Tragedy*, pp. 226-7. Although the formal agreement between Churchill and Stalin was reached in 1944, it is now clear that, from 1941 onwards, they had been negotiating such an agreement, with Anthony Eden, as Foreign Secretary, the go-between: see E. Barker, "Greece in the Framework of Anglo-Soviet Relations 1941-47" in M. Sarafis, op. cit.

49. Churchill is reported to have regarded a possible EAM victory as "a reign of terror": E. Barker, op. cit., p. 25.

50. E. Barker, op. cit., p. 25.

51. M. Mazower, *The Balkans*, p. 119.

52. John Iatrides, op. cit., p. 79.

53. E. Kazantzakis, *Nikos Kazantzakis*, pp. 484, 491.

54. See my *The Disappointed Bridge*, chapter 11, "Map-making".

55. R. Beaton, *An Introduction to Modern Greek Literature*, p. 244.

56. Quoted in P. Bien, *Kazantzakis*, p. 329.

57. The acronym IDEA represents the Greek title *Ierós Desmós Ellínon – Holy Band of Greek Officers*.

58 See N. Panourgiá, *Dangerous Citizens*, pp. 58-9.

59. C. Tsoucalas, *The Greek Tragedy*, p. 117.

60. He has been described as "a weak man, devoid of imagination and initiative": George Alexander, "The Unnamed Round" in M. Sarafis, op. cit., p. 44.

61. John O. Iatrides, op. cit., p. 83.

62. Panagiota Bitsika, *To Vima*, 26 April 1998.

63. Quoted by T.A. Couloumbis et al., *Foreign Interference in Greek Politics: An Historical Perspective*, p. 137.

64. P. Levi, *Hill of Kronos*, pp. 134-5.

65. Quoted in K. Legg, *Politics in Modern Greece*, p. 221.

66. Quoted in R. Clogg, "The Ideology of the 'Revolution of 21 April 1967" in Clogg and Yannopoulos (eds.), *Greece Under Military Rule*, p. 38.

67. Quoted in Clogg and Yannopoulos, "Editors' Introduction", *Greece Under Military Rule*, p. xv.

68. Quoted in R. Beaton, *Seferis: Waiting for the Angel*, p. 390.

69. S.V. Papacosma, "Military in Greek Politics" in J. Koumoulides (ed.), *Greece in Transition*, p. 185.

70. P. Levi, *Hill of Kronos*, p. 139. Another ordinary citizen, quoted by Sofka Zinovieff in *Eurydice Street* (p. 24), thought that "a little dictatorship, just for a few years, to get the country back on its feet again" was not harmful.

71. Ibid., p. 138.

72. Quoted in ibid. pp. 152-3.

73. Th. Angelopoulos, interview (2006), accessed at http://www.altfg.com/blog/film-reviews/days-of-36-d-theo-angelopoulos/ 23 February 2015.

74. P. Mackridge, op. cit., p. 1.

75. P. Mackridge, email to the author, 21 February 2015.

76. P. Mackridge, op. cit., p. 7.

77. Quoted in P. Levi, op. cit., pp. 132-3.

78. M. Mazower, "Kings of Europe", *Times Literary Supplement*, 9 July 2009.

Chapter 3 – Geopolitics: Greece, the Balkans and the Levant

1. I am deliberately withholding the name of my correspondent.

2. M. Mazower, *The Balkans*, p. 9.

3. Elisabeth Barker, "Greece in the Framework of Anglo-Soviet Relations 1941-

1947" in M. Sarafis (ed.), *Greece: From Resistance to Civil War*, p. 30.

4. Loukas Tsoukalis, "The Future of Greece in the European Union", in Th. Couloumbis et al. (eds.), *Greece in the Twentieth Century*, p. 326.

5. For whom a main street is named in Corfu Town.

6. L. Stavrianos, *Balkan Federation*, quoted in M. Glenny, *The Balkans*, p. 111.

7. M. Mazower, op.cit., p. 90.

8. Ibid., p. 104.

9. The expression occurs in a review by Richard Crampton of E. Pond's *Endgame in the Balkans: Regime Change, European style*, *Times Literary Supplement*, 28 September 2007.

10. Later still, the break-up of the Soviet bloc has led to a "balkanisation" of its constituent parts, with Poland, Hungary and the Baltic states regaining independence. The term "balkanisation" has also been applied to the uncertainty and the activities of separatist movements in the Middle East, India and Africa.

11. G. Augustinos, "Greece and the Balkans between the World Wars: Self-identity, the Other and national development", in D. Tziovas (ed.), *Greece and the Balkans*, p. 84.

12. M. Mazower, op. cit., p. 77.

13. A.J.P. Taylor, *The Struggle for Mastery in Europe*, p. 568.

14. A. Papachelas, "Facts and Pipedreams", *Kathimerini*, 7 December 2014.

15. M. Mazower, op. cit., p. 103.

16. The Greek population of Alexandria has shrunk from 150,000 in 1937 to 65,000 in 1960 to 3,000 in 1973 and is less than 1,000 today. The Jewish population has today almost completely disappeared.

17. Neil Barnett, "Introduction" to Leon Sciaky, *Farewell to Salonica*, p. 9.

18. M. Mazower, op. cit., p. 6.

19. J. Mansel, *Levant*, p. 169.

20. E. Durham, *The Burden of the Balkans*, pp. 286-7.

21. M. Glenny, *The Balkans*, p. 569.

22. In the early 1980s I was witness to a statement by a Muslim living in the UK, whose brother was on trial for the "honour killing" of his own daughter (she had defied his wishes in seeing a non-Muslim): he told me, "We regard the law of Islam as superior to that of the United Kingdom, and we deny that my brother has committed any crime. He was defending the honour of the family."

23. The quotations which follow, and associated statistics, are derived from Tanya Mangalakova, "The *Kanun* in present-day Albania, Kosovo and Montenegro".

24. In 2003, the Albanian newspaper *Shekulli* reported that 3000 families were confined to their homes as a result of blood feuds.

25. Following the appearance of the "Letter" from which the foregoing is drawn (26 June 2009), I received a reader's comment from an Albanian, which called my article "a malicious lie", and a "fabrication", asserting that I "have enough information to know how the truth stands, and deliberately have chosen to distort

it". In fact, all statements in my article were sourced from Albanian government information bulletins and ministries, and from international agencies.

26. Paul Adamidi-Frascheri also told me that, on the eve of a royalist counter-coup against the communist government, in 1952, the royalist agents in Albania were all exterminated. The list of these agents had been supplied to the communists by Kim Philby, at that time a Soviet spy occupying a high-ranking British diplomatic post in Washington.

27. M. Glenny, op. cit., p. 158.

28. N. Kazantzakis, *The Fratricides*, pp. 114-5.

29. Quoted in M. Dragoumis, *Greece on the Couch: Session 2*, p. 117.

30. J. Psaropoulos, "Skopje touts ethnicity", *Athens News*, 26 August 2008.

31. The following paragraphs appeared in my "Letter from Greece" in *The Irish Tmes*, 30 April. 2011.

32. W. Mallinson, *Britain and Cyprus*, pp. 67-70, 162-64.

33. The revelation of this previously unsuspected facility was made by "whistle-blower" Edward Snowden in 2013; details were published in the Greek newspaper *Ta Nea* and on the Alpha television channel.

34. R. Clogg, "Lives and times: new opportunities for truth in Greece", *Times Literary Supplement*, 22 June 2007.

35. P. Levi, *Hill of Kronos*, p. 185.

36. A. Eden, *Full Circle*, p. 315.

37. N. Malkoutzis, "Between the olive branch and the sword of justice", *Kathimerini*, 6 November 2014.

38. Panos Kammenos, quoted in *International New York Times*, 17 February 2015.

39. Reported in *Athens News*, 27 June 2014.

40. Reported in *EnetEnglish.gr*, 14 July 2014.

41. M. Mazower, op. cit., p. 134.

Chapter 4 – People

1. The Greek word for a city, *póli* [πόλη] remains linked not only to the original Greek sense of a city-state, but also to *the* city, Constantinople, which in the national/ethnic memory is *I Póli* [η Πόλη]. The nearest Latin term for *politismós* would be *civitas* – citizenship.

2. H.D.F. Kitto, *The Greeks*, p. 7.

3. L. Durrell, *Spirit of Place*, pp. 156-8.

4. H.D.F. Kitto, op. cit., p. 169.

5. Ibid., p. 213.

6. A. Papachelas, *Kathimerini*, 21 January 2015.

7. One, Yannis Makriyannis, despite being a successful merchant, general in the revolution and a party to the first Constitution (1821), was virtually illiterate, and only taught himself to write at the age of thirty. His *Memoirs* were notable for the fact that they were written in demotic, and, a century later, when Greece was

threatened by, and suffering from fascism, the *Memoirs*, for that reason, were acclaimed as a monument of modern Greek literature.

8. P. Mackridge, "The Re-Hellenization of Greek since 1750", a lecture to the Society for Modern Greek Studies, London, 17 May 2014.

9. Examples of fictional and non-fictional accounts of Greeks returning to the ancestral home from the *diasporá* include: Natalie Bakopoulos, *The Green Shore* (2012) – a fictionalised account of her family's Athenian background under the military junta 1967-74; Kay Cicellis [*recte* Tstitselis], *Death of a Town* (1954) – a depiction of her paternal town in Cephalonia during the disastrous earthquake of 1953; Eleni Gage, *North of Ithaka: One Woman's Journey into Her Family's Extraordinary Past* (2004) – return to her father's natal village of Liá, Epirus [see below, note 19]; Elias Kulukundis, *The Feasts of Memory: A Journey to a Greek Island* (1967) – return to the Dodecanese island of Kasos.

10. T. Gallant, *Modern Greece*, p. 80.

11. See Renée Hirschon, "Presents, Promises and Punctuality: Accountability and Obligations in Greek Social Life" in M. Mazower (ed.), *Networks of Power in Modern Greece.*

12. Tsipouro is a Greek bootleg liquor similar to Irish *poitín*; try it at your peril.

13. V. Alexiadou, "Introduction" to *Vefa's Kitchen.*

14. N. Kazantzakis, *Zorba the Greek*, p. 69.

15. Z. Lorenzatos, *Aegean Notebooks*, p. 65.

16. In Theodorakis' *Zorba the Greek*, Zorba woos Madame Hortense as "Bouboulina", thus giving the ailing and hopeless woman a sense of dignity.

17. J. Dubisch, *In a Different Place: Pilgrimage, Gender and Politics at a Greek Island Shrine*, p. 133.

18. N. Gage, *Hellas*, p. 39.

19. Gage, née Gatzoyannis, was born in the Epirot village of Liá, the setting for his account (in *Eleni*) of the sacrifice of her life by his mother in order to secure his escape during the civil war.

20. I was sitting at a café with the British consul in Corfu when a passing boy snatched a piece of food from her plate; she remonstrated, he spat at her. I rose to hit the boy and was restrained by all the horrified women at our table who explained how un-PC it would be for me to do so. The boy subsequently threw his mother's handbag across the street and shouted at her that she was a bad mother; the mother did nothing.

21. Eleni Stamiris, "The Women's Movement in Greece", *New Left Review*, 1/158, 1986.

22. A. Papadiamandis, *The Murderess* (*I Fonissa*, trans. Liadain Sherrard), p. 3.

23. "A Greek Politician Willing to Face the People", *New York Times*, 26 September 2014.

24. E. Stamiris, op. cit.

25. E. Friedl, "The Position of Women: Appearance and Reality" in J. Dubisch (ed.), *Gender and Power in Rural Greece*, p. 51.

26. Quoted by M. Herzfield, "Within and Without: the Category of 'Female' in the Ethnography of Modern Greece", in J. Dubisch (ed.), *Gender and Power*, pp. 224-5.

27. In 1961, 36 per cent of girls and 50 per cent of boys attended secondary school; in 1981 that had risen to 51 per cent and 61 per cent respectively. In 1961 only 1 per cent of women and 3 per cent of men graduated from university; in 1981 the figures were 3.5 per cent and 6.8 per cent respectively, but by 2014 the majority of graduates were women, but they only constituted 37 per cent of the workforce.

28. A. Karamanou, "The Changing Role of Women in Greece", in Couloumbis et al (eds.), *Greece in the Twentieth Century*, p. 274.

29. J.B. Keane, *Sive*, p. 27.

30. J. Dubisch, "Gender, Kinship and Religion" in Loizos and Papataxiarchis (eds.), *Contested Identies: Gender and Kinship in Modern Greece*, p. 45.

31. J. du Boulay, "Women: Images of their Nature and Destiny in Rural Greece", in J Dubisch (ed.), *Gender and Power*, p. 139.

32. A. Karamanou, op. cit., p. 287.

33. S.D. Salamone and J.B. Stanton, "Introducing the *Nikokyra*: Ideality and Reality in Social Process", in J Dubisch (ed.), *Gender and Power*, p. 99.

34. R. Kennedy, "Women's Friendships on Crete: A Psychological Perspective", in J Dubisch (ed.), *Gender and Power*, p. 122.

35. T. Theodoropoulos, *Athens News*, 15 July 2014. Theodoropoulos is not only a journalist but a prolific author of at least ten novels, of which only one, *The Power of the Dark God* (*I Dyname tou Skateinou Theou*, 1999) seems to have been translated into English (by David Connolly).

36. *Kathimerini*, 7 September 2010. The following paragraphs appeared in my "Letter from Greece", *Irish Times*, 17 December 2010.

37. *Kathimerini*, 19 January 2011.

38. Nikos Louvros, quoted in *AthensPlus*, 3 September 2010.

39. Going back to the earliest days of the State, in 1856 smoking was banned in state buildings (to prevent the risk of fire); in 1945 tobacconists were forbidden to offer inducements such as vouchers, to smokers; in 1952 all smoking in vehicles was prohibited; in 1980, on smoking in enclosed public places; in 1989, advertising of tobacco was banned in educational and sporting areas, and two years later on television advertising.

40. *AthensPlus*, 3 September 2010.

41. The following paragraphs appeared in *The Irish Times*, 28 August 2014.

42. See Vassilis Nedo, "Thrity years of big mistakes empty out Greece's countryside", *Kathimerini*, 14-15 February 2009.

43. Z. Lorenzatos, *Aegean Notebooks*, p. 81.

Chapter 5 – Structures of Power and Dissent

1. Quoted by Psaropoulos' wife, A.E. Stallings, *Times Literary Supplement*, 5 December 2014.

2. The pre-independence Constitution of 1822 not only concentrated almost

exclusively on the establishment of a provisional government and administration but also deliberately avoided any statement of principle such as might be derived from either the French or American constitutions.

3. Two textbooks (in Greek) are used for teaching fundamental rights, and two (in English): *Constitution, Law and Rights in the Welfare State* (George S. Katrougalos, 1988) and *Constitutional Law in Hellas* (Philippos C. Spyropoulos, 1995).

4. See Adamantia Pollis, "The State, the Law, and Human Rights in Modern Greece", *Human Rights Quarterly*, vol.9 (1987): rights are "group rights"; "there are no fundamental principles or doctrines, other than nationalism, which legitimate the Greek polity"; "the Greek courts have functioned as the legitimators of the prevailing regime and bulwarks of the status quo [...] while providing little defense for citizens against arbitrary state power"; the problem confronting the authors of the 1975 Constitution was "to draft a constitution which established a democratic institutional framework and incorporated detailed guarantees of individual freedoms and liberties without challenging the supremacy of the state".

5. A. Pollis, op. cit.

6. Quoted in *To Vima*, 2 December 2014.

7. The Article is entitled Άσυλο της κατοικίας (The Sanctuary of the Home); κατοικία can mean dwelling, residence, domicile or home. The Greek text employs the same word, *ásilo* [άσυλο] for "sanctuary" and "asylum", possibly because to announce baldly that "the home is an asylum" might give the wrong impression. *Ásilo* has many meanings and inferences: while "asylum" is a literal translation, it also represents the concepts of a place of safety, a shelter, a harbour.

8. I discuss this more fully, in the context of a specific location in Corfu, in a "Letter" in *The Irish Times*, 15 December 2014.

9. In their introduction to Couloumbis et al. (eds.), *Greece in the Twentieth Century*, p. 1.

10. The remark, from a sermon in Tinos (the principal site of pilgrimage on the feast of the Annunciation), is quoted in J. Dubisch, *In a Different Place*, p. 173.

11. Quoted in Jeremy Morris, *The Church in the Modern Age*, p. 38.

12. J. Dubisch, *In a Different Place*, p. 164.

13. Y. Palaiologos, *Kathimerini*, 20 October 2014.

14. C. Frazee, "The Orthodox Church of Greece", in J. Koumoulides (ed.), *Hellenic Perspectives: Essays in the History of Greece*, p. 148.

15. The islet of Lazareto in Corfu Bay was the site of numerous executions and remains a place of pilgrimage for descendants of the dead, mainly communist guerrillas.

16. Subsequently bishop of Galway; he was bishop of Galway when the "Annie Murphy" story broke, and resigned shortly afterwards.

17. *AthensPlus*, 30 April 2009.

18. "Kallikrates" was preceded in 1998 by an equally evocatively named "Kapodistrias Plan" which reduced municipalities from 5,775 to the 1,033 which was the starting-point for the "Kallikrates" reduction.

19. Athens News Agency, 26 May 2010.

20. In 2004, Mark Mazower referred to the current politics as "Karamanlis the Second against Papandreou the Third": "Kings of Europe", *Times Literary Supplement*, 9 July 2009.

21. S. Zinovieff, *Eurydice Street*, p. 150.

22. M. Dragoumis, *Greece on the Couch: Session 2*, p. 22.

23. N. Papandreou, *Father Dancing: An Invented Memoir*, p. 5.

24. E. Royidis, *Works* (1978) vol. 2, quoted in Koliopoulos and Veremis, *Greece: The Modern Sequel*, p. 62.

25. Christopher Torchia, "Greek feud: 2 rival leaders share common bond", *Kathimerini*, 28 November 2011.

26. In Greece, the Syriza victory in 2015 brought it within two seats of an overall majority (149 out of 300 seats).

27. In Ireland, the announcement by Lucinda Creighton, a former Fine Gael TD, of a new party, "Renua", in 2014-15, was greeted by a government minister as a sign that "the coming years would see 'flash-in-the-pan new parties' doing well in one election": *Irish Times* report, 3 January 2015.

28. In the 2015 election, Syriza, with 36.3 per cent of the national vote, had 149 seats (99 on election plus 50 as the largest party in the new parliament); ND, with 27.8 per cent, 76 seats; Golden Dawn, with 6.3 per cent, 17 seats; To Potámi, with 6.1 per cent, 17 seats (its first time in parliament); KKE, with 5.5 per cent, 15 seats; ANEL, with 4.8 per cent, 13 seats; PASOK, with 4.7 per cent, 13 seats. Democratic Left, which had been the third member of the ND-PASOK coalition, from which it departed in 2013, had merely 0.5 per cent of the vote in 2015.

29. These include RIZES Radical National Rally; LAOS Popular Orthodox Rally; Greeks Initiative; Drachma Five Star Movement; Drasis (Action); Panhellenic Citizen Chariot.

30. Quoted by Th. Veremos, "Andreas Papandreou, Radical without a Cause", in M. Mazower (ed.), *Networks of Power in Modern Greece*, p. 140.

31. A. Karakousis, "The weak Greek political system", *To Vima*, 30 November 2014.

32. Quoted in *Athens News*, 13 December 2013.

33. The following paragraphs appeared in *The Irish Times*, 13 August 2013.

34. Quoted in *GRReporter*, 4 July 2013.

35. Athens has no purpose-built mosque (having been postponed on several occasions and leaving it the only European capital without one), but Muslims have established places of worship which have been subject to attack by GD, as have the mosques (dating mostly from much earlier times) in other parts of Greece.

36. "Many Greeks have had enough of democracy", *Irish Times*, 27 November 2013.

37. N. Panourgiá, *Dangerous Citizens: The Greek Left and the Terror of the State*, p.xxiii.

38. Neni Panourgiá remarks that one cannot refer to parties of the Left as "outside

politics" since they have been represented in parliament since 1923 (the Agrarian Party) – email to the author, 23 April 2015. But the metaphorical point is that this was an absent presence of marginalisation and exclusion rather than inclusion. The Left, in effect, was there but not there.

39. N. Panourgiá, op. cit., p. 7.

40. Ibid., p. 14.

41. N. Panourgiá, New School for Social Research website.

42. B. Friel, *Plays 1*, p.419; Friel himself adapted the expression from George Steiner's *After Babel*.

43. Panourgiá would use *vasanistírio* rather than *martírio* for the word "pain", but would not exclude the relevance also of *martírio*: email to the author, 23 April 2015.

44. Panourgiá offers the word "convictions" rather than "faith", since "the language used by the Left is that of convictions (*ta pistevo mas*) and ideas (*oi idees mas*), not faith (*pisti*)": email to the author, 23 April 2015.

45. N. Panourgiá, op. cit., p. 153.

46. C. Whitman, "Foreword" to *Eighteen Texts*, p. xi.

47. The following paragraphs appeared in *The Irish Times*, 6 February 2014.

48. B. Friel, *Essays, Diaries, Interviews 1964-1999* (ed. C. Murray), p. 52.

49. The series, starring Benedict Cumberbatch as a modern-day Sherlock Holmes, was screened by the BBC, 2010-14.

50. Quoted in Y. Alexander and D. Pluchinsky, *Europe's Red Terrorists: Fighting Communist Organisations*, p. 94.

51. M. Mazower, "Kings of Europe", *Times Literary Supplement*, 9 July 2004.

52. N. Konstandaras, "Young rebels and our collective delusion", *Kathimerini*, 12 February 2013.

53. BBC News, 20 January 2014.

54. Quoted in *Athens News*, 13 March 2009.

55. Quoted in *AthensPlus*, 13 March 2009.

56. Personal email to the author, 27 February 2009.

57. Quoted in *Athens News*, 13 March 2009.

58. The attack on Microsoft, in June 2012, was claimed by the "Informal Anarchist Federation-International Revolutionary Front". It was followed by another attack in April 2015.

59. Quoted in *AthensPlus*, 16 January 2009.

60. Quoted in *AthensPlus*, 13 March 2009.

61. Quoted in *To Vima*, 10 November 2014.

62. Mary Bossi, of the University of Piraeus, points out that "the name is just a name. The personnel pool is common to these organisations": *Athens News*, 29 November 2013.

63. The names of terrorist organisations translated into English vary from one source to another; for example, "Revolutionary Sect" is also "Sect of Revolutionaries".

64. Its speciality, when posting to government ministers, is the "cooking-pot bomb": one wonders how many wary politicians would accept delivery of a cooking pot.

65. N. Konstandaras, "Can the Greek Center Hold?", *International New York Times*, 12 November 2013.

66. Quoted by Liz Alderman, "Greek crackdown blamed for attacks", *International Herald Tribune*, 21 January 2013.

67. See in particular Pavlos Eleftheriadis (associate professor of law at Oxford University), "Misrule of the Few: how the oligarchs ruined Greece", *Foreign Affairs*, November/December 2014.

68. A. Papachelas, "Fighting the technocrats of violence", *Kathimerini*, 28 January 2011.

69. Quoted in Renee Maltezou and Deepa Barrington, "Inside Greece's violent new anarchist groups", Reuters report, 14 August 2013.

70. Leonidas Chrysanthopoulos, a former Greek ambassador to Poland and Canada, and Secretary-General of Black Sea Economic Co-operation.

71. Following the Syntagma sit-ins, the *indignados* formed a political party, EPAM (United People's Front), but, despite the mass support that their protest had elicited in the sit-ins and the letter to Barroso, it failed to translate into votes at the 2012 election (less than 1%) and no candidates were presented at the 2015 election.

72. HK Bhabha, *The Location of Culture*, p. 164.

73. The Latin word "translation" meaning "carrying across" has its exact equivalent in the Greek "metaphor".

74. R. Hirschon, "Presents, Promises and Punctuality" in M. Mazower (ed.), *Networks of Power in Greece*, p. 201.

Chapter 6 – A Failed State?

1. E. Royidis, *Works* vol. 2, translated by Koliopoulos and Veremis, *Greece: The Modern Sequel*, p. 62.

2. R. Clogg, review of Koliopoulos and Veremis, *Greece: The Modern Sequel*, *Times Literary Supplement*, 26 September 2003.

3. *Kathimerini*, 12 February 2012.

4. Stournaras was head of the Foundation for Economic and Industrial Research and a lecturer in macroeconomics before becoming Finance Minister in 2012, until his resignation in 2014 and appointment as Governor of the Central Bank of Greece. He was an adviser to the Ministry of Finance during Greece's negotiations for entry to the eurozone.

5. Quoted in Dody Tsianter, "Greek Tragedy", *Time*, 15 February 2010.

6. C. Spanou, "The Quandary of Administrative Reform: Institutional and Performance Modernization", in Kalyvas et al. (eds.), *From Stagnation to Forced Adjustment: Reforms in Greece 1974-2010*, pp. 171, 189.

7. Y. Palaiologos, *The 13th Labour of Hercules*, p. 43.

8. M. Matsaganis, "Prerequisites to the Revival of Public Health Care in Greece",

in Kalyvas et al., op. cit., pp. 134-5.

9. Couloumbis et al., *Foreign Interference in Greek Politics: An Historical Perspective*, p. 143.

10. K. Legg, "The Nature of the Modern Greek State", in J. Koumolides (ed.), *Greece in Transition: Essays on the History of Modern Greece 1821-1974*, p. 283.

11. K. Legg, "The Nature of the Modern Greek State", in J. Koumoulides, op. cit., p. 291.

12. *Kathimerini*, 8 November 2012.

13. N. Malkoutzis, interview with the author, Athens, 4 March 2015.

14. Y. Palaiologos, interview with the author, Athens, 5 March 2015.

15. T. Veremis, "Andreas Papandreou: Radical Without a Cause", in M. Mazower (ed.), *Networks of Power in Modern Greece*, p. 143.

16. C. Spanou, "The Quandary of Administrative Reform", pp. 177-8.

17. See M.D. Higgins, *Causes for Concern: Irish Politics, Culture and Society*; Brian Girvin, however, states that "this is not a feature of politics in the Republic, where *brokerage* is more common: this is where elected representatives act as intermediaries for individuals dealing with public bodies [...] The politician anticipates support as a result, but this is not guaranteed": "Clientelism in the Republic", in B. Lalor (ed.), *The Encyclopaedia of Ireland*, p. 209. In his chairman's address to the Labour Party in 1985 Higgins recalled the time when policies seemed to be irrelevant: "'Give us the seats first, and then the policies will follow' was their cry. They sought to divides the party's options between policies on one hand and financial solvency and good organisation on the other. This is a false choice. Policies must be the outcome of a process that encourages participation if they are to be meaningful": M.D. Higgins, "Ideology and the Left in Ireland", *Crane Bag* 9/2.

18. M.D. Higgins, "The Limits of Clientelism", op. cit., pp. 73-96. See also M.D. Higgins and Peter Gibbon, "Patronage, tradition and modernisation: The case of the Irish 'Gombeenman'", *Economic and Social Review* vol. 6, 1974, and Lee Komito, "Irish Clientelism: A Reappraisal", *Economic and Social Review* 15/3, 1984.

19. Y. Palaiologos, "Greece's closed society is central to its current malaise", *Kathimerini*, 20 October 2014.

20. Gikas Hardouvelis, quoted by Reuters, 19 January 2011.

21. T. Cambanis, "Why is corruption so hard to shake?", *Boston Globe*, 22 August 2014; subsequent quotations from Cambanis are from this source.

22. S. Zinovieff, *Eurydice Street*, p. 19.

23. Interview with Tom Ellis, *Kathimerini*, 26 November 2013.

24. One is reminded of the old joke about how many people worked in the Irish civil service; answer: about half.

25. James Petras, "The Contradictions of Greek Socialism" in T.C. Kariotis (ed.), *The Greek Socialist Experiment: Papandreou's Greece 1981-1989*, p. 109.

26. The saga of the CDs appeared in *The Irish Times*, 8 April 2014.

27. Y. Palaiologos, *The 13ᵗʰ Labour of Hercules*, p. 35.

28. Theocharis was speaking to a member of the EU Task Force who relayed the conversation to the author.

29. Th. Cambanis, *Boston Globe*, 22 August 2014.

30. K. Vaxevanis, *New York Times*, 6 January 2013.

31. Quoted in *Daily Telegraph*, 31 January 2015 and *To Vima*, 2 February 2015.

32. Nikos Alivazatos, University of Athens, quoted in *International New York Times*, 16 October 2014.

33. *Kathimerini*, 23 April 2011.

34. *Kathimerini*, 21 January 2011.

35. Reported in *AthensPlus*, 5 June 2010.

36. Siemens have in fact been exposed as having a worldwide bribery budget for ploughing 10 per cent of its profits on such contracts back into the cycle of corruption. Countries in which this operated were Italy, Nigeria and Argentina. Until 1999, paying bribes abroad was legal in Germany, but Siemens continued a practice which was, of course, beneficial to its business. Since 2006, Siemens has paid €1.6bn. in fines in Germany and the USA and dismissed 80 per cent of its senior staff. As one investigator put it: "Bribery was Siemens' business model": Bruce Watson, "Siemens and the battle against bribery and corruption", *Guardian*, 18 September 2013.

37. This agreement was challenged in 2015 on the grounds that there was further evidence of bribery by Siemens for which the company was culpable.

38. The narrative of this long-running scandal is told in the biography of the "whistle-blower", developer Tom Gilmartin: Frank Connolly, *Tom Gilmartin* (2014).

39. Quoted in *Kathimerini*, 19 March 2012.

40. Other companies which have used the Luxembourg system include Pepsi, Ikea, Heinz and Amazon, while the EFG international banking group, with huge participation by companies controlled by the Latsis family, including Eurobank, was also implicated in the disclosures.

41. Quoted in the *New York Times*, 14 October 2010.

42. The legal profession in Greece numbers 70,000 members; doctors number 60,000, and engineers 81,000; there are approximately 600,000 civil servants.

43. Boots, a family-run traditional English chemists founded in 1849, with a presence in most British towns, was acquired by the global Walgreen company in 2014 and currently operates not only in an extensive chain in the UK and Ireland, but also in Canada and online in the USA, Norway, Romania, Russia, Taiwan, United Arab Emirates, Kuwait and Thailand.

44. *London Review of Books*, 1 January 2009.

45. Quoted by T. Cambanis, *Boston Globe*, 22 August 2014.

46. D. Tziovas, quoted in P. Mackridge, *Language and National Identity in Greece 1776-1976*, p. vi.

47. Mackridge's remarks are to be found in his lecture to the Society for Modern

Greek Studies (London), on 17 May 2014, published in part in the *Anglo-Hellenic Review* no. 50, Autumn 2014; the full text is at: http://www.moderngreek.org.uk/society/node/216.

48. See P. Mackridge, op. cit., p. 209.

49. Quoted in ibid., p. 282.

50. Quoted in ibid., p. 319.

51. 12 September 2006, accessed at http://www.in.gr/news/article.asp?ingEntityID=737870.

52. Information in this and the preceding paragraph is taken from E. Sjöberg, "The Past in Peril: Greek History Controversy and the Macedonian Crisis", *Education Inquiry* 2/1, March 2011.

53. This column appeared in the *Irish Times*, 11 December 2013.

54. C. Tsoucalas and R. Panagiotopoulou, "Education in Socialist Greece: Between Modernization and Democratization" in T.C. Kariotis (ed.), *The Greek Socialist Experiment*, p. 315.

55. N. Konstandaras, "Torpedoing the future", *Kathimerini*, 27 August 2010.

56. Anastassios Mantos, quoted in *AthensPlus*, 27 February 2009; he had called in the police to arrest a female student who was subsequently jailed for making petrol bombs.

57. EBU News Bulletin, 12 June 2013.

58. Stylianos Papathanassopoulos, "The Politics and the Effects of the Deregulation of Greek Television", *European Journal of Communications* 12/3 (1997).

59. Although I am bound in fairness to point out that whereas, in Ireland, the RTÉ NSO is the country's sole symphony orchestra, in Greece there still remained a national orchestra in Athens and another in Thessaloniki.

60. See Pavlos Eleftheriadis, *Foreign Affairs*, November/December 2014.

61. Rosemary Brady, "Erin go drill", *Forbes*, 132/6, 12 September 1983.

62. *Independent*, 4 January 2010.

63. K. Vaxevanis, "Greece gave birth to democracy. Now it has been cast out by a powerful elite", *Guardian*, 30 October 2012.

64. G. Durrell, "Impressions in the Sand: Corfu", *Sunday Times*, 24 January 1987.

65. H. Brody, *Inishkillane: Change and Decline in the West of Ireland*, pp. 32, 40, 41-42.

66. V. Calotychos, *Modern Greece: A Cultural Poetics*, p. 12.

67. Pavlos Zafiropoulos, www.thepressproject.net, 25 July 2014.

Chapter 7 – Literature

1. F.S.L. Lyons, *Culture and Anarchy in Ireland 1890-1939*, p. 4.

2. The expression was made by Anagnostakis to Yiorgos Chouliaras – email to the author from Chouliaras, 12 March 2015.

3. R. Beaton, *Introduction to Modern Greek Literature*, p. 288.

4. For an account of translation of Greek writers into English, see my column in

The Irish Times, 14 October 2014.

5. Koumandareas (b. 1931) was murdered in 2014.

6. W.B. Yeats, *The Celtic Twilight*, p. 131.

7. N. Gage, *Hellas*, p. 17.

8. P. Levi, *Hill of Kronos*, p. 27.

9. N. Kazantzakis, *Travels in Greece*, p. 171.

10. G. Seferis, "Mythistorema" in *Collected Poems 1924-1955*, p. 7.

11. A. Horton, *The Films of Theo Angelopoulos: A Cinema of Contemplation*, p. 35.

12. L. Politis, *History of Modern Greek Literature*, p. 83.

13. V. Hatziyannidis, *Four Walls*, p. 36.

14. Both quoted by Alexander Kazamias, in a review of Richard Clogg (ed.), *Minorities in Greece*, *Times Literary Supplement*, 11 July 2003.

15. See R. Deane, "The Honour of Non-Existence" in G. Gillen and H. White (eds.), *Music and Irish Cultural History*, pp. 199-211.

16. L. Durrell, "Landscape and Character" in *Spirit of Place*, p. 157.

17. See S. Constantinidis, *Modern Greek Theatre: A Quest for Hellenism*, p. 26.

18. The expression of the Mayor of the Aegean island of Lesvos, quoted in *Kathimerini*, 23 October 2014.

19. One negative side-effect of the war had been the evacuation of children (estimated at 28,000), chiefly by the communists, to eastern bloc countries, mainly Bulgaria, Romania, Hungary and Czechoslovakia, but in some cases as far away as northern Poland. The return to Greece of some of these would prove a traumatic experience. In addition, the Greek government took a further 14,700 "unclaimed" children into state care.

20. A. Horton, op. cit., p. 51.

21. L. Durrell, *Prospero's Cell*, pp. 47, 56.

22. See K. Myrsiades and L. Myrsiades, *The Karagiózis Heroic Performance in Greek Shadow Theater*, p. 1.

23. See Myrsiades and Myrsiades, ibid., p. 41.

24. Quoted in Myrsiades and Myrsiades, ibid., p. 34.

25. L. Durrell, *Prospero's Cell*, p. 53.

26. Tony Klein, *Mortika*, p. 7; *mórtis* refers to "persons who are both tough and elegant [...] a counterpart to the 'apache' of Paris" (p. 4).

27. G. Holst, *Road to Rembetika: Music of a Greek Sub-culture, Songs of Love, Sorrow and Hashish*, p. 45.

28. Elias Petropoulos in K. Butterworth and Sara Schneider, *Rebetika: Songs from the Old Greek Underworld*, p. 13.

29. Micheál Ó Suilleabháin, *Irish Times*, 10 January 2015.

30. Stathis Damianakis and Yorgos Rovertakis, quoted in N. Papandreou, *Mikis and Manos*, p.105.

31. N. Papandreou, *Mikis and Manos*, pp. 103, 107.

Endnotes

32. See R. Pine, *The Disappointed Bridge*, chapter 4, "A Guest of Cultural Politics".

33. T. Klein, *Mortika*, p. 11.

34. Y. Stamatis, "Rebetiko Nation: Hearing Pavlos Vassiliou's Alternative Greekness Through Rebetiko Song", PhD diss., University of Michigan, 2011, p. 1.

35. N. Papandreou, op. cit., p. 103.

36. G. Holst, op. cit., p. 56.

37. Yona Stamatis, op. cit., p. 4.

38. Ibid., p. 4.

39. Ibid., p. 7.

40. *Times Literary Supplement*, 9 June 2006.

41. N. Theodorakis, *Symposium* [1918-20; trans. 1974], p. 45.

42. See my discussion of *testimonio* in *The Disappointed Bridge, passim*; the most explicit statement of the need to bear witness is a Chilean woman quoted by André Brink: "I can't keep silent because I have lived it".

43. R. Beaton, "The Greek novel and the rise of the European genre" in J. Mander (ed.), *Remapping the Rise of the European Novel*, p. 226.

44. R. Pine, *The Disappointed Bridge*, p. x.

45. D.Kiberd, "Inventing Irelands", *Crane Bag* 8/1, 1984

46. See R. Pine, *The Disappointed Bridge*, chapter 8.

47. P. Levi, *Hill of Kronos*, p. 31. To this we should add the words of Sofka Zinovieff's Greek husband: "You can't even start to understand anything about Greece if you don't realize that everything is expressed through poetry and song. It's not chance that almost every other person in Greece is a poet": *Eurydice Street*, p. 30.

48. Ersi Sotiropoulos writes in the conventional style as "Ersi Sotiropoulou", which diminishes her as a female (and therefore subordinate) member of the Sotiropoulos family, despite her personal wish to assume her full patronymic. The same may be observed of the Corfiot singer known in the west as Vicky Leandros, whose recordings in Greece are sung by "Vicky Leandrou" (her original name was Vassiliki Papathanasiou, and "Leandros" was in fact her father's first name, thus adding to the irony of the genitive possessiveness.) (In 2000 she scored a hit with her album *Now* which included a duet with Chris de Burgh.) Sotiropoulos' titles (in translation) include the novel *Zigzag Through the Bitter-Orange Trees*.

49. Mavili Collective was formed during 2010, in its self-description, "as an autonomous collective structure for emergent practitioners and came together in order to re-think and re-imagine the current Greek cultural landscape and propose structures, platforms collaborations, projects that produce new alternatives. Mavili Collective is committed to produce nomadic, autonomous collective cultural zones that appear and disappear beyond the logics of the market."

50. Quoted on Enet.gr, 21 February 2014.

51. Seferis was Greek Ambassador to the Court of St James's, 1957-61.

52. The paraphrase of Elytis is quoted in V. Calotychos, *Modern Greece: A Cultural Poetics*, p. 173.

53. Quoted in Philip Sherrard, "Odysseas Elytis and the Discovery of Greece", *Journal of Modern Greek Studies* 1/2 (1983), pp. 274-5.

54. P. Sherrard, Ibid., pp. 274-5.

55. P. Sherrard, Ibid.

56. G. Seferis, *On the Greek Style*, p. 96.

57. N. Kazantzakis, *Symposium*, pp. 39-40.

58. V. Calotychos, *Modern Greece: A Cultural Poetics*, p. 221.

59. Z. Lorenzatos, *Aegean Notebooks*, p. 37; the following quotations from *Aegean Notebooks* can be found on pp. 65, 36 and 88 respectively.

60. N. Kazantzakis, Symposium, p. 61.

61. Ibid., p. 14

62. One of my sons-in-law suggested "Zeus on the Loose" as a possible title for this book; he is still in detention.

63. Quoted in E. Kazantzakis, *Nikos Kazantzakis: A Biography Based on His Letters*, p. 566.

64. Quoted in E. Kazantzakis, op. cit., p. 445.

65. *Freedom or Death* (its Greek title is Ελευθερία ί Θάνατος) was published under its original title in 1956 in the UK and USA but subsequently as *Freedom and Death.*

66. G. Theotokas, *Free Spirit*, p. 6.

67. Y. Chouliaras, "Greek Culture in the New Europe", in H. Psomiades and S. Thomadakis (eds.), *Greece, the New Europe and the Changing International Order*, p. 89. The following quotations from Chouliaras are taken from this source.

68. J. du Boulay, "Cosmos and Gender in Village Greece" in *Contested Identities: Gender and Kinship in Modern Greece*, edited by Peter Loizos and Evthymios Papataxiarchis, p. 77 n. 16.

69. See R. Pine, *The Disappointed Bridge*, chapter 7.

70. O. Elytis, *Carte Blanche: Selected Writings* (trans. D. Connolly), p. 5.

71. R. Beaton, *Introduction to Modern Greek Literature*, p. 77.

72. D. Weinberg, "The Literary Art of Alxandros Papadiamantis", L. Coustelle et al. (eds.), *A Greek Triptych: Dionysios Solomos and Alexandros Papadiamantis*, p. 101

73. D. Tziovas, *The Other Self: Selfhood and Society in Modern Greek Fiction*, p. 84.

74. R. Beaton, *Introduction to Modern Greek Literature*, p. 99.

75. D. Ricks, "Papadiamandis, Paganism and the Sanctity of Place", *Journal of Mediterranean Studies* 2/2 (1992), p. 176.

76. A. Papadiamandis, "The Fey Folk", *The Boundless Garden*, p. 241.

77. Z. Lorenzatos, *The Drama of Quality: Selected Essays* (trans. L Sherrard), p. 25.

78. D. Weinberg, op. cit., pp. 104-5.

79. A. Papadiamandis, "Black Scarf Rock", *The Boundless Garden*, p. 36 n.1.

80. A. Keselopoulos, in conversation with Andrew Herman Middleton, "Greece's Dostoevsky", *Road to Emmaus* IX/3.

81. Z. Lorenzatos, *Aegean Notebooks*, pp. 73-75.

82. J. Evans, review of *The Boundless Garden*, *Times Literary Supplement*, 25 July 2008.

83. A. Papadiamandis, "At St. Anastasia's", *The Boundless Garden*, p. 190.

84. Z. Lorenzatos, *The Drama of Quality*, p. 9.

85. Th. Stavrou, "Preface" in L. Coutelle et al. (eds.), *A Greek Diptych*, p. x.

86. A version of this section appeared in R. Pine and E. Patten (eds.), *The Literatures of War*.

87. Stratis Haviaras, *The Heroic Age*, pp. 229-30.

88. A. Stevens, *Roots of War and Terror*, pp. 9-10.

89. R. Beaton, op. cit., p. 289.

90. G. Theotokas, *Argo* (trans. E. Margaret Brooke and Ares Tsatsopoulos), p. vi.

91. In her notes for *Mrs Dalloway*, quoted in Helen Wussow, *Virginia Woolf, The Hours, the British Museum Manuscript of Mrs. Dalloway*.

92. C. Taktsis, *The Third Wedding*, trans. Leslie Finer, pp. 1, 2, 12.

93. Originally published in *Tachydromos*, reproduced as blurb for the dustjacket of the English translation of *The Third Wedding*.

94. I. Venezis, *Aeolia*, p. 244.

95. Ibid., pp. 247-8.

96. M. Douka, *Fool's Gold* (trans. Roderick Beaton), pp. 29-30.

97. Ibid., p. 9.

98. Ibid., p. 10.

99. Ibid., p. 312.

Chapter 8 – Drama, Film and Music

1. *Athens News*, 27 May 2011.

2. Quoted in Aliki Bacopoulou-Halls, *Modern Greek Theater: Roots and Blossoms*, p. 114.

3. Quoted in ibid., p. 137.

4. Quoted in ibid., p. 111.

5. Ibid., p. 10.

6. S. Constantinidis, *Modern Greek Theatre: a quest for Hellenism*, p. 25.

7. Reported in *AthensPlus*, 30 July 2010.

8. Quoted in R.Rehm, *Radical Theatre: Greek Tragedy and the Modern World*, p. 60.

9. See R. Pine, *The Disappointed Bridge*, pp. 115-19.

10. B. Kennelly, *When Then is Now*, pp. 7-8.

11. C. Nixey, "It's tragic to pretend we all like classical drama", *Times*, 28 February 2015.

12. R. Rehm, op. cit., p. 86.

13. Ibid., p. 51.

14. Ibid., p. 108.

15. See S. Constantinidis, op. cit., pp. 148-9.

16. S. Constantinidis, op. cit., p. 150.

17. Although in *Zorba* Cacoyannis created a stereotypical image of Greece, he also pursued more compelling and less superficial images and issues in *The Girl in Black* (1956). Despite the acclaim for *Zorba*, he found it necessary to sidestep censorship by adapting the classics: *Electra* (1962) which allegorised the civil war, *The Trojan Women* (1971) which suggested the junta, and *Iphigenia* (1977) the Turkish invasion of Cyprus. The fact that Theodorakis composed the score for all three films was a sign to the public that these were statements of resistance not only to the military junta but to earlier autocratic and anti-popular regimes. This strategy helps us to see *Zorba* in a less popular light, as a celebration of Greek abandon to the pursuit of freedom.

18. Katerina Zacharia, "'Reel' Hellenisms: perceptions of Greece in Greek cinema" in K. Zacharia (ed.), *Hellenisms: Culture, Identity and Ethnicity from Antiquity to Modernism*, p. 327.

19. "Guests" in Amorgos included George Mylonas, Minister of Education, whose escape is recorded in Elias Kulukundis' *The Amorgos Conspiracy* (2013).

20. To call Costas-Gavras diasporic would be inaccurate. He is an outsider, in an industry of outsiders. If all serious modern Greek cinema is unconventional and tending towards the subversive, Costas-Gavras is far to the left of the others, not merely in political terms but in aesthetic and moral terms.

21. Another (short) film was made on the assassination of Lambrakis: *Hundred Hours in May*, directed 1968 by Dimosthenis Theos.

22. We should not overlook *Power* (1977) directed by Manoussos Manoussakis, which portrays universal corruption among government, church, army and business.

23. See R. Pine, *The Disappointed Bridge*, chapter 6, "Migrations".

24. Th. Angelopoulos, "Interview", *Cinephile* 16 December 2011.

25. Th. Angelopoulos, transcript of an interview with Geoff Andrew at the National Film Theatre, London, n.d. [2011].

26. Th. Angelopoulos, "Interview", *Cinephile*.

27. A. Horton, op. cit., p. 57.

28. Th. Angelopoulos, transcript of an interview with Geoff Andrew.

29. Th. Angelopoulos, "Interview", *Cinephile*.

30. British Film Institute, 2003.

31. http://www.imdb.com/title/tt0114863/plotsummary?ref_=tt_ov_pl.

32. Th. Angelopoulos, transcript of an interview with Geoff Andrew.

33. Th. Angelopoulos, "Interview", *Cinephile*.

34. Th. Angelopoulos, transcript of an interview with Geoff Andrew.

35. Estimates of casualties vary in every case. Voulgaris' figures may err on the conservative side, and his figure for the second world war is limited to the fighting in 1940-41, without taking into account the subsequent guerrilla war. Figures from both sides in the civil war in fact estimate government losses at 70,000 and the resistance at 38,000, with as many as 80-100,000 refugees leaving Greece.

36. The "world premiere" is not strictly accurate: napalm was first used by the US Air Force over Berlin and the Pacific in 1944-45; the bombers loaned to Greece were the Cubiss SB2C Helldiver.

37. On *Dogtooth*, see Stamos Metzidakis, "No Bones to Pick with Lanthimos' Film *Dogtooth*", *Journal of Modern Greek Studies* 32/2.

38. Damian Mac Con Uladh blog, 15 October 2014.

39. Karatzaféres has always been a thorn in the establishment: in October 2012 he was arrested after he appeared on television stating that he held documents obtained from the finance ministry, which he was about to make public. His arrest coincided with that of journalist Kostas Vaxevanis who leaked the names on the "Lagarde list".

40. In old age, Metallinos produced many sexually explicit sculptures, including women exposing their genitalia very similar to the Sile-ni-gig sculptures to be found in Irish churchyards, although it is unlikely that Metallinos intended the same precautionary warning of the sins of the flesh.

41. Foreword by Paul Dujardin et al. to the exhibition catalogue.

42. K. Gregos, "When the Music Stopped", exhibition catalogue pp. 11-12.

43. B. Friel, *Essays, Diaries, Interviews 1964-1999* (ed. Christopher Murray), p. 50.

44. Exhibition catalogue, p. 41.

45. Ibid., p. 29.

46. Ibid., p. 57. "I feel I owe my moments of pleasure to the great texts of your S. Beckett which are very often my only inspiration" (email to the author, 3 April 2015).

47. The work is akin to Angelopoulos' film *Days of '36*, in that it relates an incident in a strike in Thessaloniki in 1936; in the case of Ritsos' poem, it depicts a woman mourning her son, killed during a demonstration in the strike.

48. Quotations from Theodorakis are taken from N. Papandreou's *Mikis and Manos*.

49. Among twentieth-century composers we must also take note, among symphonists particularly, of Yannis Papaioannou (1910-1989) and Yanni Christou (1926-1970), Dimitris Dragatakis (1916-2001), Antiochos Evangelatos (1904-1981), A. Kudorov (1897-1969), Petros Petridis (1892-1977) and Leonidas Zervos (1905-1987), if only because they are "unknown" outside Greece except to musicologists. The opera composer Manolis Kalomiris (1883-1962) should also be mentioned if only because he wrote the opera *Constantine Palaeologos* (*The City is Taken*) referring to that great event of Greek history, the Ottoman defeat of Constantinople in 1453. Kostas Kardamis notes that the works of symphonists in the early twentieth century within a "National School" focussed mainly on tradition, "which gave them aesthetic homogeneity" ("Symphonic Music in Greece during 19th and 20th Century", *Works by Greek Composers*, p. 48). The

advent of modernism, serialism and atonalism created problems for composers working within traditional modes.

50. Quoted in Giorgos Sakallianos, "The Greek Symphony (1900-1950): oscillating between Greek nationalism and Western art-music tradition", in Nika-Sampson et al. (eds.), *Crossroads: Greece as an Intercultural Pole of Musical Thought and Creativity*, p. 36.

51. Ibid., p. 37.

52. K. Levidou, "A Dubious Mission: Skalkottas's Vision of Truly Greek Music and his *36 Greek Dances*", in Nika-Sampson et al., op. cit., p. 256.

53. Quoted in Katarina Levidou, op. cit., p. 255.

54. I am indebted to Katerina Levidou for clarification on this issue: email to the author, 21 April 2015.

55. Quoted by George Zervos, "Aspects of Hellenicity in Nikos Skalkottas' Music", in N. Maliaras (ed.), *The National Element in Music*, p. 288.

56. Quoted by G. Zervos, op. cit., p. 293.

57. N. Papandreou, *Mikis and Manos*, p. 86.

58. Ibid., p. 94.

59. Quoted in Papandreou, op. cit., p. 85.

60. R. Beaton, *Introduction to Modern Greek Literature*, p. 226.

61. Notes to Symphony No.4, recording by Athens Symphony Orchestra and Chorus cond. Loukas Karytinos, Intuition Classics label no. INT 3136.2.

62. Actually numbered 1, 2, 3, 4, 7: numbers 5 and 6 do not exist.

63. In later years he wrote four operas based on classical themes: *Medea* (1988–90), *Elektra* (1992–93) *Antigone* (1995–96) and *Lysistrata* (1999–2001).

64. Theodorakis has also composed for stage productions of most of the classics over a forty-year period, and – one link with Ireland – Brendan Behan's *The Hostage* in 1961. There have also been scores for films of the classics, including *Phaedra* (1961), *Elektra* (1961-62), *Trojan Women* (1971) and *Iphigenia* (1977-78), in addition to *Zorba the Greek* (1964), *Z* (1969) and *Ill Met By Moonlight* (the 1956 film of the capture in Crete of a German general by Patrick Leigh Fermor and Stanley Moss).

65. Sleeve note for *State of Siege*, on Intuition Classics label no.INT 3299.2.

66. Theodorakis Home Page, "On Axion Esti", 3 August 2004.

67. Quoted in Papandreou, op. cit., pp. 92-93.

68. N. Papandreou, op. cit., p. 82.

69. Ibid., p. 91.

70. Ibid., pp. 93-94.

71. Ibid., pp. 81-82.

72. S. Zinovieff, *Eurydice Street*, p. 111.

73. N. Papandreou, op. cit., p. 119.

74. Sleeve note for *Sinfonietta/State of Siege* on Intuition Classics label INT 3299.2

Endnotes

Chapter 9 – Crisis

1. Sophocles, *Ajax*, ll. 485-6.

2. *Kathimerini*, 29 October 2011.

3. M. Mitsopoulos and Th. Pelagidis, *Understanding the Greek Crisis*, p. 3.

4. Yeats was referring to James Joyce, and spoke of "the new naturalism that leaves man helpless before the contents of his own mind": "Ideas of Good and Evil", *Essays and Introductions*, p. 405.

5. S. Heaney, *The Cure at Troy*, p. 77.

6. *International Herald Tribune*, 24 February 2012.

7. Ray Kinsella, "Greece and the European Union", *Irish Times*, 23 March 2015; he was referring to the Nobel economics laureate, who has written extensively on the issue of the markets and national debt, such as "We need a fair system for restructuring sovereign debt", *Guardian*, 4 September 2013.

8. N. Malkoutzis, "Greece, land of pain and joy", *Kathimerini*, 23 April 2011.

9. *Kathimerini*, 10 November 2014.

10. *Irish Times*, 6 January 2015.

11. *Irish Times*, 23 June 2011.

12. V. Vassilikos, *International Herald Tribune*, 13 February 2010.

13. *Guardian Weekly*, 12 February 2010.

14. Reported in *Wall Street Journal*, 27 January 2011.

15. *Irish Times*, 23 June 2011.

16. Christos Douzinas, *Guardian*, 4 February 2010.

17. Official website of the Prime Minister, primeminister.gov.gr, 11 July 2011.

18. *International Herald Tribune*, 13-14 February 2010.

19. *International Herald Tribune*, 13-14 February 2010.

20. The IFRS (International Finance Reporting Standards watchdog) notes that in 2013 Greece stated that it was moving towards a "single set of high quality global accounting standards" and had made a public commitment to doing so: "IFRS Application Around the World: Jurisdictional Profile: Greece", 2 September 2013.

21. Interview with Nikos Chrysoloras, *Kathimerini*, 29 July 2013.

22. Gikas Hardouvelis, minister of finance in 2014, reported in *To Vima*, 28 November 2014.

23. Interview with Tom Ellis, *Kathimerini*, 26 November 2013.

24. Quoted in *Irish Times*, 8 February 2015.

25. Larry Elliott, *Guardian Weekly*, 12 February 2010.

26. O. Elytis, "Introduction" to *The Greeks* by John Veltri et al., p. 10.

27. Kimon Friar in *The Greeks*, p. 141.

28. K. Tsapogas, *International Herald Tribune*, 14 February 2013.

29. Quoted in *Irish Times*, 28 June 2011.

30. *New York Times*, 20 October 2012.

31. *Kathimerini*, 31 October 2011.

32. *Irish Times*, 28 April 2012.

33. W.B. Yeats, *The Poems*, pp. 346-8.

34. G. Soros, "Does the Euro Have a Future?", *New York Review of Books*, 13 October 2011.

35. Letter to *Irish Times*, 11 February 2015.

36. greekindependentnews.net, 15 September 2014.

37. Quoted in *Kathimerini*, 23 December 2014.

38. Quoted in *International Herald Tribune*, 24 July 2013.

39. V. Vassilikos, *International Herald Tribune*, 13 February 2010.

40. A. Karakousis, "The International Monetary Fund's Great Shame", *To Vima*, 21 November 2014.

41. Quoted in *Kathimerini*, 22 August 2012.

42. Interview with Simon Carswell, *Irish Times*, 19 January 2015.

43. Derek Scally and Damian Mac Con Uladh, *Irish Times*, 23 March 2015.

44. Desmond FitzGerald, "Debt relief and Greece", *Irish Times*, 3 February 2015.

45. Quoted in *Kathimerini*, 10 March 2015.

46. The ten specific cadres of the EU Task Force and their remits are: acceleration of EU-funded projects; access to finance; public administration reform; budget and taxation; anti-corruption; business environment; public health; reform of the judiciary; migration, asylum and borders; labour market and social security.

47. *New York Times*, 20 October 2012.

48. Quoted in *Kathimerini*, 16 May 2014.

49. Efthimios Tsiliopoulos, *Athens News*, 23 August 2013.

50. Interview in *Bloomberg*, quoted in *To Vima*, 21 November 2014.

51. J.M. Keynes, "Notes on an Indemnity", 21 October 1918.

52. *Irish Times* editorial, 20 June 2011.

53. *Kathimerini*, 15 September 2012.

54. *Irish Times*, 15 December 2010.

55. The Greek-born philosopher Panagiotis Kondylis (1943-1998) quoted in *Kathimerini*, 6 December 2014.

56. N. Konstandaras, *Kathimerini*, 20 October 2010.

57. C. Simitis, *The European Debt Crisis*, p. 97.

58. Ibid., p. 150.

59. *Kathimerini*, 8 August 2012.

60. *Financial Times*, 27 January 2015.

61. We should recall Ivan Kastev's observation, "in a democracy without choices… governments get elected by making love to the electorate, but are married to the international donors": I. Kristev, "The Balkans: Democracy without Choices", Journal of Democracy 13/3, 2002.

62. N. Malkoutzis, *Kathimerini*, 9 May 2012.

Chapter 10 – Greece, Ireland and the European Union

1. The eradication of the "bendy cucumber" and the "knobbly carrot" was the subject of Commission Regulation (EEC) no.1677/88; the other offending deviant fruits and vegetables were: apples, apricots, artichokes, asparagus, aubergines, avocadoes, beans, Brussel [*sic*] Sprouts, cabbage, cauliflowers, celery, cherries, chicory, courgettes, garlic, hazelnuts, leeks, melons, mushrooms, onions, peas, plums, spinach, strawberries, tmatoes, walnuts and water melons. The prohibited sale of unwarranted examples of these items was rescinded in 2009, although varieties that did not conform to the desired shape or size were still to be labelled as inferior. The relevant EU Commissioner stated that "this is a concrete example of our drive to cut unnecessary red tape. We don't need to regulate this sort of thing at EU level. It makes no sense to throw perfectly good products away, just because they are the wrong size and shape": European Parliament press release, 30 June 2009.

2. Quoted by Hermann von Rompuy, President of the European Council, 7 May 2013.

3. S. Constantinidis, *Modern Greek Theatre*, pp. 24, 27.

4. This is not a joke: Peter Murtagh saw such a man in a queue at a soup-kitchen: *Irish Times*, 28 April 2012.

5. Quoted in *To Vima*, 12 December 2014.

6. Quoted in *Kathimerini*, 17 December 2014.

7. Quoted in *Kathimerini*, 17 December 2014.

8. Quoted in the *Irish Times*, 12 January 2015.

9. Interview with Simon Carswell, *Irish Times*, 19 January 2015.

10. Quoted in *To Vima*, 28 January 2015.

11. *New York Times*, 9 January 2015.

12. *Irish Times*, 12 February 2015.

13. Quoted in *Irish Times*, 12 February 2015.

14. *Irish Times*, 14 February 2015.

15. *Financial Times*, 19 February 2015.

16. Quoted in *Irish Times*, 20 February 2015.

17. Quoted in *Kathimerini*, 29 December 2014.

18. Quoted in *Irish Times*, 31 January 2015.

19. Before his entry into government, Varoufakis had taught game theory as one of his courses as professor at Athens University.

20. Quoted in *Kathimerini*, 24 April 2015.

21. Quoted in *To Vima*, 4 February 2015.

22. Daniel Hannan, "A lesson in Newspeak", *New Criterion*, January 2015.

23. J. Rifkin, *The European Dream: How Europe's Vision of the Future is Quickly Eclipsing the American Dream*, p. 268.

24. Y. Chouliaras, "Greek Culture in the New Europe" in Psomiades and Thomadakis (eds.), *Greece, the New Europe, and the Changing International Order*, pp. 101, 120.

25. *Irish Times*, 1 June 2013.

26. Iain Banks' *The Business* describes a global corporation which controls almost everything, its one remaining goal being a seat at the United Nations: to which end it sets about "buying" an independent Himalayan kingdom which can deliver its ultimate goal.

27. *Irish Times*, 6 November 2014.

28. C. Tsatsos, *Greece and Europe, passim.*

29. *Irish Times*, 16 September 2014.

30. C. Douzinas, *Guardian*, 4 February 2010.

31. *Financial Times*, 15 March 2013.

32. *Boston Globe*, 18 March 2013.

33. *Irish Times*, 12 August 2013.

34. Quoted in *Irish Times*, 7 July 2013.

35. N. Malkoutzis *Athens Plus*, 18 December 2009.

36. S. Rushdie, *Midnight's Children*, p. 119.

37. C. Achebe, *The Trouble with Nigeria* p. 1.

38. Speaking at the European Parliament, 23 October 1999: http.//www.global-vision.net/facts/fact5.2.asp.

39. Quoted in "Introduction" to Deniz Göktörk et al., *Orienting Istanbul: Cultural Capital of Europe?*

40. See M. Dragoumis, *Greece on the Couch: I*, p.34.

41. Hellen Wallace and William Wallace, *Flying Together in a Larger and More Diverse European Union*, p.12.

42. J. Rifkin, op. cit., p. 247.

43. S. Heaney, "The Tollund Man", *Opened Ground*, pp. 63-64.

44. J. Zielanka, *Europe as Empire: The Nature of the Enlarged European Union*, pp. 1, 2.

45. Ibid., p. 171.

46. D. Hannan, "The Objective Correlative of the EU", *New Criterion*, February 2015.

47. The texts of these lectures can be accessed at: www.SilentMajority.co.UK/EUroRealist/Germany1942.

48. Alison Smale, *International Herald Tribune*, 29 October 2012.

49. Jean Asselborn, quoted in *Reuters Business*, 26 March 2013.

50. Quoted in M. Dragoumis, *Greece on the Couch: 1*, p. 51.

51. S. Verney, "Waking the 'sleeping giant' or expressing somestic dissent? Mainstreaming Euroscepticism in crisis-stricken Greece": *International Political Science Review* 36/3, 2015

52. Padraic Halpin and Harry Papachristou, "Greece too far behind to copy Irish bailout model", *Reuters Economy*, 11 July 2012.

53. *Irish Times*, 3 November 2014.

54. The title of the project was my suggestion.

55. The towns were varied and included: Palaio Faliro (a waterfront suburb of Athens), Castlebar (a small regional centre in the west of Ireland), Eindhoven (a major industrial city in Holland), and Koivukylä, a new urban development to the north of Helsinki).

56. Quoted by Enda O'Doherty, *Irish Times*, 26 June 2013.

57. Quoted by Elaine Sciolino, "Visions of a Union", *New York Times*, 15 December 2002.

58. W. Kok, *Enlarging the European Union: Achievements and Challenges*, p. 2.

59. D. Hannan, "Objective Correlative".

60. Desmond Fisher, email to the author, 30 April 2011.

Afterword

1. O. Elytis, *Hartia*, quoted in P. Sherrard, "Odysseas Elytis and the Discovery of Greece", *Journal of Modern Greek Studies* 1/2 (1983), p. 286.

2. Artemis Leontis: *Typographies of Hellenism: Mapping the Homeland*.

3. Y. Varoufakis, "No Time for Games in Europe", *International New York Times*, 17 February 2015.

4. N. Kazantzakis, *Travels in Greece*, p. 165.

5. C.M. Woodhouse, *The Struggle for Greece*, p. 4.

6. J. Fowles, *The Magus*, p. 112.

7. G. Seferis, *Collected Poems*, p. 107.

8. *Kathimerini*, 25 April 2011.

9. W.B. Yeats, *Essays and Introductions*, p. 204.

10. P. Sherrard, "The Other Mind of Europe", pp. 37, 40.

Appendix

1. J.P. Mahaffy, *What Have the Greeks Done for Modern Civilization*, pp. 14-15.

2. L. Durrell, *From the Elephant's Back*, p. 32.

3. Quoted in R. Clogg, "The Ideology of the 'Revolutionof 21ˢᵗ April 1967'", in Clogg and Yannopoulos (eds.), *Greece Under Military Rule*, p. 41.

4. I am grateful to William and Kalypso Mallinson for drawing these speeches to my attention.

5. L. Durrell, *Bitter Lemons*, p. 131.

FURTHER READING

This reading list is not an exhaustive bibliography: it aims to give the reader an indication of what is available in English. Wherever possible I have included works still in print, marked "*", which can be obtained from good bookshops and, of course, increasingly through the internet. Regrettably, many academic studies are prohibitively expensive. Out-of-print books can sometimes be found at surprisingly low prices on the internet.

Specialist bookshops which may be in reach of English speakers (unfortunately none in Ireland) and highly recommended are Zeno Booksellers and Hellenic Book Service (both based in London), and June Samaras' Kalamos Books (in Toronto).

General Introductions

Of the many titles one could list, the two from which I have quoted extensively are Peter Levi, **The Hill of Kronos* (London: Zenith Books, 1980, frequently reprinted), and Nicholas Gage, **Hellas: A Portrait of Greece* (Athens: Efstathiadis, 1987, repr. 2002). A volume which resembles a coffee-table book but shouldn't be mistaken for one is *The Greeks* (New York: Doubleday, 1984), which contains artistic photography by John Veltri and a text by Odysseas Elytis (foreword by Lawrence Durrell). Lawrence Durrell's **The Greek Islands*, was originally published with copious photography by Faber and Faber, 1978, and reprinted as a paperback 2002, minus the photographs, which greatly diminishes the text. Durrell's **Spirit of Place* (originally 1968; repr. Axios Press, 2011) contains valuable essays on the Greek character and spirit.

General Histories

There are many histories of Greece; the following are a few, which I have found very useful:

John Campbell and Philip Sherrard's *Modern Greece* (London: Ernest Benn, 1968) is probably the most sympathetic and well-considered study, but has been superseded by more recent works. *Modern Greece: A Short History* by C.M. Woodhouse (London: Faber and Faber, 1999), an informative and comprehensive guide from the Foundation of Constantine (324 AD) to the 1980s. So too is *A Concise History of Greece* by Richard Clogg (Cambridge: Cambridge University Press, second edition, 2002). A very valuable study by two Greeks, J.S. Koliopoulos and Thanos Veremis, *Greece: The Modern Sequel, from 1821 to the Present* (London: Hurst, 2004) is thematic rather than chronological in its approach, so it's best to know the basic history first. Other concise histories are: Nicholas Doumanis, *A History of Greece* (Houndmills: Palgrave Macmillan, 2010), one of a multi-volume series and therefore suffering from a formulaic treatment, and Thomas Gallant's *Modern Greece* (London: Hodder, 2001), in a "Brief Histories" series, which is also structured to fit the publishers' pattern; Gallant, however, is not to be dismissed as a serious historian of modern Greece.

A more politically-oriented study is Constantine Tsoucalas, *The Greek Tragedy* (London: Penguin, 1969) which is well worth reading for its insights by an expatriate Greek. *The Making of Modern Greece: Nationalism, Romanticism and the Uses of the Past (1797-1896)* (Farnham: Ashgate, for King's College London: Centre for Hellenic Studies, 2009), edited by Roderick Beaton and David Ricks, is, as its title suggests, a survey of the role of nationalism, religion, language and literature in the evolution of Greece as nation-state. *Greece in Transition: Essays in the History of Modern Greece 1821-1974* (London: Zeno, 1977), edited by John Koumoulides, attempts a panoramic survey of the period; it can be read as a companion volume to Koumoulides' edited *Hellenic Perspectives: Essays in the History of Greece* (Lanham, Md.: University of America Press, 1980).

In 2008, Mark Mazower published an edited volume in honour of the late John Campbell, *Networks of Power in Modern Greece* (New York: Columbia University Press, 2008) which surveys this subject from pre-independence through to the PASOK of Andreas Papandreou.

A vital element in the evolution of modern Greece has been the divisive issue of an "official" Greek language. Peter Mackridge's *Language and National Identity in Greece, 1766-1976* (Oxford: Oxford University Press, 2009) is the most comprehensive, erudite and politically sensitive study of the subject.

Ours Once More: Folklore, Ideology and the Making of Modern Greece by Michael Herzfeld (New York: Pella, 1986) is an account of how the nineteenth-century study of folklore provided the idea of continuity between ancient and modern Greeks.

The Ionian Islands

Of the, literally, hundreds of books about these islands, the following concentrate on the period of the British protectorate (1815-64): Robert Holland, *Blue-Water Empire: The British in the Mediterranean since 1800* (London: Allen Lane, 2012), Robert Holland and Diana Markides, *The British and the Hellenes: Struggles for Mastery in the Eastern Mediterranean 1850-1960* (Oxford: Oxford University Press, 2006), and Thomas Gallant, *Experiencing Dominion: Culture, Identity and Power in the British Mediterranean* (Notre Dame, Indiana: Notre Dame University Press, 2002). The period immediately before British withdrawal is well documented by eye-witness David Thomas Ansted, whose *The Ionian Islands in the Year 1863* (London: W.H. Allen, 1863) is available in a facsimile edition. Henry Jervis-White-Jervis's *History of the Island of Corfu and of the Republic of the Ionian Islands* (London: Colburn, 1852; repr. Elibron Classics, 2005) is also valuable, as is Viscount Kirkwall's eye-witness account of British withdrawal *Four Years in the Ionian Islands: Their Political and Social Conditions with a History of the British Protectorate* (London: Chapman and Hall, 1864; repr. Kessinger n.d.).

The most comprehensive general survey of the Ionian islands is Jim Potts, *The Ionian Islands and Epirus: A Cultural History* (Oxford: Signal Books, 2010). A valuable collection of essays (proceedings of a Durrell School of Corfu seminar) is *The Ionian Islands: Aspects of Their History and Culture* (Newcastle: Cambridge Scholars Publishing, 2014), edited by Anthony Hirst and Patrick Sammon.

For sympathetic accounts of Corfu in the 1930s, see the charming memoir by Gerald Durrell, in *The Corfu Trilogy* (London: Penguin, 2006) which contains *My Family and Other Animals* (1956), *Birds,*

Beasts and Relatives (1969) and *The Garden of the Gods* (1978). The memoir by his brother, Lawrence Durrell, *Prospero's Cell: A Guide to the Landscape and Manners of the Island of Corcyra* (London: Faber and Faber, 1945) has been reprinted many times.

The novel *Slaves in Their Chains*, by Konstantine Theotoki, published in 1922, was translated (for the first time) into English by Mark Davies in 2014 (London: Angel Classics); it's a view, by one of the Corfiot aristocracy, of the decline of his class, in the light of the *enosis* of the islands with Greece in 1864.

A contemporary volume of stories of Corfu is Maria Strani-Potts' *The Cat of Portovecchio* (Blackheath NSW: Brandl and Schlesinger, 2007).

War of Independence

The Struggle for Greek Independence, edited by Richard Clogg (London: Macmillan, 1973) is valuable for its collection of essays on almost every aspect of the war of independence. The many studies of this crucial period of history include David Brewer's *The Greek War of Independence* (Woodstock and NY: Overlook Press, 2001), C.M. Woodhouse, *The Philhellenes* (London: Hodder and Stoughton, 1969), and Roderick Beaton's prize-winning *Byron's War* (Cambridge: Cambridge University Press, 2013). Woodhouse's biography *Capodistria* (Oxford: Oxford University Press, 1963) is probably his masterpiece.

A valuable collection of images from the war of independence was published by the National Gallery of Greece to accompany its permanent exhibition in its annexe in Nauplion (one of the major centres of the war): *1821: Figures & Themes from the Greek War of Independence.*

Two novels of the nineteenth century offer insights into social conditions in the light of political change: Pavlos Kalligas *Thanos Vlekas* (published 1855; trans. Thomas Doulis, Evanston, Ill.: Northwestern University Press, 2001) and Andreas Karkavitsas' *The Beggar* (published 1891; trans. William Wyatt, New York: Caratzas, 1982).

Twentieth Century

i) The Anatolian Catastrophe of 1920-22

The Blight of Asia (Reading: Sterndale, 2003) by George Horton, the American Consul in Smyrna at the time of the catastrophe, is highly prejudiced, but valuable for its eye-witness account. Giles Milton's *Paradise Lost: Smyrna 1922* (London: Sceptre, 2000) is one of a number of studies describing (rather more objectively) the destruction of the city and its Greek culture. Bruce Clark's *Twice a Stranger: How Mass Expulsion Forged Modern Greece and Turkey* (London: Granta, 2007) studies the effects of the population exchanges in the aftermath of the catastrophe, as does *Crossing the Aegean: An Appraisal of the 1923 Compulsory Population Exchange between Greece and Turkey* (New York: Berghahn, 2003) edited by a notable anthropologist, Renée Hirschon, whose *Heirs of the Greek Catastrophe: The Social Life of Asia Minor Refugees in Piraeus* (New York: Berghahn, 1998) follows the refugees in their attempt to find a new home in mainland Greece.

Ionian Vision: Greece in Asia Minor 1919-1922 (London: Allen Lane, 1973, repr. Hurst, 2005) by Michael Llewellyn Smith, remains the authoritative study of the subject.

ii) Eleftherios Venizelos

Venizelos was one of the dominant figures in modern Greek history: *Eleftherios Venizelos: The Trials of Statesmanship*, edited by Paschalis Kitromilides (Edinburgh: Edinburgh University Press, 2006), is the most up-to-date and comprehensive collection of studies; the biography by Michael Llewellyn Smith is long-awaited. Other works on Venizelos are: Andrew Dalby's *Eleftherios Venizelos* (London: Haus, 2010), one of a series of "Makers of the Modern World", and Nikolaos Emm. Papadakis, *Eleftherios K. Venizelos* (Chania: National Research Foundation "Eleftherios K. Venizelos", 2006), a written-to-order hagiography which, however, contains helpful photographs.

iii) The Second World War and the Civil War

Several volumes on this subject have been written by members of the British forces during the second world war and its immediate aftermath. Of these, the most valuable, but also the most contentious, is C.M. Woodhouse's *The Struggle for Greece 1941-49* (London: Hart-

Davis McKibbon, 1976, repr. Hurst, 2002). Other British participants to leave a record are F.W.D. Deakin, *The Embattled Mountain* (London: Oxford University Press, 1971), Geoffrey Chandler, *The Divided Land: An Anglo-Greek Tragedy* (London: Macmillan, 1959), Nigel Clive, *The Greek Experience 1943-48* (Salisbury: Russell, 1985), *Greek Entanglement* by Brigadier E.C.W. Myers (London: Hart-Davis, 1955) and Kenneth Matthews, *Memories of a Mountain War: Greece 1944-49* (London: Longman, 1972). Two journalists who observed the civil war were F.A. Voigt. *The Greek Sedition* (London: Hollis & Carter, 1949) and, later, Edgar O'Ballance, *The Greek Civil War 1944-1949* (London: Faber and Faber, 1966). The expatriation of women and children by communist partisans to neighbouring communist states during the civil war, and their subsequent repatriation, is the subject of *After the War Was Over: Reconstructing the Family, Nation and State in Greece 1943-1960* (Princeton: Princeton University Press, 2000) edited by Mark Mazower.

The authority on Greece's experience under German occupation remains Mark Mazower's *Inside Hitler's Germany: The Experience of Occupation 1941-44* (New Haven: Yale University Press, 1973, repr. 2001). A first-hand account of soldiering during the war is *Written on the Knee: A Diary from the Greek-Italian Front* by Theodore Electris, as told by his daughter (London: Scarletta Press, 2008).

The partisan side of the civil war is the subject of *The Kapetanios: Partisans and Civil War in Greece, 1943-1949* (London: New Left Books, 1972) by Dominique Eudes. *Greece: From Resistance to Civil War* (Nottingham: Spokesman, 1980) edited by Marion Sarafis, is a collection of conference papers, some of them by participants in the civil war; the bias of individual authors, and the contested narratives in the exchanges between contributors, is evident.

A non-partisan (in every sense) study of British-Greek relations leading up to the world war is J.S. Koliopoulos, *Greece and the British Connection 1935-41* (Oxford: Clarendon Press, 1977).

The experiences of the (mostly) communist partisans in the civil war is discussed by Polymeris Voglis in *Becoming a Subject: Political Prisoners during the Greek Civil War* (New York: Berghahn, 2002).

iv) Post-1950s Politics and Reconstruction

US economic intervention in Greece is chronicled in William McNeill, *The Metamorphosis of Greece since World War II* (Chicago: University of Chicago Press, 1978); McNeill, who also published *The Greek Dilemma: War and Aftermath* (London: Gollancz, 1947) was one of a team appointed to assess progress of the US aid package: the result is *Report on the Greeks: Findings of a Twentieth Century Fund Team which Surveyed Conditions in Greece in 1947* by F. Smothers, W.H. McNeill and E.D. McNeill (New York: Twentieth Century Fund, 1948). Bickham Sweet-Escott's *Greece: A Political and Economic Survey 1939-1953* (London: Royal Institute of International Affairs, 1954) is also a useful sourcebook, especially as it encompasses Cyprus.

George Papandreou was Prime Minister during the government-in-exile during the second world war and one of the architects of post-war political stability; his collected essays, *The Third War* (Athens: *Hellas* newspaper, 1948) is an invaluable guide to his political thoughts at that time.

v) Cyprus

The outstanding expert on modern Cyprus is William Mallinson: his *Cyprus: A Modern History* (2005) and *Cyprus: Diplomatic History and the Clash of Theory in International Relations* (2010) are backed up by *Britain and Cyprus: Key Themes and Documents since World War II* (2011), all published by Tauris (London).

vi) Politics and Political Life since 1960

Two early studies of modern Greek politics are: *The Web of Modern Greek Politics* (New York: Columbia University Press, 1968) by J.P.C. Carey and A.G. Carey, and *Politics in Modern Greece* (Stanford, Ca.: Stanford University Press, 1969) by Keith R. Legg; both have been superseded in many respects by later studies, but are solid accounts of the role of politics in Greek society and the structure of politics, including the junta, during whose regime the books appeared.

The Greek Socialist Experiment: Papandreou's Greece 1981-1989 (New York: Pella, 1999), edited by Theodore Kariotis, is an assessment of this crucial period in Greek political and social transition; its subtitle indicates the significance placed on the political leadership of Andreas Papandreou.

vii) The Military Junta, 1967-74

Greece under Military Rule (London: Secker and Warburg, 1972), edited by Richard Clogg and George Yannopoulos, is a collection of essays, critical of the military regime which was still in power at the time of publication.

Elias Kulukundis' *The Amorgos Conspiracy: A True Story* (Athens: Eleftheroudakis, 2013; originally published by Scribner, 1974) is an account of the rescue of the author's father-in-law, George Mylonas (minister of education from 1964 until his imprisonment), from the junta's prison camp on the island of Amorgos.

Although it belongs, strictly speaking, to the "literature" category, *Eighteen Texts* (Cambridge, Mass.: Harvard University Press, 1972), containing work by George Seferis, Kay Cicellis, Rodis Roufos, Manolis Anagnostakis and others must be mentioned here as responses to the junta.

A contemporary account written during the junta, by "Athenian" [the distinguished Greek writer Rodos Roufos] who, for reasons of security was obliged to write pseudonymously, is *Inside the Colonels' Greece* (London: Chatto and Windus, 1972). From the outside, in *The Rape of Greece: The King, the Colonels and the Resistance* (London: Simon and Schuster, 1994), Peter Murtagh, then a journalist with the *Guardian* and today with *The Irish Times*, analysed the political background to the 1967 coup and its aftermath, providing in particular details of interrogations, torture and exile carried out by the junta. *Children of the Dictatorship: Student Resistance, Cultural Politics and the Long 1960s* by Kostas Kornetis (London: Berghahn, 2013) concentrates on the activities of young Greeks under the junta.

One of the major figures in modern Greek politics, Andreas Papandreou, was held under house arrest by the junta, and died during its regime; his *Democracy at Gunpoint: The Greek Front* (London: André Deutsch, 1971; repr. Penguin, 1973) outlines the political events in Greece following the second world war and the advent of the Colonels.

The uses of classical drama as an allegory of resistance on the part of internal exiles during the junta is described by Gonda van Steen in *Theatre of the Condemned: Classical Tragedy on Greek Prison Islands* (Oxford: Oxford University Press, 2010).

The position of the Greek "Left" has been trenchantly and passionately described by Neni Panourgiá in *Dangerous Citizens: The Greek Left and the Terror of the State* (New York: Fordham University Press, 2009).

Terrorism has yet to be widely written about, but (too late for consideration in this book) *Greek Urban Warriors: Resistance and Terrorism 1967-2014* by a former US diplomat, Brady Kiesling (Athens: Lycabettus Press, 2015) explores an area of politics with which the author was professionally aware while stationed in Athens (where he still lives).

Social, Cultural and Economic Developments in the Late Twentieth Century

In 1977 the then President of Greece, Constantine Tsatsos, published a brief *Greece and Europe* (Athens: General Secretariat for Press and Information, 1977), in which he argued the case for EU membership and entered caveats about Greece's readiness.

Greece in the Twentieth Century (London: Frank Cass, 2003), edited by Theodore Couloumbis, Theodore Kariotis and Fotini Bellou, is a useful survey of Greece's relations with the USA, the Balkans and Cyprus, and its developments in the media, education, science and technology, women's issues, Church-State relations and the economy. *Modern Greece: A Cultural Poetics* by Vangelis Calotychos (Oxford: Berg, 2003) is a challenging survey of modern Greek culture in the broadest sense of the term. *Greece Prepares for the Twenty-First Century* (published jointly by the Woodrow Wilson Center Press and John Hopkins University Press, 1995), edited by Dimitri Constas and Theofanis Stavrou, assesses the social, institutional, political, economic, foreign policy and economic challenges to Greece in the global and European contexts.

A trenchant journalist, with a background in diplomacy, Mark Dragoumis collected two volumes of his contributions to *Athens News*, 2001-2005: *Greece on the Couch: Sessions 1 and 2* (Athens: *Athens News*, 2004 and 2006). Dragoumis is also the author of *The Greek Economy 1940-2004* (Athens: *Athens News*, 2004).

A collection of essays edited by Dimitris Tziovas entitled *Greek Modernism and Beyond* (Oxford: Rowman and Littlefield, 1997) examines the issues of Greek traditional cultural forms as they encounter the modernisation of Greece.

More recently, the Greek crisis has provoked several studies, including *From Stagnation to Forced Adjustment: Reforms in Greece 1974-2010* edited by S. Kalyvas, G. Pagloulatos and H. Tsoukas (London: Hurst, 2012) which unfortunately could not deal with the ongoing crisis but is extremely valuable as a study of its causes. *Understanding the Crisis in Greece: From Boom to Bust* by Michael Mitsopoulos and Theodore Pelagidis (Houndmills: Palgrave Macmillan, 2012) is an attempt by two economists (and former government advisers) to explain the causes of Greece's financial crisis. More recently, investigative journalist Yannis Palaiologos has produced *The 13ᵗʰ Labour of Hercules: Inside the Greek Crisis* (London: Portobello Books, 2014), which offers case studies of the reasons for Greece's systemic crisis. Readers of Chapter 9 will realise that I do not accept the self-serving account in *Costas Simitis' The European Debt Crisis: The Greek Case* (Manchester: Manchester University Press, 2012), but it nevertheless merits inclusion.

On the issue of minorities and minority culture, *Minorities in Greece: Aspects of a Plural Society*, edited by Richard Clogg (London: Hurst, 2003) and Dimitri Pentzopoulos' *The Balkan Exchange of Minorities and its Impact on Greece* (London: Hurst, 2003) are both valuable. A firsthand account of the experiences of a Pontic Greek is *Not Even My Name* by Thea Halo (New York: Picador, 2000).

Women's Studies and the Family

Jill Dubisch has been a pioneering scholar in the fields of anthropology and sociology. Her *In a Different Place: Pilgrimage, Gender and Politics of a Greek Island Shrine* (Princeton, NJ: Princeton University Press, 1995) takes the Mariolatry centring on the Aegean island of Tinos and extrapolates a valuable exercise in the relation of gender to nationhood. It extends the arguments in her earlier, edited, volume, *Gender and Power in Rural Greece* (Princeton, NJ: Princeton University Press, 1986). *Contested Identities: Gender and Kinship in Modern Greece*, edited by Peter Loizos and Evthymios Papataxiarchis (Princeton, NJ: Princeton University Press, 1991) also explores gender relationships inside and outside marriage.

Social and Anthropological Studies

The study of rural Greece, which, until recently, was the predominant aspect of Greek society and demography, has set international standards which it would be difficult to meet in descriptions of other societies. The leading expert was John Campbell, whose *Honour, Family and Patronage: A Study in the Institutions and Moral Values in a Greek Mountain Community* (Oxford: Clarendon Press, 1964) remains in print; a study of the nomadic, or transumant, Sarakatsani shepherds of north-west Greece, the book is in fact an invaluable introduction to the structures of rural Greek society and the values, such as *honour*, which it embodies. Another pioneer of rural anthropology is Juliet du Boulay, whose *Portrait of a Greek Mountain Village* (Oxford: Oxford University Press, 1974; repr. Denise Harvey, 1994) and *Cosmos, Life, and Liturgy in a Greek Orthodox Village* (Limni, Greece: Denise Harvey, 2009) mark her out as Campbell's equal in her sympathetic portrayal of the underlying motivations of Greek rural folk.

Other similar studies of importance are: Ernestine Friedl, *Vasilika: A Village in Modern Greece* (New York: Holt, Rinehart and Winston, 1962), David E. Sutton's *Memories Cast in Stone: The Relevance of the Past in Everyday Life* (Oxford: Berg, 1998), which analyses life in the island of Kalymnos; and Roger Just's *A Greek Island Cosmos: Kinship and Community on Meganisi* (Oxford: James Currey, 2000), which studies the Ionian islet of Meganisi, adjacent to Lefkada.

The fortunes and misfortunes of the city of Thessaloniki [Salonika] have been recalled in Leon Sciaky's memoir *Farewell Salonika: City at the Crossroads*, written in 1946 (London: WH Allen) and re-published in 2007 (London: Haus Books). The city has been extensively chronicled by Mark Mazower, in *Salonika: City of Ghosts: Christians, Muslims and Jews 1430-1950* (London: Harper Collins, 2004).

Cuisine

The classic text on Greek food is *Greek Cookery* by Nicholas Tselementes (New York: Divry, 1985 reprint of the 1950 original). The most comprehensive, regarded as the "bible" of modern Greek cuisine, is Vefa Alexiadou, *Vefa's Kitchen* (London: Phaidon, 2009) which surveys the regional "dialects" of traditional Greek cooking. There are many regional studies: I shall mention only those relating to the Ionian islands: *Prospero's Kitchen: Island Cooking of Greece* (originally published 1995-2000 with the subtitle *Mediterranean Cooking of the Ionian Islands*) by Diana Farr Louis and June Marinos (London: Tauris, 2012); Vicky Bennison's *A Taste of a Place: Corfu*

(London: Wittersham Publishing, 2002); *Corfiot Delicacies* (Corfu: Bookshop Plous, 2003) by Toula Katsarou-Vergeti, whose taverna at Agni is internationally renowned; and *Corfiot Cuisine* by Vasiliki Karounou (Corfu: Ambelonas, 2014).

Geopolitics

Among the many studies of Greece's geopolitical position, *Foreign Interference in Greek Politics*, by T.A. Couloumbis, J.A. Petropoulos and H.J. Psomiades (New York: Pella, 1976), takes a long historical perspective, from the Ottoman period through to the end of the junta, with particular reference to US involvement in Greece. John A Levandis' *The Greek Foreign Debt and the Great Powers 1821-1898* (New York, 1944) does much to explain the continued indebtedness of Greece since the war of independence.

Balkans and Levant

The most comprehensive survey of modern Balkan history is Misha Glenny's *The Balkans 1804-2012: nationalism, war and the Great Powers* (London: Granta Books, 1999, updated 2012). More concise, but equally incisive, is Mark Mazower's *The Balkans* (London: Weidenfeld and Nicolson, 2000), with a new edition, subtitled *From the End of Byzantium to the Present Day*, appearing in 2002 (London: Phoenix Books).

Also of value is André Gerolymatos, *The Balkan Wars: Conquest, Revolution, and Retribution from the Ottoman Empire to the Twentieth Century and Beyond* (Staplehurst: Spellmount, 2004).

Middle Eastern studies which are highly relevant to the Levant are: Robert Fisk *The Great War for Civilisation: The Conquest of the Middle East* (London: Harper Perennial, 2006) and David Fromkin, *A Peace to End All Peace: The Fall of the Ottoman Empire and the Creation of the Modern Middle East* (London: Phoenix, 2000).

Philip Mansel's *Levant: Splendour and Catastrophe on the Mediterranean* (London: John Murray, 2010), is a fascinating view of the region through the lenses of Smyrna, Alexandria and Beirut.

One of the most enlightening studies, which challenges preconceptions of the Balkans, is Maria Todorova, *Imagining the Balkans* (Oxford: Oxford University Press, 1997, updated 2009). Todorova has also edited *Balkan Identities: Nation and Memory* (New York: New York University Press, 2004). Another study of the complexities of the Balkans is Scott L Malcomson's *Borderlands: Nation and Empire* (London: Faber and Faber, 1994). An intriguing study is *Larry Wolff, Inventing Eastern Europe: The Map of Civilization on the Mind of the Enlightenment* (Stanford, Ca.: Stanford University Press, 1994). Greece's relations with its Balkan neighbours are studied in *Greece and the Balkans: Identities, Perceptions and Cultural Encounters since the Enlightenment* (Aldershot: Ashgate, 2003), edited by Dimitri Tziovas. A summing up of the literature is Elizabeth Pond's *Endgame in the Balkans: Regime Change, European Style* (Washington DC.: Brookings Institution Press, 2006) which optimistically addresses what the author sees as a stabilising of the region through the extension of European polity.

Macedonian issues are discussed in *Ourselves and Others: The Development of a Greek-Macedonian Cultural Identity since 1912* (Oxford: Berg, 1997), edited by Peter Mackridge and Eleni Yannakakis; unfortunately their promised sequel, on the contribution of literature to the development of Greek Macedonian cultural identity, has not materialised. Other Macedonian studies include: John Phillips, *Macedonia: Warlords and Rebels in the Balkans* (London: Tauris, 2004), Dimitris Livanios, *The Macedonian Question: Britain and the Southern Balkans 1939-1949* (Oxford: Oxford University Press, 2008) and Vangelis Calotychos, *The Balkan Prospect: Identity, Culture and Politics in Greece after 1989* (Houndmills: Palgrave Macmillan, 2013).

The background to contemporary Albanian history is well told in Jason Tomes' *King Zog: Self-made Monarch of Albania* (Stroud: Sutton Publishing, 2003). An illustration of the effect of the *kanun* on the lives of women is given in the novel *Sworn Virgin* by Elvira Dones (London: And Other Stories, 2014). The novels of Ismail Kadaré are too numerous to list, but *Broken April* (London: Vintage, 2003) and *Spring Flowers, Spring Frost* (London: Vintage, 2003) are further pictures of the effects of the *kanun*, while his non-fiction includes an analysis of Albania under the Hoxha regime, *Albanian Spring* (London: Saqi, 1995).

Travellers' accounts of Albania have in common the depiction of a mountainous region populated by tribal peoples: from Edith Durham's *High Albania* (originally published 1909, repr. Phoenix Press, 2000) to Nigel Heseltine's *Scarred Background* (London: Lovat Dickson, 1938) and Robert Carver's *The Accursed Mountains* (London: John Murray, 1998).

The classic history of the Ottoman Empire is (Lord) Patrick Kinross's *The Ottoman Centuries: The Rise and Fall of the Turkish Empire* (London: Cape, 1977, republished by the Folio Society, 2003 as *The Ottoman Empire*). A more succinct study is Donald Quataert, *The Ottoman Empire 1700-1922* (Cambridge: Cambridge University Press, 2nd edn. 2005).

Literature

There are many histories of modern Greek literature, but the single most comprehensive and unbiased study is the indispensable *An Introduction to Modern Greek Literature* by Roderick Beaton (Oxford: Clarendon Press, 1999). Beaton has also edited *The Greek Novel AD1-1985* (Beckenham: Croom Helm, 1988). Other works which should be consulted on the evolution of a modern Greek identity in fiction are: Dimitri Tziovas, *The Other Self: Selfhood and Society in Modern Greek Fiction* (Oxford: Lexington Books, 2003) and Vassilis Lambropoulos, *Literature as National Institution: Studies in the Politics of Modern Greek Criticism* (Princeton, NJ: Princeton University Press, 1988).

Modern Greek Novels/Stories Relating to Periods of War (a select list)

As I pointed out in Chapter 7, the principal novels to be translated into English concern war at various periods in Greek modern history. Regretfully, limitations of space persuade me to include only books currently in print (therefore all the following can be taken as carrying the '*' indicator). Many of the translations have appeared from the Greek publisher Kedros in their extensive "Modern Greek Writers" series. Full citations are mostly omitted from this section, since many of the titles are available in various editions. Where two dates are given, the first is the date of original publication in Greek; the second, of the translation into English.

First World War

Stratis Myrivilis: *Life in the Tomb* 1924/1977; repr. 1987, Quartet

'Anatolian Catastrophe' 1922

Stratis Doukas: *A Prisoner of War's Story* 1929/1999, University of Birmingham Press

Panos Karnezis: *The Maze* 2004, Jonathan Cape

Dido Sotiriou: *Farewell Anatolia* 1962/1991, Kedros

Second World War and Aftermath

Andreas Franghias: *The Courtyard* 1976/1995, Kedros

Stratis Haviaras: *When the Tree Sings*, 1980 Picador

Nikos Kokantzis: *Gioconda* 1975/1997, Kedros repr. 2014

Alexandros Kotzias: *Jaguar* 1991, Kedros

Pavlos Matesis: *The Daughter* 1990/2002, Arcadia

Stratis Tsirkas: *Drifting Cities* 1960, '62, '65/1995, Kedros

Greek Civil War, 1945-48/9

Aris Alexandrou: *The Mission Box* 1974/1996, Kedros

Nicholas Gage: *Eleni* 1983, Ballantine

Stratis Haviaras: *The Heroic Age* 1984, Simon & Schuster; Penguin 1985

Sophia Nikolaidou: *The Scapegoat* (London: Melville, 2015)

Colonels' Dictatorship, 1967-74

Nick Papandreou: *Father Dancing* 1996, Viking

Vassilis Vassilikos: *Z* (New York: Farrar Straus Giroux, 1968; repr. 1988 Random House)

Natalie Bakopoulos: *The Green Shore* (New York: Simon and Schuster, 2012)

Elias Maglinis: *The Interrogation* (Birmingham: University of Birmingham Press, 2013)

General

Nikos Bakolas: *The Crossroads* [Thessaloniki 1930s-40s] 1987/1997, Kedros

Sotiris Dimitriou: *May Your Name be Blessed* [Epirus: border crossings] 1993/2000, University of Birmingham Press

Alki Zei: *Achilles' Fiancée* 1991, Kedros

A valuable introduction to modern writing (poetry and prose) since 1821 is the anthology *Modern Greek Writing*, edited by David Ricks with helpful biographical introductions (London: Peter Owen, 2003), while a bilingual edition, *A Century of Greek Poetry 1900-2000* is edited by Peter Bien, Peter Constantine, Edmund Keeley and Karen van Dyck (River Vale, NJ: Cosmos, 2004). There have been several collections of short stories; those in print are *Beyond the Broken Statues* , translated by Nikolas Kostis and *Angelic & Black* , translated by David Connolly (both from River Vale, NJ: Cosmos, 2006)

Works which are *not* explicitly concerned with war include:

Petros Abatzoglou: *What Does Mrs Freeman Want?* (1988/1991; 2005 Dalkey Archive Press

Sotoris Dimitriou: *Woof Woof, Dear Lord* (1995) Kedros

Apostolos Doxiadis: *Uncle Petros and Goldbach's Conjecture* (London: Faber and Faber, 2000)

Eugenia Fakinou: *Astradeni* 1982/1991, Kedros

Rhea Galanaki: *Eleni or Nobody* (Evanston, Ill.: Northwestern University Press, 2003); *I Shall Sign as Loui* (Evanston, Ill.: Northwestern University Press, 2000)

Vangelis Hatziyannidis: *Four Walls* (2000/2006) and *Stolen Time* (2004/2007), both London: Marion Boyars

Margarita Karapanou: *Kassandra and the Wolf* (1974/1977; repr. 2009); *The Sleepwalker* (1997/2011) Both: Northampton, Mass.: Clockroot Books.

Panos Karnezis: *The Convent* (London: Norton, 2010), *The Birthday Party* (London: Jonathan Cape, 2007) and his short stories *Little Infamies* (New York: Farrar Straus Giroux, 2002)

Ioanna Karystiani: *The Jasmine Isle* (1997/2006); *Swell* (2006-2010); *Back to Delphi* (2010/2013). All New York, Europa

Menis Koumandareas: *Koula* (Dalkey Archive Press, 2005).

Costas Montis: *Afentis Batistas* (1980/2006) Dayton, OH.: Feather Star

Stratis Myrivilis: *The Mermaid Madonna* (London: Hutchinson, 1959)

Aristotelis Nikolaidis: *Vanishing-Point* 1975/1995, Kedros

Nikos Gabriel Pentzikis: *Mother Thessaloniki* 1998, Kedros

Theodore Pitsios: *The Bellmaker's House* (River Vale, NJ: Cosmos, 2007)

Spyros Plaskovits: *The Façade Lady of Corfu* 1995, Kedros

Vangelis Raptopoulos: *The Cicadas* 1985/1996, Kedros

Antonis Samarakis: *The Passport* (short stories) (River Vale, NJ: Cosmos, 2006)

Aris Sfakianakis: *The Emptiness Beyond* 1996, Kedros

Yannis Skarimbas: *Mariambas* (University of Birmingham Press, 2015)

Ersi Sotiropoulos: *Zigzag Through the Bitter-Orange Trees* (Northampton, Mass.: Interlink, 2007)

Irini Spanidou: *God's Snake* (London: Penguin, 1986; repr. Vintage 1998)

Costas Taktsis: *The Third Wedding* (London: Alan Ross, 1967; repr. 1986 Red Dust)

Takis Theodoropoulos: *The Power of the Dark God* 2000 (River Vale, NJ: Cosmos, 2007)

Thanassis Valtinos: *Data from the Decade of the Sixties* (Minnesota, Minn.: Northwestern University Press, 2000)

Georgios Vizyenos: *Thracian Tales*; *Moskov Selim*. Both Athens: Aiora (2014, 2015)

Yorgis Yatromanolakis: *The Spiritual Meadow* (1974/2000); *The History of a Vendetta* (1982/1991); *A Report of a Murder* (1993/1995), all published in London by Dedalus.

Vassa Solomou Xanthaki: *The Marriage* (Evia: Denise Harvey, 2010).

Petros Markaris has created the character of "Inspector Costas Haritos" whose investigations illuminate many dark corners of the

Greek underworld: translations to date are: *Deadline in Athens* (New York: Grove Press, 2004); *The Late-Night News* (London: Vintage, 2004); *Zone Defence* (London: Vintage, 2007); *Che Committed Suicide* (London: Arcadia, 2009).

Four authors whose work has featured extensively in this book are: Odysseas Elytis, Nikos Kazantzakis, Alexandros Papadiamandis and George Seferis.

Odysseas Elytis

Selected Poems 1940-1979 (London: Anvil Press, 1981).

Carte Blanche: selected writings (trans. David Connolly: Amsterdam: Harwood Academic Publishers, 1999)

Nikos Kazantzakis

It's unnecessary to list all Kazantzakis' works, but those referred to in this book include: *Zorba the Greek* (London: Faber and Faber, 1961, many reprints); *The Last Temptation of Christ* (New York: Simon and Schuster, 1960); *The Fratricides* (London: Faber and Faber, 1974, many reprints); *Freedom or Death* (New York: Simon and Schuster, 1966); *Christ Recrucified* (Oxford: Cassirer, 1954, many reprints).

Much harder to find are Kazantzakis' *Symposium* (New York: Minerva Press, 1974) and his passionate journal of his *Travels in Greece* (Oxford: Cassirer, 1966).

Kazantzakis' widow, Eleni (Helen) compiled a biography based on his letters, *Kazantzakis: a biography* which has appeared in many editions from 1968 onwards, of which the most recent is: Berkeley, Ca.: Creative Arts, 1983. This biography has in many respects been superseded by Peter Bien's magisterial 2-volume study *Kazantzakis: Politics of the Spirit* (Princeton NJ: Princeton University Press, 1989-2007).

Alexandros Papadiamandis

The first volume of a projected three-volume edition of Papadiamandis' stories is *The Boundless Garden* edited by Lambros Kamperidis and Denise Harvey (Evia: Denise Harvey, 2007). His novella, *The Murderess* has appeared in two editions: translated by Peter Levi (London: Writers & Readers, 1983) and *translated by Liadain Sherrard (Evia: Denise Harvey, 2011). Further stories were translated by Elizabeth Constantinides as *Tales from a Greek Island* (Baltimore: John Hopkins University Press, 1987).

Studies of Papadiamandis' work include: Louis Coutelle et al., eds., *A Greek Triptych: Dionysios Solomos and Alexandros Papadiamantis* (Minneapolis, Minn.: Nostos Books, 1986) and Anestis Keselopoulos, *Greece's Dostoevsky: The Theological Vision of Alexandros Papadiamandis* (Thessaloniki: Protecting Veil, 2011).

George Seferis

The most complete and authoritative edition of Seferis' poetry is *Collected Poems 1924-1955*, translated by Edmund Keeley and Philip Sherrard (Princeton, NJ: Princeton University Press, 1967); a bilingual edition was published in 2014.

In addition to his poetry, Seferis published one novel, *Six Nights on the Acropolis*, originally in Greek in 1974, and translated by Susan Matthias (River Vale, NJ: Cosmos, 2007).

On the Greek Style (Boston: Little Brown, 1966; repr. Denise Harvey, 2000)

A Poet's Journal: Days of 1945-1951 (Cambridge, Mass.: Harvard University Press, 1974, repr. 2014)

A Levant Journal (Jerusalem: Ibis, 2007) covers the years 1941-44 and 1955-56 during Seferis' diplomatic postings.

The outstanding biography of Seferis is Roderick Beaton, * *George Seferis: Waiting for the Angel* (London: Yale University Press, 2003).

Music

The book accompanying the 12-disc collection of Greek composers is *Works by Greek Composers: 19th-20th Century* (Hellenic Ministry of Culture: 2004): for an account of the mystery surrounding this production, see above, pp. 158-59.

The phenomenon of *rebétiko* and its place in modern Greek culture is studied in *Rebetika: Songs from the Old Greek Underworld*, edited by Katharine Butterworth and Sara Schneider (originally published 1975 in Athens by Komboloi Press and reprinted 2014 by Aiora Press). Charles Howard's CD compilation *Mortika: Rare Vintage Recordings from a Greek Underworld* (Arko Records: ARKO CD008, 2005) is accompanied by valuable essays on the origins of the genre. An important study is Elias Petropoulos' *Songs of the Greek Underworld: The Rebetika Tradition* (London: Saqi, 2000). Gail Holst is probably the foremost published author on *Rebétiko*: her *Road to Rembetika: Music of a Greek Sub-culture, Songs of Love, Sorrow & Hashish* has been reprinted: Evia, Greece: Denise Harvey, 1994.

Histories of Greek music and studies of its contemporary development are the province primarily of academics. The only major composer to have received critical attention is Mikis Theodorakis: Gail Holst's *Theodorakis: Myth & Politics in Modern Greek Music* (Amsterdam: Hakkert, 1979) is valuable but restricted to the earlier work. The relationship of Theodorakis and Manos Hadjidakis is explored in Nikos Papandreou, *Mikis and Manos: A Tale of Two Composers* (Athens, Kerkyra Publications, 2004).

Drama

The definitive work on the *Karagiózis* shadow theatre is *The Karaghiozis Heroic Performance in Greek Shadow Theater* by Linda S Myriades, trans. Kostas Myrsiades (Hanover NH: University Press of New England, 1988), and several other studies include a consideration of the *Karagiózis* influence on modern Greek drama, including Aliki Bacopoulou-Halls, *Modern Greek Theater: Roots and Blossoms* (Athens: Diogenis, 1982), which takes *Rebétiko* as a starting-point for her discussions. Rush Rehm's *Radical Theatre: Greek tragedy and the modern world* (London: Duckworth, 2003) explores contemporary presentation of classic Greek drama, while Stratos Constantinidis' *Modern Greek Theatre: A Quest for Hellenism* (Jefferson, NC: McFarland, 2001) discusses approaches to "Greekness" on the modern Greek stage.

Film

The guide to all Greek films is Dimitris Koliodimos, *The Greek Filmography 1914 through 1996* (originally published Jefferson, NC: McFarland, 1999 and reprinted in 2 volumes, 2005); regrettably the reprint does not bring the book up to date. Mel Schuster's *The Contemporary Greek Cinema* (Metuchen, NJ: Scarecrow Press, 1979) is valuable as far as it goes, but many of the filmmakers listed have since developed their careers. There is a dearth of study of modern Greek cinema, with the exception of Theo Angelopoulos: see Andrew

Horton, *Theo Angelopoulos: A Cinema of Contemplation* (Princeton, NJ: Princeton University Press, 1997) which unfortunately could not cover the works of the director's final years. *Theo Angelopoulos: Interviews* edited by Dan Fainaru (London: University Press of Mississippi, 2001) collects many of his interviews.

Most of Angelopoulos' films are available in three collections:

Vol. I: *The Reconstruction* (1970), *Days of '36* (1972), *The Travelling Players* (1975), *The Hunters* (1977).

Vol. II: *Alexander the Great* (1980), *Voyage to Cythera* (1984), *The Beekeeper* (1986), *Landscape in the Mist* (1988), *The Suspended Step of the Stork* (1991).

Vol. III: *Ulysses' Gaze* (1995), *Eternity and a Day* (1998), *The Weeping Meadow* (2004), *The Dust of Time* (2009).

INDEX

Index